EXAM✓CRAM

CompTIA®
Security+

SYO-201 Practice Questions
Exam Cram, Second Edition

Diane Barrett

CompTIA® Security+ SYO-201 Practice Questions Exam Cram, Second Edition

Copyright ® 2010 by Pearson Education, Inc.

ISBN-13: 978-0-7897-4258-2
ISBN-10: 0-7897-4258-6
Library of Congress Cataloging-in-Publication data is on file.

Printed in the United States of America

First Printing: October 2009

10   09   08   07   06   4   3   2   1

Trademarks

Warning and Disclaimer

Bulk Sales

Que Publishing offers excellent discounts on this book when ordered in quantity for bulk purchases or special sales. For more information, please contact

U.S. Corporate and Government Sales

1-800-382-3419

corpsales@pearsontechgroup.com

For sales outside the U.S., please contact

International Sales

international@pearsoned.com

Publisher
Paul Boger

Associate Publisher
David Dusthimer

Acquisitions Editor
Betsy Brown

Senior Development Editor
Christopher Cleveland

Managing Editor
Patrick Kanouse

Technical Editor
Pawan Bhardwaj

Project Editor
Seth Kerney

Copy Editor
Keith Cline

Proofreader
Water Crest Publishing, Inc.

Publishing Coordinator
Vanessa Evans

Multimedia Developer
Dan Scherf

Cover Designer
Gary Adair

Page Layout
Bronkella Publishing LLC

Table of Contents

Chapter 3:
Domain 3.0: Access Control **141**

About the Author

Diane Barrett has been involved in the IT industry for about 20 years. She spent 7 years in software development before becoming involved in education, security, and forensics. Currently she is the Faculty Council Chair for the Systems Development Group at the University of Advancing Technology and both develops curriculum and teaches in the Computer Forensics and Network Security programs. In addition, she does contract forensic and security work. Diane belongs to the local chapters of several security user groups, including HTCIA, ISSA, and InfraGard. She holds about 15 industry certifications, including CISSP, ISSMP, and Security+. She has also authored several other security and forensic books. Diane received her master of science degree in computer technology with a specialization in information security from Capella University and is currently working on a Ph.D. in business administration with a specialization in information security.

Dedication

To my nephew Ryan, who is always a bright spot in my day.

Acknowledgments

Publishing a book takes the collaboration and teamwork of many individuals. Thanks to everyone involved in this process at Pearson Education, especially Betsy and Chris. To the editorial and technical reviewers, thank you for making sure that my work was sound and on target. Special thanks to my husband for all his support and patience while I worked on this project.

We Want to Hear from You!

As the reader of this book, *you* are our most important critic and commentator. We value your opinion and want to know what we're doing right, what we could do better, what areas you'd like to see us publish in, and any other words of wisdom you're willing to pass our way.

As an Associate Publisher for Pearson, I welcome your comments. You can email or write me directly to let me know what you did or didn't like about this book—as well as what we can do to make our books better.

Please note that I cannot help you with technical problems related to the topic of this book. We do have a User Services group, however, where I will forward specific technical questions related to the book.

When you write, please be sure to include this book's title and author as well as your name, email address, and phone number. I will carefully review your comments and share them with the author and editors who worked on the book.

Email: feedback@pearson.com

Mail: David Dusthimer
       Associate Publisher
       Pearson
       800 East 96th Street
       Indianapolis, IN 46240 USA

Reader Services

Visit our website and register this book at www.examcram.com/register for convenient access to any updates, downloads, or errata that might be available for this book.

Introduction

Welcome to *Security+ Practice Questions Exam Cram 2*. The sole purpose of this book is to provide you with practice questions and answers and explanations that will help you learn, drill, and review for the Security+ Certification (2008 Edition) exam. The book offers a large number of questions to practice each exam objective and will help you assess your knowledge before you take the real exam. The detailed answers to every question will help reinforce your knowledge about different concepts covered on the Security+ (2008 Edition) exam.

Who This Book Is For

If you have studied the SY0-201 exam's content and think you are ready to put your knowledge to the test, but you are not sure that you want to take the real exam yet, this book is for you! Maybe you have answered other practice questions or unsuccessfully taken the real exam, reviewed, and want to do more practice questions before going to take the real exam; this book is for you, too! Even when the exam is done and you have passed with flying colors and got the Security+ Certification in your pocket, keep the book handy on your desktop to look for answers to your everyday security issues.

What You Will Find in This Book

This book is all about practice questions! The practice questions in the book, some very easy and others a bit more difficult (perhaps with a little complicated problem scenario, for example), are all aimed at raising your confidence level before taking the real exam. In fact, you will even find questions that you will face in real life.

This book is organized according to the objectives published by CompTIA for the SY0-201: CompTIA Security+ (2008 Edition) exam. Each chapter corresponds to an exam objective, and in every chapter you will find the following three elements:

▸ **Practice questions**: These are the numerous questions that will help you learn, drill, and review exam objectives. All the questions in this section are multiple-choice type. Choose the correct answer based on your knowledge of security.

▶ **Quick-check answer key**: After you have finished answering the questions, you can quickly grade your exam from this section. Only correct answers are given in this section. No explanations are offered yet! Even if you have answered a question incorrectly, do not be discouraged. Just move on! Keep in mind that this is not the real exam. You can always review the topic and do the questions again.

▶ **Answers and explanations**: This section provides you with correct answers and further explanations about the content addressed in that question. Use this information to learn why an answer is correct and to reinforce the content in your mind for the exam day.

> **NOTE**
>
> It is not possible to reflect a real exam on a paper product. As mentioned earlier, the purpose of the book is to help you prepare for the exam, not to provide you with real exam questions. Neither the author nor the publisher can guarantee that you will pass the exam just by memorizing the practice questions in this book.

You will also find a Cram Sheet at the beginning of the book specifically written for the exam day. The Cram Sheet contains core knowledge that you need for the exam and is also found in the book *CompTIA Security+ Exam Cram, Second Edition* (ISBN: 0-7897-3804-X). The Cram Sheet condenses all the necessary facts covered on the exam into an easy-to-handle tear card. It is something you can carry with you to the testing center and use as a last-second study aid. Be aware that you cannot take the Cram Sheet into the exam room, though!

Hints for Using This Book

Because this book is a practice product on paper, you might want to complete your exams on a separate piece of paper so that you can reuse the exams over and over without having previous answers in your way. Also, a general rule of thumb across all practice questions products is to make sure that you are scoring well into the high 80% to 90% range on all topics before attempting the real exam. The higher percentages you score on practice question products, the better your chances for passing the real exam. Of course, we cannot guarantee a passing score on the real exam, but we can offer you plenty of opportunities to practice and assess your knowledge levels before you enter the real exam.

When you have completed the exam on paper, use the companion CD to take a timed exam. Doing so will help build your confidence and help you determine whether you need to study more. Your results will indicate the exam objectives in which you need further study or hand-on practice.

Need Further Study?

Are you having a hard time correctly answering these questions? If so, you probably need further review of all exam objectives. Be sure to see the following sister products to this book:

CompTIA Security+ Exam Cram, Second Edition, by Diane Barrett, Kalani K. Hausman, Martin Weiss (ISBN: 0-7897-3804-X).

CompTIA Security+ Cert Flash Cards Online Series, by Diane Barrett (ISBN: 978-0-7897-4204-9)

CHAPTER ONE

Domain 1.0: Systems Security

Securing your resources is a challenge in any working environment. After all, resources are now commonly attacked through software, hardware, and peripherals. Domain 1 of the Security+ exam requires that you understand how to minimize system threats and thus thwart would-be attackers and that you understand the different types of potential attacks. Be sure to give yourself plenty of time to review all of these concepts. The following list identifies the key areas from Domain 1.0 (which counts as 21% of the exam) that you need to master:

▶ Differentiate among various systems security threats.

▶ Explain the security risks pertaining to system hardware and peripherals.

▶ Implement OS hardening practices and procedures to achieve workstation and server security.

▶ Carry out the appropriate procedures to establish application security.

▶ Implement security applications.

▶ Explain the purpose and application of virtualization technology.

Practice Questions

Objective 1.1: Differentiate among various systems security threats.

1. Which of the following is the most common result of a buffer overflow?

   - O **A.** Privilege escalation
   - O **B.** Disguised malicious programs
   - O **C.** Code replication
   - O **D.** Collection of personal data

   Quick Answer: **41**
   Detailed Answer: **44**

2. Which of the following best describes a virus?

   - O **A.** An action that exceeds the storage-space allocation of an application
   - O **B.** A program disguised as a useful application
   - O **C.** A program designed to attach itself to other code and replicate
   - O **D.** Software that communicates information from a user's system without notifying the user

   Quick Answer: **41**
   Detailed Answer: **44**

3. Which of the following is best describes a Trojan?

   - O **A.** It infects other systems only after a user executes the application that it is buried in.
   - O **B.** It sends messages to a computer with an IP address indicating that the message is coming from a trusted host.
   - O **C.** It collects personal information, or changes your computer configuration without appropriately obtaining prior consent.
   - O **D.** It is self-replicating and therefore needs no user intervention.

   Quick Answer: **41**
   Detailed Answer: **44**

4. Which of the following best describes a rootkit?

   - O **A.** Software used for the collection of personal data
   - O **B.** Software hidden on a computer for the purpose of compromising the system
   - O **C.** Software that provides the originator with the venue to propagate
   - O **D.** Software that reports data such as surfing habits and sites visited

   Quick Answer: **41**
   Detailed Answer: **44**

5. Which of the following is considered a worm?

- ○ **A.** Melissa
- ○ **B.** Acid Rain
- ○ **C.** Code Red
- ○ **D.** Mocmex

Quick Answer: **41**
Detailed Answer: **45**

6. A disgruntled employee creates a utility for purging old emails from the server. Inside the utility is code that will erase the server's hard drive contents on January 1, 2010. This is an example of which of the following attacks?

- ○ **A.** Virus
- ○ **B.** Logic bomb
- ○ **C.** Spoofing
- ○ **D.** Trojan horse

Quick Answer: **41**
Detailed Answer: **45**

7. Which of the following best describes spyware?

- ○ **A.** Software used for the collection of personal data
- ○ **B.** Software hidden on a computer for the purpose of compromising the system
- ○ **C.** Software that provides the originator with the venue to propagate
- ○ **D.** Software that reports data such as surfing habits and sites visited

Quick Answer: **41**
Detailed Answer: **45**

8. Which of the following is the best reason not to request to be removed from a mailing list in a reply to an unsolicited email?

- ○ **A.** It allows the sender to spoof your email address.
- ○ **B.** It is a waste of time because the sender very seldom removes you from the list.
- ○ **C.** It verifies that you have a legitimate, working email address.
- ○ **D.** It allows the sender to collect personal data.

Quick Answer: **41**
Detailed Answer: **45**

9. Which of the following are methods by which email spam lists are created? (Select all correct answers.)

- ○ **A.** Searching the Web for addresses
- ○ **B.** Scanning newsgroup postings
- ○ **C.** Stealing Internet mailing lists
- ○ **D.** Stealing user email address books

Quick Answer: **41**
Detailed Answer: **45**

10. Which of the following best describes programming errors that result in allowing someone to gain unauthorized administrative access?

Quick Answer: **41**
Detailed Answer: **46**

- ○ **A.** Buffer overflow
- ○ **B.** Virus
- ○ **C.** Trojan
- ○ **D.** Logic bomb

11. Which of the following best describes malware that takes advantage of a security hole, and then automatically replicates to other systems running the same software?

Quick Answer: **41**
Detailed Answer: **46**

- ○ **A.** Spyware
- ○ **B.** Virus
- ○ **C.** Trojan
- ○ **D.** Worm

12. Which of the following is a type of malware that is disguised as a useful application?

Quick Answer: **41**
Detailed Answer: **46**

- ○ **A.** Spyware
- ○ **B.** Virus
- ○ **C.** Trojan
- ○ **D.** Worm

13. Which of the following is a type of malware is associated with collecting personal information without appropriately obtaining prior consent?

Quick Answer: **41**
Detailed Answer: **46**

- ○ **A.** Spyware
- ○ **B.** Virus
- ○ **C.** Trojan
- ○ **D.** Worm

14. Which of the following is a type of malware hidden on a computer mainly for the purpose of compromising the system and getting escalated privileges?

Quick Answer: **41**
Detailed Answer: **47**

- ○ **A.** Spyware
- ○ **B.** Spam
- ○ **C.** Adware
- ○ **D.** Rootkit

15. Which of the following is a type of malware that provides the spam or virus originator with a venue to propagate?

- ○ **A.** Logic bomb
- ○ **B.** Botnet
- ○ **C.** Adware
- ○ **D.** Rootkit

16. Which of the following is true with regard to antispyware programs?

- ○ **A.** They must be updated regularly.
- ○ **B.** They can detect rootkits.
- ○ **C.** They can detect botnets.
- ○ **D.** They do not have to be updated.

17. Which of the following best describes the primary security issue with botnets?

- ○ **A.** They are malicious.
- ○ **B.** They can remain undetected.
- ○ **C.** They can execute code.
- ○ **D.** They are remotely controlled.

18. Which of the following is also referred to as slag code?

- ○ **A.** Logic bomb
- ○ **B.** Botnet
- ○ **C.** Adware
- ○ **D.** Rootkit

19. A buffer overflow can result in which of the following? (Select all correct answers.)

- ○ **A.** Overwriting of data or memory storage
- ○ **B.** A denial of service
- ○ **C.** Automatic code replication to other hosts
- ○ **D.** Execution of arbitrary code at a privileged level

20. Which of the following are virus types? (Select all correct answers.)

    ○ **A.** Polymorphic

    ○ **B.** Polynomial

    ○ **C.** Stealth

    ○ **D.** Covert

Quick Answer: **41**
Detailed Answer: **48**

21. Which of the following best describes a boot sector virus?

    ○ **A.** Can change each time it is executed to avoid detection

    ○ **B.** Uses techniques to avoid detection

    ○ **C.** Is placed into the first sector of the hard drive

    ○ **D.** Infects executable program files and becomes active in memory

Quick Answer: **41**
Detailed Answer: **48**

22. Which of the following is another name for a botnet?

    ○ **A.** Privilege escalation

    ○ **B.** Global hook

    ○ **C.** Honeynet

    ○ **D.** Zombie army

Quick Answer: **41**
Detailed Answer: **48**

23. Which of the following is most like spyware?

    ○ **A.** Virus

    ○ **B.** Trojan

    ○ **C.** Spam

    ○ **D.** Worm

Quick Answer: **41**
Detailed Answer: **48**

24. Which of the following best describes what rootkits use for stealth activity?

    ○ **A.** Global hooks

    ○ **B.** Tracking software/adware

    ○ **C.** Privilege escalation

    ○ **D.** Social engineering

Quick Answer: **41**
Detailed Answer: **48**

25. Which of the following is the most effective method to avoid rootkit infection?

Quick Answer: **41**
Detailed Answer: **48**

- ○ **A.** Never responding to the sender of an unsolicited email message
- ○ **B.** Running operating systems from an account with lesser privileges
- ○ **C.** Properly disabling the accounts of all terminated employees
- ○ **D.** Only downloading trusted applications

26. Which of the following best describes a botnet?

Quick Answer: **41**
Detailed Answer: **48**

- ○ **A.** A program designed to execute malicious actions when a certain event occurs or a period of time goes by
- ○ **B.** A large number of programs disguised as useful applications
- ○ **C.** A large number of computers that forward transmissions to other computers on the Internet
- ○ **D.** Exploitation in software code that takes advantage of a programming flaw

27. Which of the following terms is most closely related to software exploitation that crashes the system and leaves it in a state where arbitrary code can be executed?

Quick Answer: **41**
Detailed Answer: **49**

- ○ **A.** Logic bomb
- ○ **B.** Privilege escalation
- ○ **C.** Spam
- ○ **D.** Trojan

28. Which of the following are the most effective ways to prevent an attacker from exploiting software? (Select all correct answers.)

Quick Answer: **41**
Detailed Answer: **49**

- ○ **A.** Apply current patches
- ○ **B.** Do not allow Internet access
- ○ **C.** Apply current service packs
- ○ **D.** Monitor the Web for newly discovered vulnerabilities

29. Which of the following virus is a hybrid of boot and program viruses?

Quick Answer: **41**
Detailed Answer: **49**

- ○ **A.** Polymorphic
- ○ **B.** Macro
- ○ **C.** Stealth
- ○ **D.** Multipartite

30. Which of the following malware finds other systems running the same vulnerable software and then replicates itself without any user interaction?

Quick Answer: **41**
Detailed Answer: **49**

- ○ **A.** Virus
- ○ **B.** Trojan
- ○ **C.** Worm
- ○ **D.** Logic bomb

31. Which of the following is the main difference between a Trojan and a virus?

Quick Answer: **41**
Detailed Answer: **49**

- ○ **A.** A Trojan requires user interaction and a virus does not.
- ○ **B.** A Trojan does not replicate itself and a virus does.
- ○ **C.** A virus does not require user interaction and a Trojan does.
- ○ **D.** A virus does not replicate itself and a Trojan does.

32. Which of the following are indications that a computer may contain spyware? (Select all correct answers.)

Quick Answer: **41**
Detailed Answer: **49**

- ○ **A.** The browser home page changes.
- ○ **B.** It takes a long time for the Windows desktop to come up.
- ○ **C.** Clicking a link does nothing or goes to an unexpected website.
- ○ **D.** The email inbox contains an unsolicited email message.

33. Which of the following are acceptable ways of dealing with spam? (Select all correct answers.)

Quick Answer: **41**
Detailed Answer: **50**

- ○ **A.** Delete the email without opening it.
- ○ **B.** Reply back and try to identify the spammer.
- ○ **C.** Turn off the preview function of your email software.
- ○ **D.** Immediately call the local law enforcement office.

34. Which of the following are ways a rootkit can be installed? (Select all correct answers.)

Quick Answer: **41**
Detailed Answer: **50**

    ○ **A.** By accessing documents on the local intranet.

    ○ **B.** Included as part of software package.

    ○ **C.** An unpatched vulnerability.

    ○ **D.** The user downloads it.

35. Which of the following is a type of malware that can use encryption to protect outbound communications and piggyback on commonly used ports to communicate without interrupting other applications that use that port?

Quick Answer: **41**
Detailed Answer: **50**

    ○ **A.** Logic bomb

    ○ **B.** Botnet

    ○ **C.** Adware

    ○ **D.** Rootkit

36. The system administrator abruptly leaves the organization after being passed over for a promotion. Two weeks later, employees report they cannot access files. It has been determined that at midnight the system suddenly began deleting files. Which of the following is the most likely type of malicious code that caused this event?

Quick Answer: **41**
Detailed Answer: **50**

    ○ **A.** Logic bomb

    ○ **B.** Botnet

    ○ **C.** Adware

    ○ **D.** Rootkit

37. Which of the following would best describe the type of malicious code that enters a system through a freeware program that the user installed?

Quick Answer: **41**
Detailed Answer: **50**

    ○ **A.** Virus

    ○ **B.** Trojan

    ○ **C.** Worm

    ○ **D.** Logic bomb

38. Which of the following type of virus avoids antivirus software detection by changing form each time it is executed?

Quick Answer: **41**
Detailed Answer: **50**

    ○ **A.** Polymorphic

    ○ **B.** Macro

    ○ **C.** Stealth

    ○ **D.** Multipartite

39. Which of the following is an automated computer program controlled by outside sources with the intention of forwarding transmissions to other computers on the Internet?

Quick Answer: **41**
Detailed Answer: **51**

  ○ **A.** Logic bomb

  ○ **B.** Adware

  ○ **C.** Bot

  ○ **D.** Virus

40. Which of the following are steps taken to protect a network from malicious code? (Select all correct answers.)

Quick Answer: **41**
Detailed Answer: **51**

  ○ **A.** Do not use any type of removable media from another user without first scanning the disk.

  ○ **B.** Open all attachments sent to you by people you might know.

  ○ **C.** Install firewalls or intrusion-prevention systems on client machines.

  ○ **D.** Subscribe to security newsgroups.

Objective 1.2: Explain the security risks pertaining to system hardware and peripherals.

1. Which of the following type of hardware vulnerability can allow local users to cause a denial of service or the system not to boot?

Quick Answer: **41**
Detailed Answer: **51**

  ○ **A.** USB

  ○ **B.** BIOS

  ○ **C.** NAS

  ○ **D.** PDA

2. Which of the following is an inherent security risk when using network attached storage?

Quick Answer: **41**
Detailed Answer: **51**

  ○ **A.** It is easy to lose this type of storage device.

  ○ **B.** Running applications this way leaves little trace on the host system.

  ○ **C.** Organizations often fail to protect data on storage subsystems.

  ○ **D.** Antivirus software cannot be installed on large storage systems.

3. Which of the following is the primary security concern associated with cell phones and other mobile devices?

Quick Answer: **41**
Detailed Answer: **51**

- ○ **A.** This type of storage device can easily be lost or stolen.
- ○ **B.** Antivirus software cannot be installed on this type of storage device.
- ○ **C.** The data cannot be encrypted on this type of storage device.
- ○ **D.** It is easy to crack the password on this type of storage device.

4. Which of the following can result in the exploitation of a BIOS vulnerability? (Select all correct answers.)

Quick Answer: **41**
Detailed Answer: **51**

- ○ **A.** Hard drive failure
- ○ **B.** System not to boot
- ○ **C.** System to lock up
- ○ **D.** Denial of service

5. Which of the following is the greatest security risk when allowing personal small, high-capacity, removable storage devices on the network?

Quick Answer: **41**
Detailed Answer: **52**

- ○ **A.** A disgruntled employee can easily misuse data.
- ○ **B.** There is no way scan the device for malware.
- ○ **C.** The data transferred cannot be encrypted.
- ○ **D.** The device can easily break off in the attached computer.

6. Which of the following is the most appropriate method to disable unauthorized users from accessing USB storage devices?

Quick Answer: **41**
Detailed Answer: **52**

- ○ **A.** Edit the Registry.
- ○ **B.** Fill the USB slots with glue.
- ○ **C.** Edit Security Accounts Manager.
- ○ **D.** Use Group Policy.

7. Which of the following are ways the BIOS can be compromised? (Select all correct answers.)

Quick Answer: **41**
Detailed Answer: **52**

- ○ **A.** Modifying Registry keys
- ○ **B.** Known vulnerabilities
- ○ **C.** Bypassing access control
- ○ **D.** The BIOS password

8. Which of the following is an inherent security risk associated when allowing cell phones and other mobile devices on the network?

Quick Answer: **41**
Detailed Answer: **52**

   ○ **A.** The data transferred cannot be encrypted.

   ○ **B.** The device can be synched to the user desktop.

   ○ **C.** The device can easily be compromised.

   ○ **D.** Employee productivity is greatly reduced.

9. Which of the following is the primary method used to reduce the risks associated with allowing email to cell phone access?

Quick Answer: **41**
Detailed Answer: **52**

   ○ **A.** Limiting email address access

   ○ **B.** Encrypting the communication

   ○ **C.** Not allowing attachments

   ○ **D.** Requiring both to be password protected

10. Which of the following methods can be used to bypass BIOS access control? (Select all correct answers.)

Quick Answer: **41**
Detailed Answer: **52**

   ○ **A.** Cracking the BIOS password

   ○ **B.** Deleting the contents of the MBR

   ○ **C.** Deleting the contents of the CMOS RAM

   ○ **D.** Overloading the keyboard buffer

11. System access to the BIOS configuration utility is controlled by which of the following?

Quick Answer: **41**
Detailed Answer: **52**

   ○ **A.** Hardware token

   ○ **B.** Lock

   ○ **C.** Password

   ○ **D.** ACL

12. Which of the following is a correct statement regarding the BIOS passwords on a desktop and on a laptop?

Quick Answer: **41**
Detailed Answer: **52**

   ○ **A.** Desktop passwords are automatically encrypted.

   ○ **B.** Laptop passwords are automatically encrypted.

   ○ **C.** Desktop passwords are usually flashed into firmware.

   ○ **D.** Laptop passwords are usually flashed into firmware.

13. Which of the following may be used to bypass the password on a laptop? (Select all correct answers.)

Quick Answer: **41**
Detailed Answer: **52**

- ○ **A.** Special loopback device
- ○ **B.** Lock pick
- ○ **C.** Hardware dongle
- ○ **D.** Removing the CMOS battery

14. Which of the following can minimize the risks associated BIOS vulnerabilities? (Select all correct answers.)

Quick Answer: **41**
Detailed Answer: **53**

- ○ **A.** Using the same BIOS password for all machines
- ○ **B.** Creating a BIOS password policy
- ○ **C.** Changing the BIOS password frequently
- ○ **D.** Using an HDD password

15. Which of the following is the main underlying concern when allowing small, high-capacity, removable storage devices on the corporate network?

Quick Answer: **41**
Detailed Answer: **53**

- ○ **A.** Data encryption
- ○ **B.** Accessibility of multiple computers
- ○ **C.** Malware infection
- ○ **D.** Accessibility of information

16. Which of the following best describes the probable cause when employee handheld devices send large quantities of text messages to random numbers?

Quick Answer: **41**
Detailed Answer: **53**

- ○ **A.** Virus
- ○ **B.** Rootkit
- ○ **C.** Too low of a workload
- ○ **D.** Theft of proprietary information

17. Which of the following should be implemented when employee handheld devices send large quantities of text messages to random numbers?

Quick Answer: **41**
Detailed Answer: **53**

- ○ **A.** Increased work loads
- ○ **B.** Intrusion detection
- ○ **C.** Antivirus software
- ○ **D.** Data encryption

18. Which of the following are security concerns when allowing removable hard drives such as small passport types on the network? (Select all correct answers.)

- ○ **A.** Malware infection
- ○ **B.** Data theft
- ○ **C.** Reduced productivity
- ○ **D.** Information leakage

19. Which of the following is the best approach to prevent unauthorized use of removable storage and portable devices?

- ○ **A.** Placing a USB lock on ports
- ○ **B.** Issuing authorized devices and access
- ○ **C.** Prohibiting the use of media including CDs
- ○ **D.** Requiring device registration with the IT department

20. Which of the following is currently the most effective method to minimize data theft if a storage device is lost?

- ○ **A.** Encryption
- ○ **B.** Password protection
- ○ **C.** Immediate dismissal of the employee
- ○ **D.** Policies dictating proper employee remediation

21. Which of the following are essential parts of SAN or NAS security? (Select all correct answers.)

- ○ **A.** USB locks on ports
- ○ **B.** Secure passwords
- ○ **C.** Antivirus software
- ○ **D.** Data encryption

22. Which of the following security mechanisms should be considered when dealing with large data repositories? (Select all correct answers.)

- ○ **A.** Key management
- ○ **B.** Secure logging
- ○ **C.** Authentication devices
- ○ **D.** Encryption

23. Which of the following storage devices would require protection for data considered "at rest?"

- ○ **A.** USB
- ○ **B.** PDA
- ○ **C.** NAS
- ○ **D.** BIOS

Quick Answer: **41**
Detailed Answer: **54**

24. Which of the following in an inherent risk associated with BIOS passwords?

- ○ **A.** They can easily be guessed.
- ○ **B.** Manufacturer created backdoors.
- ○ **C.** Too many incorrect guesses can lock it out forever.
- ○ **D.** Too many incorrect guesses can destroy the BIOS.

Quick Answer: **41**
Detailed Answer: **54**

25. Which of the following is the most likely result of the physical compromise of the BIOS?

- ○ **A.** A DoS attack.
- ○ **B.** A virus infection.
- ○ **C.** The MBR has been changed.
- ○ **D.** The system boot order has been changed.

Quick Answer: **41**
Detailed Answer: **54**

Objective 1.3: Implement OS hardening practices and procedures to achieve workstation and server security.

1. Which of the following are basic areas of hardening? (Select all correct answers.)

- ○ **A.** Operating system
- ○ **B.** Application
- ○ **C.** Internet
- ○ **D.** Network

Quick Answer: **42**
Detailed Answer: **54**

2. In which of the following hardening areas would file-level security solutions occur? (Select all correct answers.)

Quick Answer: **42**
Detailed Answer: **54**

- ○ **A.** Operating system
- ○ **B.** Application
- ○ **C.** Internet
- ○ **D.** Network

3. In which of the following hardening areas would disabling unnecessary protocols and services occur?

Quick Answer: **42**
Detailed Answer: **55**

- ○ **A.** Operating system
- ○ **B.** Application
- ○ **C.** Internet
- ○ **D.** Network

4. In which of the following hardening areas would hotfixes, patches, and service packs occur? (Select all correct answers.)

Quick Answer: **42**
Detailed Answer: **55**

- ○ **A.** Operating system
- ○ **B.** Application
- ○ **C.** Internet
- ○ **D.** Network

5. Which of the following is critical in hardening a network?

Quick Answer: **42**
Detailed Answer: **55**

- ○ **A.** File-level security
- ○ **B.** Configuring log files
- ○ **C.** Configuring auditing
- ○ **D.** Mapping avenues of access

6. Which of the following updates are very specific and targeted toward an exact problem?

Quick Answer: **42**
Detailed Answer: **55**

- ○ **A.** Service pack
- ○ **B.** Hotfix
- ○ **C.** Patch
- ○ **D.** Maintenance release

7. Which of the following updates is a major revision of functionality and operation?

    O   **A.** Service pack

    O   **B.** Hotfix

    O   **C.** Patch

    O   **D.** Maintenance release

8. Which of the following updates is generally used to eliminate security vulnerabilities?

    O   **A.** Service pack

    O   **B.** Hotfix

    O   **C.** Patch

    O   **D.** Maintenance release

9. Application hardening practices should include reviewing which of the following? (Select all correct answers.)

    O   **A.** Key management

    O   **B.** Default administration accounts

    O   **C.** Standard passwords

    O   **D.** Behavior-based profiles

10. Which of the following best describes why regular update reviews for all deployed operating systems is imperative?

    O   **A.** Default administration accounts may have been compromised.

    O   **B.** Behavior-based profiles may have changed.

    O   **C.** Automated attacks make use of common vulnerabilities.

    O   **D.** Firmware updates may have been accidentally missed.

11. Which of the following best describes why public key infrastructure (PKI) implementations must be properly configured and updated?

    O   **A.** Behavior-based profiles may have changed.

    O   **B.** To maintain key and ticket stores.

    O   **C.** Automated attacks make use of common vulnerabilities.

    O   **D.** To isolate access attempts.

12. Hardening of the operating system includes which of the following? (Select all correct answers.)

Quick Answer: **42**
Detailed Answer: **57**

  ○ **A.** Updating the system firmware

  ○ **B.** Configuring log files and auditing

  ○ **C.** Implementation of account lockout policies

  ○ **D.** Changing default account names and passwords

13. Hardening of the network includes which of the following? (Select all correct answers.)

Quick Answer: **42**
Detailed Answer: **57**

  ○ **A.** Configuring devices and firewalls

  ○ **B.** Configuring log files and auditing

  ○ **C.** Securing the file system selection

  ○ **D.** Updating the hardware firmware

14. Which of the following is the primary reason public areas of the network should be included in a site survey?

Quick Answer: **42**
Detailed Answer: **57**

  ○ **A.** It mitigates unsecure access to a secured network.

  ○ **B.** It addresses emergent hardware-related vulnerabilities.

  ○ **C.** It isolates access attempts within the operating system environment.

  ○ **D.** It allows the proper level of access control.

15. Which of the following is the primary reason regular log review is critical for web servers?

Quick Answer: **42**
Detailed Answer: **57**

  ○ **A.** To prevent SMTP relay from being used by spammers

  ○ **B.** To verify URL values are not exploiting unpatched buffer overruns

  ○ **C.** To confirm that password details are not being intercepted

  ○ **D.** To prevent poisoning by unauthorized zone transfers

16. Which of the following is the primary reason hardening is necessary for email servers?

Quick Answer: **42**
Detailed Answer: **57**

  ○ **A.** To prevent SMTP relay from being used by spammers

  ○ **B.** To verify URL values are not exploiting unpatched buffer overruns

  ○ **C.** To confirm that password details are not being intercepted

  ○ **D.** To prevent poisoning by unauthorized zone transfers

17. NNTP servers raise many of the same security considerations risks as which of the following server types?

- ○ **A.** Database
- ○ **B.** DNS
- ○ **C.** Email
- ○ **D.** DHCP

18. Which of the following is the primary reason hardening is necessary for DNS servers?

- ○ **A.** To prevent SMTP relay from being used by spammers
- ○ **B.** To verify URL values are not exploiting unpatched buffer overruns
- ○ **C.** To confirm that password details are not being intercepted
- ○ **D.** To prevent poisoning from forged query results

19. Which of the following is the primary reason regular log review is critical for FTP servers?

- ○ **A.** To prevent SMTP relay from being used by spammers
- ○ **B.** To verify URL values are not exploiting unpatched buffer overruns
- ○ **C.** To confirm that password details are not being intercepted
- ○ **D.** To prevent poisoning by unauthorized zone transfers

20. Which of the following is the primary reason hardening is necessary for print servers?

- ○ **A.** To prevent SMTP relay from being used by spammers
- ○ **B.** To prevent exposure of access credentials to packet sniffing
- ○ **C.** To prevent client leases from rogue servers
- ○ **D.** To prevent DoS attacks by unauthorized parties

21. DHCP servers raise many of the same security considerations risks as which of the following server types?

- ○ **A.** Database
- ○ **B.** DNS
- ○ **C.** Email
- ○ **D.** NNTP

22. Data repositories of any type might require specialized security considerations due to which of the following? (Select all correct answers.)

Quick Answer: **42**
Detailed Answer: **59**

- ○ **A.** Access requirements
- ○ **B.** Bandwidth requirements
- ○ **C.** Processing resources requirements
- ○ **D.** Lease requirements

23. Which of the following is true of network file shares?

Quick Answer: **42**
Detailed Answer: **59**

- ○ **A.** Scope address pools will flood with insufficient lease duration.
- ○ **B.** They are not secure until default access permissions are removed.
- ○ **C.** If not secured, DoS attacks can prevent proper name resolution.
- ○ **D.** The password is always encrypted in all network file-sharing systems.

24. Which of the following best describes why operating systems that support DHCP server authentication should be used?

Quick Answer: **42**
Detailed Answer: **59**

- ○ **A.** To prevent SMTP relay from being used by spammers
- ○ **B.** To prevent exposure of access credentials to packet sniffing
- ○ **C.** To prevent client leases from rogue servers
- ○ **D.** To prevent DoS attacks by unauthorized parties

25. Which of the following are appropriate methods to improve the security of data repositories? (Select all correct answers.)

Quick Answer: **42**
Detailed Answer: **59**

- ○ **A.** Use of role-based access control
- ○ **B.** Elimination of unneeded connection libraries
- ○ **C.** Use of discretionary-based access control
- ○ **D.** Elimination of bandwidth restrictions

26. Which of the following enables an administrator to set consistent common security standards for a certain group of computers and enforce common computer and user configurations?

   ○ **A.** Group Policy

   ○ **B.** User Manager

   ○ **C.** Task Manager

   ○ **D.** Network Monitor

Quick Answer: **42**
Detailed Answer: **59**

27. Which of the following best describes the default behavior of a group policy?

   ○ **A.** Hierarchical and proportionate

   ○ **B.** Hierarchical and singular

   ○ **C.** Inherited and singular

   ○ **D.** Inherited and cumulative

Quick Answer: **42**
Detailed Answer: **59**

28. Which of the following is the most appropriate method to apply a security update to 1000 client machines?

   ○ **A.** Use role-based access control

   ○ **B.** Use a Group Policy object

   ○ **C.** Use a distribution server

   ○ **D.** Use Resultant Set of Policy

Quick Answer: **42**
Detailed Answer: **60**

29. Which of the following are the most compelling reasons that configuration baselines have been established? (Select all correct answers.)

   ○ **A.** Industry standards

   ○ **B.** Organizational requests

   ○ **C.** Governmental mandates

   ○ **D.** Regulatory bodies

Quick Answer: **42**
Detailed Answer: **60**

30. Which of the following would an administrator apply to reflect an appropriate level of baseline security based on server role?

   ○ **A.** Group Policy

   ○ **B.** Configuration baseline

   ○ **C.** Security template

   ○ **D.** Active Directory

Quick Answer: **42**
Detailed Answer: **60**

Objective 1.4: Carry out the appropriate procedures to establish application security.

Quick Answer: **42**
Detailed Answer: **60**

1. Which of the following are identified vulnerabilities of the Java language? (Select all correct answers.)

   ○ **A.** Buffer overflows

   ○ **B.** Unauthorized file upload

   ○ **C.** Email exposure

   ○ **D.** Unexpected redirection

Quick Answer: **42**
Detailed Answer: **60**

2. Which of the following most accurately describes how Java applets execute?

   ○ **A.** When the web server retrieves the directory web page

   ○ **B.** When the web server's browser loads the hosting web page

   ○ **C.** When the client machine's browser loads the hosting web page

   ○ **D.** When the operating system loads the hosting web page

Quick Answer: **42**
Detailed Answer: **60**

3. Which of the following best describes the reason Java applets are a security risk?

   ○ **A.** Java is compiled on the client browser.

   ○ **B.** Java is a precompiled language.

   ○ **C.** Java is compiled by the client operating system.

   ○ **D.** Java applets execute on the hosting web server.

Quick Answer: **42**
Detailed Answer: **60**

4. Which of the following are identified vulnerabilities of JavaScript? (Select all correct answers.)

   ○ **A.** Buffer overflows

   ○ **B.** Unauthorized file upload

   ○ **C.** Email exposure

   ○ **D.** Unexpected redirection

Quick Answer: **42**
Detailed Answer: **61**

5. Which of the following is the most effective method to mitigate vulnerabilities exposed by earlier forms of Java?

Quick Answer: **42**
Detailed Answer: **61**

- ○ **A.** Keeping machines up-to-date with new version releases
- ○ **B.** Disabling third-party browser extensions
- ○ **C.** Setting the pop-up blocker setting to high
- ○ **D.** Enabling Integrated Windows Authentication

6. ActiveX and its controls share many of the same vulnerabilities present in which of the following?

Quick Answer: **42**
Detailed Answer: **61**

- ○ **A.** Cookies
- ○ **B.** JavaScript
- ○ **C.** Embedded Java applets
- ○ **D.** Common Gateway Interface script

7. Which of the following is the most realistic method to mitigate having cookies expose long-term browsing habits?

Quick Answer: **42**
Detailed Answer: **61**

- ○ **A.** Disabling third-party browser extensions
- ○ **B.** Regularly clearing the browser cookie cache
- ○ **C.** Configuring client browsers to block all cookies
- ○ **D.** Disabling automatic code execution on client browsers

8. Which of the following is the most effective method to mitigate buffer overflows or cross-site scripting attacks?

Quick Answer: **42**
Detailed Answer: **61**

- ○ **A.** Blocking third-party cookies
- ○ **B.** Accepting only numeric data input
- ○ **C.** Disabling third-party browser extensions
- ○ **D.** Validating data input

9. Which of the following is most likely to use a tracking cookie?

Quick Answer: **42**
Detailed Answer: **61**

- ○ **A.** Spyware
- ○ **B.** Credit Union
- ○ **C.** Trojan
- ○ **D.** Shopping cart

10. Which of the following best describes what the exploitation of
Simple Mail Transport Protocol (SMTP) relay agents is used for?

   ○ **A.** Buffer overflow

   ○ **B.** Logic bomb

   ○ **C.** Spyware

   ○ **D.** Spam

Quick Answer: **42**
Detailed Answer: **62**

11. Which of the following best describes a tracking cookie?

   ○ **A.** Beneficial

   ○ **B.** Permanent

   ○ **C.** Temporary

   ○ **D.** Valuable

Quick Answer: **42**
Detailed Answer: **62**

12. S-HTTP communicates over which of the following ports?

   ○ **A.** 80

   ○ **B.** 443

   ○ **C.** 110

   ○ **D.** 4445

Quick Answer: **42**
Detailed Answer: **62**

13. HTTPS communicates over which of the following ports?

   ○ **A.** 80

   ○ **B.** 443

   ○ **C.** 110

   ○ **D.** 4445

Quick Answer: **42**
Detailed Answer: **62**

14. Which of the following exploits are associated with SSL certificates? (Select all correct answers.)

   ○ **A.** Ill-formatted requests

   ○ **B.** Small key sizes

   ○ **C.** Outdated CRLs

   ○ **D.** Buffer overflows

Quick Answer: **42**
Detailed Answer: **62**

15. Which of the following vulnerabilities are associated with LDAP?
(Select all correct answers.)

   ○ **A.** Ill-formatted requests

   ○ **B.** Small key sizes

   ○ **C.** Outdated CRLs

   ○ **D.** Buffer overflows

Quick Answer: **42**
Detailed Answer: **62**

16. Which of the following vulnerabilities are associated with FTP? (Select all correct answers.)

- ○ **A.** Buffer overflows
- ○ **B.** Anonymous file access
- ○ **C.** Unencrypted authentication
- ○ **D.** Improper formatted requests

Quick Answer: **42**
Detailed Answer: **63**

17. FTP over SSL communicates over which of the following ports?

- ○ **A.** 21
- ○ **B.** 80
- ○ **C.** 22
- ○ **D.** 81

Quick Answer: **42**
Detailed Answer: **63**

18. Which of the following are security concerns when allowing IM applications on the network? (Select all correct answers.)

- ○ **A.** The capture of cached logs containing conversations
- ○ **B.** Malware spreading through IM contacts
- ○ **C.** Unauthorized data and video sharing
- ○ **D.** Improper formatted requests

Quick Answer: **42**
Detailed Answer: **63**

19. Which of the following are exploits for CGI scripts? (Select all correct answers.)

- ○ **A.** Buffer overflows.
- ○ **B.** Anonymous file access.
- ○ **C.** Arbitrary commands may be executed on the server.
- ○ **D.** Arbitrary commands may be executed on the client.

Quick Answer: **42**
Detailed Answer: **63**

20. An attacker places code within a web page that redirects the client's browser to attack yet another site when a client's browser opens the web page. This is an example of what type of attack?

- ○ **A.** Unencrypted authentication
- ○ **B.** Session hijacking
- ○ **C.** Buffer overflow
- ○ **D.** Cross-site scripting

Quick Answer: **42**
Detailed Answer: **63**

21. Which of the following best describes Java or JavaScript?

   ○ **A.** Java applets allow access to cache information.

   ○ **B.** JavaScript can provide access to files of known name.

   ○ **C.** JavaScript runs even after the applet is closed.

   ○ **D.** Java applets can execute arbitrary instructions on the server.

Quick Answer: **42**
Detailed Answer: **63**

22. Which of the following is another name for identification of configuration details of the server that may be helpful to later identify unauthorized access attempts?

   ○ **A.** Profiling

   ○ **B.** Reporting

   ○ **C.** Abstracting

   ○ **D.** Hyperlinking

Quick Answer: **42**
Detailed Answer: **64**

23. Which of the following is the most likely reason it is dangerous to maintain cookie session information?

   ○ **A.** It provides custom user configuration settings.

   ○ **B.** It may expose sensitive information about secured sites.

   ○ **C.** It allows multiple actual connections to a web server.

   ○ **D.** It may allow automatic code execution on client browsers.

Quick Answer: **42**
Detailed Answer: **64**

24. Which of the following are browser-based vulnerabilities? (Select all correct answers.)

   ○ **A.** Session hijacking

   ○ **B.** SQL injection

   ○ **C.** Buffer overflows

   ○ **D.** Social engineering

Quick Answer: **42**
Detailed Answer: **64**

25. Which of the following is of most concern for a security administrator when allowing peer-to-peer networking?

   ○ **A.** Buffer-overflow attacks can go unnoticed.

   ○ **B.** Unauthorized file upload to network servers.

   ○ **C.** Connections are negotiated directly between clients.

   ○ **D.** Arbitrary commands may be executed on the server.

Quick Answer: **42**
Detailed Answer: **64**

Objective 1.5: Implement security applications.

1. Which of the following most accurately describes personal firewall design?

   ○ **A.** Closes off systems by integrity checking

   ○ **B.** Closes off systems by blocking port access

   ○ **C.** Closes off systems by blacklisting applications

   ○ **D.** Closes off systems by blocking BIOS access

Quick Answer: **43**
Detailed Answer: **64**

2. Which of the following best describes where host intrusion prevention system software resides?

   ○ **A.** Between the system's Registry and OS kernel

   ○ **B.** At the application level

   ○ **C.** Between the system's applications and OS kernel

   ○ **D.** At the network layer

Quick Answer: **43**
Detailed Answer: **64**

3. Which of the following types of detection does a host intrusion detection system use? (Select all correct answers.)

   ○ **A.** Anomaly detection

   ○ **B.** Misuse detection

   ○ **C.** Blacklist detection

   ○ **D.** Outbound detection

Quick Answer: **43**
Detailed Answer: **64**

4. Which of the following is the most appropriate reason for firewalls to monitor outbound connections?

   ○ **A.** To track the collection of personal data

   ○ **B.** To track users going to inappropriate sites

   ○ **C.** To monitor excessive user bandwidth usage

   ○ **D.** To catch malware that transmits information

Quick Answer: **43**
Detailed Answer: **65**

5. Which of the following is most common detection method used in antivirus programs?

   ○ **A.** Anomaly detection

   ○ **B.** Misuse detection

   ○ **C.** Scanning

   ○ **D.** Filtering

Quick Answer: **43**
Detailed Answer: **65**

6. Which of the following is most common main component of anti-spam software?

   ○ **A.** Anomaly detection

   ○ **B.** Misuse detection

   ○ **C.** Scanning

   ○ **D.** Filtering

Quick Answer: **43**
Detailed Answer: **65**

7. Which of the following best describes antivirus scanning technology?

   ○ **A.** Identifies virus code based on a unique behavior pattern

   ○ **B.** Identifies virus code based on a unique set of Registry keys

   ○ **C.** Identifies virus code based on a unique string of characters

   ○ **D.** Identifies virus code based on a unique set of commands

Quick Answer: **43**
Detailed Answer: **65**

8. Which of the following are unintended consequences of using pop-up blockers with high settings? (Select all correct answers.)

   ○ **A.** Applications or programs might not install.

   ○ **B.** Firewall applications might not work properly.

   ○ **C.** It verifies a legitimate working user account.

   ○ **D.** Information entered is deleted by reloading the page.

Quick Answer: **43**
Detailed Answer: **65**

9. Which of the following best describes heuristic scanning behavior?

   ○ **A.** Searches for operating system kernel-level changes

   ○ **B.** Looks for instructions not typically found in the application

   ○ **C.** Identifies virus code based on a unique string of characters

   ○ **D.** Monitors both incoming and outgoing connections

Quick Answer: **43**
Detailed Answer: **65**

10. Which of the following are known issues with using heuristic scanning methods? (Select all correct answers.)

   ○ **A.** Buffer overflow

   ○ **B.** Susceptible to false positives

   ○ **C.** Cannot identify new viruses without database update

   ○ **D.** Logic bomb

Quick Answer: **43**
Detailed Answer: **65**

11. Which of the following best describes a false positive?

   ○ **A.** The software classifies a nonintrusive action as a possible intrusion.

   ○ **B.** The software detects virus-like behavior and pops up a warning.

   ○ **C.** The software classifies an intrusive as a nonintrusive action.

   ○ **D.** The software fails to detects virus-like behavior.

Quick Answer: **43**
Detailed Answer: **66**

12. When an organization implements a decentralized antispam software solution, which of the following will happen?

   ○ **A.** A central server pushes updates to the client machines.

   ○ **B.** The antispam vendor is responsible for the updates.

   ○ **C.** The department manager is responsible for updates.

   ○ **D.** The individual users are responsible for updates.

Quick Answer: **43**
Detailed Answer: **66**

13. Which of the following will result when the antispam software filter level is set to high? (Select all correct answers.)

   ○ **A.** Fewer false positives

   ○ **B.** More false positives

   ○ **C.** Less spam will be filtered

   ○ **D.** More spam will be filtered

Quick Answer: **43**
Detailed Answer: **66**

14. Which of the following best describes the result of adding an email address to the approved list?

   ○ **A.** It is considered part of the white list.

   ○ **B.** It is considered part of the black list.

   ○ **C.** It is considered part of the gray list.

   ○ **D.** It is considered part of the brown list.

Quick Answer: **43**
Detailed Answer: **66**

15. Which of the following best describes the result of adding an email address to the blocked list?

   ○ **A.** It is considered part of the white list.

   ○ **B.** It is considered part of the black list.

   ○ **C.** It is considered part of the gray list.

   ○ **D.** It is considered part of the brown list.

Quick Answer: **43**
Detailed Answer: **66**

16. Which of the following are characteristics of pop-ups? (Select all correct answers.)

Quick Answer: **43**
Detailed Answer: **66**

  ○ **A.** Some are helpful.

  ○ **B.** Most are integrated in toolbars.

  ○ **C.** Many are an annoyance.

  ○ **D.** Some are malicious.

17. Which of the following is true about pop-up blockers? (Select all correct answers.)

Quick Answer: **43**
Detailed Answer: **66**

  ○ **A.** Most block only JavaScript.

  ○ **B.** Many are integrated into toolbars.

  ○ **C.** Flash can bypass a pop-up blocker.

  ○ **D.** The user cannot adjust the settings.

18. Which of the following pop-up blocker settings will block most automatic pop-ups but still allow functionality?

Quick Answer: **43**
Detailed Answer: **67**

  ○ **A.** Low

  ○ **B.** Medium

  ○ **C.** High

  ○ **D.** Custom

19. Which of the following best describes a pop-under ad?

Quick Answer: **43**
Detailed Answer: **67**

  ○ **A.** Pop-up used to install software

  ○ **B.** Pop-up used to fill-in forms

  ○ **C.** Unseen until the current window is closed

  ○ **D.** Floating pop-up in a web page

20. Which of the following best describes a hover ad?

Quick Answer: **43**
Detailed Answer: **67**

  ○ **A.** Pop-up used to install software

  ○ **B.** Pop-up used to fill-in forms

  ○ **C.** Unseen until the current window is closed

  ○ **D.** Floating pop-up in a web page

21. Which of the following is the most likely reason that certain mes-
    sages continue to pass though the spam filter even though they
    are set to the organizational specifications?

    ○ **A.** The software is inferior and should be returned.

    ○ **B.** The software settings need to be adjusted.

    ○ **C.** The software can't assign meaning to words.

    ○ **D.** The software needs to be retrained.

22. Which of the following is a part of heuristic antispam filtering?

    ○ **A.** A predefined rule set

    ○ **B.** A predefined character set

    ○ **C.** A predefined set of commands

    ○ **D.** A predefined set of Registry keys

23. Which of the following best describes the term for a unique string
    of characters used in antivirus software?

    ○ **A.** Heuristic

    ○ **B.** Signature

    ○ **C.** Misnomer

    ○ **D.** Anomaly

24. Which of the following best describes the characteristics of host-
    based IDSs? (Select all correct answers.)

    ○ **A.** Good at detecting unauthorized user activity

    ○ **B.** Good at detecting unauthorized file modifications

    ○ **C.** Good at detecting denial of service attacks

    ○ **D.** Good at detecting unauthorized user access

25. Which of the following is the main purpose of a host-based IDS?

    ○ **A.** Prevent attacks in real time

    ○ **B.** Locate packets not allowed on the network

    ○ **C.** Proactively protect machines against attacks

    ○ **D.** Analyze data that originates on the local machine

Objective 1.6: Explain the purpose and application of virtualization technology.

1. Which of the following is an inherent security risk in using virtual machines?

   Quick Answer: **43**
   Detailed Answer: **68**

   ○ **A.** The BIOS can easily be compromised.

   ○ **B.** The boot order can be easily changed.

   ○ **C.** Security measures are nonexistent.

   ○ **D.** The entire machine can be compromised.

2. Which of the following would be the most effective method to protect a virtual environment hosting medical data?

   Quick Answer: **43**
   Detailed Answer: **68**

   ○ **A.** Using segmented physical hardware for the virtual servers

   ○ **B.** Using shared physical hardware with virtual machines for testing

   ○ **C.** Using segmented physical hardware for each virtual server

   ○ **D.** Using shared physical hardware with virtual machines for web applications

3. Which of the following are appropriate reasons to use virtualized environments? (Select all correct answers.)

   Quick Answer: **43**
   Detailed Answer: **68**

   ○ **A.** Reduces threat risk

   ○ **B.** Allows isolation of applications

   ○ **C.** Reduces equipment costs

   ○ **D.** Allows environments on USB devices

4. Which of the following controls how access to a computer's processors and memory is shared in a virtual environment?

   Quick Answer: **43**
   Detailed Answer: **68**

   ○ **A.** BIOS

   ○ **B.** Hypervisor

   ○ **C.** Operating system

   ○ **D.** Virtual machine applications

5. In which of the following ways would a forensic analyst mostly likely use a virtual environment? (Select all correct answers.)

Quick Answer: **43**
Detailed Answer: **68**

- ○ **A.** To view the environment the same way the criminal did
- ○ **B.** To load multiple cases at once
- ○ **C.** To image hard drives and removable media
- ○ **D.** To examine environments that may contain malware

6. Which of the following is true in regard to a compromised virtual machine environment?

Quick Answer: **43**
Detailed Answer: **68**

- ○ **A.** It is contained in its own environment.
- ○ **B.** It can provide access to the network.
- ○ **C.** Any threat can easily be addressed by deletion.
- ○ **D.** It can be replaced by a backup copy immediately.

7. Which of the following is true about virtual machine environments? (Select all correct answers.)

Quick Answer: **43**
Detailed Answer: **69**

- ○ **A.** They are susceptible to the same issues as a host operating system.
- ○ **B.** They do not need antivirus or malware protection.
- ○ **C.** They need to be patched just like host environments.
- ○ **D.** They are contained environments that do not need patching.

8. In which of the following areas should the vulnerabilities of existing virtual environments be addressed?

Quick Answer: **43**
Detailed Answer: **69**

- ○ **A.** Change management policy
- ○ **B.** Business continuity plan
- ○ **C.** Organizational security policy
- ○ **D.** Disaster recovery plan

9. Which of the following are areas where virtual environments can be used to improve security? (Select all correct answers.)

Quick Answer: **43**
Detailed Answer: **69**

- ○ **A.** Scanning for malicious software
- ○ **B.** Reducing internal data aggregation
- ○ **C.** Allowing unstable applications to be isolated
- ○ **D.** Providing better disaster recovery solutions

10. Which of the following is the most effective method to reduce server power consumption?

Quick Answer: **43**
Detailed Answer: **69**

- ○ **A.** Replacing older servers with newer low wattage servers
- ○ **B.** Combining all physical hardware into one virtualized server
- ○ **C.** Using segmented physical hardware for like-kind servers
- ○ **D.** Using shared physical hardware for all virtual servers

11. On which of the following types of technology can virtual environments be run? (Select all correct answers.)

Quick Answer: **43**
Detailed Answer: **69**

- ○ **A.** Servers
- ○ **B.** Desktops
- ○ **C.** USB drives
- ○ **D.** Routers

12. Which of the following best describes a hypervisor?

Quick Answer: **43**
Detailed Answer: **69**

- ○ **A.** Acts as an intermediary between the kernel and the OS
- ○ **B.** Provides multiple hardware systems to run one OS
- ○ **C.** Acts as an intermediary between the kernel and the hardware
- ○ **D.** Provides more than one operating system to run on a computer

13. Which of the following best describes a Type 1 hypervisor?

Quick Answer: **43**
Detailed Answer: **70**

- ○ **A.** Runs directly on the hardware platform
- ○ **B.** Runs at the second level above the hardware
- ○ **C.** Runs within an operating system environment
- ○ **D.** Runs at the third level above the hardware

14. Which of the following best describes a Type 2 hypervisor?

Quick Answer: **43**
Detailed Answer: **70**

- ○ **A.** Runs directly on the hardware platform
- ○ **B.** Runs at the second level above the hardware
- ○ **C.** Runs within an operating system environment
- ○ **D.** Runs at the third level above the hardware

15. Security concerns of virtual environments begin with which of the following?

    ○ **A.** The underlying hardware

    ○ **B.** The guest operating system

    ○ **C.** The host operating system

    ○ **D.** The virtual machine files

Quick Answer: **43**
Detailed Answer: **70**

16. Which of the following is an unintended security risk in using virtual machines?

    ○ **A.** The BIOS can easily be compromised.

    ○ **B.** Disaster recovery becomes more complex.

    ○ **C.** Most virtual machines run with high privileges.

    ○ **D.** Technology is advancing faster than security.

Quick Answer: **43**
Detailed Answer: **70**

17. Which of the following is the most effective method to secure a virtualized environment?

    ○ **A.** Using encryption for all communication

    ○ **B.** Locking down the host machine as tightly as possible

    ○ **C.** Hosting as many virtual machines per server as possible

    ○ **D.** Segmenting by the sensitivity of the contained information

Quick Answer: **43**
Detailed Answer: **70**

18. Which of the following are areas that need special consideration when used in a virtualized environment? (Select all correct answers.)

    ○ **A.** Web servers in a virtualized demilitarized zone

    ○ **B.** Secure storage on virtualized SAN technologies

    ○ **C.** Financial applications on virtualized shared hosting

    ○ **D.** Multiple virtualized email applications on the same server

Quick Answer: **43**
Detailed Answer: **71**

19. Preconfigured virtual appliances are available for which of the following? (Select all correct answers.)

    ○ **A.** Output devices

    ○ **B.** Operating systems

    ○ **C.** Networking components

    ○ **D.** Applications

Quick Answer: **43**
Detailed Answer: **71**

20. When using a Type 2 hypervisor, the guest operating system runs where?

Quick Answer: **43**
Detailed Answer: **71**

- ○ **A.** Directly on the hardware platform
- ○ **B.** At the second level above the hardware
- ○ **C.** Within an operating system environment
- ○ **D.** At the third level above the hardware

Quick-Check Answer Key

Objective 1.1: Differentiate among various systems security threats.

1. A	15. B	29. D
2. C	16. A	30. C
3. A	17. B	31. B
4. B	18. A	32. A, B, C
5. C	19. A, B, D	33. A, C
6. B	20. A, C	34. B, C, D
7. A	21. C	35. D
8. C	22. D	36. A
9. A, B, C	23. B	37. B
10. A	24. A	38. A
11. D	25. B	39. C
12. C	26. C	40. A, C, D
13. A	27. B	
14. D	28. A, C, D	

Objective 1.2: Explain the security risks pertaining to system hardware and peripherals.

1. B	10. A, C, D	19. B
2. C	11. C	20. A
3. A	12. D	21. C, D
4. B, D	13. A, C	22. A, B, C, D
5. A	14. B, C	23. C
6. D	15. D	24. B
7. B, C, D	16. A	25. D
8. B	17. C	
9. B	18. A, B, D	

Objective 1.3: Implement OS hardening practices and procedures to achieve workstation and server security.

1. A, B, C	11. B	21. B
2. A, B	12. B, C, D	22. A, B, C
3. D	13. A, B, D	23. B
4. A, B	14. A	24. C
5. D	15. B	25. A, B
6. B	16. A	26. A
7. A	17. C	27. D
8. C	18. D	28. B
9. B, C	19. C	29. A, C, D
10. C	20. D	30. C

Objective 1.4: Carry out the appropriate procedures to establish application security.

1. A, D	10. D	19. A, C
2. C	11. B	20. D
3. B	12. A	21. B
4. B, C	13. B	22. A
5. A	14. B, C	23. B
6. C	15. A, D	24. A, C
7. B	16. B, C	25. C
8. D	17. A	
9. A	18. A, B, C	

Objective 1.5: Implement security applications.

1. B
2. C
3. A,
4. D
5. C
6. D
7. C
8. A, D
9. B
10. B, C
11. A
12. D
13. B, D
14. A
15. B
16. A, C, D
17. A, B, C
18. B
19. C
20. D
21. C
22. A
23. B
24. A, B
25. D

Objective 1.6: Explain the purpose and application of virtualization technology.

1. D
2. A
3. B, C
4. B
5. B, D
6. B
7. A, C
8. C
9. C, D
10. C
11. A, B, C, D
12. D
13. A
14. C
15. B
16. C
17. D
18. B, C
19. B, C, D
20. D

Answers and Explanations

Objective 1.1: Differentiate among various systems security threats.

1. **Answer: A.** Perhaps the most popular method of privilege escalation is a buffer over-flow attack. Buffer overflows cause disruption of service and lost data. This condition occurs when the data presented to an application or service exceeds the storage-space allocation that has been reserved in memory for that application or service. Answer B is incorrect because programs disguised as useful applications are Trojans. Trojans do not replicate themselves like viruses, but they can be just as destructive. Code is hidden inside the application that can attack your system directly or allow the system to be compromised by the code's originator. The Trojan is typically hidden, so its ability to spread depends on the popularity of the software (such as a game) and a user's willingness to download and install the software. Answer C is incorrect because a virus is a program or piece of code designed to attach itself to other code and replicate. It replicates when an infected file is executed or launched. Answer D is incorrect because spyware is associated with behaviors such as advertising, collecting personal information, or changing you computer configuration without appropriately obtaining prior consent. Basically, spyware is software that communicates information from a user's system to another party without notifying the user.

2. **Answer: C.** A program or piece of code that runs on your computer without your knowledge is a virus. It is designed to attach itself to other code and replicate. It replicates when an infected file is executed or launched. Answer A is incorrect. Buffer over-flows cause disruption of service and lost data. This condition occurs when the data presented to an application or service exceeds the storage-space allocation that has been reserved in memory for that application or service. Answer B is incorrect because programs disguised as useful applications are Trojans. Trojans do not repli-cate themselves like viruses, but they can be just as destructive. Code is hidden inside the application that can attack your system directly or allow the system to be compro-mised by the code's originator. The Trojan is typically hidden, so its ability to spread depends on the popularity of the software and a user's willingness to download and install the software. Answer D is incorrect because spyware is associated with behav-iors such as advertising, collecting personal information, or changing your computer configuration without appropriately obtaining prior consent. Basically, spyware is soft-ware that communicates information from a user's system to another party without notifying the user.

3. **Answer: D.** A Trojan horse appears to be useful software but has code hidden inside that will attack your system directly or allow the system to be infiltrated by the origina-tor of the code after it has been executed. Answer A is incorrect because it describes a worm. Worms are similar in function and behavior to a virus with the exception that worms are self-replicating. Answer B is incorrect because it describes IP spoofing. Answer C is incorrect because it describes spyware.

4. **Answer: B.** A rootkit is a piece of software that can be installed and hidden on a computer mainly for the purpose of compromising the system and getting escalated privileges such as administrative rights. Answer A is incorrect because spyware is associated with behaviors such as advertising, collecting personal information, or changing your computer configuration without appropriately obtaining prior consent. Basically, spyware is software that communicates information from a user's system to another party without notifying the user. Answer C is incorrect. A bot provides a spam or virus originator with the venue to propagate. Many computers compromised in this way are unprotected home computers (although recently it has become known that many computers in the corporate world are bots, too). A botnet is a large number of computers that forward transmissions to other computers on the Internet. You may also hear a botnet referred to a zombie army. Answer D is incorrect. Adware is a form of advertising that installs additional tracking software on your system that keeps in contact with the company through your Internet connection. It reports data to the company, such as your surfing habits and which sites you have visited.

5. **Answer: C.** Code Red is an exploit is used to spread a worm. This threat affects only web servers running Microsoft Windows 2000. Answers A, B, and D are incorrect; Melissa, Acid Rain, and Mocmex are not worms. Melissa is a virus. Acid Rain and Mocmex are Trojans.

6. **Answer: B.** A logic bomb is a virus or Trojan horse that is built to go off when a certain event occurs or a period of time goes by. Answers A and D are incorrect because a specified time element is involved. Answer C is incorrect because spoofing involves modifying the source address of traffic or the source of information.

7. **Answer: A.** Spyware is associated with behaviors such as advertising, collecting personal information, or changing your computer configuration without appropriately obtaining prior consent. Basically, spyware is software that communicates information from a user's system to another party without notifying the user. Answer B is incorrect because a piece of software that can be installed and hidden on a computer mainly for the purpose of compromising the system and getting escalated privileges such as administrative rights is a rootkit. Answer C is incorrect because a large number of computers that forward transmissions to other computers on the Internet, allowing the originator a venue to propagate, is a botnet. Answer D is incorrect because a form of advertising that installs additional tracking software on your system that keeps in contact with the company through your Internet connection is adware. It reports data to the company, such as your surfing habits and which sites you have visited.

8. **Answer: C.** Requesting to be removed from junk email lists often results in more spam because it verifies that you have a legitimate, working email address. Therefore answers A, B, and D are incorrect.

9. **Answer: A, B, C.** Email spam lists are often created by scanning newsgroup postings, stealing Internet mailing lists, or searching the Web for addresses. Spammers use automated tools to subscribe to as many mailing lists as possible. From those lists, they capture addresses or use the mailing list as a direct target for their attacks. Answer D is incorrect because email spam lists are not created in this manner.

10. **Answer: A.** Perhaps the most popular method of privilege escalation is a buffer over-flow attack. Buffer overflows cause disruption of service and lost data. This condition occurs when the data presented to an application or service exceeds the storage-space allocation that has been reserved in memory for that application or service. Answer B is incorrect because a virus is a program or piece of code designed to attach itself to other code and replicate. It replicates when an infected file is executed or launched. Answer C is incorrect. A Trojan horse appears to be useful software but has code hidden inside that will attack your system directly or allow the system to be infiltrated by the originator of the code after it has been executed. Answer D is incorrect. A logic bomb is a virus or Trojan horse designed to execute malicious actions when a certain event occurs or a period of time goes by.

11. **Answer: D.** Worms are similar in function and behavior to a virus with the exception that worms are self-replicating. A worm is built to take advantage of a security hole in an existing application or operating system and then find other systems running the same software and automatically replicate itself to the new host. Answer A is incorrect. Spyware is associated with behaviors such as collecting personal information or changing your computer configuration without appropriately obtaining prior consent. Basically, spyware is software that communicates information from a user's system to another party without notifying the user. Answer B is incorrect because a virus is a program or piece of code designed to attach itself to other code and replicate. It repli-cates when an infected file is executed or launched. Answer C is incorrect. A Trojan horse appears to be useful software but has code hidden inside that will attack your system directly or allow the system to be infiltrated by the originator of the code after it has been executed.

12. **Answer: C.** A Trojan horse appears to be useful software but has code hidden inside that will attack your system directly or allow the system to be infiltrated by the origina-tor of the code after it has been executed. Answer A is incorrect. Spyware is associat-ed with behaviors such as collecting personal information or changing your computer configuration without appropriately obtaining prior consent. Basically, spyware is soft-ware that communicates information from a user's system to another party without notifying the user. Answer B is incorrect because a virus is a program or piece of code designed to attach itself to other code and replicate. It replicates when an infected file is executed or launched. Answer D is incorrect. Worms are similar in function and behavior to a virus with the exception that worms are self-replicating. A worm is built to take advantage of a security hole in an existing application or operating system and then find other systems running the same software and automatically replicate itself to the new host.

13. **Answer: A.** Spyware is associated with behaviors such as collecting personal informa-tion or changing your computer configuration without appropriately obtaining prior consent. Basically, spyware is software that communicates information from a user's system to another party without notifying the user. Answer B is incorrect because a virus is a program or piece of code designed to attach itself to other code and repli-cate. It replicates when an infected file is executed or launched. Answer C is incorrect. A Trojan horse appears to be useful software but has code hidden inside that will attack your system directly or allow the system to be infiltrated by the originator of the code after it has been executed. Answer D is incorrect. Worms are similar in function and behavior to a virus with the exception that worms are self-replicating. A worm is

built to take advantage of a security hole in an existing application or operating system and then find other systems running the same software and automatically replicate itself to the new host.

14. **Answer: D.** A rootkit is a piece of software that can be installed and hidden on a computer mainly for the purpose of compromising the system and getting escalated privileges such as administrative rights. Answer A is incorrect. Spyware is associated with behaviors such as advertising, collecting personal information, or changing your computer configuration without appropriately obtaining prior consent. Basically, spyware is software that communicates information from a user's system to another party without notifying the user. Answer B is incorrect. Spam is a term that refers to the sending of unsolicited commercial email. Email spam targets individual users with direct mail messages. Answer C is incorrect because adware is a form of advertising that installs additional tracking software on your system that keeps in contact with the company through your Internet connection.

15. **Answer: B.** A botnet is a large number of computers that forward transmissions to other computers on the Internet. You may also hear a botnet referred to a zombie army. Answer A is incorrect. A logic bomb is a virus or Trojan horse designed to execute malicious actions when a certain event occurs or a period of time goes by. Answer C is incorrect. Adware is a form of advertising that installs additional tracking software on your system that keeps in contact with the company through your Internet connection. It reports data to the company, such as your surfing habits and which sites you have visited. Answer D is incorrect. A rootkit is a piece of software that can be installed and hidden on a computer mainly for the purpose of compromising the system and getting escalated privileges such as administrative rights.

16. **Answer: A.** Many spyware-eliminator programs are available. These programs scan your machine, similarly to how antivirus software scans for viruses; and just as with antivirus software, you should keep spyware-eliminator programs updated and regularly run scans. Therefore, answer D is incorrect. Answers B and C are incorrect because antispyware programs cannot detect rootkits or botnets.

17. **Answer: B.** The main issue with botnets is that they are securely hidden. This allows the botnet masters to perform tasks, gather information, and commit crimes while remaining undetected. Answers A, C, and D are concerns, but the main security concern it is they can remain undetected.

18. **Answer: A.** A logic bomb is also referred to as slag code. It is malicious in intent, and usually planted by a disgruntled employee. Answer B is incorrect. A botnet is a large number of computers that forward transmissions to other computers on the Internet. You may also hear a botnet referred to a zombie army. Answer C is incorrect. Adware is a form of advertising that installs additional tracking software on your system that keeps in contact with the company through your Internet connection. It reports data to the company, such as your surfing habits and which sites you have visited. Answer D is incorrect. A rootkit is a piece of software that can be installed and hidden on a computer mainly for the purpose of compromising the system and getting escalated privileges such as administrative rights.

19. **Answer: A, B, D.** A buffer overflow can result in the overwriting of data or memory storage, a denial of service due to overloading the input buffer's ability to cope with the additional data, or the originator can execute arbitrary code, often at a privileged level. Answer C is incorrect because a buffer overflow is targeted toward an individual machine.

20. **Answer: A, C.** There are several types of viruses, including boot sector, polymorphic, macro, program, stealth, and multipartite. Answers B and D are incorrect because they do not describe types of viruses.

21. **Answer: C.** A boot sector is placed into the first sector of the hard drive so that when the computer boots, the virus loads into memory. Answer A is incorrect because it describes a polymorphic virus. Answer B is incorrect because it describes a stealth virus. Answer D is incorrect because it describes a program virus.

22. **Answer: D.** A botnet is a large number of computers that forward transmissions to other computers on the Internet. You may also hear a botnet referred to a zombie army. Answer A is incorrect because a popular method of privilege escalation is a buffer-overflow attack. Answer B is incorrect because most rootkits use global hooks for stealth activity. Answer C is incorrect because a honeynet is used for monitoring large networks.

23. **Answer: B.** A Trojan horse appears to be useful software but has code hidden inside that will attack your system directly or allow the system to be infiltrated by the origina-tor of the code after it has been executed. Answer A is incorrect because a virus is a program or piece of code designed to attach itself to other code and replicate. It repli-cates when an infected file is executed or launched. Answer C is incorrect because spam is a term that refers to the sending of unsolicited commercial email. Email spam targets individual users with direct mail messages. Answer D is incorrect. Worms are similar in function and behavior to a virus with the exception that worms are self-repli-cating. A worm is built to take advantage of a security hole in an existing application or operating system and then find other systems running the same software and auto-matically replicate itself to the new host.

24. **Answer: A.** Most rootkits use global hooks for stealth activity. So, if you use security tools that can prevent programs from installing global hooks and stop process injec-tion, you can prevent rootkit functioning. Answer B is incorrect because adware uses tracking software. Answer C is incorrect because privilege escalation is associated with buffer overflows. Answer D is incorrect because social engineering is taking advantage of human nature.

25. **Answer: B.** Rootkit functionality requires full administrator rights. Therefore, you can avoid rootkit infection by running Windows from an account with lesser privileges. Answer A is incorrect; it describes an effective way to deal with spam. Answer C is incorrect; it describes an effective way to deal with user account exploitation. Answer D is incorrect because it describes an effective way to deal with spyware.

26. **Answer: C.** A botnet is a large number of computers that forward transmissions to other computers on the Internet. You may also hear a botnet referred to a zombie army. Answer A is incorrect because it describes a logic bomb. Answer B is incorrect because it describes Trojans. Answer D is incorrect because it describes a buffer over-flow.

27. **Answer: B.** Privilege escalation takes advantage of a program's flawed code, which then crashes the system and leaves it in a state where arbitrary code can be executed or an intruder can function as an administrator. Answer A is incorrect because a logic bomb is a virus or Trojan horse designed to execute malicious actions when a certain event occurs or a period of time goes by. Answer C is incorrect; spam is a term that refers to the sending of unsolicited commercial email. Email spam targets individual users with direct mail messages. Answer D is incorrect Trojans are programs disguised as useful applications.

28. **Answer: A, C, D.** Currently, the most effective way to prevent an attacker from exploiting software is to keep the manufacturer's latest patches and service packs applied and to monitor the Web for newly discovered vulnerabilities. Answer B is incorrect because it not feasible to disconnect the network from the Internet.

29. **Answer: D.** A multipartite virus is a hybrid of boot and program viruses. It first attacks a boot sector and then attacks system files or vice versa. Answer A is incorrect because a polymorphic virus can change each time it is executed. It was developed to avoid detection by antivirus software. Answer B is incorrect because a macro virus is inserted into a Microsoft Office document and emailed to unsuspecting users. Answer C is incorrect because a stealth virus uses techniques to avoid detection, such as temporarily removing itself from an infected file or masking a file's size.

30. **Answer: C.** Worms are similar in function and behavior to a virus with the exception that worms are self-replicating. A worm is built to take advantage of a security hole in an existing application or operating system and then find other systems running the same software and automatically replicate itself to the new host. Answer A is incorrect because a virus is a program or piece of code designed to attach itself to other code and replicate. It replicates when an infected file is executed or launched. Answer B is incorrect because a Trojan appears to be useful software but has code hidden inside that will attack your system directly or allow the system to be infiltrated by the originator of the code after it has been executed. Answer D is incorrect because a logic bomb is a virus or Trojan horse designed to execute malicious actions when a certain event occurs or a period of time goes by.

31. **Answer: B.** Trojans are programs disguised as useful applications. Trojans do not replicate themselves like viruses, but they can be just as destructive. Code hidden inside the application can attack your system directly or allow the system to be compromised by the code's originator. The Trojan is typically hidden, so its ability to spread depends on the popularity of the software and a user's willingness to download and install the software. Answer A is incorrect because Trojans can perform actions without the user's knowledge or consent, such as collecting and sending data or causing the computer to malfunction. Answers C and D are incorrect; a virus is a program or piece of code that runs on your computer without your knowledge. It is designed to attach itself to other code and replicate.

32. **Answer: A, B, C.** Indications that a computer may contain spyware include: the system is slow, (especially when browsing the Internet), it takes a long time for the Windows desktop to come up, clicking a link does nothing or goes to an unexpected website, the browser home page changes (and you might not be able to reset it), and web pages are automatically added to your favorites list. Answer D is incorrect because it describes spam.

33. **Answer: A, C.** When dealing with spam, the user should delete the email without opening it and turn off the preview function of the mail software. Answer B is incorrect because this is an inappropriate action. There are specific laws that deal with spamming, and trying to conduct your own investigation can be dangerous. Answer D is incorrect because local law enforcement does not investigate a single spam incident.

34. **Answer: B, C, D.** Rootkits can be included as part of software package, and can be installed by way of an unpatched vulnerability or by the user downloading and installing it. Answer A is incorrect because accessing documents on the local intranet should not result in a rootkit installation

35. **Answer: D.** Rootkits have also been known to use encryption to protect outbound communications and piggyback on commonly used ports to communicate without interrupting other applications that use that port. Answer A is incorrect. A logic bomb is a virus or Trojan horse designed to execute malicious actions when a certain event occurs or a period of time goes by. Answer B is incorrect. A botnet is a large number of computers that forward transmissions to other computers on the Internet. You may also hear a botnet referred to a zombie army. Answer C is incorrect. Adware is a form of advertising that installs additional tracking software on your system that keeps in contact with the company through your Internet connection. It reports data to the company, such as your surfing habits and which sites you have visited.

36. **Answer: A.** A logic bomb is a virus or Trojan horse designed to execute malicious actions when a certain event occurs or a period of time goes by Answer B is incorrect. A botnet is a large number of computers that forward transmissions to other computers. Answer C is incorrect. Adware is a form of advertising that installs additional tracking software on your system that keeps in contact with the company through your Internet connection. It reports data to the company, such as your surfing habits and which sites you have visited. Answer D is incorrect. A rootkit is a piece of software that can be installed and hidden on a computer mainly for the purpose of compromising the system and getting escalated privileges such as administrative rights.

37. **Answer: B.** A Trojan appears to be useful software but has code hidden inside that will attack your system directly or allow the system to be infiltrated by the originator of the code after it has been executed. Answer A is incorrect because a virus is a program or piece of code designed to attach itself to other code and replicate. It replicates when an infected file is executed or launched. Answer C is incorrect because a worm is built to take advantage of a security hole in an existing application or operating system and then find other systems running the same software and automatically replicate itself to the new host. Answer D is incorrect because a logic bomb is a virus or Trojan horse designed to execute malicious actions when a certain event occurs or a period of time goes by.

38. **Answer: A.** A polymorphic virus can change each time it is executed. It was developed to avoid detection by antivirus software. Answer B is incorrect because a macro virus is inserted into a Microsoft Office document and emailed to unsuspecting users. Answer C is incorrect because a stealth virus uses techniques to avoid detection, such as temporarily removing itself from an infected file or masking a files size. Answer D is incorrect because multipartite virus is a hybrid of boot and program viruses. It first attacks a boot sector then attacks system files or vice versa.

39. Answer: C. A bot, short for robot, is an automated computer program that needs no user interaction. Bots are systems that outside sources can control. A bot provides a spam or virus originator with the venue to propagate. Answer A is incorrect because a logic bomb is a virus or Trojan horse designed to execute malicious actions when a certain event occurs or a period of time goes by Answer B is incorrect. Adware is a form of advertising that installs additional tracking software on your system that keeps in contact with the company through your Internet connection. It reports data to the company, such as your surfing habits and which sites you have visited. Answer D is incorrect because a virus is a program or piece of code designed to attach itself to other code and replicate.

40. Answer: A, C, D. You can take steps to protect your network from malicious code such as not using any type of removable media from another user without first scanning for malware, performing backups on a daily basis, installing firewalls or intrusion-prevention systems on client machines, and subscribing to newsgroups and checking antivirus websites on a regular basis. Answer B is incorrect. Opening all attachments will mostly likely infect a machine.

Objective 1.2: Explain the security risks pertaining to system hardware and peripherals.

1. **Answer: B.** A vulnerability in the BIOS can allow local users to cause a denial of service and the system not to boot. Answers A, C, and D are incorrect because they are all types of storage devices.

2. **Answer: C.** Organizations fail to protect data when it reaches its final resting on these storage subsystems. Although many organizations protect data in motion using encryption, they fail to protect that same data when it reaches its final resting on storage subsystems. Answer A is incorrect. Network attached storage is a large-capacity device, and it not easy to lose. Answer B is incorrect because it describes virtualization. Answer D is incorrect because antivirus software can be installed on large storage systems.

3. **Answer: A.** Just about everyone carries a cell phone, and most corporate workers have PDAs. These devices have associated risks. The first is theft or loss. It is estimated that eight million cell phones are lost or stolen every year. For many organizations, losing a cell phone or a PDA loaded with contacts, emails, and client data can be a severe detriment to business. Handheld devices are rarely password protected, even though they contain a remarkable amount of data. Answer B is incorrect antivirus software can be installed on mobile systems. Answer C is incorrect because encryption can be used with handheld devices. Answer D is incorrect because cracking the password on handheld devices is no easier than regular password cracking.

4. **Answer: B, D.** A vulnerability in the BIOS can allow local users to cause a denial of service and the system not to boot. Answer A is incorrect because a hard drive failure has to do with the hard disk itself and nothing to do with the BIOS. Answer C is incorrect because system lockup implies that the machine was already booted and is associated more with attacks that happen after the machine is up and running.

5. **Answer: A.** Small, high-capacity, removable storage devices present a concern when it comes to corporate security and protecting proprietary information. It is quite simple for a disgruntled employee to take data and sell it. Answers B and C are incorrect because the devices can be scanned for malware and can also be encrypted. Answer D is incorrect because having the device break off in the computer is not a security risk.

6. **Answer: D.** Group Policy can be used to disable the capacity for unauthorized users to use any USB storage devices. Another layer of protection can be applied by encrypting and properly securing sensitive corporate information. Answer A is incorrect because editing the Registry can cause harm. Answer B is incorrect because filling the USB slots with glue can cause harm to the computer. Answer C is incorrect because the Security Accounts Manager (SAM) stores password information.

7. **Answer: B, C, D.** The BIOS can be compromised in several ways: the BIOS password, known vulnerabilities, and bypassing access control. Answer A is incorrect because editing the Registry is done after the system had already booted.

8. **Answer: B.** To provide convenience and redundancy, technology such as WLAN, USB, and Bluetooth connections are used with client software to sync PDAs and cell phones to a user's desktop computer. There are also enterprise-level product suites. Although this might prevent lost data, it also presents other risks. New security threats targeting cell phones and other mobile devices could quickly become bigger than anything the industry has seen so far. Therefore, answers A, C, and D are incorrect.

9. **Answer: B.** Security policy should dictate that sensitive data be encrypted. Answer A is incorrect because the limiting email address access would cause excessive overhead. Answer C is incorrect because eliminating attachments would not secure the communication. Answer D is incorrect because the use of passwords would not secure the communication.

10. **Answer: A, C, D.** BIOS access control can be bypassed by cracking the BIOS password, overloading the keyboard buffer, and deleting the contents of the CMOS RAM. Answer B is incorrect because the MBR is part of the hard disk configuration and has nothing to do with the BIOS.

11. **Answer: C.** System access to the BIOS configuration utility is controlled by a password. After the password is set, the configuration of the computer cannot be changed without inputting the password. Answers A and B are incorrect because they are hardware devices. Answer D is incorrect because access control lists are used on routers and operating systems but not on the BIOS.

12. **Answer: D.** The BIOS passwords of laptops are a bit different in that the passwords are usually flashed into firmware. Answers A and B are incorrect because encryption is not automatic for all BIOS versions. Answer C is incorrect because desktop BIOS passwords and stored in the CMOs and are not flashed into the firmware.

13. **Answer: A, C.** Depending on the manufacturer, the laptop may have a hardware dongle or special loopback device to bypass the password. Answer B is incorrect because a lock pick is used for breaking standard locking mechanisms such as a door lock. Answer D is incorrect because removing the CMOS battery will not reset a password that is flashed into the firmware.

14. **Answer: B, C.** Many organizations do not have a policy for BIOS passwords. In many organizations, most computers share the same BIOS password, and that password is seldom changed. If an attacker manages to gain physical access, a large portion of the network could be compromised. Answer A is incorrect because sharing the same BIOS password is not good practice and leaves the machine vulnerable. Answer D is incorrect because a hard disk drive password is used after the system boots.

15. **Answer: D.** It is quite simple for a disgruntled employee to misuse data (take the data and sell it, for instance). Of course, the real issue is access to the information. However, if the information is readily available, even employees with good intentions might misplace or have a removable storage device stolen. Answers A, B, and C are incorrect; the main underlying concern is the amount of data that is available to employees, not unencrypted data, the ability to access multiple machines, or malware infection.

16. **Answer: A.** The more capabilities a device has, the more vulnerable the device. The Cabir virus has been found in about 15 different variations. According to a report from an Ireland-based cell phone security company, in mid-2008 the security company tracked 100,000 virus incidents per day. Answer B is incorrect because rootkits are normally not found on handheld devices. Answers C and D are incorrect because they both imply that the users are the ones sending the text messages.

17. **Answer: C.** The more capabilities a device has, the more vulnerable the device. The Cabir virus has been found in about 15 different variations. According to a report from an Ireland-based cell phone security company, in mid-2008 the security company tracked 100,000 virus incidents per day. Answer A is incorrect because it implies that the users are the ones sending the text messages. Answer B is incorrect because not all devices currently have intrusion detection software available. Answer D is incorrect because encryption will not eliminate virus threats.

18. **Answer: A, B, D.** Removable hard drives, especially the small passport types, afford users the convenience to carry files for both their work environment and their home environment in one device. This convenience provides an opportunity for viruses and other malware to spread between networks and physical locations as they share files in both environments and with other users. In addition to malware infections, these devices have a large amount of storage space, so they lend themselves to data theft and information leakage. Answer C is incorrect. Reduced productivity should not be a byproduct of allowing removable hard drives.

19. **Answer: B.** A better approach is to combine security policies with purchasing and issuing removable storage devices and encrypting them as necessary. Then allowing only the approved devices and blocking all unauthorized devices. Although answers A and C are viable solutions, they are not the best approach. Answer D is incorrect because it causes undue administrative overhead.

20. **Answer: A.** An organization should consider implementing controls that ensure all portable devices and removable media are encrypted and accounted for. The security policy should require encryption of all data on portable computers and removable storage. Answer B is incorrect because as of this writing, the device is still undergoing internal testing, and consideration for the device becoming an actual product will come later. Answers C and D are incorrect because they are not types of viruses.

21. **Answer: C, D.** A good antivirus solution is essential to protect the integrity of stored data and to prevent malware from spreading to other parts of the network through the storage system. Additional considerations when dealing with large data repositories should include encryption, authentication devices, secure logging, and key management. Answer A is incorrect because it describes a solution for small storage devices. Answer B is incorrect because it does not address data at rest.

22. **Answer: A, B, C, D.** A good antivirus solution is essential to protect the integrity of stored data and to prevent malware from spreading to other parts of the network through the storage system. Additional considerations when dealing with large data repositories should include encryption, authentication devices, secure logging, and key management.

23. **Answer: C.** Some security appliances sit on a SAN or are connected to NAS to protect data considered "at rest." Answers A and B are incorrect because they are handheld devices and the data changes. Answer D is incorrect. The BIOS is not considered data at rest.

24. **Answer: B.** Many BIOS manufacturers build in backdoor passwords. Often, they are simple, such as the name of the BIOS manufacturer. In addition, lists of known backdoor passwords are available on the Internet. Because this method of access has become so public, BIOS manufacturers have become more secretive about any backdoors they may now use. Answer A is incorrect because secure BIOS passwords can be made. Answer C is incorrect because the BIOS does not lock the user out after too many bad passwords. This is a condition set with Group Policy. Answer D is incorrect because too many incorrect BIOS password guesses will not destroy it, but improperly flashing it will.

25. **Answer: D.** If an attacker gains physical access to the machine and changes the boot order, there is no way to protect the system from compromise. An attacker could boot the system from a device that contains software to change the administrative password, extract password information for a later attack, directly access data on the hard disk, or install a backdoor or Trojan. Answers A and B are incorrect; a DoS attack and virus do not require physical access to the machine. Answer C is incorrect because the MBR is concerned with operating system boot order, not BIOS boot order.

Objective 1.3: Implement OS hardening practices and procedures to achieve workstation and server security.

1. **Answer: A, B, D.** The three basic areas of hardening are operating system, application, and network. Answer C is incorrect because the Internet is a shared public network and is not hardened.

2. **Answer: A, B.** Operating system hardening includes encrypted file support and secured file system selection that allows the proper level of access control. Application hardening includes default application administration accounts, standard passwords,

and common services installed by default should also be reviewed and changed or disabled as required. Answer C is incorrect because the Internet is a shared public network and is not hardened. Answer D is incorrect because network hardening involves access restrictions to network services, updates to security hardware and software, and disabling unnecessary protocol support and services.

3. **Answer: D.** Network hardening involves access restrictions to network services, updates to security hardware and software, and disabling unnecessary protocol support and services. Answer A is incorrect; operating system hardening includes encrypted file support and secured file system selection that allows the proper level of access control. Answer B is incorrect; application hardening includes default application administration accounts, standard passwords, and common services installed by default should also be reviewed and changed or disabled as required. Answer C is incorrect because the Internet is a shared public network and is not hardened.

4. **Answer: A, B.** Operating system hardening includes encrypted file support and secured file system selection. This allows the proper level of access control and allows you to address newly identified exploits and apply security patches, hotfixes, and service packs. Application hardening includes default application administration accounts, standard passwords, and common services installed by default should also be reviewed and changed or disabled as required. Applications must be maintained in an updated state through the regular review of hotfixes, patches, and service packs. Answer C is incorrect because the Internet is not a shared public network and is not hardened. Answer D is incorrect because network hardening involves access restrictions to network shares and services, updates to security hardware and software, and disabling unnecessary protocol support and services.

5. **Answer: D.** Mapping avenues of access is critical in hardening a network. This process is a part of the site survey that should be performed for any network, especially those that involve public areas where a simple connection through a workstation might link the protected internal network directly to a public broadband connection. Answers A, B, and C are incorrect because they are part of operating system hardening.

6. **Answer: B.** Hotfixes are, typically, small and specific-purpose updates that alter the behavior of installed applications in a limited manner. These are the most common type of update. A hotfix is related to a service pack and should be deployed with this in mind. Answer A is incorrect because service packs are major revisions of functionality or service operation in an installed application. Service packs are the least common type of update, often requiring extensive testing to ensure against service failure in integrated network environments before application. Answer C is incorrect because patches are similar to hotfixes; security patches eliminate security vulnerabilities. They may be mandatory if the circumstances match and need to be deployed quickly. Answer D is incorrect because maintenance releases are incremental updates between service packs or software versions to fix multiple outstanding issues.

7. **Answer: A.** Service packs are major revisions of functionality or service operation in an installed application or operating system. Service packs are the least common type of update, often requiring extensive testing to ensure against service failure in integrated network environments before application. Answer B is incorrect because hotfixes are, typically, small and specific-purpose updates that alter the behavior of installed applications in a limited manner. These are the most common type of update. Answer C is incorrect because patches are similar to hotfixes; patches are typically focused updates that affect installed applications. Security patches eliminate security vulnerabilities. They may be mandatory if the circumstances match and need to be deployed quickly. Answer D is incorrect because maintenance releases are incremental updates between service packs or software versions to fix multiple outstanding issues.

8. **Answer: C.** Patches are similar to hotfixes; patches typically focus on updates that affect installed applications. Security patches eliminate security vulnerabilities. They may be mandatory if the circumstances match and need to be deployed quickly Answer A is incorrect because service packs are major revisions of functionality or service operation in an installed application. Service packs are the least common type of update, often requiring extensive testing to ensure against service failure in integrated network environments before application. Answer B is incorrect; hotfixes are, typically, small and specific-purpose updates that alter the behavior of installed applications in a limited manner. These are the most common type of update. Answer D is incorrect because maintenance releases are incremental updates between service packs or software versions to fix multiple outstanding issues.

9. **Answer: B, C.** In application hardening, default application administration accounts, standard passwords, and common services installed by default should also be reviewed and changed or disabled as required. Answer A is incorrect because key management has to do with certificates. Answer D is incorrect because behavior-based profiles are associated with intrusion detection.

10. **Answer: C.** It is also imperative to include regular update reviews for all deployed operating systems, to address newly identified exploits and apply security patches, hotfixes, and service packs. Answer A is incorrect; update reviews will not reveal compromised administrative accounts. Answer B is incorrect because behavior-based profiles are associated with intrusion detection. Answer D is incorrect. Firmware updates have to do with hardware, not operating systems.

11. **Answer: B.** IP Security (IPsec) and public key infrastructure (PKI) implementations must be properly configured and updated to maintain key and ticket stores. Some systems may be hardened to include specific levels of access, gaining the C2 security rating required by many government deployment scenarios. Answer A is incorrect because behavior-based profiles are associated with intrusion detection. It is also imperative to include regular update reviews for all deployed operating systems, to address newly identified exploits and apply security patches, hotfixes, and service packs. Answer C is incorrect; regular update reviews for all deployed operating systems will address newly identified exploits as well as application of security patches, hotfixes, and service packs. Answer D is incorrect. IPsec and PKI have nothing to do with isolating access attempts.

12. **Answer: B, C, D.** Operating system hardening includes configuring log files and auditing, changing default administrator account names and default passwords, and the institution of account lockout and password policies to guarantee strong passwords that can resist brute-force attacks. File-level security and access control mechanisms serve to isolate access attempts within the operating system environment. Answer A is incorrect because regularly reviewing applied firmware updates and applying those that are required for the network configuration and hardware solutions in use are associated with network hardening practices.

13. **Answer: A, B, D.** Network hardening practices include configuring log files, auditing, and configuring network devices and firewalls to exclude unsecure protocols, such as raw Telnet sessions that transfer logon and session details in plain-text format. Routing hardware must also be maintained in a current state by regularly reviewing applied firmware updates and applying those that are required for the network configuration and hardware solutions in use. Answer C is incorrect because securing the file system is an operating system hardening activity.

14. **Answer: A.** Mapping avenues of access is critical in hardening a network. This process is a part of the site survey that should be performed for any network, especially those that involve public areas where a simple connection through a workstation might link the protected internal network directly to a public broadband connection. Wireless networks also create significant avenues for unsecure access to a secured network. A user who configures a PC card on his workstation to allow synchronization of his 802.11-compliant wireless PDA may have inadvertently bypassed all security surrounding an organization's network. Answer B is incorrect; hardware-related vulnerabilities are associated with network hardening practices. Answer C is incorrect; hardware-related vulnerabilities are associated with operating system hardening practices. Answer D is incorrect; access control is associated with operating system hardening practices.

15. **Answer: B.** Regular log review is critical for web servers, to ensure that submitted URL values are not used to exploit unpatched buffer overruns or to initiate other forms of common exploits. Answer A is incorrect. Email service hardening includes preventing SMTP relay from being used by spammers, and limiting attachment and total storage per user to prevent denial-of-service attacks using large file attachments. Answer C is incorrect. Because of limitations in FTP, unless an encapsulation scheme is used between the client and host systems the logon and password details are passed in clear text and may be subject to interception by packet sniffing. Answer D is incorrect. Unauthorized DNS zone transfers should also be restricted to prevent DNS poisoning attacks.

16. **Answer: A.** Email service hardening includes preventing SMTP relay from being used by spammers, and limiting attachment and total storage per user to prevent denial-of-service attacks using large file attachments. Answer B is incorrect. Regular log review is critical for web servers, to ensure that submitted URL values are not used to exploit unpatched buffer overruns or to initiate other forms of common exploits. Answer C is incorrect. Because of limitations in FTP, unless an encapsulation scheme is used between the client and host systems the logon and password details are passed in clear text and may be subject to interception by packet sniffing. Answer D is incorrect. Unauthorized DNS zone transfers should also be restricted to prevent DNS poisoning attacks.

17. **Answer: C.** Network News Transfer Protocol (NNTP) servers providing user access to newsgroup posts raise many of the same security considerations risks as email servers. Answers A, B, and D are incorrect. Access control for newsgroups may be somewhat more complex, with moderated groups allowing public anonymous submission (and authenticated access required for post approval). This type of control is not addressed with database, DNS, or DHCP servers.

18. **Answer: D.** Query results that are forged and returned to the requesting client or recursive DNS query can poison the DNS records. Answer A is incorrect. Email service hardening includes preventing SMTP relay from being used by spammers, and limiting attachment and total storage per user to prevent denial-of-service attacks using large file attachments. Answer B is incorrect. Regular log review is critical for web servers, to ensure that submitted URL values are not used to exploit unpatched buffer overruns or to initiate other forms of common exploits. Answer C is incorrect. Because of limitations in the FTP protocol, unless an encapsulation scheme is used between the client and host systems the logon and password details are passed in clear text and may be subject to interception by packet sniffing.

19. **Answer: C.** FTP logs should be spot-checked for password-guessing and brute-force attacks. Because of limitations in FTP, unless an encapsulation scheme is used between the client and host systems the logon and password details are passed in clear text and may be subject to interception by packet sniffing. Answer A is incorrect. Email service hardening includes preventing SMTP relay from being used by spammers, and limiting attachment and total storage per user to prevent denial-of-service attacks using large file attachments. Answer B is incorrect. Regular log review is critical for web servers, to ensure that submitted URL values are not used to exploit unpatched buffer overruns or to initiate other forms of common exploits. Answer D is incorrect. Unauthorized DNS zone transfers should also be restricted to prevent DNS poisoning attacks.

20. **Answer: D.** Print servers pose several risks, including possible security breaches in the event that unauthorized parties access cached print jobs or sensitive printed material. DoS attacks may be used to disrupt normal methods of business, and network-connected printers require authentication of access to prevent attackers from generating printed memos, invoices, or any other manner of printed materials. Answer A is incorrect. Email service hardening includes preventing SMTP relay from being used by spammers, and limiting attachment and total storage per user to prevent denial-of-service attacks using large file attachments. Answer B is incorrect. Because of limitations in FTP, unless an encapsulation scheme is used between the client and host systems the logon and password details are passed in clear text and may be subject to interception by packet sniffing. Answer C is incorrect. If the operating system in use does not support DHCP server authentication, attackers may also configure their own DHCP servers within a subnet, taking control of the network settings of clients and obtaining leases from these rogue servers.

21. **Answer: B.** Dynamic Host Configuration Protocol (DHCP) servers share many of the same security problems associated with other network services, such as DNS servers. DHCP servers may be overwhelmed by lease requests if bandwidth and processing resources are insufficient. Answer A is incorrect because data repositories of any type

might require specialized security considerations. Answers C and D are incorrect. Network News Transfer Protocol (NNTP) servers providing user access to newsgroup posts raise many of the same security considerations risks as email servers.

22. **Answer: A, B, C.** Data repositories of any type might require specialized security considerations, based on the bandwidth and processing resources required to prevent DoS attacks, removal of default password and administration accounts such as the SQL default sa account, and security of replication traffic to prevent exposure of access credentials to packet sniffing. Answer D is incorrect because lease requirements are associated with DHCP servers.

23. **Answer: B.** Network file shares are not secure until you remove default access permissions. Answer A is incorrect scope address pools have to do with DHCP servers. Answer C is incorrect because proper name resolution is associated with DNS servers. Answer D is incorrect. The password is not encrypted in many network file-sharing systems.

24. **Answer: C.** If the operating system in use does not support DHCP server authentication, attackers may also configure their own DHCP servers within a subnet, taking control of the network settings of clients and obtaining leases from these rogue servers. Answer A is incorrect. Email service hardening includes preventing SMTP relay from being used by spammers, and limiting attachment and total storage per user to prevent denial-of-service attacks using large file attachments. Answer B is incorrect. Because of limitations in FTP, unless an encapsulation scheme is used between the client and host systems the logon and password details are passed in clear text and may be subject to interception by packet sniffing. Answer D is incorrect. Unauthorized DNS zone transfers should also be restricted to prevent DNS poisoning attacks.

25. **Answer: A, B.** Data repositories of any type might require specialized security considerations, based on the bandwidth and processing resources required. Role-based access control may be used to improve security, and the elimination of unneeded connection libraries and character sets may help to alleviate common exploits. Answers C and D are incorrect; using discretionary-based access control and eliminating bandwidth restrictions would relax security, not improve it.

26. **Answer: A.** Group Policy can be used for ease of administration in managing the environment of users. This can include installing software and updates or controlling what appears on the desktop based on the user's job function and level of experience. The Group Policy object (GPO) is used to apply Group Policy to users and computers. Answer B is incorrect because User Manager is used to create and manage user accounts. Answers C and D are incorrect because Active Directory and Directory services store information and settings in a central database.

27. **Answer: D.** Group policies are applied in a specific order or hierarchy. By default, a group policy is inherited and cumulative. Answer A is incorrect because group policies are cumulative not proportionate. Answer B is incorrect; group policies are inherited, not singular. Answer C is incorrect because group policies are cumulative, not singular.

28. **Answer: B.** Group Policy enables you to set consistent common security standards for a certain group of computers and enforce common computer and user configurations. It also simplifies computer configuration by distributing applications and restricting the distribution of applications that may have limited licenses. To allow this wide range of administration, GPOs can be associated with or linked to sites, domains, or organizational units. Answer A is incorrect role-based access control allow access to resources based on the user role. Answer C is incorrect. Using a distribution server may be helpful, but the update is mandatory, and therefore it needs to be pushed out. Answer D is incorrect. RSoP is used for predicting the affect of a policy.

29. **Answer: A, C, D.** Security baselines are often established by governmental mandate, regulatory bodies, or industry representatives, such as the PCI requirements established by the credit card industry for businesses collecting and transacting credit information. Answer B is incorrect because organizational requests are merely requests, and security baselines are often established due to some type of regulation or standard.

30. **Answer: C.** Security templates are sets of configurations that reflect a particular role or standard established through industry standards or within an organization, assigned to fulfill a particular purpose. Examples include a "minimum access" configuration template assigned to limited access kiosk systems, whereas a "high-security" template could be assigned to systems requiring more stringent logon and access control mechanisms. Answer A is incorrect because Group Policy enables you to set consistent common security standards for a certain group of computers and enforce common computer and user configurations. Answer B is incorrect because security baselines are often established by governmental mandate, regulatory bodies, or industry representatives, such as the PCI requirements established by the credit card industry for businesses collecting and transacting credit information. Answer D is incorrect because Active Directory stores information and settings in a central database.

Objective 1.4: Carry out the appropriate procedures to establish application security.

1. **Answer: A, D.** Some identified vulnerabilities of the Java language include buffer overflows, ability to execute instructions, resource monopolization, and unexpected redirection. Answers B and C are incorrect because unauthorized file upload and email exposure are associated with JavaScript, not the Java language.

2. **Answer: C.** Java applets execute when the client machine's browser loads the hosting web page. Vulnerabilities are based on the Java language. JavaScript vulnerabilities must be addressed based on the operating system and browser version in use on each client. Answers A and B are incorrect because JavaScript vulnerabilities must be addressed based on the operating system and browser version in use on each client, not the server. Answer D is incorrect the operating system does not load the hosting web page an application and browser do.

3. **Answer: B.** Java is a precompiled language. Before it can be executed, it undergoes a Just In Time (JIT) compilation into the necessary binary bytes. A Java-based mini-program, called an applet, may present many security risks to the client. Applets execute when the client machine's browser loads the hosting web page. Answers A and C are

incorrect because Java is a precompiled language. Answer D is incorrect because applets execute when the client machine's browser loads the hosting web page.

4. **Answer: B, C.** JavaScript is a client-side interpreted language that mainly poses privacy-related vulnerability issues such as unauthorized file upload and email exposure. Answers A and D are incorrect because they are associated with the Java language. Some identified vulnerabilities of the Java language include buffer overflows, ability to execute instructions, resource monopolization, and unexpected redirection.

5. **Answer: A.** To avoid vulnerabilities exposed by earlier forms of Java and ActiveX development, all machines should be kept up-to-date with new version releases. Scripting language vulnerabilities may be addressed in this manner, as well as by turning off or increasing the client's browser security settings to prevent automatic code execution. Answer B is incorrect because this setting controls third-party tool bands and browser helper objects. Answer C is incorrect because increasing the pop-up setting will not mitigate Java vulnerabilities. Answer D is incorrect because Integrated Windows Authentication has to do with logon information, not Java vulnerabilities.

6. **Answer: C.** Microsoft developed a precompiled application technology that can be embedded in a web page in the same way as Java applets. This technology is referred to as ActiveX, and its controls share many of the same vulnerabilities present in embedded Java applets. Answer A is incorrect because cookies are temporary files stored in the client's browser cache to maintain settings across multiple pages, servers, or sites. Answer B is incorrect because JavaScript is a smaller language that does not create applets or standalone applications. Answer D is incorrect because CGI (Common Gateway Interface) scripts are programs that run on the server to service client requests.

7. **Answer: B.** Clients should regularly clear their browser cookie cache to avoid exposing long-term browsing habits in this way. Where possible, client browsers may also be configured to block third-party cookies, although many online commerce sites require this functionality for their operation. Answer A is incorrect because this setting controls third-party tool bands and browser helper objects. Answer C is incorrect because blocking all cookies would hamper the functionality for many online commerce sites. Answer D is incorrect because disabling automatic code execution on client browsers has more to do with Java applets and ActiveX controls.

8. **Answer: D.** By restricting the data that can be input and using proper input validation, application designers can reduce the threat posed by maliciously crafted URL references and redirected web content. Answer A is incorrect because third-party cookies would limit exposing long-term browsing habits. Answer B is incorrect because accepting only numeric data input is not feasible, and if it not validated, it will not mitigate attacks. Answer C is incorrect because this setting controls third-party tool bands and browser helper objects.

9. **Answer: A.** Whereas cookies generally provide benefits to the end users, spyware would be most likely to use a tracking cookie. A tracking cookie is a particular type of permanent cookie that stays around, whereas a session cookie stays around only for the particular visit to a website. Answers B and D are incorrect because these sites would use session cookies, not tracking cookies. Answer C is incorrect because a Trojan appears to be useful software but has code hidden inside that will attack your system directly or allow the system to be infiltrated by the originator of the code after it has been executed.

10. **Answer: D.** Spammers search for unprotected SMTP relay services running on public servers, which may then be used to resend SMTP messages to obscure their true source. Answer A is incorrect because buffer overflows are associated not using proper input validation. Answer B is incorrect. A logic bomb is a virus or Trojan horse designed to execute malicious actions when a certain event occurs or a period of time goes by. Answer C is incorrect. Spyware is associated with behaviors such as advertising, collecting personal information, or changing your computer configuration without appropriately obtaining prior consent.

11. **Answer: B.** A tracking cookie is a particular type of permanent cookie that stays around, whereas a session cookie stays around only for the particular visit to a website. Therefore, answer C is incorrect. Answers A and D are incorrect because tracking cookies are beneficial or valuable only to the tracking party, not the user.

12. **Answer: A.** Secure Hypertext Transport Protocol (S-HTTP) operates over port 80 along with regular HTTP traffic. Answer B is incorrect because HTTPS (HTTP over SSL) and SSL employ X.509 digital certificates and operate over port 443. Answer C is incorrect. Email clients connect to port 110 of a remote email server, and then use the POP3 protocol to retrieve email. Answer D is incorrect. Port 4445 uses TCP/UDP for service type upnotifyp.

13. **Answer: B.** HTTPS (HTTP over SSL) and SSL employ X.509 digital certificates and operate over port 443. Answer A is incorrect because Secure Hypertext Transport Protocol (S-HTTP) operates over port 80 along with regular HTTP traffic. Answer C is incorrect. Email clients connect to port 110 of a remote email server, and then use the POP3 protocol to retrieve email. Port 4445 uses TCP/UDP for service type upnotifyp, therefore Answer D is incorrect.

14. **Answer: B, C.** Malformed certificates may be used to exploit the parsing libraries used by SSL agents. SSL certificates may also be used to establish links vulnerable to packet sniffing by using compromised self-signed or expired certificates. Other exploits include the use of small key sizes, outdated certificate revocation lists, and other mechanisms intended to provide weak or compromised SSL certificates. Answers A and D are incorrect because they are associated with programming errors. Buffer-overflow vulnerabilities may be used to enact arbitrary commands on a server. Format string vulnerabilities may result in unauthorized access to enact commands on a server or impair its normal operation. Improperly formatted requests may be used to create an effective denial-of-service (DoS) attack against the server, preventing it from responding to normal requests.

15. **Answer: A, D.** Buffer-overflow vulnerabilities may be used to enact arbitrary commands on the LDAP server. Format string vulnerabilities may result in unauthorized access to enact commands on the LDAP server or impair its normal operation. Improperly formatted requests may be used to create an effective denial-of-service (DoS) attack against the LDAP server, preventing it from responding to normal requests. Answers B and C are incorrect because they are associated with SSL certificate vulnerabilities. Malformed certificates may be used to exploit the parsing libraries used by SSL agents. SSL certificates may also be used to establish links vulnerable to packet sniffing by using compromised self-signed or expired certificates. Other exploits include the use of small key sizes, outdated certificate revocation lists, and other mechanisms intended to provide weak or compromised SSL certificates.

16. **Answer: B, C.** FTP servers provide user access to upload or download files between client systems and a networked FTP server. FTP servers include many potential security issues, including anonymous file access and unencrypted authentication. Answers A and D are incorrect because they are associated with programming errors. Buffer-overflow vulnerabilities may be used to enact arbitrary commands on a server. Format string vulnerabilities may result in unauthorized access to enact commands on a server or impair its normal operation. Improperly formatted requests may be used to create an effective denial-of-service (DoS) attack against the server, preventing it from responding to normal requests.

17. **Answer: A.** FTPS (FTP over SSL) using TCP port 21. Answer B is incorrect because HTTP operates over port 80. Answer C is incorrect. A more secure version of FTP (S/FTP) has been developed, including SSL encapsulation. This is referred to as FTP over SSH using the Secure Shell (SSH) TCP port 22. Answer D is incorrect because port 81 is used as an alternate port for hosting a website.

18. **Answer: A, B, C.** Attackers develop viral malware capable of spreading through contact lists within IM clients. Others focus on capturing IM traffic and cached logs of past conversations, in an attempt to obtain useful or harmful information. The file-transfer and desktop-sharing capabilities of many clients present challenges against unauthorized data sharing, while creative attackers make use of the audio and video capabilities to directly "tap" unwary IM users. Answer D is incorrect. Improperly formatted requests may be used to create an effective denial-of-service (DoS) attack against servers, preventing them from responding to normal requests.

19. **Answer: A, C.** CGI scripts may be exploited to leak information including details about running server processes and daemons, samples included in some default installations are not intended for security and include well-known exploits, and buffer overflows may allow arbitrary commands to be executed on the server. Answer B is incorrect because anonymous file access is associated with FTP servers. Answer D is incorrect because CGI scripts do not run on the client system.

20. **Answer: D.** When a website redirects the client's browser to attack yet another site, this is referred to as cross-site scripting. Answer A is incorrect because unencrypted authentication is associated with FTP servers. Answer B is incorrect because a session hijack occurs when an attacker causes the client's browser to establish a secure connection to a compromised web server acting as a proxy or redirecting traffic to a secure target site, exposing traffic as it passes through the compromised system. Answer C is incorrect because a buffer overflow occurs when data input exceeds the memory space allocated and injects unanticipated data or programmatic code into executable memory.

21. **Answer: B.** An early exploit of JavaScript allowed access to files located on the client's system if the name and path were known. Answers A and D are incorrect because incorrect because JavaScript, not Java, can be used to execute arbitrary instructions on the server, send email as the user, and allow access to cache information. Answer C is incorrect because Java, not JavaScript, can continue running even after the applet has been closed.

22. **Answer: A.** Exploits may allow the identification of configuration details of the server that may be helpful to later unauthorized access attempts, a process often referred to as profiling. Answer B is incorrect because reporting portrays information collected in a particular area. Answer C is incorrect because abstracting is used to understand and solve problems. Answer D is incorrect because hyperlinking is associated with web pages.

23. **Answer: B.** The danger to maintaining session information is that sites may access cookies stored in the browser's cache that may contain details on the user's e-commerce shopping habits, along with many user details that could possibly include sensitive information identifying the user or allowing access to secured sites. Answers A and C are incorrect because these actions prove helpful for the client. Answer D is incorrect because this action is associated with Java.

24. **Answer: A, C.** Browser-based vulnerabilities include session hijacking, buffer overflows, cross-site scripting, and add-in vulnerabilities. Answer B is incorrect because SQL injection is associated with SQL database servers. Answer D is incorrect because social engineering is taking advantage of human nature.

25. **Answer: C.** The common BitTorrent file-sharing application is an example of resource-sharing peer-to-peer (P2P) solution, allowing users to transport files between remote clients without passing through a central server for access. This presents difficulties for access restriction, because any two clients may negotiate connections using random ports and protocols, bypassing traffic analysis and access control restrictions. Answer A is incorrect; it describes a vulnerability exploitation of Java, CGI scripts, and LDAP. Answer B is incorrect; anonymous file upload is associated with FTP servers. Answer D is incorrect because it describes a CGI script exploit.

Objective 1.5: Implement security applications.

1. **Answer: B.** Like most other solutions, firewalls have strengths and weaknesses. By design, firewalls close off systems to scanning and entry by blocking ports or non-trusted services and applications. However, they require proper configuration. Answers A and C are incorrect because they describe behaviors associated with antivirus software. Answer D is incorrect because blocking off the system through BIOS access would cause it not to boot.

2. **Answer: C.** A host intrusion prevention system software resides between your system's applications and OS kernel. A HIPS consists of software that sits between your system's applications and OS kernel. The HIPS will monitor suspicious activity; then it will either block or allow the activity based on the predefined rule set. Therefore, answers A, B, and D are incorrect.

3. **Answer: A, B.** A host intrusion detection system uses either misuse detection or anomaly detection. A HIDS monitors events for suspicious activity. This can be done by using either misuse detection or anomaly detection. In misuse detection, a database of signatures is used, and the information monitored is compared to the database. This is similar to the way antivirus software works. Answer C is incorrect

because black lists are associated with email. Answer D is incorrect because outbound monitoring is usually done by a firewall.

4. **Answer: D.** Monitoring outbound connections is important in the case of malware that "phones home." Without this type of protection, the environment is not properly protected. Answer A is incorrect because behaviors such as collecting personal information or changing your computer configuration without appropriately obtaining prior consent are associated with spyware. Answer B is incorrect because tracking users inappropriate site visits is associated with content filtering. Answer C is incorrect. Monitoring bandwidth usage is a function of a network tool.

5. **Answer: C.** The most common method used in an antivirus program is scanning. Scanning searches files in memory, the boot sector, and on the hard disk for identifiable virus code. Scanning identifies virus code based on a unique string of characters known as a signature. Answers A and B are incorrect. A host intrusion detection system uses either misuse detection or anomaly detection. Answer D is incorrect because filtering is associated with antispam programs.

6. **Answer: D.** The main component of antispam software is heuristic filtering. Heuristic filtering has a predefined rule set that compares incoming email information against the rule set. Answers A and B are incorrect. A host intrusion detection system uses either misuse detection or anomaly detection. Answer C is incorrect because scanning is associated with antivirus programs.

7. **Answer: C.** The most common method used in an antivirus program is scanning. Scanning searches files in memory, the boot sector, and on the hard disk for identifiable virus code. Scanning identifies virus code based on a unique string of characters known as a signature. Answer A is incorrect because behavior patterns are associated with intrusion detection systems. Answers B and D are incorrect because antivirus software does not base its technologies on Registry keys or commands. It will scan Registry keys, but the technology is based on a unique set of characters to identify malware.

8. **Answer: A, D.** If all pop-ups are blocked, the user might not be able to install applications or programs. Field help for fill-in forms is often in the form of a pop-up. Some pop-up blockers may delete the information already entered by reloading the page, causing the users unnecessary grief. Answer B is incorrect because firewalls are not affected by pop-up blocker settings. Answer C is incorrect because the answer is associated with email lists.

9. **Answer: B.** Heuristic scanning looks for instructions or commands that are not typically found in application programs. Answer A is incorrect because it describes rootkit software. Answer C is incorrect because it describes antivirus scanning software. Answer D is incorrect because it describes firewall software.

10. **Answer: B, C.** Heuristic scanning looks for instructions or commands that are not typically found in application programs. The issue with these methods is that they are susceptible to false positives and cannot identify new viruses until the database is updated. Answers A and D are incorrect. Buffer overflows and logic bombs are malware that have nothing to do with heuristic scanning methods.

11. **Answer: A.** A false positive occurs when the software classifies an action as a possible intrusion when it is actually a nonthreatening action. Answer B is incorrect because it describes antivirus scanning software. Answer C is incorrect because it describes a false negative. Answer D is incorrect because the end result is a false negative.

12. **Answer: D.** When antispam software and updates are installed on a central server and pushed out to the client machines, this is called a centralized solution. When the updates are left up to the individual users, you have a decentralized environment. Answer A is incorrect because it describes a centralized solution. Answer B is incorrect. Vendors are never responsible for updating applications on client machines. Answer C is incorrect because making the manager responsible for the updates is not necessarily a decentralized solution.

13. **Answer: B, D.** Specific spam filtering levels can be set on the user's email account. If the setting is high, more spam will be filtered, but it may also filter legitimate email as spam, thus causing false positives. Therefore, answers A and C are incorrect because they depict just the opposite.

14. **Answer: A.** In general, an email address added to the approved list is never considered spam. This is also known as a white list. Using white lists allows more flexibility in the type of email you receive. Putting the addresses of your relatives or friends in your white list allows you to receive any type of content from them. An email address added to the blocked list is always considered spam. This is also known as a black list. Answer B is incorrect. Blacklisting is blocking an email address. Answer C is incorrect. Graylisting is related to whitelisting and blacklisting. What happens is that each time a given mailbox receives an email from an unknown contact (IP), that mail is rejected with a "try again later." Answer D is incorrect because brownlisting is a concept based on a CBL type system driven by tokens from blocked sites.

15. **Answer: B.** In general, an email address added to the approved list is never considered spam. This is also known as a white list. Using white lists allows more flexibility in the type of email you receive. Putting the addresses of your relatives or friends in your white list allows you to receive any type of content from them. An email address added to the blocked list is always considered spam. This is also known as a black list. Answer A is incorrect. Whitelisting is allowing an email address. Answer C is incorrect. Graylisting is related to whitelisting and blacklisting. What happen is that each time a given mailbox receives an email from an unknown contact (IP), that mail is rejected with a "try again later." Answer D is incorrect because brownlisting is a concept based on a CBL type system driven by tokens from blocked sites.

16. **Answer: A, C, D.** Although some pop-ups are helpful, many are an annoyance, and others can contain inappropriate content or entice the user to download malware. Answer B is incorrect because it describes pop-up blockers, not pop-ups.

17. **Answer: A, B, C.** Many pop-up blockers are integrated into vendor toolbars. You can circumvent pop-up blockers in various ways. Most pop-up blockers block only the JavaScript; therefore, technologies such as Flash bypass the pop-up blocker. On many Internet browsers, holding down the Ctrl key while clicking a link will allow it to bypass the pop-up filter. Answer D is incorrect because users can adjust the settings on pop-up blockers.

18. **Answer: B.** Set the software to medium so that it will block most automatic pop-ups but still allow functionality. Keep in mind that you can adjust the settings on pop-up blockers to meet the organizational policy or to best protect the user environment. Answer A is incorrect because it will allow most pop-ups. Answer C is incorrect because it will affect functionality. Answer D is incorrect because the custom setting is not needed.

19. **Answer: C.** There are several variations of pop-up windows. A pop-under ad opens a new browser window under the active window. These types of ads often are not seen until the current window is closed. They are essentially "floating pop-ups" in a web page. Answers A and B are incorrect because they describe useful pop-ups and are not ads. Answer D is incorrect because it describes a hover ad. Hover ads are Dynamic Hypertext Markup Language (DHTML) pop-ups.

20. **Answer: D.** There are several variations of pop-up windows. A pop-under ad opens a new browser window under the active window. These types of ads often are not seen until the current window is closed. Hover ads are Dynamic Hypertext Markup Language (DHTML) pop-ups. They are essentially "floating pop-ups" in a web page. Answers A and B are incorrect because they describe useful pop-ups and are not ads. Answer C is incorrect because it describes a pop-under ad.

21. **Answer: C.** It is important to understand that the spam filter software cannot assign meaning to the words examined. It just tracks and compares the words used. Answer A is incorrect because chances are there is nothing wrong with the software. Answer B is incorrect because adjusting the settings may cause legitimate email to be filtered. Answer D is incorrect because chances are there is nothing wrong with the software. Training the software to recognize spam takes time and often the process must be repeated.

22. **Answer: A.** Heuristic filtering has a predefined rule set that compares incoming email information against the rule set. The software reads the contents of each message and compares the words in that message against the words in typical spam messages. Each rule assigns a numeric score to the probability of the message being spam. This score is then used to determine whether the message meets the acceptable level set. Answers B, C, and D are incorrect because heuristic filtering is not based on character sets, commands, or Registry keys.

23. **Answer: B.** Scanning identifies virus code based on a unique string of characters known as a signature. Answer A is incorrect because heuristic filtering has a predefined rule set that compares incoming email information against the rule set. Answer C is incorrect because a misnomer has nothing to do with security. Answer D is incorrect. Anomaly detection is associated with a HIDS.

24. **Answer: A, B.** HIDSs monitor communications on a host-by-host basis and try to filter malicious data. These types of IDSs are good at detecting unauthorized file modifications and user activity. NIDSs monitor the packet flow and try to locate packets that may have gotten through misconfigured firewalls and are not allowed for one reason or another. They are best at detecting DoS attacks and unauthorized user access. Answers C and D are incorrect because they are associated with a NIDS.

25. **Answer: D.** NIDSs try to locate packets not allowed on the network. HIDSs collect and analyze data that originates on the local machine or a computer hosting a service. NIDSs tend to be more distributed. Answers A, B, and C are incorrect because they describe features of a NIDS.

Objective 1.6: Explain the purpose and application of virtualization technology.

1. **Answer: D.** If attackers can compromise the virtual machines, they will likely have control of the entire machine. Most virtual machines run with very high privileges on the host because a virtual machine needs access to the host's hardware so that it can map the physical hardware into virtualized hardware. Answer A is incorrect because although compromising the BIOS is possible, the inherent risk is to the other environments. Answer B is incorrect because physical access is usually required to change the boot order. Answer C is incorrect because virtual environments can be secured.

2. **Answer: A.** Segmenting virtual machines by the information they handle will keep highly sensitive data from being on the same physical hardware as virtual machines used for testing or lower security applications. The organization should have a policy in place that states that high-security virtual machines containing vital information never share the same hardware as virtual machines for testing. Answers B and D are incorrect because the environments the virtual machines will be shared with are less secure. Answer C is incorrect because this it defeats the purpose of using virtual environments.

3. **Answer: B, C.** Virtual environments can be used to improve security by allowing unstable applications to be used in an isolated environment and providing better disaster recovery solutions. Virtual environments are used for cost-cutting measures, too. One well-equipped server can host several virtual servers. This reduces the need for power and equipment. Forensic analysts often use virtual environments to examine environments that may contain malware or as a method of viewing the environment the same way the criminal did. Answer A is incorrect because virtualized environments, if compromised, can provide access to not only the network, but also any virtualization infrastructure. This puts a lot of data at risk. Answer D is incorrect because the ability to store environments on USB devices puts data at risk.

4. **Answer: B.** The hypervisor controls how access to a computer's processors and memory is shared. A hypervisor or virtual machine monitor (VMM) is a virtualization platform that provides more than one operating system to run on a host computer at the same time. Answer A is incorrect. The BIOS holds information necessary to boot the computer. Answer C is incorrect. The operating system interfaces between the hardware and the user and provides an environment for programs and applications to run. Answer D is incorrect because it is the hypervisor, not the virtual machine applications, that controls how the virtual environment uses the host resources.

5. **Answer: A, D.** Forensic analysts often use virtual environments to examine environments that may contain malware or as a method of viewing the environment the same way the criminal did. Answer B is incorrect. It is not good forensic practice to load multiple cases on one machine, virtual or real. Answer C is incorrect because imaging

hard drive and removable media should be done using a write-blocker to avoid data alteration.

6. **Answer: B.** Virtualized environments, if compromised, can provide access to not only the network, but also any virtualization infrastructure. This puts a lot of data at risk. Security policy should address virtual environments. Answer A is incorrect. It is possible that other virtual machines have been compromised, too. Answers C and D are incorrect because deleting the virtual machine or replacing it by a backup copy will not guarantee that the rest of the machine or network has not been compromised.

7. **Answer: A, C.** Vulnerabilities also come into play in virtual environments. For example, a few years ago, VMware's NAT service had a buffer-overflow vulnerability that allowed remote attackers to execute malicious code by exploiting the virtual machine itself. Virtual machine environments need to be patched just like host environments and are susceptible to the same issues as a host operating system. You should be cognizant of share files among guest and host operating systems. Answers B and D are incorrect because virtual machines need to be patched just like host environments and are susceptible to the same issues as a host operating system, including malware infection.

8. **Answer: C.** Security policy should address virtual environment vulnerabilities. Any technology software without a defined business need should not be allowed on systems. This applies to all systems, including virtual environments. Answer A is incorrect because change management policy deals with how environmental changes are addressed. Answer B is incorrect because business continuity planning addresses how a business will survive in the long term after a mishap. Answer D is incorrect because disaster recovery planning deals with how the organization will react to a disaster.

9. **Answer: C, D.** Hardware vendors are rapidly embracing virtualization and developing new features to simplify virtualization techniques. Virtual environments can be used to improve security by allowing unstable applications to be used in an isolated environment and providing better disaster recovery solutions. Answer A is incorrect because virtual environments do not scan for viruses. Answer B is incorrect virtual environments have nothing to do with reducing data aggregation. Data aggregation is used to gather statistics about user habits mostly for online advertising purposes.

10. **Answer: C.** Segmenting virtual machines by the information they handle will keep highly sensitive data from being on the same physical hardware as virtual machines used for testing or lower security applications. The organization should have a policy in place that states that high-security virtual machines containing vital information never share the same hardware as virtual machines for testing. Answer A is incorrect because although replacing the servers may reduce the power consumption, it will be costly. Answer B is incorrect. Combining all physical hardware into one virtual server might not even be possible, and there is no guarantee this will not create additional issues. Answer D is incorrect because it does not take the security of the data into consideration.

11. **Answer: A, B, C, D.** Virtual environments are available to run on just about everything from servers and routers to USB thumb drives.

12. **Answer: D.** A hypervisor or virtual machine monitor (VMM) is a virtualization platform that provides more than one operating system to run on a host computer at the same time. Answers A and C are incorrect because hypervisors do not interact with the OS kernel. Answer B is incorrect. This describes a mainframe environment.

13. **Answer: A.** A Type 1 native or bare-metal hypervisor is software that runs directly on a hardware platform. The guest operating system runs at the second level above the hardware. This technique allows full guest systems to be run in a relatively efficient manner. The guest OS is not aware it is being virtualized and requires no modification. Answer B is incorrect because it describes where a Type 1 guest operating systems runs. Answer C is incorrect because it describes where a Type 2 or hosted hypervisor runs. Answer D is incorrect because it describes where a Type 2 guest operating systems runs.

14. **Answer: C.** A Type 2 or hosted hypervisor is software that runs within an operating system environment, and the guest operating system runs at the third level above the hardware. The hypervisor runs as an application or shell on another already running operating system. Answer A is incorrect because it describes where a Type 1 native or bare-metal hypervisor runs. Answer B is incorrect because it describes where a Type 1 guest operating systems runs. Answer D is incorrect because it describes where a Type 2 guest operating systems runs.

15. **Answer: B.** The security concerns of virtual environments begin with the guest operating system. If a virtual machine is compromised, an intruder can gain control of all the guest operating systems. In addition, because hardware is shared, most virtual machines run with very high privileges. This can allow an intruder who compromises a virtual machine to compromise the host machine, too. Answer A is incorrect because the underlying hardware security will only be affected if the guest operating system is compromised. Answer C is incorrect. Although the host operating system needs to be secure, the immediate concerns are with the guest operating system. Answer D is incorrect. The virtual machine files are what make up the virtual machine and are part of the way the environment loads.

16. **Answer: C.** The security concerns of virtual environments begin with the guest operating system. If a virtual machine is compromised, an intruder can gain control of all the guest operating systems. In addition, because hardware is shared, most virtual machines run with very high privileges. This can allow an intruder who compromises a virtual machine to compromise the host machine, too. Answer A is incorrect because although compromising the BIOS is possible, the unintended risk is high privileges need to run the virtual environment. Answer B is incorrect because disaster recovery is easier using virtual machines. Answer D is incorrect because although technology advances quite rapidly, virtual environments can be secured.

17. **Answer: D.** To secure a virtualized environment, machines should be segmented by the sensitivity of the information they contain. A policy should be in place that specifies that hardware is not shared for test environments and sensitive data. Answer A is incorrect because although encryption is a viable solution, it might not be possible and is not always the correct solution for an organization. Answer B is incorrect. Although the host operating system needs to be secure, the immediate concerns are with the guest operating systems. Answer C is incorrect because high-security virtual machines containing vital information should never share the same hardware as virtual machines for testing.

18. **Answer: B, C.** A policy should be in place that specifies that hardware is not shared for test environments and sensitive data. Another way to secure a virtualized environment is to use standard locked-down images. Other areas that present issues for a virtualized environment and need special consideration are deploying financial applications on virtualized shared hosting and secure storage on storage-area network (SAN) technologies. Answer A is incorrect. Web servers in a DMZ are generally less secure because of the nature of the environment. Answer D is incorrect. Multiple email applications on the seam server are similar to web servers in that they would generally be the DMZ and a bit less secure.

19. **Answer: B, C, D.** Preconfigured virtual appliances are available for operating systems, networking components, and applications. Answer A is incorrect because output devices such as monitors and printers are not currently virtualized.

20. **Answer: D.** A Type 2 or hosted hypervisor is software that runs within an operating system environment, and the guest operating system runs at the third level above the hardware. The hypervisor runs as an application or shell on another already running operating system. Answer A is incorrect because it describes where a Type 1 native or bare-metal hypervisor runs. Answer B is incorrect because it describes where a Type 1 guest operating systems runs. Answer C is incorrect because it describes where a Type 2 or hosted hypervisor runs.

CHAPTER TWO

Domain 2.0: Network Infrastructure

The network infrastructure is subject to myriad internal and external attacks through services, protocols, and open ports. It is imperative that you understand how to eliminate nonessential services and protocols, especially if the network has been in existence for some period of time and some services are no longer needed or have been forgotten. To stop many would-be attackers, you must understand the different types of attacks that can happen, along with how to implement a network design, components, and tools that can protect the infrastructure. Be sure to give yourself plenty of time to review all of these concepts. The following list identifies the key areas from Domain 2.0 (which counts as 20% of the exam) that you need to master:

- ▶ Differentiate between the different ports and protocols, their respective threats and mitigation techniques.

- ▶ Distinguish between network design elements and components.

- ▶ Determine the appropriate use of network security tools to facilitate network security.

- ▶ Apply the appropriate network tools to facilitate network security.

- ▶ Explain the vulnerabilities and mitigations associated with network devices.

- ▶ Explain the vulnerabilities and mitigations associated with various transmission media.

- ▶ Explain the vulnerabilities and implement mitigations associated with wireless networking.

Practice Questions

Objective 2.1: Differentiate between the different ports & protocols, their respective threats, and mitigation techniques.

1. Which of the following ports should be blocked when it has been determined that an intruder has been using Telnet for unauthorized access?

   ○ **A.** 110

   ○ **B.** 21

   ○ **C.** 23

   ○ **D.** 443

Quick Answer: **107**
Detailed Answer: **110**

2. Which of the following ports should be blocked when it has been determined that an intruder has been using SNMP for unauthorized access? (Select all correct answers.)

   ○ **A.** 161

   ○ **B.** 162

   ○ **C.** 443

   ○ **D.** 4445

Quick Answer: **107**
Detailed Answer: **110**

3. Which of the following best describes TCP/IP hijacking?

   ○ **A.** Providing false identity information to gain unauthorized access

   ○ **B.** An established connection without specifying a username or password

   ○ **C.** An attacker takes control of a session between the server and a client

   ○ **D.** Redirecting traffic by changing the IP record for a specific domain

Quick Answer: **107**
Detailed Answer: **110**

4. Which of the following best describes spoofing?

Quick Answer: **107**
Detailed Answer: **110**

- ○ **A.** Providing false identity information to gain unauthorized access
- ○ **B.** An established connection without specifying a username or password
- ○ **C.** An attacker takes control of a session between the server and a client
- ○ **D.** Redirecting traffic by changing the IP record for a specific domain

5. Which of the following best describes a null session?

Quick Answer: **107**
Detailed Answer: **110**

- ○ **A.** Providing false identity information to gain unauthorized access
- ○ **B.** An established connection without specifying a username or password
- ○ **C.** An attacker takes control of a session between the server and a client
- ○ **D.** Redirecting traffic by changing the IP record for a specific domain

6. Which of the following best describes DNS poisoning?

Quick Answer: **107**
Detailed Answer: **110**

- ○ **A.** Providing false identity information to gain unauthorized access
- ○ **B.** An established connection without specifying a username or password
- ○ **C.** An attacker taking control of a session between the server and a client
- ○ **D.** Redirecting traffic by changing the IP record for a specific domain

7. Which of the following best describes a man-in-the-middle attack?

Quick Answer: **107**
Detailed Answer: **111**

- ○ **A.** An attacker takes advantage of the add/grace period to monopolize names without ever paying for them.
- ○ **B.** Packets are captured, the pertinent information is extracted, and then packets are placed back on the network.
- ○ **C.** An attack that typically involves flooding a listening port on a machine with packets to disrupt service.
- ○ **D.** An attacker intercepts traffic and then tricks the parties at both ends into believing that they are communicating with each other.

8. Which of the following best describes a relay attack?

   ○ **A.** An attacker takes advantage of the add/grace period to monopolize names without ever paying for them.

   ○ **B.** Packets are captured, the pertinent information is extracted, and then packets are placed back on the network.

   ○ **C.** An attack that typically involves flooding a listening port on a machine with packets to disrupt service.

   ○ **D.** An attacker intercepts traffic and then tricks the parties at both ends into believing that they are communicating with each other.

Quick Answer: **107**
Detailed Answer: **111**

9. Which of the following best describes a DDoS attack?

   ○ **A.** An attacker takes advantage of the add/grace period to monopolize names without ever paying for them.

   ○ **B.** Packets are captured, the pertinent information is extracted, and then packets are placed back on the network.

   ○ **C.** An attack that typically involves flooding a listening port on a machine with packets to disrupt the resources.

   ○ **D.** An attacker intercepts traffic and then tricks the parties at both ends into believing that they are communicating with each other.

Quick Answer: **107**
Detailed Answer: **111**

10. Which of the following best describes DNS kiting?

   ○ **A.** An attacker takes advantage of the add/grace period to monopolize names without ever paying for them.

   ○ **B.** Packets are captured, the pertinent information is extracted, and then packets are placed back on the network.

   ○ **C.** An attack that typically involves flooding a listening port on a machine with packets to disrupt the resources.

   ○ **D.** An attacker intercepts traffic and then tricks the parties at both ends into believing that they are communicating with each other.

Quick Answer: **107**
Detailed Answer: **111**

11. Which of the following methods can be used to mitigate DDoS attacks? (Select all correct answers.)

Quick Answer: **107**
Detailed Answer: **111**

- ○ **A.** Setting up filters on external routers to drop all ICMP packets
- ○ **B.** Reducing the amount of time before the reset of an unfinished TCP connection
- ○ **C.** Increasing the amount of time before the reset of an unfinished TCP connection
- ○ **D.** Setting up a filter that denies traffic originating from the Internet that shows an internal network address

12. Which of the following best describes the practice of deleting a domain name during the five-day AGP and immediately re-registering it for another five-day period?

Quick Answer: **107**
Detailed Answer: **112**

- ○ **A.** TCP/IP hijacking
- ○ **B.** DNS tasting
- ○ **C.** DNS kiting
- ○ **D.** Domain spoofing

13. Which of the following best describes ARP poisoning?

Quick Answer: **107**
Detailed Answer: **112**

- ○ **A.** Broadcasting a fake or reply to an entire network
- ○ **B.** Changing the IP record for a specific domain
- ○ **C.** Sending fragmented UDP packets
- ○ **D.** Distributing zombie software

14. Which of the following attacks is associated with services using an interprocess communication share such as network file and print sharing services?

Quick Answer: **107**
Detailed Answer: **112**

- ○ **A.** DNS spoofing
- ○ **B.** Null sessions
- ○ **C.** ARP poisoning
- ○ **D.** DNS kiting

15. Which of the following hundreds of ICMP packets have been sent to the host?

Quick Answer: **107**
Detailed Answer: **112**

- ○ **A.** DNS spoofing
- ○ **B.** ARP poisoning
- ○ **C.** Man-in-the-middle
- ○ **D.** Denial of service

16. Which of the following type of attacks is most likely being executed when an unauthorized service is relaying information to a source outside the network?

Quick Answer: **107**
Detailed Answer: **112**

- ○ **A.** DNS spoofing
- ○ **B.** ARP poisoning
- ○ **C.** Man-in-the-middle
- ○ **D.** Denial of service

17. Which of the following best describes the primary security issue with null sessions?

Quick Answer: **107**
Detailed Answer: **112**

- ○ **A.** The sessions are not terminated properly.
- ○ **B.** The connection is not authenticated.
- ○ **C.** The connection is not encrypted.
- ○ **D.** The sessions are remotely controlled.

18. Which of the following is most effective way to reduce null session vulnerability?

Quick Answer: **107**
Detailed Answer: **113**

- ○ **A.** Reducing the reset time of an unfinished TCP connection
- ○ **B.** Using the signing capabilities of certificates
- ○ **C.** Setting up filters to drop all ICMP packets
- ○ **D.** Disabling NetBIOS over TCP/IP

19. Which of the following are effective ways to mitigate spoofing attacks? (Select all correct answers.)

Quick Answer: **107**
Detailed Answer: **113**

- ○ **A.** Editing the Registry on Windows-based computers to restrict anonymous access
- ○ **B.** Using IPsec to secure transmissions between critical servers and clients
- ○ **C.** Denying traffic originating from the Internet that shows an internal network address
- ○ **D.** Using the signing capabilities of certificates on servers and clients

20. Running which of the following commands is the quickest way to tell which ports are open and which services are running on the machine?

Quick Answer: **107**
Detailed Answer: **113**

- ○ **A.** `netstat`
- ○ **B.** `nbtstat`
- ○ **C.** `ipconfig`
- ○ **D.** `msconfig`

21. Which of the following protocols is used for monitoring the health of network equipment, computer equipment, and devices?

- ○ **A.** SNAP
- ○ **B.** SMTP
- ○ **C.** SDLC
- ○ **D.** SNMP

Quick Answer: **107**
Detailed Answer: **113**

22. Which of the following are effective ways to protect the network infrastructure from attacks aimed at antiquated or unused ports and protocols? (Select all correct answers.)

- ○ **A.** Keeping only protocols installed by default
- ○ **B.** Allowing traffic only on necessary ports
- ○ **C.** Removing any unnecessary protocols
- ○ **D.** Allowing only traffic requested by users

Quick Answer: **107**
Detailed Answer: **113**

23. Which of the following sessions can typically result in TCP/IP hijacking? (Select all correct answers.)

- ○ **A.** Telnet
- ○ **B.** Web
- ○ **C.** Email
- ○ **D.** Samba

Quick Answer: **107**
Detailed Answer: **113**

24. Which of the following is the most effective method to mitigate session hijacking?

- ○ **A.** Denying traffic originating from the Internet that shows an internal network address
- ○ **B.** Forcing users to re-authenticate before allowing transactions to occur
- ○ **C.** Reducing the amount of time before the reset of an unfinished TCP connection
- ○ **D.** Setting up filters on external routers to drop all incoming ICMP packets

Quick Answer: **107**
Detailed Answer: **113**

25. When mitigating null session vulnerability, which of the following ports should be closed? (Select all correct answers.)

- ○ **A.** 161
- ○ **B.** 162
- ○ **C.** 139
- ○ **D.** 445

Quick Answer: **107**
Detailed Answer: **114**

26. When editing the Registry on Windows-based computers to restrict anonymous access, which of the following key values is restrictive without interfering with application functionality?

- ○ **A.** 0
- ○ **B.** 1
- ○ **C.** 2
- ○ **D.** 3

27. Which of the following sessions can typically result in a man-in-the-middle attack? (Select all correct answers.)

- ○ **A.** Telnet
- ○ **B.** Wireless
- ○ **C.** Email
- ○ **D.** Samba

28. Which of the following are issues associated with kited domains? (Select all correct answers.)

- ○ **A.** Search engines return more-relevant results.
- ○ **B.** Search engines return less-relevant results.
- ○ **C.** Capitalization on slight variations of website addresses.
- ○ **D.** Domain names that legitimate businesses use may be tied up.

29. Which of the following are ways to minimize the effects of DNS poisoning when hosting your own DNS? (Select all correct answers.)

- ○ **A.** Checking that the hosting server is not open-recursive
- ○ **B.** Running operating systems from an account with lesser privileges
- ○ **C.** Using different servers for authoritative and recursive lookups
- ○ **D.** Disabling recursive access for networks to resolve names that are not in zone files

30. Which of the following are the most effective methods to mitigate ARP poisoning on a large network? (Select all correct answers.)

○ **A.** Using equipment that offers port security

○ **B.** Using static mapping for IP addresses and ARP tables

○ **C.** Using script-based mapping for IP addresses and ARP tables

○ **D.** Deploying monitoring tools or an intrusion detection system (IDS)

Quick Answer: **107**
Detailed Answer: **114**

Objective 2.2: Distinguish between network design elements and components.

1. The organization requires email traffic in a DMZ segment, which of the following TCP ports will be open? (Select all correct answers.)

○ **A.** 110

○ **B.** 21

○ **C.** 25

○ **D.** 443

Quick Answer: **107**
Detailed Answer: **114**

2. Which of the following UDP ports must be open to allow SNMP traffic through the router?

○ **A.** 161

○ **B.** 162

○ **C.** 443

○ **D.** 4445

Quick Answer: **107**
Detailed Answer: **114**

3. Which of the following best describes a demilitarized zone (DMZ)?

○ **A.** A small network between the database servers and file servers

○ **B.** A small network between the internal network and the Internet

○ **C.** A portion of the internal network that uses web-based technologies

○ **D.** A portion of the internal infrastructure used in business-to-business relationships

Quick Answer: **107**
Detailed Answer: **114**

4. Which of the following best describes a virtual local-area network (VLAN)?

Quick Answer: **107**
Detailed Answer: **115**

- ○ **A.** A method to allow multiple computers to connect to the Internet using one IP address
- ○ **B.** A method to unite network nodes physically into the same broadcast domain
- ○ **C.** A method to split one network into two using routers to connect them together
- ○ **D.** A method to unite network nodes logically into the same broadcast domain

5. Which of the following best describes Network Address Translation (NAT)?

Quick Answer: **107**
Detailed Answer: **115**

- ○ **A.** A method to allow multiple computers to connect to the Internet using one IP address
- ○ **B.** A method to unite network nodes physically into the same broadcast domain
- ○ **C.** A method to split one network into two using routers to connect them together
- ○ **D.** A method to unite network nodes logically into the same broadcast domain

6. Which of the following best describes subnetting?

Quick Answer: **107**
Detailed Answer: **115**

- ○ **A.** A method to allow multiple computers to connect to the Internet using one IP address
- ○ **B.** A method to unite network nodes physically into the same broadcast domain
- ○ **C.** A method to split one network into two using routers to connect them together
- ○ **D.** A method to unite network nodes logically into the same broadcast domain

7. Which of the following is the most important security aspect of using Network Address Translation (NAT)?

Quick Answer: **107**
Detailed Answer: **115**

- ○ **A.** It unites network nodes logically into the same broadcast domain.
- ○ **B.** It hides the internal network from the outside world.
- ○ **C.** It allows users to be grouped by department rather than location.
- ○ **D.** It allows external users to access necessary information.

8. Which of the following is the most common reason networks are subnetted?

- ○ **A.** To allow logical division on the same broadcast domain
- ○ **B.** To hide the internal network from the outside world
- ○ **C.** For easier application of security policies
- ○ **D.** To control network traffic

9. Which of the following private IP address ranges should be used for the internal network when there are 100 host systems?

- ○ **A.** 10.x.x.x
- ○ **B.** 172.16.x.x
- ○ **C.** 192.168.1.x
- ○ **D.** 224.1.1.x

10. When a client machine receives an IP address of 169.254.0.15, it is an indication of which of the following?

- ○ **A.** The client cannot contact the DHCP server.
- ○ **B.** The client has a corrupt routing table.
- ○ **C.** The client has a manually configured address.
- ○ **D.** The client cannot contact the DNS server.

11. Automatic Private IP Addressing (APIPA) is denoted by which of the following IP addresses?

- ○ **A.** 192.168.1.10
- ○ **B.** 169.254.0.5
- ○ **C.** 224.223.10.1
- ○ **D.** 172.16.15.84

12. Which of the following best describes network access control (NAC)?

- ○ **A.** A method to allow multiple computers to connect to the Internet using one IP address
- ○ **B.** A method to split one network into two using routers to connect them together
- ○ **C.** A method to unite network nodes logically into the same broadcast domain
- ○ **D.** A method of enforcement that helps ensure computers are properly configured

13. Which of the following IP address ranges can be used for the internal network when using NAT? (Select all correct answers.)

    ○ **A.** 10.x.x.x
    ○ **B.** 172.16.x.x
    ○ **C.** 192.168.1.x
    ○ **D.** 224.1.1.x

Quick Answer: **107**
Detailed Answer: **116**

14. Which of the following are basic components of NAC? (Select all correct answers.)

    ○ **A.** Access requestor
    ○ **B.** Network redirector
    ○ **C.** Policy enforcement point
    ○ **D.** Policy decision point

Quick Answer: **107**
Detailed Answer: **117**

15. Which of the following devices can be a policy enforcement point in NAC? (Select all correct answers.)

    ○ **A.** Hub
    ○ **B.** Switch
    ○ **C.** Firewall
    ○ **D.** Router

Quick Answer: **107**
Detailed Answer: **117**

16. Which of the following best describes the NAC method that performs an assessment as hosts come online, and then grants appropriate access?

    ○ **A.** Inline
    ○ **B.** Out-of-band
    ○ **C.** Switch based
    ○ **D.** Host based

Quick Answer: **107**
Detailed Answer: **117**

17. Which of the following is a business benefit associated with the use of NAC? (Select all correct answers.)

    ○ **A.** Compliance
    ○ **B.** Separation of duties
    ○ **C.** Improved security posture
    ○ **D.** Operational cost management

Quick Answer: **107**
Detailed Answer: **117**

18. Which of the following are ways to mitigate vulnerabilities associated with a PBX? (Select all correct answers.)

    Quick Answer: **107**
    Detailed Answer: **117**

    ○ **A.** Changing any default passwords have been change

    ○ **B.** Physically securing the area where the PBX resides

    ○ **C.** Implementing an encryption solution

    ○ **D.** Putting a data-validation system in place

19. Which of the following type of attacks is associated with the use of a PBX?

    Quick Answer: **107**
    Detailed Answer: **117**

    ○ **A.** Man-in-the-middle

    ○ **B.** Buffer overflows

    ○ **C.** Denial of service

    ○ **D.** Social engineering

20. Which of the following type of attacks are associated with the use of VoIP? (Select all correct answers.)

    Quick Answer: **107**
    Detailed Answer: **118**

    ○ **A.** Man-in-the-middle

    ○ **B.** Buffer overflows

    ○ **C.** Denial of service

    ○ **D.** Social engineering

21. Which of the following is an inherent security risk associated with using SIP as an alternative for VoIP?

    Quick Answer: **107**
    Detailed Answer: **118**

    ○ **A.** It leaves the network open to long-distance toll fraud.

    ○ **B.** It leaves the network open to war-dialing attacks.

    ○ **C.** It leaves the network open to unauthorized transport of data.

    ○ **D.** It leaves the network open to war-driving attacks.

22. Which of the following is an inherent security risk associated with using a PBX?

    Quick Answer: **107**
    Detailed Answer: **118**

    ○ **A.** It leaves the network open to long-distance toll fraud.

    ○ **B.** It leaves the network open to war-dialing attacks.

    ○ **C.** It leaves the network open to unauthorized transport of data.

    ○ **D.** It leaves the network open to war-driving.

23. Which of the following is an inherent security risk associated with using a modem pool?

- ○ **A.** It leaves the network open to long-distance toll fraud.
- ○ **B.** It leaves the network open to war-dialing attacks.
- ○ **C.** It leaves the network open to unauthorized transport of data.
- ○ **D.** It leaves the network open to war-driving.

Quick Answer: **107**
Detailed Answer: **118**

24. Which of the following solutions can help mitigate the risks and vulnerabilities associated with VoIP? (Select all correct answers.)

- ○ **A.** Authentication
- ○ **B.** Setting the callback features
- ○ **C.** Data validation
- ○ **D.** Implementing a firewall solution

Quick Answer: **107**
Detailed Answer: **118**

25. Which of the following solutions can help mitigate the risks and vulnerabilities associated with modems? (Select all correct answers.)

- ○ **A.** Authentication
- ○ **B.** Setting the callback features
- ○ **C.** Data validation
- ○ **D.** Implementing a firewall solution

Quick Answer: **107**
Detailed Answer: **118**

Objective 2.3: Determine the appropriate use of network security tools to facilitate network security.

1. Which of the following are functions of an intrusion detection system? (Select all correct answers.)

- ○ **A.** Prevent attacks
- ○ **B.** Analyze data
- ○ **C.** Identify attacks
- ○ **D.** Respond to attacks

Quick Answer: **108**
Detailed Answer: **119**

2. Which of the following best describes the difference between an intrusion detection system and a firewall?

Quick Answer: **108**
Detailed Answer: **119**

- ○ **A.** IDSs control the information coming in and out of the network, whereas firewalls actually prevent attacks.

- ○ **B.** Firewalls control the information coming in and out of the network, whereas IDSs identifies unauthorized activity.

- ○ **C.** Firewalls control the information coming in and out of the network, whereas IDSs actually prevent attacks.

- ○ **D.** IDSs control the information coming in and out of the network, whereas firewalls identifies unauthorized activity.

3. Which of the following best describes a host intrusion detection system?

Quick Answer: **108**
Detailed Answer: **119**

- ○ **A.** Examines the information exchanged between machines

- ○ **B.** Attempts to prevent attacks in real time

- ○ **C.** Controls the information coming in and out of the network

- ○ **D.** Collects and analyzes data that originates on the local machine

4. Which of the following best describes a network intrusion detection system?

Quick Answer: **108**
Detailed Answer: **119**

- ○ **A.** Examines the information exchanged between machines

- ○ **B.** Attempts to prevent attacks in real time

- ○ **C.** Controls the information coming in and out of the network

- ○ **D.** Collects and analyzes data that originates on the local machine

5. Which of the following best describes a network intrusion prevention system?

Quick Answer: **108**
Detailed Answer: **119**

- ○ **A.** Examines the information exchanged between machines

- ○ **B.** Attempts to prevent attacks in real time

- ○ **C.** Controls the information coming in and out of the network

- ○ **D.** Collects and analyzes data that originates on the local machine

6. Which of the following best describes an inline NIPS?

  ○ **A.** Sits inside the network to detect attacks after they occur

  ○ **B.** Sits outside of the network to detect attacks after they occur

  ○ **C.** Sits between the network and the Internet

  ○ **D.** Sits between the protected systems and the rest of the network

Quick Answer: **108**
Detailed Answer: **119**

7. Which of the following is true when implementing a NIPS? (Select all correct answers.)

  ○ **A.** The sensors must be placed on domain controllers to function properly.

  ○ **B.** The sensors must be physically inline to function properly.

  ○ **C.** It adds single points of failure to the network.

  ○ **D.** It adds additional redundancy to the network.

Quick Answer: **108**
Detailed Answer: **119**

8. Which of the following best describes fail-open technology in reference to the implementation of NIPS?

  ○ **A.** If the device fails, it provides application redundancy.

  ○ **B.** If the device fails, it will prevents a fire from starting.

  ○ **C.** If the device fails, it causes a complete network outage.

  ○ **D.** If the device fails, a complete network outage will be avoided.

Quick Answer: **108**
Detailed Answer: **120**

9. Which of the following best describes a firewall?

  ○ **A.** Examines the information exchanged between machines

  ○ **B.** Attempts to prevent attacks in real time

  ○ **C.** Controls the information coming in and out of the network

  ○ **D.** Collects and analyzes data that originates on the local machine

Quick Answer: **108**
Detailed Answer: **120**

10. Which of the following firewall technologies can distinguish between FTP commands?

Quick Answer: **108**
Detailed Answer: **120**

- ○ **A.** Application-level gateway
- ○ **B.** Circuit-level gateway
- ○ **C.** Proxy gateway
- ○ **D.** SOCKS proxy

11. Which of the following best describes a packet-filtering firewall?

Quick Answer: **108**
Detailed Answer: **120**

- ○ **A.** Relies on algorithms to process application layer data
- ○ **B.** Operates at the OSI network layer
- ○ **C.** Operates at the OSI session layer
- ○ **D.** Examines traffic for application layer protocols

12. Which of the following best describes a stateful-inspection firewall?

Quick Answer: **108**
Detailed Answer: **120**

- ○ **A.** Relies on algorithms to process application layer data
- ○ **B.** Operates at the OSI network layer
- ○ **C.** Operates at the OSI session layer
- ○ **D.** Examines traffic for application layer protocols

13. Which of the following best describes a circuit-level firewall?

Quick Answer: **108**
Detailed Answer: **120**

- ○ **A.** Relies on algorithms to process application layer data
- ○ **B.** Operates at the OSI network layer
- ○ **C.** Operates at the OSI session layer
- ○ **D.** Examines traffic for application layer protocols

14. Which of the following best describes an application-level firewall?

Quick Answer: **108**
Detailed Answer: **121**

- ○ **A.** Relies on algorithms to process application layer data
- ○ **B.** Operates at the OSI network layer
- ○ **C.** Operates at the OSI session layer
- ○ **D.** Examines traffic for application layer protocols

15. Which of the following are functions of proxy servers? (Select all correct answers.)

Quick Answer: **108**
Detailed Answer: **121**

- ○ **A.** Caching
- ○ **B.** Logging
- ○ **C.** Addressing
- ○ **D.** Filtering

16. Which of the following are examples of a bastion host? (Select all correct answers.)

Quick Answer: **108**
Detailed Answer: **121**

   ○ **A.** Web server

   ○ **B.** Email server

   ○ **C.** Database server

   ○ **D.** DHCP server

17. Which of the following should be implemented if the organization wants to substantially reduce Internet traffic?

Quick Answer: **108**
Detailed Answer: **121**

   ○ **A.** Content filter

   ○ **B.** Proxy server

   ○ **C.** Protocol analyzer

   ○ **D.** Packet-filtering firewall

18. Which of the following should be implemented if the organization wants a simple, good first line of defense?

Quick Answer: **108**
Detailed Answer: **122**

   ○ **A.** Content filter

   ○ **B.** Proxy server

   ○ **C.** Protocol analyzer

   ○ **D.** Packet-filtering firewall

19. Which of the following should be implemented if the organization wants to monitor unauthorized transfer of confidential information?

Quick Answer: **108**
Detailed Answer: **122**

   ○ **A.** Content filter

   ○ **B.** Proxy server

   ○ **C.** Protocol analyzer

   ○ **D.** Packet-filtering firewall

20. Which of the following should be implemented if the organization wants to troubleshoot network issues?

Quick Answer: **108**
Detailed Answer: **122**

   ○ **A.** Content filter

   ○ **B.** Proxy server

   ○ **C.** Protocol analyzer

   ○ **D.** Packet-filtering firewall

21. Which of the following should be implemented if the organization wants to capture proper documentation for forensic investigations and litigation purposes?

    ○ **A.** Content filter

    ○ **B.** Proxy server

    ○ **C.** Protocol analyzer

    ○ **D.** Packet-filtering

22. Content filtering is integrated at which of the following levels?

    ○ **A.** Network level

    ○ **B.** Application level

    ○ **C.** System kernel level

    ○ **D.** Operating system level

23. Which of the following is the biggest drawback of using content filtering?

    ○ **A.** Network bandwidth is reduced.

    ○ **B.** Daily updates required.

    ○ **C.** Terminology must be defined.

    ○ **D.** Opens the system to DoS attacks.

24. Which of the following are functions of a protocol analyzer? (Select all correct answers.)

    ○ **A.** Monitor for unexpected traffic

    ○ **B.** Identify unnecessary protocols

    ○ **C.** Prevent SMTP relay from being exploited

    ○ **D.** Prevent DoS attacks by unauthorized parties

25. Which of the following is true about the use of content filtering?

    ○ **A.** It will report all violations identified in one group of applications.

    ○ **B.** It will report only violations identified in the specified applications.

    ○ **C.** It will report only violations identified in one application at a time.

    ○ **D.** It will report all violations identified in all applications.

Objective 2.4: Apply the appropriate network tools to facilitate network security.

1. Which of the following are objectives for the placement of firewalls? (Select all correct answers.)

   ○ **A.** Identify unnecessary protocols

   ○ **B.** Allow only traffic that is necessary

   ○ **C.** Provide notification of suspicious behavior

   ○ **D.** Monitor unauthorized transfer of information

Quick Answer: **108**
Detailed Answer: **123**

2. Which of the following is the most likely placement of each firewall when an organization is deploying only two of them?

   ○ **A.** One behind the DMZ and one between the intranet and the extranet

   ○ **B.** One in front of the DMZ and one between the intranet and the extranet

   ○ **C.** One in front of the DMZ and one between the DMZ and the internal network

   ○ **D.** One in front of the DMZ and one between the financial data and the user data

Quick Answer: **108**
Detailed Answer: **124**

3. Which of the following best describes the reason packet-filtering firewalls are considered unsecure as compared to other types of firewalls?

   ○ **A.** They allow packets regardless of communication patterns.

   ○ **B.** Due to physical placement, they are very accessible.

   ○ **C.** It is impossible to create a secure password for them.

   ○ **D.** They can be compromised with very little effort.

Quick Answer: **108**
Detailed Answer: **124**

4. Which of the following best describes why an organization would implement a proxy service firewall?

   ○ **A.** To prevent DoS attacks by unauthorized parties

   ○ **B.** To monitor unauthorized transfer of confidential information

   ○ **C.** To capture proper documentation for forensic investigations

   ○ **D.** To prevent user computers from directly accessing the Internet

Quick Answer: **108**
Detailed Answer: **124**

5. Which of the following best describes what governs the traffic of proxy service firewalls?

Quick Answer: **108**
Detailed Answer: **124**

- ○ **A.** Settings
- ○ **B.** Rules
- ○ **C.** Policies
- ○ **D.** Guidelines

6. Which of the following technologies would you implement when setting up a switched network and want to group users by department?

Quick Answer: **108**
Detailed Answer: **124**

- ○ **A.** VPN
- ○ **B.** NAT
- ○ **C.** VLAN
- ○ **D.** DMZ

7. Where would an organization place a web server that needs to be accessed by both the employees and by external customers?

Quick Answer: **108**
Detailed Answer: **124**

- ○ **A.** VPN
- ○ **B.** NAT
- ○ **C.** VLAN
- ○ **D.** DMZ

8. Which of the following would an organization implement to monitor the internal network and external traffic when the source of recent security breaches is unknown? (Select all correct answers.)

Quick Answer: **108**
Detailed Answer: **125**

- ○ **A.** Firewall
- ○ **B.** Content filter
- ○ **C.** Host-based IDS
- ○ **D.** Network-based IDS

9. Which of the following is the most likely placement of a proxy server when a small organization is deploying it for Internet connectivity?

Quick Answer: **108**
Detailed Answer: **125**

- ○ **A.** On the internal network
- ○ **B.** Between the internal network and the Internet
- ○ **C.** Between the web server and file server
- ○ **D.** In parallel with IP routers

10. Which of the following is the most likely placement of a proxy server when a small organization is deploying it for content caching?

Quick Answer: **108**
Detailed Answer: **125**

  ○ **A.** On the internal network

  ○ **B.** Between the internal network and the Internet

  ○ **C.** Between the web server and file server

  ○ **D.** In parallel with IP routers

11. Which of the following is the most likely placement of a proxy server when a small organization is deploying it both Internet connectivity and web content caching?

Quick Answer: **108**
Detailed Answer: **125**

  ○ **A.** On the internal network

  ○ **B.** Between the internal network and the Internet

  ○ **C.** Between the web server and file server

  ○ **D.** In parallel with IP routers

12. Which of the following is the most likely placement of a proxy server when a large organization is deploying it for Internet connectivity?

Quick Answer: **108**
Detailed Answer: **126**

  ○ **A.** On the internal network

  ○ **B.** Between the internal network and the Internet

  ○ **C.** Between the web server and file server

  ○ **D.** In parallel with IP routers

13. Which of the following best describes the mechanics of Internet content filtering?

Quick Answer: **108**
Detailed Answer: **126**

  ○ **A.** Analyzes data against a database contained in the software

  ○ **B.** Analyzes data by scanning against a vendor provided rule base

  ○ **C.** Analyzes data against preset rules contained in the software

  ○ **D.** Analyzes data by matching against predefined traffic patterns

14. Which of the following would be likely placements of a hardware network Internet content filtering device? (Select all correct answers.)

- ○ **A.** Behind the proxy/NAT point
- ○ **B.** On the individual user machines
- ○ **C.** In a DMZ with public addresses behind a packet-filtering router
- ○ **D.** Connected to the same network segment as the users monitored

Quick Answer: **108**
Detailed Answer: **126**

15. Which of the following is the most likely reason to place a proxy server in parallel with IP routers?

- ○ **A.** To allow for better content caching
- ○ **B.** To prevent direct access to the Internet
- ○ **C.** To allow for network load balancing
- ○ **D.** To prevent unauthorized transfer of data

Quick Answer: **108**
Detailed Answer: **126**

16. Which of the following are most likely placements of a network protocol analyzer? (Select all correct answers.)

- ○ **A.** Inline
- ○ **B.** On the outside of the DMZ
- ○ **C.** On the outside the Internet router
- ○ **D.** Between the devices of the traffic capture

Quick Answer: **108**
Detailed Answer: **126**

17. Which of the following is the most likely placement of placement of a packet-filtering firewall?

- ○ **A.** In the DMZ, between it and the internal network
- ○ **B.** On the internal network between servers
- ○ **C.** Between the Internet and the protected network
- ○ **D.** Securing the main perimeter

Quick Answer: **108**
Detailed Answer: **127**

18. Which of the following is the most common unintended consequence when deploying multiple firewalls?

- ○ **A.** Legitimate traffic gets blocked.
- ○ **B.** Increased network latency.
- ○ **C.** Increased attack vector.
- ○ **D.** Troubleshooting becomes complex.

Quick Answer: **108**
Detailed Answer: **127**

19. Which of the following is the most likely placement of placement of a proxy service firewall?

Quick Answer: **108**
Detailed Answer: **127**

   ○ **A.** In the DMZ, between it and the internal network

   ○ **B.** On the internal network between servers

   ○ **C.** Between the Internet and the protected network

   ○ **D.** Securing the main perimeter

20. Which of the following is the most likely placement of placement of a stateful-inspection firewall?

Quick Answer: **108**
Detailed Answer: **127**

   ○ **A.** In the DMZ, between it and the internal network

   ○ **B.** On the internal network between servers

   ○ **C.** Between the Internet and the protected network

   ○ **D.** Securing the main perimeter

Objective 2.5: Explain the vulnerabilities and mitigations associated with network devices.

1. Which of the following best describes privilege escalation?

Quick Answer: **108**
Detailed Answer: **128**

   ○ **A.** A default set of user credentials

   ○ **B.** Data transmitted that can be easily sniffed

   ○ **C.** Accidental or intentional access to resources

   ○ **D.** Application code functions allowing unauthorized access

2. Which of the following best describes a back door?

Quick Answer: **108**
Detailed Answer: **128**

   ○ **A.** A default set of user credentials

   ○ **B.** Data transmitted that can be easily sniffed

   ○ **C.** Accidental or intentional access to resources

   ○ **D.** Application code functions allowing unauthorized access

3. Which of the following satisfies organizational requirements for password complexity based on best practices?

Quick Answer: **108**
Detailed Answer: **128**

   ○ **A.** Derived from common words found in the dictionary

   ○ **B.** A mixture of character case, numbers, and/or symbols

   ○ **C.** A random-generated password created by a program

   ○ **D.** Derived from personal information such as birthdates

4. In a corporate environment, which of the following is most vulnerable to DoS attacks?

- ○ **A.** Internal user systems
- ○ **B.** Network resources
- ○ **C.** Network storage
- ○ **D.** Internal servers

Quick Answer: **108**
Detailed Answer: **128**

5. Which of the following best describes a denial-of-service (DoS) attack?

- ○ **A.** Intentional access to resources not intended for access by the user
- ○ **B.** Application code functions that allow unauthorized access to network resources
- ○ **C.** Attempt to block access attempt to block access by overwhelming network availability
- ○ **D.** Attempt to directly access the resources through unauthorized means

Quick Answer: **108**
Detailed Answer: **128**

6. Which of the following will reduce the vulnerability of a broadcast packet sniffer readily identifying a WAP?

- ○ **A.** Requiring WPA2 encryption
- ○ **B.** Turning off SSID broadcast
- ○ **C.** Turning off DHCP on the WAP
- ○ **D.** Restricting access by MAC addresses

Quick Answer: **108**
Detailed Answer: **129**

7. Which of the following is the best method to mitigate attacks against networking devices and services installed with a default set of user credentials?

- ○ **A.** Replacing them on an as-needed basis
- ○ **B.** Replacing them when an attack has been detected
- ○ **C.** Replacing them with unique strong logon credentials
- ○ **D.** Replacing them with the same strong logon credential

Quick Answer: **108**
Detailed Answer: **129**

8. Which of the following are ways to mitigate the vulnerabilities of wireless networks? (Select all correct answers.)

- ○ **A.** Requiring WPA2 encryption
- ○ **B.** Turning off SSID broadcast
- ○ **C.** Turning on DHCP on the WAP
- ○ **D.** Restricting access by MAC addresses

Quick Answer: **108**
Detailed Answer: **129**

9. Which of the following is the most common origin of back doors?

   ○ **A.** Created during application development

   ○ **B.** Created during system certification

   ○ **C.** Created during user interface testing

   ○ **D.** Created during implementation

Quick Answer: **108**
Detailed Answer: **129**

10. Which of the following should be performed when implementing distributed wireless network configurations spanning multiple buildings or open natural areas?

   ○ **A.** Land survey

   ○ **B.** Building inspection

   ○ **C.** OSHA inspection

   ○ **D.** Site survey

Quick Answer: **108**
Detailed Answer: **130**

11. Which of the following is most closely linked to privilege escalation?

   ○ **A.** SSID broadcast

   ○ **B.** Application flaws

   ○ **C.** Application development

   ○ **D.** Automated attacks

Quick Answer: **108**
Detailed Answer: **130**

12. Which of the following is most closely linked to packet sniffing?

   ○ **A.** SSID broadcast

   ○ **B.** Application flaws

   ○ **C.** Application development

   ○ **D.** Automated attacks

Quick Answer: **108**
Detailed Answer: **130**

13. Which of the following is most closely linked to weak passwords?

   ○ **A.** SSID broadcast

   ○ **B.** Application flaws

   ○ **C.** Application development

   ○ **D.** Automated attacks

Quick Answer: **108**
Detailed Answer: **130**

14. Which of the following is most closely linked to back doors?

   ○ **A.** SSID broadcast

   ○ **B.** Application flaws

   ○ **C.** Application development

   ○ **D.** Automated attacks

Quick Answer: **108**
Detailed Answer: **131**

15. Which of the following is most closely linked to default accounts?

- ○ **A.** Network resources
- ○ **B.** Application flaws
- ○ **C.** Network credentials
- ○ **D.** Automated attacks

Quick Answer: **108**
Detailed Answer: **131**

16. Which of the following is most closely linked to denial of service?

- ○ **A.** Network resources
- ○ **B.** SSID broadcast
- ○ **C.** Network credentials
- ○ **D.** Application development

Quick Answer: **108**
Detailed Answer: **131**

17. Which of the following best describes the situation where User A can read User B's email without specific authorization?

- ○ **A.** Privilege escalation
- ○ **B.** Default accounts
- ○ **C.** Weak passwords
- ○ **D.** Back door

Quick Answer: **108**
Detailed Answer: **132**

18. Which of the following best describes the situation where a software designer puts in shortcut entry points to allow rapid code evaluation and testing?

- ○ **A.** Privilege escalation
- ○ **B.** Default accounts
- ○ **C.** Weak passwords
- ○ **D.** Back door

Quick Answer: **108**
Detailed Answer: **132**

19. Which of the following attacks are associated with weak passwords? (Select all correct answers.)

- ○ **A.** Packet sniffing
- ○ **B.** Automated attacks
- ○ **C.** Social engineering
- ○ **D.** Denial of service

Quick Answer: **108**
Detailed Answer: **132**

20. Which of the following attacks are associated with fringe service industries such as online casinos?

- ○ **A.** Packet sniffing
- ○ **B.** Automated attacks
- ○ **C.** Social engineering
- ○ **D.** Denial of service

Quick Answer: **108**
Detailed Answer: **132**

Objective 2.6: Explain the vulnerabilities and mitigations associated with various transmission media.

1. Which of the following is best defense against vampire taps?

   ○ **A.** Mandatory access control

   ○ **B.** Logical access control

   ○ **C.** Physical access control

   ○ **D.** Network access control

Quick Answer: **109**
Detailed Answer: **133**

2. Which of the following is the most critical in protecting switched networks?

   ○ **A.** Mandatory access control

   ○ **B.** Logical access control

   ○ **C.** Physical access control

   ○ **D.** Network access control

Quick Answer: **109**
Detailed Answer: **133**

3. Which of the following is true with regard to the use of hubs?

   ○ **A.** Hubs do not provide data isolation between endpoint ports.

   ○ **B.** Hubs provide data isolation between endpoint ports.

   ○ **C.** Hubs provide packet forwarding for routable addresses.

   ○ **D.** Hubs provide copying of packets to a monitoring connection.

Quick Answer: **109**
Detailed Answer: **133**

4. Which of the following is an inherent security risk associated with using hubs?

   ○ **A.** They allow any node to manage traffic to and from all other nodes on the same device.

   ○ **B.** They allow any node to observe data traffic to and from all other nodes on the same device.

   ○ **C.** They allow any node to examine encryption traffic to and from all other nodes on the same device.

   ○ **D.** They allow any node to encrypt traffic to and from all other nodes on the same device.

Quick Answer: **109**
Detailed Answer: **133**

5. In which of the following allows interception of data traffic without a detectable presence on the network?

Quick Answer: **109**
Detailed Answer: **134**

   ○ **A.** Keylogger

   ○ **B.** Back door

   ○ **C.** Logic bomb

   ○ **D.** Vampire tap

Objective 2.7: Explain the vulnerabilities and implement mitigations associated with wireless networking.

1. Which of the following best describes a major security issue when implementing WAPs?

Quick Answer: **109**
Detailed Answer: **134**

   ○ **A.** WEP is the default encryption.

   ○ **B.** The SSID is broadcast in plain text.

   ○ **C.** They are hard to physically locate.

   ○ **D.** Any node can view the data of another node.

2. Which of the following best describes why data emanation is a security risk in wireless networks? (Select all correct answers.)

Quick Answer: **109**
Detailed Answer: **134**

   ○ **A.** It uses 802.1x transmissions that generate detectable radio-frequency signals funneled into one direction.

   ○ **B.** Sniffing the data may use many solutions to increase the distance over which detection is possible.

   ○ **C.** Sniffing the data may use many solutions to reduce the distance over which transmission is possible.

   ○ **D.** It uses 802.1x transmissions that generate detectable radio-frequency signals in all directions.

3. Which of the following is the primary method to mitigate the vulnerabilities associated with communication over an 802.1x wireless link?

Quick Answer: **109**
Detailed Answer: **134**

   ○ **A.** Authorization

   ○ **B.** Authentication

   ○ **C.** Encryption

   ○ **D.** Identification

4. Which of the following type of attacks are associated with the use of wireless communication? (Select all correct answers.)

    ○ **A.** Packet sniffing

    ○ **B.** Session hijacking

    ○ **C.** Man-in-the-middle

    ○ **D.** Spam relaying

Quick Answer: **109**
Detailed Answer: **134**

5. Which of the best describes why session hijacking is possible in wireless communication?

    ○ **A.** There is no authorization mechanism.

    ○ **B.** There is no authentication mechanism.

    ○ **C.** The authentication mechanism is one-way.

    ○ **D.** The authorization mechanism is one-way.

Quick Answer: **109**
Detailed Answer: **134**

6. Which of the following best describes why a man-in-the-middle attack is possible in wireless communication?

    ○ **A.** The request for connection by the client is a bidirectional open broadcast.

    ○ **B.** The request for connection by the access point is a bidirectional open broadcast.

    ○ **C.** The request for connection by the access point is an omnidirectional open broadcast.

    ○ **D.** The request for connection by the client is an omnidirectional open broadcast.

Quick Answer: **109**
Detailed Answer: **135**

7. Which of the following best describes war-driving?

    ○ **A.** Driving around with a laptop system configured to listen for open access points

    ○ **B.** Dialing a large range of telephone numbers in search of devices that can be exploited

    ○ **C.** Marking landmarks to indicate the presence of an available access point

    ○ **D.** Accessing an open public WAP for a monthly fee or commission from the end user

Quick Answer: **109**
Detailed Answer: **135**

8. Which of the following best describes war-chalking?

Quick Answer: **109**
Detailed Answer: **135**

○ **A.** Driving around with a laptop system configured to listen for open access points

○ **B.** Dialing a large range of telephone numbers in search of devices that can be exploited

○ **C.** Marking landmarks to indicate the presence of an available access point

○ **D.** Accessing an open public for a monthly fee or commission from the end user

9. Which of the following best describes bluejacking?

Quick Answer: **109**
Detailed Answer: **135**

○ **A.** Driving around system configured to listen for open access points

○ **B.** Sending broadcast spam from a nearby Bluetooth-enabled device

○ **C.** Deleting data on a Bluetooth device that has opened a connection

○ **D.** Marking landmarks to indicate an available open access point

10. Which of the following best describes bluesnarfing?

Quick Answer: **109**
Detailed Answer: **135**

○ **A.** Driving around system configured to listen for open access points

○ **B.** Sending broadcast spam from a nearby Bluetooth-enabled device

○ **C.** Deleting data on a Bluetooth device that has opened a connection

○ **D.** Marking landmarks to indicate an available open access point

11. Which of the following is the bandwidth commonly associated with 802.11b communications?

Quick Answer: **109**
Detailed Answer: **136**

○ **A.** 1.5MBps

○ **B.** 11Mbps

○ **C.** 100Mbps

○ **D.** 19.2Kbps

12. Which of the following best describes a WLAN technology that uses Ethernet protocols?

- ○ **A.** Wi-Fi
- ○ **B.** i-Mode
- ○ **C.** Bluetooth
- ○ **D.** WAP

Quick Answer: **109**
Detailed Answer: **136**

13. Which of the following encryption standards currently is the most secure for Wi-Fi connections?

- ○ **A.** WAP
- ○ **B.** WPA2
- ○ **C.** WEP2
- ○ **D.** WEP

Quick Answer: **109**
Detailed Answer: **136**

14. Which of the following best describes the situation that allows using reflective tube waveguides such as a Pringle's can to capture data?

- ○ **A.** Weak encryption
- ○ **B.** Session hijacking
- ○ **C.** War-driving
- ○ **D.** Data emanation

Quick Answer: **109**
Detailed Answer: **136**

15. Which of the following best describes the situation that allows a hijacker to wait until the authentication cycle is completed, then generate a signal that causes the client to think it has been disconnected from the access point?

- ○ **A.** Weak encryption
- ○ **B.** Session hijacking
- ○ **C.** War-driving
- ○ **D.** Data emanation

Quick Answer: **109**
Detailed Answer: **136**

16. Which of the following best describes what might allow data transacted over an 802.1x wireless link to be passed in clear form?

- ○ **A.** Weak encryption
- ○ **B.** Session hijacking
- ○ **C.** War-driving
- ○ **D.** Data emanation

Quick Answer: **109**
Detailed Answer: **136**

17. Which of the following best describes the situation where an attack is aimed at pairing with the attacker's device for unauthorized access, modification, or deletion of data?

- ○ **A.** Bluejacking
- ○ **B.** Bluesnarfing
- ○ **C.** War-driving
- ○ **D.** War-chalking

Quick Answer: **109**
Detailed Answer: **137**

18. Which of the following best describes the situation that allows an attack aimed at the identification of existing wireless networks, the SSID used, and any known WEP keys?

- ○ **A.** Weak encryption
- ○ **B.** Session hijacking
- ○ **C.** War-driving
- ○ **D.** Data emanation

Quick Answer: **109**
Detailed Answer: **137**

19. Which of the following best describes the situation where an attack is aimed at generating messages that appear to be from the device itself?

- ○ **A.** Bluejacking
- ○ **B.** Bluesnarfing
- ○ **C.** War-driving
- ○ **D.** War-chalking

Quick Answer: **109**
Detailed Answer: **137**

20. In which of the following attacks would the implementation of a rogue AP with stronger signal strength than more remote permanent installations be found?

- ○ **A.** Weak encryption
- ○ **B.** Man-in-the-middle
- ○ **C.** War-driving
- ○ **D.** Data emanation

Quick Answer: **109**
Detailed Answer: **138**

21. When a client attempts to make an 802.1x-compliant connection, which of the following best describes how the AP authenticates the client?

- ○ **A.** Users provide a shared password.
- ○ **B.** Through hardware token authentication.
- ○ **C.** Through a basic challenge-response method.
- ○ **D.** Users provide an identifier along with a password.

Quick Answer: **109**
Detailed Answer: **138**

22. Using the Temporal Key Integrity Protocol (TKIP) or Wi-Fi Protected Access (WPA/WPA2) standards would be most useful in preventing which of the following attacks?

 ○ **A.** Weak encryption

 ○ **B.** Data emanation

 ○ **C.** Bluejacking

 ○ **D.** War-driving

23. Which of the following are standard specifications included in the WAP standard?

 ○ **A.** Wireless Application Environment (WAE)

 ○ **B.** Wireless Session Layer (WSL)

 ○ **C.** Wireless Transport Layer Security (WTLS)

 ○ **D.** Wired Equivalent Privacy (WEP)

24. The Wi-Fi Protected Access standards were developed by the Wi-Fi Alliance to replace which of the following?

 ○ **A.** DES

 ○ **B.** WAP

 ○ **C.** AES

 ○ **D.** WEP

25. WSL is equivalent to which of the following layers of the OSI model?

 ○ **A.** Session

 ○ **B.** Transport

 ○ **C.** Network

 ○ **D.** Presentation

Quick-Check Answer Key

Objective 2.1: Differentiate between the different ports & protocols, their respective threats, and mitigation techniques.

1. C	11. A, B, D	21. D
2. A, B	12. C	22. B, C
3. C	13. A	23. A, B
4. A	14. B	24. B
5. B	15. D	25. C, D
6. D	16. C	26. B
7. D	17. B	27. A, B
8. B	18. D	28. B, C, D
9. C	19. B, C, D	29. A, C, D
10. A	20. C	30. A, D

Objective 2.2: Distinguish between network design elements and components.

1. A, C	10. A	19. D
2. A, B	11. B	20. A, B, C
3. B	12. D	21. C
4. D	13. A, B, C	22. A
5. A	14. A, C, D	23. B
6. C	15. B, C, D	24. A, C
7. B	16. B	25. B, D
8. D	17. A, C, D	
9. C	18. A, B	

Objective 2.3: Determine the appropriate use of network security tools to facilitate network security.

1. B, C, D	10. A	19. A
2. B	11. B	20. C
3. D	12. A	21. A
4. A	13. C	22. D
5. B	14. D	23. C
6. D	15. A, B, C	24. A, B
7. B, C	16. A, B	25. B
8. D	17. B	
9. C	18. D	

Objective 2.4: Apply the appropriate network tools to facilitate network security.

1. B, C	8. C, D	15. C
2. C	9. B	16. A, D
3. A	10. A	17. C
4. D	11. B	18. B
5. B	12. D	19. A
6. C	13. A	20. D
7. D	14. A, C, D	

Objective 2.5: Explain the vulnerabilities and mitigations associated with network devices.

1. C	8. A, B, D	15. C
2. D	9. A	16. A
3. B	10. D	17. A
4. B	11. B	18. D
5. C	12. A	19. B, C
6. B	13. D	20. D
7. C	14. C	

Objective 2.6: Explain the vulnerabilities and mitigations associated with various transmission media.

1. C   3. A   5. D
2. C   4. B

Objective 2.7: Explain the vulnerabilities and implement mitigations associated with wireless networking.

1. B   10. C   19. A
2. D   11. B   20. B
3. C   12. A   21. C
4. A, B, C   13. B   22. A
5. C   14. D   23. A
6. D   15. B   24. D
7. A   16. A   25. A
8. C   17. B
9. B   18. C

Answers and Explanations

Objective 2.1: Differentiate between the different ports & protocols, their respective threats, and mitigation techniques.

1. **Answer: C.** Telnet uses port 23. Answer A is incorrect because port 110 is used for POP3 incoming mail. Answer B is incorrect because port 21 is used for FTP. Port 443 is used by HTTPS; therefore, answer D is incorrect.

2. **Answer: A, B.** UDP ports 161 and 162 are used by SNMP. Answer C is incorrect because port 443 is used by HTTPS. Answer D is incorrect because port 4445 uses TCP/UDP for service type upnotifyp.

3. **Answer: C.** TCP/IP hijacking is the term used when an attacker takes control of a session between the server and a client. This can occur due to the TCP three-way handshake. The three-way handshake is the method used to establish and tear down network connections. Answer A is incorrect because it describes spoofing. Spoofing is a method of providing false identity information to gain unauthorized access. Answer B is incorrect because it describes a null session. A null session is a connection without specifying a username or password. Answer D is incorrect because it describes DNS poisoning. DNS poisoning allows a perpetrator to redirect traffic by changing the IP record for a specific domain, thus permitting the attacker to send legitimate traffic anywhere they choose.

4. **Answer: A.** Spoofing is a method of providing false identity information to gain unauthorized access. Answer B is incorrect because it describes a null session. A null session is a connection without specifying a username or password. Answer C is incorrect because it describes TCP/IP hijacking. TCP/IP hijacking is the term used when an attacker takes control of a session between the server and a client. Answer D is incorrect because it describes DNS poisoning. DNS poisoning allows a perpetrator to redirect traffic by changing the IP record for a specific domain, thus permitting the attacker to send legitimate traffic anywhere they choose.

5. **Answer: B.** A null session is a connection without specifying a username or password. Answer A is incorrect because it describes spoofing. Spoofing is a method of providing false identity information to gain unauthorized access. Answer C is incorrect because it describes spoofing. TCP/IP hijacking is the term used when an attacker takes control of a session between the server and a client. Answer D is incorrect because it describes DNS poisoning. DNS poisoning allows a perpetrator to redirect traffic by changing the IP record for a specific domain, thus permitting the attacker to send legitimate traffic anywhere they choose.

6. **Answer: D.** DNS poisoning allows a perpetrator to redirect traffic by changing the IP record for a specific domain. Query results that are forged and returned to the requesting client or recursive DNS query can poison the DNS records, thus permitting the attacker to send legitimate traffic anywhere they choose. Answer A is incorrect because it describes spoofing. Spoofing is a method of providing false identity information to gain unauthorized access. Answer B is incorrect because it describes a null

session. A null session is a connection without specifying a username or password. Answer C is incorrect because it describes TCP/IP hijacking. TCP/IP hijacking is the term used when an attacker takes control of a session between the server and a client.

7. **Answer: D.** The man-in-the-middle attack takes place when an attacker intercepts traffic and then tricks the parties at both ends into believing that they are communicating with each other. Answer A is incorrect; it describes DNS kiting. DNS kiting refers to the practice of taking advantage of the add/grace period (AGP) to monopolize domain names without ever paying for them. Answer B is incorrect; it describes a replay attack. In a replay attack, packets are captured by using sniffers. After the pertinent information is extracted, the packets are placed back on the network. Answer C is incorrect; it describes a denial-of-service attack. The purpose of a DoS attack is to disrupt the resources or services that a user would expect to have access to.

8. **Answer: B.** In a replay attack, packets are captured by using sniffers. After the pertinent information is extracted, the packets are placed back on the network. Answer A is incorrect; it describes DNS kiting. DNS kiting refers to the practice of taking advantage of the AGP to monopolize domain names without ever paying for them. Answer C is incorrect; it describes a denial-of-service attack. The purpose of a DoS attack is to disrupt the resources or services that a user would expect to have access to. Answer D is incorrect; it describes a man-in-the-middle attack. The man-in-the-middle attack takes place when an attacker intercepts traffic and then tricks the parties at both ends into believing that they are communicating with each other.

9. **Answer: C.** The purpose of a denial of service (DoS) attack is to disrupt the resources or services that a user would expect to have access to. Answer A is incorrect; it describes DNS kiting. DNS kiting refers to the practice of taking advantage of the AGP to monopolize domain names without ever paying for them. Answer B is incorrect; it describes a replay attack. In a replay attack, packets are captured by using sniffers. After the pertinent information is extracted, the packets are placed back on the network. Answer D is incorrect; it describes a man-in-the-middle attack. The man-in-the-middle attack takes place when an attacker intercepts traffic and then tricks the parties at both ends into believing that they are communicating with each other.

10. **Answer: A.** DNS kiting refers to the practice of taking advantage of the AGP to monopolize domain names without ever paying for them. Answer B is incorrect; it describes a replay attack. In a replay attack, packets are captured by using sniffers. After the pertinent information is extracted, the packets are placed back on the network. Answer C is incorrect; it describes a denial-of-service attack. The purpose of a DoS attack is to disrupt the resources or services that a user would expect to have access to. Answer D is incorrect; it describes a man-in-the-middle attack. The man-in-the-middle attack takes place when an attacker intercepts traffic and then tricks the parties at both ends into believing that they are communicating with each other.

11. **Answer: A, B, D.** To help protect your network, you can set up filters on external routers to drop packets involved in these types of attacks. You should also set up another filter that denies traffic originating from the Internet that shows an internal network address. If the operating system allows it, reduce the amount of time before the reset of an unfinished TCP connection. Doing so makes it harder to keep resources unavailable for extended periods of time. Answer C is incorrect; increasing the amount of time before the reset of an unfinished TCP connection makes the resources unavailable for a longer period of time.

12. **Answer: C.** DNS kiting refers to the practice of taking advantage of the AGP to monopolize domain names without ever paying for them. How domain kiting works is that a domain name is deleted during the five-day AGP and immediately re-registered for another five-day period. Answer A is incorrect. TCP/IP hijacking is the term used when an attacker takes control of a session between the server and a client. Answer B is incorrect. Besides automatically registering domain names and placing advertising, domain kiters can track the amount of revenue generated. This is called domain tasting. It is used to test the profitability of domain names. Answer D is incorrect. Spoofing is a method of providing false identity information to gain unauthorized access.

13. **Answer: A.** Because ARP does not require any type of validation, as ARP requests are sent, the requesting devices believe that the incoming ARP replies are from the correct devices. This can allow a perpetrator to trick a device into thinking any IP is related to any MAC address. Answer B is incorrect because it describes DNS poisoning. Answer C is incorrect. A Teardrop attack sends fragmented UDP packets. Answer D is incorrect. In a DDoS attack, the attacker distributes zombie software that allows the attacker partial or full control of the infected computer system.

14. **Answer: B.** A null session is a connection without specifying a username or password. Null sessions are a possible security risk because the connection is not really authenticated. Answer A is incorrect because spoofing involves modifying the source address of traffic or source of information. Answer C is incorrect because ARP poisoning allows a perpetrator to trick a device into thinking that an incorrect IP address is related to a MAC address. The implementation of the ARP protocol is simple. The receipt of an ARP reply at any time causes the receiving computer to add the newly received information to its ARP cache without any type of verification. Answer D is incorrect because domain kiting refers to the practice of taking advantage of this AGP period to monopolize domain names without ever paying for them.

15. **Answer: D.** A denial-of-service (DoS) attack that attempts to block service or reduce activity on a host by sending ping requests directly to the victim using ICMP is called a ping flood. Answer A is incorrect because spoofing involves modifying the source address of traffic or source of information. Answer C is incorrect because a man-in-the middle attack is commonly used to gather information in transit between two hosts. Answer B is incorrect because the purpose of a DoS attack is to disrupt the resources or services that a user would expect to have access to.

16. **Answer: C.** A man-in-the-middle attack is commonly used to gather information in transit between two hosts. Answer A is incorrect because spoofing involves modifying the source address of traffic or source of information. ARP poisoning allows a perpetrator to trick a device into thinking any IP is related to any MAC address; therefore, Answer B is incorrect. Because the purpose of a DoS attack is to deny use of resources or services to legitimate users, answer D is incorrect.

17. **Answer: B.** A null session is a connection without specifying a username or password. Null sessions are a possible security risk because the connection is not really authenticated. Answer A is incorrect because the session is not abnormally terminated. Although answer C may be a concern, it is not the primary issue. Answer D is incorrect because null sessions are direct connections and are not remote controlled.

18. **Answer: D.** The most effective way to reduce null session vulnerability is by disabling NetBIOS over TCP/IP. Editing the Registry to restrict anonymous access is another method used to control null session access. After you have done this, verify that ports 139 and 445 are closed. Answer A is incorrect; reducing the amount of time before the reset of an unfinished TCP connection deals with DoS attacks. Answers B and C are incorrect; using the signing capabilities of certificates and denying traffic originating from the Internet that shows an internal network address are protective measures against spoofing.

19. **Answer: B, C, D.** To mitigate the effects of spoofing, you should set up a filter that denies traffic originating from the Internet that shows an internal network address. Using the signing capabilities of certificates on servers and clients allows web and email services to be more secure. The use of IPsec can secure transmissions between critical servers and clients. Answer A is incorrect because editing the Registry to restrict anonymous access is a method used to control null session access.

20. **Answer: A.** The quickest way to tell which ports are open and which services are running is to do a `netstat` operation on the machine. Answer B is incorrect; `nbtstat` is designed to help troubleshoot NetBIOS name resolution problems. Answer C is incorrect; `ipconfig` is used to troubleshoot IP address configuration. Answer D is incorrect; `msconfig` is used to configure startup services and on Windows computers.

21. **Answer: D.** SNMP is used for monitoring the health of network equipment, computer equipment, and devices like uninterruptible power supplies (UPS). Answer A is incorrect because SubNetwork Access Protocol (SNAP) defines how data is formatted for transmission and how access to the network is controlled. Answer B is incorrect because SMTP is used for email. Answer C is incorrect because The Synchronous Data Link Control (SDLC) protocol was developed by IBM to be used as the Layer 2 of the SNA hierarchical network.

22. **Answer: B, C.** The best way to protect the network infrastructure from attacks aimed at antiquated or unused ports and protocols is to remove any unnecessary protocols and create access control lists to allow traffic on necessary ports only. By doing so, you eliminate the possibility of unused and antiquated protocols being exploited and minimize the threat of an attack. Answer A is incorrect. It is not always necessary to keep protocols installed by default. Answer D is incorrect. Users should never control what goes in and out of the network.

23. **Answer: A, B.** TCP/IP hijacking commonly happens during Telnet and web sessions where security is lacking or when session timeouts are not configured properly. Answer C is incorrect because email is susceptible to spoofing not hijacking. Answer D is incorrect. Samba provides file and print services to SMB/CIFS clients for Linux-based operating systems.

24. **Answer: B.** Forcing a user to re-authenticate before allowing transactions to occur could help prevent this type of attack. Protection mechanisms include the use of unique initial sequence numbers (ISNs) and web session cookies. Answer A is incorrect because to mitigate the effects of spoofing, you should set up a filter that denies traffic originating from the Internet that shows an internal network address. Answers C and D are incorrect; to mitigate the vulnerability of DDoS attacks, reduce the amount of time before the reset of an unfinished TCP connection and set up filters on external routers.

25. **Answer: C, D.** The most effective way to reduce null session vulnerability is by disabling NetBIOS over TCP/IP. After you have this, verify that ports 139 and 445 are closed. Answers A and B are incorrect; Simple Network Management Protocol (SNMP) is often overlooked when checking for vulnerabilities because it uses User Datagram Protocol (UDP) ports 161 and 162.

26. **Answer: B.** The key default value is 0. Changing this value to 1, which is more restrictive, keeps a null session from seeing user accounts and admin shares. Changing the value to 2 is the most restrictive. This disables null session without explicit permissions. However, this setting may conflict with some applications that rely on null sessions. Keep in mind that even though you can change the Registry settings to try to prevent this type of attack, some tools sidestep this measure. If security is a major concern, you might have to consider not allowing any null sessions on your public and private networks. Based on this information, answers A, C, and D are incorrect.

27. **Answer: A, B.** The man-in-the-middle attack takes place when an attacker intercepts traffic and then tricks the parties at both ends into believing that they are communicating with each other. This attack is common in Telnet and wireless technologies. Answer C is incorrect because email is susceptible to spoofing not hijacking. Answer D is incorrect. Samba provides file and print services to SMB/CIFS clients for Linux-based operating systems.

28. **Answer: B, C, D.** Kited domains present several issues. They force search engines to return less-relevant results, tie up domain names that legitimate businesses may want to use, and capitalize on slight variations of personal or business website addresses. Answer A is incorrect; kiting has just opposite effect.

29. **Answer: A, C, D.** To minimize the effects of DNS poisoning, check the DNS setup if you are hosting your own DNS. Be sure the DNS server is not open-recursive. An open-recursive DNS server responds any lookup request, without checking where it originates. Disable recursive access for other networks to resolve names that are not in your zone files. You can also use different servers for authoritative and recursive lookups and require that caches discard information except from the .com servers, and the root servers. Answer B is incorrect because it describes an effective way to deal with rootkits.

30. **Answer: A, D.** ARP poisoning is limited to attacks that are local based, so an intruder needs either physical access to your network or control of a device on your local network. To mitigate ARP poisoning on a small network, you can use static or script-based mapping for IP addresses and ARP tables. For large networks, use equipment that offers port security. Answers B and C are incorrect; they are solutions for small networks, not large networks.

Objective 2.2: Distinguish between network design elements and components.

1. **Answer: A, C.** Port 110 is used for POP3 incoming mail and port 25 is used for SMTP mail. Answer B is incorrect because port 21 is used for FTP. Port 443 is used by HTTPS; therefore, answer D is incorrect.

2. **Answer: A, B.** UDP ports 161 and 162 are used by SNMP. Answer C is incorrect because port 443 is used by HTTPS. Answer D is incorrect because port 4445 uses TCP/UDP for service type upnotifyp.

3. **Answer: B.** A demilitarized zone (DMZ) is a small network between the internal network and the Internet that provides a layer of security and privacy. Answer A is incorrect it describes a separate subnetwork. Answer C is incorrect because it describes an intranet. An intranet is a portion of the internal network that uses web-based technologies. The information is stored on web servers and accessed using browsers. Answer D is incorrect because it describes an extranet. An extranet is the public portion of the company's IT infrastructure that allows resources to be used by authorized partners and resellers that have proper authorization and authentication. This type of arrangement is commonly used for business-to-business relationships.

4. **Answer: D.** The purpose of a virtual local-area network (VLAN) is to unite network nodes logically into the same broadcast domain regardless of their physical attachment to the network. VLANs provide a way to limit broadcast traffic in a switched network. Answer A is incorrect because it describes NAT, which allows multiple computers to connect to the Internet using one IP address. Answer B is incorrect; a switch is used to unite network nodes physically into the same broadcast domain. Answer C is incorrect because subnetting splits one network into two or more, using routers to connect each subnet.

5. **Answer: A.** NAT allows multiple computers to connect to the Internet using one IP address. Answer B is incorrect; a switch is used to unite network nodes physically into the same broadcast domain Answer C is incorrect because subnetting splits one network into two or more, using routers to connect each subnet. Answer D is incorrect because the purpose of a virtual local-area network (VLAN) is to unite network nodes logically into the same broadcast domain regardless of their physical attachment to the network. VLANs provide a way to limit broadcast traffic in a switched network.

6. **Answer: C.** Subnetting splits one network into two or more, using routers to connect each subnet. Answer A is incorrect. NAT allows multiple computers to connect to the Internet using one IP address. Answer B is incorrect; a switch is used to unite network nodes physically into the same broadcast domain. Answer D is incorrect because the purpose of a virtual local-area network (VLAN) is to unite network nodes logically into the same broadcast domain regardless of their physical attachment to the network. VLANs provide a way to limit broadcast traffic in a switched network.

7. **Answer: B.** Network Address Translation (NAT) acts as a liaison between an internal network and the Internet. It allows multiple computers to connect to the Internet using one IP address. An important security aspect of NAT is that it hides the internal network from the outside world. Answers A and C are incorrect because the purpose of a virtual local-area network (VLAN) is to unite network nodes logically into the same broadcast domain regardless of their physical attachment to the network. VLANs provide a way to limit broadcast traffic in a switched network. Answer D is incorrect; a DMZ allows external users to access information that the organization deems necessary.

8. **Answer: D.** Subnetting can be done for several reasons. If you have a Class C address and 1,000 clients, you will have to subnet the network or use a custom subnet mask to accommodate all the hosts. The most common reason networks are subnetted is to control network traffic by limiting broadcast domains, which limits broadcast storms. Answers A and C are incorrect because the purpose of a virtual local-area network (VLAN) is to unite network nodes logically into the same broadcast domain regardless of their physical attachment to the network. VLANs provide a way to limit broadcast traffic in a switched network. Answer B is incorrect; an important security aspect of NAT is that it hides the internal network from the outside world.

9. **Answer: C.** There are specific reserved private IP addresses for use on an internal network. In a Class C network, valid nonroutable host IDs are from 192.168.0.1 to 192.168.255.254. Network addresses with the first byte between 192 and 223 are Class C and can have about 250 hosts. Answer A is incorrect because it is a Class A address. Valid host IDs are from 10.0.0.1 to 10.255.255.254. Network addresses with the first byte between 1 and 126 are Class A and can have about 17 million hosts each. Answer B is incorrect because it is a Class B addresses; valid host IDs are from 172.16.0.1 through 172.31.255.254. Network addresses with the first byte between 128 and 191 are Class B and can have about 65,000 hosts each. Answer D is incorrect because network addresses with the first byte between 224 and 239 are Class D and are used for multicasting.

10. **Answer: A.** Another address range to keep in mind when designing IP address space is Automatic Private IP Addressing (APIPA). In the event that no Dynamic Host Configuration Protocol (DHCP) server is available at the time that the client issues a DHCP lease request, the client is automatically configured with an address from the 169.254.0.1 through 169.254.255.254 range. Answer B is incorrect because if the client has a corrupt routing table will not be able to reach the proper destination. Answer C is incorrect because if the client has a manually configured address it is not usually in the 169.254.x.x address range. If the client cannot contact the DNS server, the message displayed is "Cannot contact DNS server, therefore Answer D is incorrect."

11. **Answer: B.** In the event that no Dynamic Host Configuration Protocol (DHCP) server is available at the time that the client issues a DHCP lease request, the client is automatically configured with an address from the 169.254.0.1 through 169.254.255.254 range. Answer A is incorrect because it is a Class C internal address. Answer C is incorrect because it is a Class D address. Answer D is incorrect because it is a Class B internal address.

12. **Answer: D.** One of the most effective ways to protect the network from malicious hosts is to use network access control (NAC). NAC offers a method of enforcement that helps ensure that computers are properly configured. The premise behind NAC is to secure the environment by examining the user's machine and, based on the results, grant access accordingly. Answer A is incorrect because it describes the function of NAT. Answer B is incorrect because it describes the function of subnetting. Answer C is incorrect because it describes the function of a VLAN.

13. **Answer: A, B, C.** In a Class C network, valid nonroutable host IDs are from 192.168.0.1 to 192.168.255.254. Network addresses with the first byte between 192 and 223 are Class C and can have about 250 hosts. Answer A is incorrect because it is a Class A address. Valid host IDs are from 10.0.0.1 to 10.255.255.254. Network

addresses with the first byte between 1 and 126 are Class A and can have about 17 million hosts each. Answer B is incorrect because it is a Class B addresses; valid host IDs are from 172.16.0.1 through 172.31.255.254. Network addresses with the first byte between 128 and 191 are Class B and can have about 65,000 hosts each. Answer D is incorrect because network addresses with the first byte between 224 and 239 are Class D and are reserved for multicasting.

14. **Answer: A, C, D.** The basic components of NAC products are the Access requestor (AR), which is the device that requests access; the policy decision point (PDP), which is the system that assigns a policy based on the assessment; and the policy enforcement point (PEP), which is the device that enforces the policy. Answer B is incorrect. The network redirector, or redirector, is an operating system driver that sends data to and receives data from a remote device.

15. **Answer: B, C, D.** The policy enforcement point is the device that enforces the policy. This device may be a switch, firewall, or router. Answer A is incorrect; a hub cannot enforce policy.

16. **Answer: B.** The four ways NAC systems can be integrated into the network are inline, out-of-band, switch based, and host based. An out-of-band intervenes and performs an assessment as hosts come online, and then grants appropriate access. Answer A is incorrect. An appliance in the line usually sits between the access and the distribution switches. Answer C is incorrect. Switch based is similar to in-band NAC except enforcement occurs on the switch itself. Answer D is incorrect. Host based relies on an installed host agent to assess and enforce access policy devices.

17. **Answer: A, C, D.** In addition to providing the ability to enforce security policy, contain noncompliant users, and mitigate threats, NAC offers a number of business benefits. The business benefits include compliance, a better security posture, and operational cost management. Answer B is incorrect. Separation of duties is one of the key concepts of internal controls. It is not a business benefit. It is the most difficult and sometimes the most costly one to achieve.

18. **Answer: A, B.** To protect your network, make sure the PBX is in a secure area, any default passwords have been changed, and only authorized maintenance is done. Many times, hackers can gain access to the phone system via social engineering because this device is usually serviced through a remote maintenance port. Answers C and D are incorrect because these are solution associated with mitigating vulnerabilities associated with VoIP.

19. **Answer: D.** Many times, hackers can gain access to the phone system via social engineering because this device is usually serviced through a remote maintenance port. To protect your network, make sure the Private Branch Exchange (PBX) is in a secure area, any default passwords have been changed, and only authorized maintenance is done. Answer A is incorrect. Man-in-the-middle attacks are executed between the SIP phone and a SIP proxy, allowing the audio to be manipulated, causing dropped, rerouted, or playback calls. Answers B and C are incorrect; they are associated with VoIP. VoIP PBX servers are susceptible to the same type of exploits as other network servers. These attacks include DoS and buffer overflows, with DoS being the most prevalent.

20. **Answer: A, B, C.** Man-in-the-middle attacks are executed between the SIP phone and a SIP proxy, allowing the audio to be manipulated, causing dropped, rerouted, or playback calls. VoIP PBX servers are susceptible to the same type of exploits as other network servers. These attacks include DoS and buffer overflows, with DoS being the most prevalent. Answer D is incorrect. Many times, hackers can gain access to the phone system via social engineering because this device is usually serviced through a remote maintenance port.

21. **Answer: C.** Session Initiation Protocol (SIP) is commonly used in instant messaging, but it can also be used as an alternative for VoIP. Using SIP can leave VoIP networks open to unauthorized transport of data. Answer A is incorrect because long-distance toll fraud is associated with a PBX. Answer B is incorrect; war-dialing attacks take advantage of unsecure modems. Answer D is incorrect because war-driving attacks take advantage of wireless networks.

22. **Answer: A.** For years, PBX-type systems have been targeted by hackers, mainly to get free long-distance service. The vulnerabilities that phone networks are subject to include social engineering, long-distance toll fraud, and breach of data privacy. Answer B is incorrect war-dialing attacks take advantage of unsecure modems. Answer C is incorrect. Session Initiation Protocol (SIP) is commonly used in instant messaging, but it can also be used as an alternative for VoIP. Using SIP can leave VoIP networks open to unauthorized transport of data. Answer D is incorrect. War-driving is used to intercept wireless communications by driving around looking for unsecured wireless networks.

23. **Answer: B.** Leaving modems open for incoming calls with little to no authentication for users dialing in can be a clear security vulnerability in the network. For example, war-dialing attacks take advantage of this situation. War-dialing is the process by which an automated software application is used to dial numbers in a given range to determine whether any of the numbers are serviced by modems that accept dial-in requests. Answer A is incorrect because long-distance toll fraud is associated with a PBX. Answer C is incorrect; using SIP can leave VoIP networks open to unauthorized transport of data. Answer D is incorrect because war-driving attacks take advantage of wireless networks.

24. **Answer: A, C.** Implementing the following solutions can help mitigate the risks and vulnerabilities associated with VoIP: encryption, authentication, data validation, and nonrepudiation. VoIP is basically based on a TCP/IP network, and Therefore, technologies that are used to secure IP networks can be used for VoIP, too. Answer B is incorrect because callback features are associated with the use of modems. Answer D is incorrect because encryption and firewall solutions are associated with the use of cable modems.

25. **Answer: B, D.** Setting the callback features to have the modem call the user back at a preset number and using encryption and firewall solutions will help keep the environment safe from attacks. Answers A and C are incorrect; implementing encryption, authentication, data validation, and nonrepudiation can help mitigate the risks and vulnerabilities associated with VoIP.

Objective 2.3: Determine the appropriate use of network security tools to facilitate network security.

1. **Answer: B, C, D.** The three basic areas of hardening are operating system, network, and application intrusion detection systems are designed to analyze data, identify attacks, and respond to the intrusion. Answer A is incorrect because preventing attacks is associated with an intrusion prevention system.

2. **Answer: B.** IDSs are different from firewalls in that firewalls control the information that gets in and out of the network, whereas IDSs can identify unauthorized activity. IDSs are also designed to catch attacks in progress within the network, not just on the boundary between private and public networks. Intrusion prevention differs from intrusion detection in that it actually prevents attacks instead of only detecting the occurrence of an attack. Based on this information, answers A, C, and D are incorrect.

3. **Answer: D.** A HIDS collects and analyzes data that originates on the local machine. Answer A is incorrect; a NIDS tries to locate packets not allowed on the network that the firewall missed and looks at the information exchanged between machines. Answer B is incorrect; intrusion prevention differs from intrusion detection in that it actually prevents attacks in real time instead of only detecting the occurrence. Answer C is incorrect because firewalls control the information that gets in and out of the network.

4. **Answer: A.** A NIDS tries to locate packets not allowed on the network that the firewall missed and looks at the information exchanged between machines. Answer B is incorrect; intrusion prevention differs from intrusion detection in that it actually prevents attacks in real time instead of only detecting the occurrence. Answer C is incorrect because firewalls control the information that gets in and out of the network. Answer D is incorrect; a HIDS collects and analyzes data that originates on the local machine.

5. **Answer: B.** Intrusion prevention differs from intrusion detection in that it actually prevents attacks in real time instead of only detecting the occurrence. Answer A is incorrect; a NIDS tries to locate packets not allowed on the network that the firewall missed and looks at the information exchanged between machines. Answer C is incorrect because firewalls control the information that gets in and out of the network. Answer D is incorrect; a HIDS collects and analyzes data that originates on the local machine.

6. **Answer: D.** An inline NIPS works like a Layer 2 bridge. It sits between the systems that need to be protected and the rest of the network. They proactively protect machines against damage from attacks that signature-based technologies cannot detect, as most NIPS solutions have the ability to look at application layer protocols such as HTTP, FTP, and SMTP. Answers A and B are incorrect because a NIPS detects attacks as they are occurring not after they occur. This is more of a function of an IDS. Answer C is incorrect because it describes a firewall.

7. **Answer: B, C.** When implementing a NIPS, keep in mind that the sensors must be physically inline to function properly. This adds single points of failure to the network. Answer A is incorrect because sensors are not placed on domain controllers. Answer D is incorrect because the sensors add single points of failure to the network, not redundancy.

8. **Answer: D.** When implementing a NIPS, keep in mind that the sensors must be physically inline to function properly. This adds single points of failure to the network. A good way to prevent this issue is to use fail-open technology. This means that if the device fails, it does not cause a complete network outage; instead, it acts like a patch cable. Answer A is incorrect because fail open has nothing to do with application redundancy. Answer B is incorrect; a NIPS fail-open has nothing to do with fire. Answer C is incorrect because it does not cause a complete network outage; instead, it acts like a patch cable.

9. **Answer: C.** A firewall is a component placed on computers and networks to help eliminate undesired access by the outside world. It can be composed of hardware, software, or a combination of both. Answer A is incorrect; a NIDS tries to locate packets not allowed on the network that the firewall missed and looks at the information exchanged between machines. Answer B is incorrect because intrusion prevention actually prevents attacks in real time instead of only detecting the occurrence. Answer D is incorrect; a HIDS collects and analyzes data that originates on the local machine.

10. **Answer: A.** An application-level gateway understands services and protocols. Answer C is too generic to be a proper answer. Answer B is incorrect because a circuit-level gateway's decisions are based on source and destination addresses. Answer D is incorrect because SOCKS proxy is an example of a circuit-level gateway.

11. **Answer: B.** A packet-filtering firewall is typically a router. Packets can be filtered based on IP addresses, ports, or protocols. They operate at the network layer (Layer 3) of the OSI model. Packet-filtering solutions are generally considered less-secure firewalls because they still allow packets inside the network, regardless of communication pattern within the session. Answer A is incorrect because it describes the function of a stateful- inspection firewall. A stateful-inspection firewall is a combination of all types of firewalls. This firewall relies on algorithms to process application layer data. Answer C is incorrect; a circuit-level gateway operates at the OSI session layer (Layer 5) by monitoring the TCP packet flow to determine whether the session requested is a legitimate one. Answer D is incorrect. With an application-level gateway, all traffic is examined to check for OSI application layer (Layer 7) protocols that are allowed. Examples of this type of traffic are File Transfer Protocol (FTP), Simple Mail Transfer Protocol (SMTP), and Hypertext Transfer Protocol (HTTP).

12. **Answer: A.** A stateful-inspection firewall is a combination of all types of firewalls. This firewall relies on algorithms to process application layer data. Answer B is incorrect. A packet-filtering firewall is typically a router. Packets can be filtered based on IP addresses, ports, or protocols. They operate at the network layer (Layer 3) of the OSI model. Packet-filtering solutions are generally considered less-secure firewalls because they still allow packets inside the network, regardless of communication pattern within the session. Answer C is incorrect; a circuit-level gateway operates at the OSI session layer (Layer 5) by monitoring the TCP packet flow to determine whether the session requested is a legitimate one. Answer D is incorrect. With an application-level gateway, all traffic is examined to check for OSI application layer (Layer 7) protocols that are allowed. Examples of this type of traffic are File Transfer Protocol (FTP), Simple Mail Transfer Protocol (SMTP), and Hypertext Transfer Protocol (HTTP).

13. **Answer: C.** A circuit-level gateway operates at the OSI session layer (Layer 5) by monitoring the TCP packet flow to determine whether the session requested is a legitimate

one. Answer A is incorrect. A stateful-inspection firewall is a combination of all types of firewalls. This firewall relies on algorithms to process application layer data. Answer B is incorrect; a packet-filtering firewall is typically a router. Packets can be filtered based on IP addresses, ports, or protocols. They operate at the network layer (Layer 3) of the OSI model. Packet-filtering solutions are generally considered less-secure firewalls because they still allow packets inside the network, regardless of communication pattern within the session. Answer D is incorrect. With an application-level gateway, all traffic is examined to check for OSI application layer (Layer 7) protocols that are allowed. Examples of this type of traffic are File Transfer Protocol (FTP), Simple Mail Transfer Protocol (SMTP), and Hypertext Transfer Protocol (HTTP).

14. **Answer: D.** With an application-level gateway, all traffic is examined to check for OSI application layer (Layer 7) protocols that are allowed. Examples of this type of traffic are File Transfer Protocol (FTP), Simple Mail Transfer Protocol (SMTP), and Hypertext Transfer Protocol (HTTP). Answer A is incorrect. A stateful-inspection firewall is a combination of all types of firewalls. This firewall relies on algorithms to process application layer data. Answer B is incorrect. A packet-filtering firewall is typically a router. Packets can be filtered based on IP addresses, ports, or protocols. They operate at the network layer (Layer 3) of the OSI model. Packet-filtering solutions are generally considered less-secure firewalls because they still allow packets inside the network, regardless of communication pattern within the session. Answer C is incorrect; a circuit-level gateway operates at the OSI session layer (Layer 5) by monitoring the TCP packet flow to determine whether the session requested is a legitimate one.

15. **Answer: A, B, D.** Proxy servers are used for security, logging, and caching. When the proxy server receives a request for an Internet service, it passes through filtering requirements and checks its local cache of previously downloaded web pages. Answer C is incorrect. Addressing is a function of a DHCP server.

16. **Answer: A, B.** An exposed server that provides public access to a critical service, such as a web or email server, may be configured to isolate it from an organization's network and to report attack attempts to the network administrator. Such an isolated server is referred to as a bastion host, named for the isolated towers that were used to provide castles advanced notice of pending assault. Answer C is incorrect. Database servers are generally contained on the internal network. Answer D is incorrect. DHCP servers give out IP addresses on the internal network.

17. **Answer: B.** When a proxy server receives a request for an Internet service, it passes through filtering requirements and checks its local cache of previously downloaded web pages. Because web pages are stored locally, response times for web pages are faster, and traffic to the Internet is substantially reduced. Answer A is incorrect. Internet content filters use a collection of terms, words, and phrases that are compared to content from browsers and applications. This type of software can filter content from various types of Internet activity and applications, such as instant messaging, email, and office documents. It can be used to monitor and stop the disclosure of the organization's proprietary or confidential information. Answer C is incorrect. Protocol analyzers help you troubleshoot network issues by gathering packet-level information across the network. These applications capture packets and decode the information into readable data for analysis. Answer D is incorrect; a packet-filtering firewall filters packets based on IP addresses, ports, or protocols and is a simple, good first line of defense.

18. **Answer: D.** A packet-filtering firewall filters packets based on IP addresses, ports, or protocols and is a simple, good first line of defense. Answer A is incorrect. Internet content filters use a collection of terms, words, and phrases that are compared to content from browsers and applications. This type of software can filter content from various types of Internet activity and applications, such as instant messaging, email, and office documents. It can be used to monitor and stop the disclosure of the organization's proprietary or confidential information. Answer B is incorrect. When a proxy server receives a request for an Internet service, it passes through filtering requirements and checks its local cache of previously downloaded web pages. Because web pages are stored locally, response times for web pages are faster, and traffic to the Internet is substantially reduced. Answer C is incorrect. Protocol analyzers help you troubleshoot network issues by gathering packet-level information across the network. These applications capture packets and decode the information into readable data for analysis.

19. **Answer: A.** Internet content filters use a collection of terms, words, and phrases that are compared to content from browsers and applications. This type of software can filter content from various types of Internet activity and applications, such as instant messaging, email, and office documents. It can be used to monitor and stop the disclosure of the organization's proprietary or confidential information. Answer B is incorrect. When a proxy server receives a request for an Internet service, it passes through filtering requirements and checks its local cache of previously downloaded web pages. Because web pages are stored locally, response times for web pages are faster, and traffic to the Internet is substantially reduced. Answer C is incorrect. Protocol analyzers help you troubleshoot network issues by gathering packet-level information across the network. These applications capture packets and decode the information into readable data for analysis. Answer D is incorrect; a packet-filtering firewall filters packets based on IP addresses, ports, or protocols and is a simple, good first line of defense.

20. **Answer: C.** Protocol analyzers help you troubleshoot network issues by gathering packet-level information across the network. These applications capture packets and decode the information into readable data for analysis. Answer A is incorrect. Internet content filters use a collection of terms, words, and phrases that are compared to content from browsers and applications. This type of software can filter content from various types of Internet activity and applications, such as instant messaging, email, and office documents. It can be used to monitor and stop the disclosure of the organization's proprietary or confidential information. Answer B is incorrect. When a proxy server receives a request for an Internet service, it passes through filtering requirements and checks its local cache of previously downloaded web pages. Because web pages are stored locally, response times for web pages are faster, and traffic to the Internet is substantially reduced. Answer D is incorrect; a packet-filtering firewall filters packets based on IP addresses, ports, or protocols and is a simple, good first line of defense.

21. **Answer: A.** Internet content filters use a collection of terms, words, and phrases that are compared to content from browsers and applications. Because content filtering uses screen captures of each violation with time-stamped data, it provides proper documentation for forensic investigations and litigation purpose. Answer B is incorrect.

When a proxy server receives a request for an Internet service, it passes through filtering requirements and checks its local cache of previously downloaded web pages. Because web pages are stored locally, response times for web pages are faster, and traffic to the Internet is substantially reduced. Answer C is incorrect. Protocol analyzers help you troubleshoot network issues by gathering packet-level information across the network. These applications capture packets and decode the information into readable data for analysis. Answer D is incorrect; a packet-filtering firewall filters packets based on IP addresses, ports, or protocols and is a simple, good first line of defense.

22. **Answer: D.** Content filtering is integrated at the operating system level so that it can monitor events such as opening files via Windows Explorer. It can be used to monitor and stop the disclosure of the organization's proprietary or confidential information. Based on the previous information, answers A, B, and C are incorrect because content filtering is integrated at the operating system level.

23. **Answer: C.** Unlike antivirus and antispyware applications, content monitoring does not require daily updates to keep the database effective and current. On the downside, content filtering needs to be "trained." For example, to filter nonpornographic material, the terminology must be input and defined in the database. Answer A is incorrect because content filtering helps control bandwidth costs. Answer B is incorrect based on the previous stated information. Answer D is incorrect. Packet-filtering solutions are generally considered less-secure firewalls because they still allow packets inside the network, regardless of communication pattern within the session. This leaves the system open to DoS attacks.

24. **Answer: A, B.** Protocol analyzers can do more than just look at packets. They prove useful in many other areas of network management, such as monitoring the network for unexpected, unwanted, and unnecessary traffic. For example, if the network is running slowly, a protocol analyzer can tell you whether necessary protocols are running on the network. Answers C and D are incorrect; attack prevention is a function of an intrusion prevention system not a protocol analyzer.

25. **Answer: B.** Content filtering will report only on violations identified in the specified applications listed for the filtering application. In other words, if the application will filter only Microsoft Office documents and a user chooses to use open Office, the content will not be filtered. Based on the above information, answers A, C, and D are incorrect; content filtering will report only on violations identified in the specified applications listed for the filtering application.

Objective 2.4: Apply the appropriate network tools to facilitate network security.

1. **Answer: B, C.** The main objective for the placement of firewalls is to allow only traffic that the organization deems necessary and provide notification of suspicious behavior. Answer A is incorrect because this is the function of a protocol analyzer. Answer D is incorrect because Internet content filters monitor unauthorized transfer of confidential information.

2. **Answer: C.** Most organizations deploy, at a minimum, two firewalls. The first firewall is placed in front of the DMZ to allow requests destined for servers in the DMZ or to route requests to an authentication proxy. The second firewall is placed to allow outbound requests. All initial necessary connections are located on the DMZ machines. For example, a RADIUS server may be running in the DMZ for improved performance and enhanced security, even though its database resides inside the company intranet. Answer A is incorrect; the first firewall should be deployed in front of the DMZ, not behind it. Answer B is incorrect; although the extranet would be located in the DMZ, and the intranet is located on the internal network, it is between the DMZ and the internal network where the firewall should be placed. Answer D is incorrect; although you may have a firewall between the user data and financial data, if you are only deploying two, the second one should go between the DMZ and the internal network.

3. **Answer: A.** A packet-filtering firewall is typically a router. Packets can be filtered based on IP addresses, ports, or protocols. They operate at the Network layer (Layer 3) of the Open Systems Interconnection (OSI) model. Packet-filtering solutions are generally considered less secure firewalls because they still allow packets inside the network, regardless of communication patterns within the session. Answer B is incorrect; all firewalls should be physically secure. Answer C is incorrect because secure passwords for firewalls can easily be created. Answer D is incorrect because compromising a secure router takes quite a bit of effort.

4. **Answer: D.** Proxy service firewalls are go-betweens for the network and the Internet. They can be used hide the internal addresses from the outside world through NAT. This does not allow the computers on the network to directly access the Internet. Answer A is incorrect because it describes the function of an intrusion detection system. Answers B and C are incorrect because they describe functions associated with an Internet content filtering system not a proxy service firewall.

5. **Answer: B.** Proxy service firewalls are go-betweens for the network and the Internet. They hide the internal addresses from the outside world and don't allow the computers on the network to directly access the Internet. This type of firewall has a set of rules that the packets must pass to get in or out. Because the firewall check traffic against a set of rules, setting, policies and guidelines are incorrect. Therefore, answers A, C, and D are incorrect.

6. **Answer: C.** The purpose of a VLAN is to unite network nodes logically into the same broadcast domain regardless of their physical attachment to the network. Answer A is incorrect because a virtual private network (VPN) is a network connection that allows you access via a secure tunnel created through an Internet connection. Answer B is incorrect because NAT acts as a liaison between an internal network and the Internet. Answer D is incorrect because a DMZ is a small network between the internal network and the Internet that provides a layer of security and privacy.

7. **Answer: D.** A DMZ is a small network between the internal network and the Internet that provides a layer of security and privacy. Answer A is incorrect because a virtual private network (VPN) is a network connection that allows you access via a secure tunnel created through an Internet connection. Answer B is incorrect because NAT acts as a liaison between an internal network and the Internet. Answer C is incorrect. The purpose of a VLAN is to unite network nodes logically into the same broadcast domain regardless of their physical attachment to the network.

8. **Answer: C, D.** Because you want to monitor both types of traffic, the IDSs should be used together. Network-based intrusion detection systems monitor the packet flow and try to locate packets that are not allowed for one reason or another and may have gotten through the firewall. Host-based intrusion detection systems monitor communications on a host-by-host basis and try to filter malicious data. These types of IDSs are good at detecting unauthorized file modifications and user activity. A firewall protects computers and networks from undesired access by the outside world; therefore, answer A is incorrect. Answer B is incorrect because Internet content filters use a collection of terms, words, and phrases that are compared to content from browsers and applications. Because content filtering uses screen captures of each violation with time-stamped data, it provides proper documentation for forensic investigations and litigation purpose.

9. **Answer: B.** Proxy servers can be placed between the private network and the Internet for Internet connectivity. If the organization is using the proxy server for both Internet connectivity and web content caching, the proxy server should be placed between the internal network and the Internet, with access for users who are requesting the web content. Answer A is incorrect; proxy servers are usually placed internally for web content caching. Answer C is incorrect. A firewall is usually placed between a web server and an internal file server. Answer D is incorrect. In some proxy server designs, such as for a large organization, the proxy server is placed in parallel with IP routers. This design allows for network load balancing by forwarding of all HTTP and FTP traffic through the proxy server and all other IP traffic through the router.

10. **Answer: A.** Proxy servers are usually placed internally for web content caching. Answer B is incorrect; Proxy servers can be placed between the private network and the Internet for Internet connectivity. If the organization is using the proxy server for both Internet connectivity and web content caching, the proxy server should be placed between the internal network and the Internet, with access for users who are requesting the web content. Answer C is incorrect. A firewall is usually placed between a web server and an internal file server. Answer D is incorrect. In some proxy server designs, such as for a large organization, the proxy server is placed in parallel with IP routers. This design allows for network load balancing by forwarding of all HTTP and FTP traffic through the proxy server and all other IP traffic through the router.

11. **Answer: B.** Proxy servers can be placed between the private network and the Internet for Internet connectivity. If the organization is using the proxy server for both Internet connectivity and web content caching, the proxy server should be placed between the internal network and the Internet, with access for users who are requesting the web content. Answer A is incorrect; proxy servers are usually placed internally for web content caching. Answer C is incorrect. A firewall is usually placed between a web server and an internal file server. Answer D is incorrect. In some proxy server designs, such as for a large organization, the proxy server is placed in parallel with IP routers. This design allows for network load balancing by forwarding of all HTTP and FTP traffic through the proxy server and all other IP traffic through the router.

12. **Answer: D.** In some proxy server designs, such as for a large organization, the proxy server is placed in parallel with IP routers. This design allows for network load balancing by forwarding of all HTTP and FTP traffic through the proxy server and all other IP traffic through the router. Answer A is incorrect; proxy servers are usually placed internally for web content caching. Answer C is incorrect. A firewall is usually placed between a web server and an internal file server. Answer B is incorrect. Proxy servers can be placed between the private network and the Internet for Internet connectivity. If the organization is using the proxy server for both Internet connectivity and web content caching, the proxy server should be placed between the internal network and the Internet, with access for users who are requesting the web content.

13. **Answer: A.** Internet content filtering works by analyzing data against a database contained in the software. Content filtering reports only on violations identified in the specified applications listed for the filtering application. In other words, if the application will only filter Microsoft Office documents and a user chooses to use Open Office, the content will not be filtered. Answers B and C are incorrect; they describe functions associated with firewalls. Answer D is incorrect; analyzing traffic patterns is associated with an intrusion detection systems.

14. **Answer: A, C, D.** Network Internet content filters can be hardware or software. Many network solutions combine both. Hardware appliances are usually connected to the same network segment as the users they will monitor. Other configurations include being deployed behind a firewall or in a DMZ, with public addresses behind a packet-filtering router. These appliances use access control filtering software on the dedicated filtering appliance. The device monitors every packet of traffic that passes over a network. Answer B is incorrect; network Internet content filters would not be placed on the individual systems. If this were true, they would become host-based content filters.

15. **Answer: C.** In some proxy server designs, the proxy server is placed in parallel with IP routers. This design allows for network load balancing by forwarding of all HTTP and FTP traffic through the proxy server and all other IP traffic through the router. Answer A is incorrect; proxy servers are usually placed internally for content caching not in parallel with IP routers. Answer B is incorrect; Proxy servers can be placed between the private network and the Internet for Internet connectivity. Answer D is incorrect because it describes Internet content filters. This type of software can filter content from various types of Internet activity and applications, such as instant messaging, email, and office documents. It can be used to monitor and stop the disclosure of the organization's proprietary or confidential information.

16. **Answer: A, D.** Protocol analyzers can be placed inline or in between the devices from which you want to capture the traffic. If you are analyzing SAN traffic, the analyzer can be placed outside the direct link with the use of an optical splitter. The analyzer is placed to capture traffic between the host and the monitored device. Answers B and C are incorrect because protocol analyzers are used to troubleshoot internal network issues and Therefore, they would not be placed outside the network.

17. **Answer: C.** A packet-filtering firewall is best suited for simple networks or used to protect a network that is used mainly for Internet access. The placement of a packet-filtering firewall is between the Internet and the protected network. It filters all traffic entering or leaving the network. Answer A is incorrect because proxy service firewalls allow organizations to offer services securely to Internet users. All servers hosting public services are placed in the demilitarized zone (DMZ) with the proxy firewall between the DMZ and the internal network. Answer B is incorrect; firewalls are not usually placed in between servers on the internal network, VLANs are used to separate resources. Answer D is incorrect because a stateful-inspection firewall is suited for main perimeter security. Stateful-inspection firewalls can thwart port scanning by closing off ports until a connection to the specific port is requested.

18. **Answer: B.** When deploying multiple firewalls, you might experience network latency. If you do, check the placement of the firewalls and possibly reconsider the topology to be sure you get the most out of the firewalls. Answer A is incorrect. If the access lists are configured correctly, legitimate traffic should not be blocked. This is true whether you are using 1 firewall or 10 firewalls. Answer C is incorrect, using multiple firewalls will reduce the attack vector, not increase it. Answer D is incorrect. Troubleshooting should become less complex because each firewall is configured for the traffic it will filter.

19. **Answer: A.** Proxy service firewalls allow organizations to offer services securely to Internet users. All servers hosting public services are placed in the demilitarized zone (DMZ) with the proxy firewall between the DMZ and the internal network. Answer B is incorrect; firewalls are not usually placed in between servers on the internal network, VLANs are used to separate resources. Answer C is incorrect because A packet-filtering firewall is best suited for simple networks or used to protect a network that is used mainly for Internet access. The placement of a packet-filtering firewall is between the Internet and the protected network. It filters all traffic entering or leaving the network. Answer D is incorrect because a stateful-inspection firewall is suited for main perimeter security. Stateful-inspection firewalls can thwart port scanning by closing off ports until a connection to the specific port is requested.

20. **Answer: D.** A stateful-inspection firewall is suited for main perimeter security. Stateful-inspection firewalls can thwart port scanning by closing off ports until a connection to the specific port is requested. Answer A is incorrect because proxy service firewalls allow organizations to offer services securely to Internet users. All servers hosting public services are placed in the demilitarized zone (DMZ) with the proxy firewall between the DMZ and the internal network. Answer B is incorrect; firewalls are not usually placed in between servers on the internal network, VLANs are used to separate resources. Answer C is incorrect because a packet-filtering firewall is best suited for simple networks or used to protect a network that is used mainly for Internet access. The placement of a packet-filtering firewall is between the Internet and the protected network. It filters all traffic entering or leaving the network.

Objective 2.5: Explain the vulnerabilities and mitigations associated with network devices.

1. **Answer: C.** Privilege escalation is a vulnerability represented by the accidental or intentional access to resources not intended for access by the user. Application flaws can allow a normal user access to administrative functions reserved for privileged accounts, or to access features of an application reserved for other users. An example of the latter would be if User A could read User B's email without specific authorization. Answer A is incorrect because it describes default accounts. Answer B is incorrect because data transmitted over a wireless network using 802.1x that can be easily "sniffed" is referred to as data emanations. Answer D is incorrect because a back door is an application code function created intentionally or unintentionally, which allow unauthorized access to networked resources.

2. **Answer: D.** A back door is an application code function created intentionally or unintentionally, which allow unauthorized access to networked resources. Answer A is incorrect because it describes default accounts. Answer B is incorrect because data transmitted over a wireless network using 802.1x that can be easily "sniffed" is referred to as data emanations. Answer C is incorrect. Privilege escalation is a vulnerability represented by the accidental or intentional access to resources not intended for access by the user. Application flaws can allow a normal user access to administrative functions reserved for privileged accounts, or to access features of an application reserved for other users. An example of the latter would be if User A could read User B's email without specific authorization.

3. **Answer: B.** Complexity means a mixture of character case, numbers, and/or symbols. Answers A and D are incorrect because automated and social-engineering assaults on passwords are easier when a password is short, and lacking in complexity, such as those derived from a common word found in the dictionary, or derived from easily guessable personal information such as birthdates, family names, pet names, and similar details. Answer C is incorrect because random generated passwords created by a program and often too complex for users to remember. This causes the users to write down the passwords and store them somewhere easily accessible. This goes against best practices.

4. **Answer: B.** Unlike resources located on the local system, network resources are much more vulnerable to DoS attacks. These attacks attempt to block access to resources by overwhelming network availability, instead of attempting to directly access the resources through unauthorized means. By blocking access to a website or network resource, the attacker effectively prevents authorized availability. Answer A is incorrect because a DoS focuses on network resources not local resources. Answer C is incorrect; viruses and worms ranked the highest for sheer number of attacks against network storage. Answer D is incorrect; DoS attacks are launched against servers in the DMZ, not the internal network, unless there is not a DMZ in place. However, corporate networks usually have some type of segmentation keeping the internal network and DMZ separated making this answer choice incorrect.

5. **Answer: C.** Unlike resources located on the local system, network resources are much more vulnerable to DoS attacks. These attacks attempt to block access to resources by overwhelming network availability, instead of attempting to directly access the

resources through unauthorized means. By blocking access to a website or network resource, the attacker effectively prevents authorized availability. Answer A is incorrect because privilege escalation is the intentional access to resources not intended for access by the user. Answer B is incorrect; a back door is an application code function created intentionally or unintentionally, which allow unauthorized access to networked resources. Answer D is incorrect; attempting to directly access the resources through unauthorized means would fall along the lines of a spoofing attack.

6. **Answer: B.** Wireless networks often announce their service set identifier (SSID) to allow mobile devices to discover available WAPs. Turning off this broadcast can reduce the vulnerability of a broadcast packet sniffer readily identifying a WAP, but is not truly secure because the SSID is broadcast in plain text whenever a client connects to the network. As long as the SSID broadcast is turned on the WAP will be identifiable. Therefore, answers A, C, and D are incorrect. These solutions can help mitigate the risks associated with using wireless communication, but they will reduce the vulnerability associated with identifying the WAP.

7. **Answer: C.** Many networking devices and services are initially installed with a default set of user credentials, such as Oracle's Scott/Tiger and IBM's qsecofr/qsecofr. Unless these credentials are removed and replaced with unique strong logon credentials, they present an avenue for network attack because they are known to potential attackers. Answer A is incorrect because replacing them on an as-needed basis is not proper policy. Answer B is incorrect; replacing them when an attack has been detracted is reactive instead of proactive. Answer D is incorrect because using the same logon credential for all devices and services leaves them all vulnerable should the password be compromised.

8. **Answer: A, B, D.** Wireless networks often announce their service set identifier (SSID) to allow mobile devices to discover available WAPs. Turning off this broadcast can reduce the vulnerability of a broadcast packet sniffer readily identifying a WAP, but is not truly secure because the SSID is broadcast in plain text whenever a client connects to the network. Turning off SSID broadcast should be considered a "best practice," along with conducting the site survey, selecting channels not already in use in the area, requiring WPA2 (or newer) encryption, and restricting access to a known list of Wi-Fi MAC addresses where possible. Answer C is incorrect because turning on DHCP will allow a rogue client to automatically connect. Therefore, it increases the vulnerability.

9. **Answer: A.** Back doors are application code functions created intentionally or unintentionally that enable unauthorized access to networked resources. Many times during application development, software designers put in shortcut entry points to allow rapid code evaluation and testing. If not removed before application deployment, such entry points can present the means for an attacker to gain unauthorized access later. Other back doors may be inserted by the application designers purposefully, presenting later threats to the network if applications are never reviewed by another application designer before deployment. Answer B is incorrect because back doors are associated with code development not system certification. Answer C is incorrect because during user interface testing, the users do not have access to the code and cannot create back doors. Answer D is incorrect because the code has already been developed and tested during the implementation phase. At this point, there is not access to the code itself.

10. **Answer: D.** To optimize network layout within each unique location, a site survey is necessary before implementing any WLAN solution. This is particularly important in distributed wireless network configurations spanning multiple buildings or open natural areas, where imposing structures and tree growth may affect network access in key areas. Answers A, B, and C are incorrect. Land surveys, building inspections, and OSHA inspections are agency-related functions and cannot be conducted by the organization.

11. **Answer: B.** Privilege escalation is a vulnerability represented by the accidental or intentional access to resources not intended for access by the user. Application flaws can allow a normal user access to administrative functions reserved for privileged accounts, or to access features of an application reserved for other users. Answer A is incorrect because it describes the vulnerability of a broadcast packet sniffer readily identifying a WAP. Answer C is incorrect. Back doors represent application code functions created intentionally or unintentionally, which allow unauthorized access to networked resources. Answer D is incorrect because automated and social-engineering assaults on passwords are easier when a password is short, lacking in complexity, derived from a common word found in the dictionary, or derived from easily guessable personal information such as birthdays, family names, pet names, and similar details.

12. **Answer: A.** Wireless networks often announce their service set identifier (SSID) to allow mobile devices to discover available WAPs. Turning off this broadcast can reduce the vulnerability of a broadcast packet sniffer readily identifying a WAP, but is not truly secure because the SSID is broadcast in plain text whenever a client connects to the network. Answer B is incorrect. Privilege escalation is a vulnerability represented by the accidental or intentional access to resources not intended for access by the user. Application flaws can allow a normal user access to administrative functions reserved for privileged accounts, or to access features of an application reserved for other users. Answer C is incorrect. Back doors represent application code functions created intentionally or unintentionally, which allow unauthorized access to networked resources. Answer D is incorrect because automated and social-engineering assaults on passwords are easier when a password is short, lacking in complexity, derived from a common word found in the dictionary, or derived from easily guessable personal information such as birthdays, family names, pet names, and similar details.

13. **Answer: D.** Automated and social-engineering assaults on passwords are easier when a password is short, lacking in complexity, derived from a common word found in the dictionary, or derived from easily guessable personal information such as birthdays, family names, pet names, and similar details. Answer A is incorrect because it describes the vulnerability of a broadcast packet sniffer readily identifying a WAP. Answer B is incorrect. Privilege escalation is a vulnerability represented by the accidental or intentional access to resources not intended for access by the user. Application flaws can allow a normal user access to administrative functions reserved for privileged accounts, or to access features of an application reserved for other users. Answer C is incorrect. Back doors represent application code functions created intentionally or unintentionally, which allow unauthorized access to networked resources.

14. **Answer: C.** Back doors represent application code functions created intentionally or unintentionally, which allow unauthorized access to networked resources. Many times during application development, software designers put in shortcut entry points to allow rapid code evaluation and testing. If not removed before application deployment, such entry points can present the means for an attacker to gain unauthorized access later. Answer A is incorrect because it describes the vulnerability of a broadcast packet sniffer readily identifying a WAP. Answer B is incorrect. Privilege escalation is a vulnerability represented by the accidental or intentional access to resources not intended for access by the user. Application flaws can allow a normal user access to administrative functions reserved for privileged accounts, or to access features of an application reserved for other users. Answer D is incorrect because automated and social-engineering assaults on passwords are easier when a password is short, lacking in complexity, derived from a common word found in the dictionary, or derived from easily guessable personal information such as birthdays, family names, pet names, and similar details.

15. **Answer: C.** Many networking devices and services are initially installed with a default set of user credentials, such as Oracle's Scott/Tiger and IBM's qsecofr/qsecofr. Unless these credentials are removed and replaced with unique strong logon credentials, they present an avenue for network attack. Answer A is incorrect. Network resources are much more vulnerable to DoS attacks. These attacks attempt to block access to resources by overwhelming network availability, instead of attempting to directly access the resources through unauthorized means. Answer B is incorrect. Privilege escalation is a vulnerability represented by the accidental or intentional access to resources not intended for access by the user. Application flaws can allow a normal user access to administrative functions reserved for privileged accounts, or to access features of an application reserved for other users. Answer D is incorrect because automated and social-engineering assaults on passwords are easier when a password is short, lacking in complexity, derived from a common word found in the dictionary, or derived from easily guessable personal information such as birthdays, family names, pet names, and similar details.

16. **Answer: A.** Network resources are much more vulnerable to DoS attacks. These attacks attempt to block access to resources by overwhelming network availability, instead of attempting to directly access the resources through unauthorized means. Answer B is incorrect. Privilege escalation is a vulnerability represented by the accidental or intentional access to resources not intended for access by the user. Application flaws can allow a normal user access to administrative functions reserved for privileged accounts, or to access features of an application reserved for other users. Answer C is incorrect. Many networking devices and services are initially installed with a default set of user credentials. Unless these credentials are removed and replaced with unique strong logon credentials, they present an avenue for network attack. Answer D is incorrect because automated and social-engineering assaults on passwords are easier when a password is short, lacking in complexity, derived from a common word found in the dictionary, or derived from easily guessable personal information such as birthdays, family names, pet names, and similar details.

17. **Answer: A.** Privilege escalation represents the accidental or intentional access to resources not intended for access by the user. Application flaws can allow a normal user access to administrative functions reserved for privileged accounts, or to access features of an application reserved for other users. An example of the latter is if User A can read User B's email without specific authorization. Answer B is incorrect. Many networking devices and services are initially installed with a default set of user credentials. Unless these credentials are removed and replaced with unique strong logon credentials, they present an avenue for network attack. Answer C is incorrect. Any resource exposed on a network may be attacked to gain unauthorized access. The most common form of authentication and user access control is the username/password combination, which can be significantly weakened as a security measure if a "weak" password is selected. Answer D is incorrect. Back doors are application code functions created intentionally or unintentionally that enable unauthorized access to networked resources. Many times during application development, software designers put in shortcut entry points to allow rapid code evaluation and testing. If not removed before application deployment, such entry points can present the means for an attacker to gain unauthorized access later.

18. **Answer: D.** Back doors are application code functions created intentionally or unintentionally that enable unauthorized access to networked resources. Many times during application development, software designers put in shortcut entry points to allow rapid code evaluation and testing. If not removed before application deployment, such entry points can present the means for an attacker to gain unauthorized access later. Answer A is incorrect. Privilege escalation represents the accidental or intentional access to resources not intended for access by the user. Application flaws can allow a normal user access to administrative functions reserved for privileged accounts, or to access features of an application reserved for other users. An example of the latter is if User A can read User B's email without specific authorization. Answer B is incorrect. Many networking devices and services are initially installed with a default set of user credentials. Unless these credentials are removed and replaced with unique strong logon credentials, they present an avenue for network attack. Answer C is incorrect. Any resource exposed on a network may be attacked to gain unauthorized access. The most common form of authentication and user access control is the username/password combination, which can be significantly weakened as a security measure if a "weak" password is selected.

19. **Answer: B, C.** Automated and social-engineering assaults on passwords are easier when a password is short, lacking in complexity (complexity here meaning a mixture of character case, numbers, and symbols), derived from a common word found in the dictionary, or derived from easily guessable personal information such as birthdays, family names, pet names, and similar details. Answer A is incorrect because it is attack associated with WAPs announcing their service set identifier (SSID). Answer D is incorrect because DoS attacks are often used for Internet extortion schemes, where an attacking botnet of tens of thousands of zombied client systems can be used to consume all available connections to a business website.

20. **Answer: D.** DoS attacks are often used for Internet extortion schemes, where an attacking botnet of tens of thousands of zombied client systems can be used to consume all available connections to a business website. Many fringe service industries,

such as online casinos, are regularly targeted with this type of attack. Answer A is incorrect because it is attack associated with WAPs announcing their service set identifier (SSID). Answers B and C are incorrect; automated and social-engineering assaults on passwords are easier when a password is short, lacking in complexity (complexity here meaning a mixture of character case, numbers, and symbols), derived from a common word found in the dictionary, or derived from easily guessable personal information such as birthdays, family names, pet names, and similar details.

Objective 2.6: Explain the vulnerabilities and mitigations associated with various transmission media.

1. **Answer: C.** Data traffic over coaxial network cabling can be intercepted and inspected by an attacker through the use of a vampire tap, which pierces the cable at an arbitrary point and allows direct connection to the data transport wiring. Similar technologies can be applied to modern fiber optic media, allowing interception of data traffic without a detectable presence on the network. Physical access control to areas where network media is exposed is critical to protecting against unauthorized taps. Vampire taps are physical in nature. Answers A, B, and D are incorrect because they controls that are configured using software and are not physical in nature.

2. **Answer: C.** Physical access control to the networking closet is critical to protect switched networks against any exposed supervisory ports that can be exploited by an attacker. Although answers A, B, and D are possible methods to control access, if physical access in not secured, the controls will not do any good. Therefore, these answers are incorrect.

3. **Answer: A.** Before the development of network switches, hubs were commonly used to distribute data packets to endpoint ports. Hubs do not provide data isolation between endpoint ports, allowing any node to observe data traffic to and from all other nodes on the same device. Answer B is incorrect because switches provide data isolation between endpoint ports, not hubs. Answer C is incorrect because routers provide packet forwarding for routable addresses, not hubs. Answer D is incorrect because in port mirroring the switch sends a copy of network packets to a monitoring network connection.

4. **Answer: B.** Certain types of networking equipment provide attackers with access to inspect network traffic for interception of user credentials, security encryption traffic, and other forms of sensitive transmitted data. Hubs do not provide data isolation between endpoint ports, allowing any node to observe data traffic to and from all other nodes on the same device. Answer A is incorrect because a network hub is a fairly unsophisticated broadcast device and it does not manage any of the traffic that comes through it. The BIOS holds information necessary to boot the computer. Answers C and D are incorrect; hubs operate at Layer 2 of the OSI model and know nothing about encryption.

5. **Answer: D.** Data traffic over coaxial network cabling can be intercepted and inspected by an attacker through the use of a vampire tap, which pierces the cable at an arbitrary point and allows direct connection to the data transport wiring. Similar technologies can be applied to modern fiber-optic media, allowing interception of data traffic without a detectable presence on the network. Answer A is incorrect; good antivirus software will find commercial keyloggers. Answer B is incorrect; there are applications available to find back doors, especially those created by malware. Answer B is incorrect; checks for unauthorized modification of code would prevent logic bombs.

Objective 2.7: Explain the vulnerabilities and implement mitigations associated with wireless networking.

1. **Answer: B.** Wireless networks often announce their service set identifier (SSID) to allow mobile devices to discover available Wireless Access Points (WAPs). Turning off this broadcast can reduce the vulnerability of a wireless packet sniffer detecting broadcasts that readily identify a WAP. In this particular instance, the WAP is not secure because the SSID is broadcast in plain text whenever a client connects to the network. Answer A is incorrect because WAPs by default do not have encryption enabled. Answer C is incorrect because if physical access is limited, the risk is mitigated. Answer D is incorrect because it describes the characteristics of a hub.

2. **Answer: D.** 802.1x transmissions generate detectable radio-frequency signals in all directions. Persons who wanting to "sniff" the data transmitted over the network may use many solutions to increase the distance over which detection is possible, including the use of reflective tube waveguides. Answer A is incorrect because the radio-frequency signals are generated in all directions not is one direction. Answers B and D are incorrect because data emanation is what allows for the sniffing of the data, not why data emanation is a risk.

3. **Answer: C.** Without the use of a mandated encryption standard, data transmitted over an 802.1x wireless link may be passed in clear form. Additional forms of encryption may be implemented, such as the Wired Equivalent Privacy (WEP) and the Advanced Encryption Standard (AES), but transport encryption mechanisms suffer from the fact that a determined listener can obtain enough traffic data to calculate the encoding key in use. Answers A, B, and D are incorrect because authorization, authentication, and identification are access control methods, not methods to mitigate data transmissions.

4. **Answer: A, B, C.** Wireless communications are susceptible to data emanation, weak encryption, session hijacking, man-in-the-middle attacks, and war-driving. Answer D is incorrect because spam relaying is associated open SMTP relays in email servers.

5. **Answer: C.** Because the authentication mechanism is one-way, it is easy for a hijacker to wait until the authentication cycle is completed and then generate a signal to the client that causes the client to think it has been disconnected from the access point, while at the same time beginning to transmit data traffic pretending to be from the original client. Answers A and D are incorrect. Both of these answers deal with authorization and session hijacking deals with authentication. Answer B is incorrect because it is not true that an authentication mechanism is not there. It exists and is one-way.

6. **Answer: D.** The request for connection by the client is an omnidirectional open broadcast. It is possible for a hijacker to act as an access point to the client, and as a client to the true network access point, allowing the hijacker to follow all data transactions with the ability to modify, insert, or delete packets at will. Answer A is incorrect because request for connection by the client is an omnidirectional open broadcast. Answers B and C are incorrect; the connection request is made by the client not the access point.

7. **Answer: A.** A popular pastime involves driving around with a laptop system configured to listen for open 802.1x access points announcing their SSID broadcasts, which is known as war-driving. Answer B is incorrect because it describes war dialing. Answer C is incorrect because it describes war-chalking. Answer D incorrect because it describes a hotspot.

8. **Answer: C.** War-chalking utilizes a set of symbols and shorthand details to provide specifics needed to connect using a business access point. This is done by marking buildings, curbs, and other landmarks to indicate the presence of an available access point and its connection details. Answer A is incorrect. A popular pastime involves driving around with a laptop system configured to listen for open 802.1x access points announcing their SSID broadcasts, which is known as war-driving. Answer B is incorrect because it describes war dialing. Answer D incorrect because it describes a hotspot.

9. **Answer: B.** Mobile devices equipped for Bluetooth short-range wireless connectivity, such as laptops, cell phones, and PDAs, are subject to receiving text and message broadcast spam sent from a nearby Bluetooth-enabled transmitting device in an attack referred to as bluejacking. Answer A is incorrect. A popular pastime involves driving around with a laptop system configured to listen for open 802.1x access points announcing their SSID broadcasts, which is known as war-driving. Answer C is incorrect because it describes bluesnarfing. Answer D is incorrect. War-chalking utilizes a set of symbols and shorthand details to provide specifics needed to connect using a business access point. This is done by marking buildings, curbs, and other landmarks to indicate the presence of an available access point and its connection details.

10. **Answer: C.** Although typically benign, attackers use bluejacking to generate messages that appear to be from the device itself. This leads users to follow obvious prompts and establish an open Bluetooth connection to the attacker's device. Once paired with the attacker's device, the user's data becomes available for unauthorized access, modification, or deletion, which is an attack referred to as bluesnarfing. Answer B is incorrect. Mobile devices equipped for Bluetooth short-range wireless connectivity, such as laptops, cell phones, and PDAs, are subject to receiving text and message broadcast spam sent from a nearby Bluetooth-enabled transmitting device in an attack referred to as bluejacking. Answer A is incorrect. A popular pastime involves driving around with a laptop system configured to listen for open 802.1x access points announcing their SSID broadcasts, which is known as war-driving. Answer D is incorrect. War-chalking utilizes a set of symbols and shorthand details to provide specifics needed to connect using a business access point. This is done by marking buildings, curbs, and other landmarks to indicate the presence of an available access point and its connection details.

11. **Answer: B.** The 802.11b WLAN specification allows up to 11Mbps wireless connectivity. Answer A is incorrect because 1.5MBps is a common speed for cable modem and T1 connectivity. Answer C is incorrect because 100Mbps is a common wired LAN data transfer rate. Answer D is incorrect because 19.2Kbps specifies a common modem bandwidth limit.

12. **Answer: A.** The 802.11b (Wi-Fi) standard uses the CSMA/CA connectivity methods commonly found in Ethernet connectivity. Answers B and D are incorrect because both WAP and i-Mode are standards used by mobile devices such as cell phones, pagers, and PDAs and are not used to specify WLAN standards. Answer C is incorrect because Bluetooth is based on a different transmission protocol.

13. **Answer: B.** The WPA2 standard implements the 802.11i-2004 protocols, and is currently the highest standard for Wi-Fi communication security. Answer A is incorrect because a WAP refers to both handheld devices as well as wireless access points. Answer C is incorrect because WEP2 is a stopgap enhancement to WEP present in some of the early 802.11i drafts. Answer D is incorrect because the WEP standard was proven to be unsecure and has been replaced by the newer WPA standards.

14. **Answer: D.** Data emanation happens because 802.1x transmissions generate detectable radio-frequency signals in all directions. Persons wanting to sniff the data transmitted over the network may use many solutions to increase the distance over which detection is possible, including the use of reflective tube waveguides (such as the popular Pringle's can) and flying devices overhead to increase detection range without interference from building structures. Answer A is incorrect because without the use of a mandated encryption standard, data transacted over an 802.1x wireless link may be passed in clear form and attackers can take advantage of this weak or nonexistent encryption. Answer B is incorrect because the wireless authentication mechanism is one-way, allowing session hijacking. Answer C is incorrect because a popular pastime involves driving around with a laptop system configured to listen for open 802.1x access points announcing their SSID broadcasts, which is known as war-driving.

15. **Answer: B.** Because the authentication mechanism is one-way, it is easy for a hijacker to wait until the authentication cycle is completed and then generate a signal to the client that causes the client to think it has been disconnected from the access point, while at the same time beginning to transact data traffic pretending to be the original client. Answer A is incorrect because without the use of a mandated encryption standard, data transacted over an 802.1x wireless link may be passed in clear form, and attackers can take advantage of this weak or nonexistent encryption. Answer C is incorrect because a popular pastime involves driving around with a laptop system configured to listen for open 802.1x access points announcing their SSID broadcasts, which is known as war-driving. Answer D is incorrect. Persons wanting to "sniff" the data transmitted over the wireless network may use many solutions to increase the distance over which detection is possible, including the use of reflective tube waveguides (such as the popular Pringle's can) and flying devices overhead to increase detection range without interference from building structures.

16. **Answer: A.** Without the use of a mandated encryption standard, data transacted over an 802.1x wireless link may be passed in clear form and attackers can take advantage of this weak or nonexistent encryption. Answer B is incorrect because the wireless authentication mechanism is one-way, allowing session hijacking. Answer C is incorrect

because a popular pastime involves driving around with a laptop system configured to listen for open 802.1x access points announcing their SSID broadcasts, which is known as war-driving. Answer D is incorrect. Persons wanting to "sniff" the data transmitted over the wireless network may use many solutions to increase the distance over which detection is possible, including the use of reflective tube waveguides (such as the popular Pringle's can) and flying devices overhead to increase detection range without interference from building structures.

17. **Answer: B.** Although typically benign, attackers can use bluejacking to generate messages that appear to be from the device itself, leading users to follow obvious prompts and establish an open Bluetooth connection to the attacker's device. Once paired with the attacker's device, the user's data becomes available for unauthorized access, modification, or deletion, which is a more aggressive attack referred to as bluesnarfing. Answer A is incorrect. Mobile devices equipped for Bluetooth short-range wireless connectivity, such as laptops, cell phones, and PDAs, are subject to receiving text and message broadcast spam sent from a nearby Bluetooth-enabled transmitting device in an attack referred to as bluejacking. Answer C is incorrect. A popular pastime involves driving around with a laptop system configured to listen for open 802.1x access points announcing their SSID broadcasts, which is known as war-driving. Answer D is incorrect. War-chalking utilizes a set of symbols and shorthand details to provide specifics needed to connect using a business access point. This is done by marking buildings, curbs, and other landmarks to indicate the presence of an available access point and its connection details.

18. **Answer: C.** War-driving is aimed at identification of existing wireless networks, the service set identifier (SSID) used to identify the wireless network, and any known WEP keys. Answer A is incorrect because without the use of a mandated encryption standard, data transacted over an 802.1x wireless link may be passed in clear form and attackers can take advantage of this weak or nonexistent encryption. Answer B is incorrect because the wireless authentication mechanism is one way, allowing session hijacking. Answer D is incorrect. Persons wanting to "sniff" the data transmitted over the wireless network may use many solutions to increase the distance over which detection is possible, including the use of reflective tube waveguides (such as the popular Pringle's can) and flying devices overhead to increase detection range without interference from building structures.

19. **Answer: A.** Mobile devices equipped for Bluetooth short-range wireless connectivity, such as laptops, cell phones, and PDAs, are subject to receiving text and message broadcast spam sent from a nearby Bluetooth-enabled transmitting device in an attack referred to as bluejacking. Answer B is incorrect. Although typically benign, attackers can use bluejacking to generate messages that appear to be from the device itself, leading users to follow obvious prompts and establish an open Bluetooth connection to the attacker's device. Once paired with the attacker's device, the user's data becomes available for unauthorized access, modification, or deletion, which is a more aggressive attack referred to as bluesnarfing. Answer C is incorrect. A popular pastime involves driving around with a laptop system configured to listen for open 802.1x access points announcing their SSID broadcasts, which is known as war-driving. Answer D is incorrect. War-chalking utilizes a set of symbols and shorthand details to provide specifics needed to connect using a business access point. This is done by marking buildings, curbs, and other landmarks to indicate the presence of an available access point and its connection details.

20. **Answer: B.** Because the request for connection by the client is an omnidirectional open broadcast, it is possible for a hijacker to act as an access point to the client, and as a client to the true network access point, allowing the hijacker to follow all data transactions with the ability to modify, insert, or delete packets at will. By implementing a rogue AP with stronger signal strength than more remote permanent installations, the attacker can cause a wireless client to preferentially connect to their own stronger nearby connection using the wireless device's standard roaming handoff mechanism. Answer A is incorrect. Without the use of a mandated encryption standard, data transacted over an 802.1x wireless link may be passed in clear form and attackers can take advantage of this weak or nonexistent encryption. Answer C is incorrect because a popular pastime involves driving around with a laptop system configured to listen for open 802.1x access points announcing their SSID broadcasts, which is known as war-driving. Answer D is incorrect. Persons wanting to "sniff" the data transmitted over the wireless network may use many solutions to increase the distance over which detection is possible, including the use of reflective tube waveguides (such as the popular Pringle's can) and flying devices overhead to increase detection range without interference from building structures.

21. **Answer: C.** When a client attempts to make an 802.1x-compliant connection, the client attempts to contact a wireless access point (AP). The AP authenticates the client through a basic challenge-response method, and then provides connectivity to a wired network or serves as a bridge to a secondary wireless AP. Answers A and D are incorrect because there is no user interaction in the authentication process. Answer B is incorrect because a hardware token is a security token that is used in multifactor authentication. It has nothing to do with how a client authenticates to a WAP.

22. **Answer: A.** New standards that involve time-changing encryption keys may help with weal key encryption, such as the Temporal Key Integrity Protocol (TKIP) and Wi-Fi Protected Access (WPA/WPA2) standard. Answer B is incorrect. Persons wanting to "sniff" the data transmitted over the wireless network may use many solutions to increase the distance over which detection is possible, including the use of reflective tube waveguides (such as the popular Pringle's can) and flying devices overhead to increase detection range without interference from building structures. Answer C is incorrect. Mobile devices equipped for Bluetooth short-range wireless connectivity, such as laptops, cell phones, and PDAs, are subject to receiving text and message broadcast spam sent from a nearby Bluetooth-enabled transmitting device in an attack referred to as bluejacking. D is incorrect because a popular pastime involves driving around with a laptop system configured to listen for open 802.1x access points announcing their SSID broadcasts, which is known as war-driving.

23. **Answer: A.** Wireless Application Environment (WAE) specifies the framework used to develop applications for mobile devices, including cell phones, data pagers, and PDAs. Answers B and C are incorrect. Wireless Session Layer (WSL), Wireless Transport Layer (WTL), and Wireless Transport Layer Security (WTLS) are the specifications that are included in the WAP standard. Answer D is incorrect because specifications for the Wired Equivalent Privacy (WEP) standard are detailed within the 802.11b (Wi-Fi) specification. This specification details a method of data encryption and authentication that may be used to establish a more secured wireless connection.

24. **Answer: D.** The Wi-Fi Protected Access (WPA and later WPA2) standards were developed by the Wi-Fi Alliance to replace the WEP protocol while the 802.11i standard was being developed. The WPA includes many of the functions of the 802.11i protocol but relies on the Rivest Cipher 4 (RC4), which is considered vulnerable to keystream attacks. The later WPA2 standard was certified to include the full 802.11i standard after its final approval. Answers A and C are incorrect because they are encryptions standards are not associated with the Wi-Fi Alliance. Answer C is incorrect because a WAP refers to both handheld devices as well as wireless access points.

25. **Answer: A.** Wireless Session Layer (WSL) is equivalent to the session layer of the Open Systems Interconnection (OSI) model. Based on this information, answers B, C, and D are incorrect.

CHAPTER THREE

Domain 3.0: Access Control

The concept of security within the network environment includes aspects drawn from all operating systems, application software packages, hardware solutions, and networking configurations present within the network to be secured, and from within any network-sharing connectivity directly or indirectly with the network to be secured. For the Security+ exam, you need to develop the broadest set of skills possible, gaining experience from the most specific to the most general of security concepts. This chapter focuses on access control mechanisms and methods for secure network authentication and physical access. A general knowledge of network terminology will aid in understanding these concepts. As a prospective security professional, you should also take every opportunity you may find to expand your skill base beyond these. The following list identifies the key areas from Domain 3.0 (which counts as 17% of the exam) that you need to master:

► Identify and apply industry best practices for access control methods.

► Explain common access control models and the differences between each.

► Organize users and computers into appropriate security groups and roles while distinguishing between appropriate rights and privileges.

► Apply appropriate security controls to file and print resources.

► Compare and implement logical access control methods.

► Summarize the various authentication models and identify the components of each.

▶ Deploy various authentication models and identify the components of each.

▶ Explain the difference between identification and authentication (identity proofing).

▶ Explain and apply physical access security methods.

Practice Questions

Objective 3.1: Identify and apply industry best practices for access control methods.

1. Which of the following security access control methods is best equated to the phrase "less is more?"

    ○ **A.** Implicit deny

    ○ **B.** Least privilege

    ○ **C.** Job rotation

    ○ **D.** Account expiration

Quick Answer: **172**
Detailed Answer: **175**

2. Which of the following security access control methods is best equated to the principal behind Microsoft's User Access Control (UAC) technology?

    ○ **A.** Implicit deny

    ○ **B.** Least privilege

    ○ **C.** Job rotation

    ○ **D.** Account expiration

Quick Answer: **172**
Detailed Answer: **175**

3. Which of the following security access control methods is best described as resource availability restricted to only those logons explicitly granted access?

    ○ **A.** Implicit deny

    ○ **B.** Least privilege

    ○ **C.** Job rotation

    ○ **D.** Account expiration

Quick Answer: **172**
Detailed Answer: **175**

4. Which of the following security access control methods is best described as the separation of logons as well as the separation of roles?

Quick Answer: **172**
Detailed Answer: **176**

- ○ **A.** Mandatory vacations
- ○ **B.** Principle of least privilege
- ○ **C.** Separation of duties
- ○ **D.** Rotation of job duties

5. Which of the following security access control methods is best described as the practice of terminating passwords on a regular basis?

Quick Answer: **172**
Detailed Answer: **176**

- ○ **A.** Rotation
- ○ **B.** Purging
- ○ **C.** Aging
- ○ **D.** Expiration

6. Which of the following security access control methods is best described as the practice of revolving administrative users between roles?

Quick Answer: **172**
Detailed Answer: **176**

- ○ **A.** Implicit deny
- ○ **B.** Least privilege
- ○ **C.** Job rotation
- ○ **D.** Account expiration

7. An organization is concerned about the proper level of access. Which of the following security access control methods would best mitigate this risk?

Quick Answer: **172**
Detailed Answer: **176**

- ○ **A.** Implicit deny
- ○ **B.** Least privilege
- ○ **C.** Job rotation
- ○ **D.** Account expiration

8. An organization is concerned about securing resource availability. Which of the following security access control methods would best mitigate this risk?

Quick Answer: **172**
Detailed Answer: **176**

- ○ **A.** Implicit deny
- ○ **B.** Least privilege
- ○ **C.** Job rotation
- ○ **D.** Account expiration

9. An organization is concerned about the fact that the programmers also test the software they are developing. Which of the following security access control methods would best mitigate this risk?

   - ○ **A.** Mandatory vacations
   - ○ **B.** Principle of least privilege
   - ○ **C.** Separation of duties
   - ○ **D.** Rotation of job duties

10. An organization is concerned about fraudulent activity. Which of the following security access control methods would best mitigate this risk?

    - ○ **A.** Implicit deny
    - ○ **B.** Least privilege
    - ○ **C.** Job rotation
    - ○ **D.** Account expiration

11. An organization is concerned about software development contractors having access to network resources after the contracted work has been completed. Which of the following security access control methods would best mitigate this risk?

    - ○ **A.** Implicit deny
    - ○ **B.** Least privilege
    - ○ **C.** Job rotation
    - ○ **D.** Account expiration

12. Which of the following best describes the security access control method that protects the network by ensuring an inadvertent malware execution during normal daily operations cannot then attack the network with full administrative privileges?

    - ○ **A.** Segregation of duties
    - ○ **B.** Separation of accounts
    - ○ **C.** Separation of roles
    - ○ **D.** Segregation of resources

13. Which of the following best describes the control within the Microsoft environment that allows lesser accounts to perform privileged processes?

    - ○ **A.** "Run as" option
    - ○ **B.** "Send to" option
    - ○ **C.** "Gpresult" command
    - ○ **D.** "Run" command

14. Which of the following best describes the protection mechanism of using the access control practice to expire passwords on a regular basis?

    ○ **A.** Spoofing attacks
    ○ **B.** Null session attacks
    ○ **C.** ARP poisoning attacks
    ○ **D.** Brute-force attacks

15. Which of the following basic access control methods would be violated when an employee is given roles that include security management procedures and compliance audit procedures?

    ○ **A.** Implicit deny
    ○ **B.** Principle of least privilege
    ○ **C.** Separation of duties
    ○ **D.** Account expiration

Objective 3.2: Explain common access control models and the differences between each.

1. Which of the following access control methods involves the assignment of labels to resources and accounts?

    ○ **A.** Mandatory access control
    ○ **B.** Discretionary access control
    ○ **C.** Role-based access control
    ○ **D.** Rule-based access control

2. Which of the following access control methods involves the explicit specification of access rights for accounts with regards to each particular resource?

    ○ **A.** Mandatory access control
    ○ **B.** Discretionary access control
    ○ **C.** Role-based access control
    ○ **D.** Rule-based access control

Quick Check

3. Which of the following access control methods commonly involves testing against an access control list that details systems and accounts with access rights?

- ○ **A.** Mandatory access control
- ○ **B.** Discretionary access control
- ○ **C.** Role-based access control
- ○ **D.** Rule-based access control

Quick Answer: **172**
Detailed Answer: **179**

4. Which of the following access control methods commonly involves access rights that may vary by account or by time of day?

- ○ **A.** Mandatory access control
- ○ **B.** Discretionary access control
- ○ **C.** Role-based access control
- ○ **D.** Rule-based access control

Quick Answer: **172**
Detailed Answer: **179**

5. Which of the following access control methods would most likely be used within governmental systems?

- ○ **A.** Mandatory access control
- ○ **B.** Discretionary access control
- ○ **C.** Role-based access control
- ○ **D.** Rule-based access control

Quick Answer: **172**
Detailed Answer: **180**

6. Which of the following access control methods would involve assignment of rights to groups for inheritance by group member account?

- ○ **A.** Mandatory access control
- ○ **B.** Discretionary access control
- ○ **C.** Role-based access control
- ○ **D.** Rule-based access control

Quick Answer: **172**
Detailed Answer: **180**

7. The network administrator is responsible for selecting the access control method that will be used for a new kiosk system. Organization members want to have full access to information about all categories of information, but visitors should have access only to general items about the organization. Which forms of access control are most appropriate to this requirement? (Select all correct answers.)

- ○ **A.** Mandatory access control
- ○ **B.** Discretionary access control
- ○ **C.** Role-based access control
- ○ **D.** Rule-based access control

Quick Answer: **172**
Detailed Answer: **180**

8. The network administrator is responsible for selecting the access control method that will be used for a new 24-hour employee cafeteria. Members of management must always be granted access, whereas other staff members should be granted access only during their assigned lunch hours. Visitors should be allowed access during normal business hours only. What form of access control is best for this scenario?

- ○ **A.** Mandatory access control
- ○ **B.** Discretionary access control
- ○ **C.** Role-based access control
- ○ **D.** Rule-based access control

Quick Answer: **172**
Detailed Answer: **180**

9. According to the TCSEC specification, which of the following are divisions of access control? (Select all correct answers.)

- ○ **A.** Minimal
- ○ **B.** Verified
- ○ **C.** Logical
- ○ **D.** Physical

Quick Answer: **172**
Detailed Answer: **180**

10. According to the TCSEC specification, which of the following is the highest level of access?

- ○ **A.** Minimal
- ○ **B.** Mandatory
- ○ **C.** Verified
- ○ **D.** Discretionary

Quick Answer: **172**
Detailed Answer: **180**

11. The organization is selecting an access control method where the objective is to assign permissions based on forms of conditional testing. Which form of access control is most appropriate to meet this requirement?

- ○ **A.** Rule-based access model
- ○ **B.** Group-based access model
- ○ **C.** Role-based access model
- ○ **D.** User-based security model

Quick Answer: **172**
Detailed Answer: **181**

12. The organization is selecting an access control method where the objective is to assign strict permissions where if the labels on the account and resource do not match, the resource remains unavailable. Which form of access control is most appropriate to meet this requirement?

- ○ **A.** Mandatory access control
- ○ **B.** Discretionary access control
- ○ **C.** Role-based access control
- ○ **D.** Rule-based access control

13. The organization is selecting an access control method in which the subject has complete control over the objects that it owns. Which form of access control is most appropriate to meet this requirement?

- ○ **A.** Mandatory access control
- ○ **B.** Discretionary access control
- ○ **C.** Role-based access control
- ○ **D.** Rule-based access control

14. In which of the following forms of access control would access be granted based on the categorical assignment such as classified, secret, or top secret be found?

- ○ **A.** Mandatory access control
- ○ **B.** Discretionary access control
- ○ **C.** Role-based access control
- ○ **D.** Rule-based access control

15. The organization is selecting an access control method of access control where the objective is to provide a great level of scalability within its large enterprise scenarios. Which form of access control is most appropriate to meet this requirement?

- ○ **A.** Rule-based access model
- ○ **B.** Group-based access model
- ○ **C.** Role-based access model
- ○ **D.** User-based security model

Objective 3.3: Organize users and computers into appropriate security groups and roles while distinguishing between appropriate rights and privileges.

1. Which of the following information is held in a user account? (Select all correct answers.)

   ○ **A.** Permissions

   ○ **B.** Password

   ○ **C.** Name

   ○ **D.** Devices

Quick Answer: **172**
Detailed Answer: **182**

2. Which of the following groups has the greatest access to data and the opportunity to either deliberately sabotage it or accidentally delete it?

   ○ **A.** Partnering vendors

   ○ **B.** Contract workers

   ○ **C.** Internal users

   ○ **D.** External users

Quick Answer: **172**
Detailed Answer: **182**

3. To which of the following types of groups would a user be assigned for applications such as Microsoft Exchange?

   ○ **A.** Mail

   ○ **B.** Distribution

   ○ **C.** Security

   ○ **D.** Administrator

Quick Answer: **172**
Detailed Answer: **182**

4. In a Microsoft Windows 2003 network, in which of the following groups could a user be placed? (Select all correct answers.)

   ○ **A.** Local

   ○ **B.** Global

   ○ **C.** Domain

   ○ **D.** Universal

Quick Answer: **172**
Detailed Answer: **182**

5. Which of the following access control methods would most likely be used to manage the access permissions in a peer-to-peer net-work or a workgroup?

Quick Answer: **172**
Detailed Answer: **182**

- ○ **A.** Rule-based access model
- ○ **B.** Group-based access model
- ○ **C.** Role-based access model
- ○ **D.** User-based security model

6. Which of the following access control methods would be used to manage the access permissions on a large numbers of user accounts?

Quick Answer: **172**
Detailed Answer: **183**

- ○ **A.** Rule-based access model
- ○ **B.** Group-based access model
- ○ **C.** Role-based access model
- ○ **D.** User-based security model

7. To which of the following types of groups would a user be assigned for access to information such as a home directory?

Quick Answer: **172**
Detailed Answer: **183**

- ○ **A.** Mail
- ○ **B.** Distribution
- ○ **C.** Security
- ○ **D.** Administrator

8. Which of the following best describe the user rights assignment? (Select all correct answers.)

Quick Answer: **172**
Detailed Answer: **183**

- ○ **A.** Segregates users
- ○ **B.** Grants specific privileges
- ○ **C.** Segregates resources
- ○ **D.** Grants logon rights

9. The organization is selecting an access control method where the objective is to assign permissions uniquely to each account. Which form of access control is most appropriate to meet this requirement?

Quick Answer: **172**
Detailed Answer: **183**

- ○ **A.** Rule-based access model
- ○ **B.** Group-based access model
- ○ **C.** Role-based access model
- ○ **D.** User-based security model

10. The organization is selecting an access control method where the objective is to assign permissions based on ease of administration. Which form of access control is most appropriate to meet this requirement?

   Quick Answer: **172**
   Detailed Answer: **183**

- ○ **A.** Rule-based access model
- ○ **B.** Group-based access model
- ○ **C.** Role-based access model
- ○ **D.** User-based security model

11. Which of the following most accurately describes user rights and user permissions? (Select all correct answers.)

   Quick Answer: **172**
   Detailed Answer: **184**

- ○ **A.** Logon rights control who and how users log on to the computer
- ○ **B.** Rights allow users to perform system tasks such as the right to back up files
- ○ **C.** Permissions control who and how users log on to the computer
- ○ **D.** Permissions allow users to perform system tasks such as the right to back up files

12. If an administrator gives a user full access in one group and no access in another group, which of the following is the end result?

   Quick Answer: **172**
   Detailed Answer: **184**

- ○ **A.** Full access
- ○ **B.** No access
- ○ **C.** Read access
- ○ **D.** Write access

13. If an administrator gives a user write access in one group and read access in another group, which of the following is the highest level of access the user is granted?

   Quick Answer: **172**
   Detailed Answer: **184**

- ○ **A.** Full access
- ○ **B.** No access
- ○ **C.** Read access
- ○ **D.** Write access

14. Which of the following is best practice when applying permissions to accounts in a domain environment?

   Quick Answer: **172**
   Detailed Answer: **184**

- ○ **A.** Apply to group accounts
- ○ **B.** Apply to individual accounts
- ○ **C.** Apply to local accounts
- ○ **D.** Apply to universal accounts

15. Which of the following is best practice when using the Administrator account?

Quick Answer: **172**
Detailed Answer: **184**

- ○ **A.** Used for all functions provided the user has administrative privileges
- ○ **B.** Used only for the purpose of logging into the server
- ○ **C.** Used only for the purpose of administering the server
- ○ **D.** Never used because it is a sensitive account

Objective 3.4: Apply appropriate security controls to file and print resources.

1. Which of the following is the most compelling reason to lock down file and print shares?

Quick Answer: **173**
Detailed Answer: **184**

- ○ **A.** Logic bombs can spread via unprotected shares
- ○ **B.** Unprotected network shares are always easy attack targets
- ○ **C.** Intrusion detections systems cannot detect attacks on unprotected shares
- ○ **D.** Unprotected network shares allow users to access shared information

2. When addressing file and print sharing, which of the following NetBIOS ports should be secured? (Select all correct answers.)

Quick Answer: **173**
Detailed Answer: **184**

- ○ **A.** 138
- ○ **B.** 135
- ○ **C.** 139
- ○ **D.** 137

3. When addressing file and print sharing that uses SMB directly over TCP/IP, which of the following ports should be secured?

Quick Answer: **173**
Detailed Answer: **185**

- ○ **A.** 110
- ○ **B.** 445
- ○ **C.** 135
- ○ **D.** 161

4. Which of the following is true of file and print sharing?

   ○ **A.** It increases unauthorized access risk.

   ○ **B.** It decreases unauthorized access risk.

   ○ **C.** It mitigates unauthorized access risk.

   ○ **D.** It protects against unauthorized access risk.

Quick Answer: **173**
Detailed Answer: **185**

5. Which of the following best describes the areas that should be examined when addressing file and print sharing? (Select all correct answers.)

   ○ **A.** Simple Mail Transfer Protocol

   ○ **B.** Common Gateway Protocol

   ○ **C.** Server Message Block

   ○ **D.** Common Internet File System

Quick Answer: **173**
Detailed Answer: **185**

6. Which of the following best practices is recommended if file and print sharing is not really needed?

   ○ **A.** Deny access to the default shares

   ○ **B.** Bind NetBIOS to TCP/IP

   ○ **C.** Unbind NetBIOS from TCP/IP

   ○ **D.** Remove the default shares

Quick Answer: **173**
Detailed Answer: **185**

7. Which of the following is an inherent risk when using a Microsoft Windows 2003 operating system?

   ○ **A.** Hidden shares are created by default.

   ○ **B.** Users can create shares without authorization.

   ○ **C.** Shares automatically grant all users full access.

   ○ **D.** Users can create undetectable hidden shares.

Quick Answer: **173**
Detailed Answer: **185**

8. Which of the following are recommendations for securing file and print sharing? (Select all correct answers.)

   ○ **A.** Install proper firewalls

   ○ **B.** Filter traffic on port 135

   ○ **C.** Bind NetBIOS to TCP/IP

   ○ **D.** Run intrusion detection tools

Quick Answer: **173**
Detailed Answer: **185**

9. Which of the following qualities would be pertinent when selecting antivirus software if open shares are a concern?

   ○ **A.** Searching for logic bombs

   ○ **B.** Searching for CIFS worms

   ○ **C.** Searching for adware

   ○ **D.** Searching for SMTP vulnerabilities

10. Which of the following can go a long way toward making sure that file sharing is not enabled unless needed? (Select all correct answers.)

    ○ **A.** Discretionary control

    ○ **B.** User education

    ○ **C.** Written warnings

    ○ **D.** Mandatory settings

Objective 3.5: Compare and implement logical access control methods.

1. Which of the following best describes an access control list?

   ○ **A.** A combination of methods to limit access to data

   ○ **B.** Underlying data that defines access permissions

   ○ **C.** A method to set consistent common security standards

   ○ **D.** A unique value that identifies a security principal

2. Which of the following best describes logical access control?

   ○ **A.** A combination of methods to limit access to data

   ○ **B.** Underlying data that defines access permissions

   ○ **C.** A method to set consistent common security standards

   ○ **D.** A unique value that identifies a security principal

3. Which of the following best describes a security identifier?

   ○ **A.** A combination of methods to limit access to data

   ○ **B.** Underlying data that defines access permissions

   ○ **C.** A method to set consistent common security standards

   ○ **D.** A unique value that identifies a security principal

4. Which of the following best describes group policy?

   ○ **A.** A combination of methods to limit access to data

   ○ **B.** Underlying data that defines access permissions

   ○ **C.** A method to set consistent common security standards

   ○ **D.** A unique value that identifies a security principal

5. Which of the following best describes a decentralized security management model?

   ○ **A.** Less secure but more scalable than a centralized model

   ○ **B.** More secure but less scalable than a centralized model

   ○ **C.** More secure and more scalable than a centralized model

   ○ **D.** Less secure and less scalable than a centralized model

6. Which of the following best describes a centralized security management model?

   ○ **A.** Less secure but more scalable than a decentralized model

   ○ **B.** More secure but less scalable than a decentralized model

   ○ **C.** More secure and more scalable than a decentralized model

   ○ **D.** Less secure and less scalable than a decentralized model

7. Which of the following best describes the general order of Group Policy object application?

   ○ **A.** Group policies get applied from the top down.

   ○ **B.** Group policies get applied based on complexity.

   ○ **C.** Group policies get applied based on alphabetic order.

   ○ **D.** Group policies get applied from the bottom up.

8. Which of the following would conform to best practices with regard to password policy?

Quick Answer: **173**
Detailed Answer: **187**

- ○ **A.** At least four characters, uppercase and lowercase letters, numbers, and special characters
- ○ **B.** At least six characters, lowercase letters, numbers, and special characters
- ○ **C.** At least eight characters, uppercase and lowercase letters, numbers, and special characters
- ○ **D.** At least twelve characters, uppercase and lowercase letters, numbers, and special characters

9. Which of the following is the correct number of domain password polices that can be set for a Windows 2003 domain?

Quick Answer: **173**
Detailed Answer: **188**

- ○ **A.** One
- ○ **B.** Three
- ○ **C.** Ten
- ○ **D.** Unlimited

10. Which of the following are best practices when formulating password account policies?? (Select all correct answers.)

Quick Answer: **173**
Detailed Answer: **188**

- ○ **A.** Set the server to not allow users to use the same password over and over again
- ○ **B.** Require password complexity for all accounts
- ○ **C.** Lock user accounts out after two failed logon attempts
- ○ **D.** Require users to change passwords every 60 to 90 days

11. An organization is implementing a domain policy where the employees are primarily shift workers. Which of the following would be the best solution to implement?

Quick Answer: **173**
Detailed Answer: **188**

- ○ **A.** Mandatory password changes
- ○ **B.** Increased account lockout time
- ○ **C.** Time-of-day restrictions
- ○ **D.** Reduced failed logon attempts

12. In Microsoft operating systems, which of the following best describes an access control entry?

- ○ **A.** A combination of methods to limit access to data
- ○ **B.** A method to set consistent common security standards
- ○ **C.** A unique value that identifies a security principal
- ○ **D.** A descriptor that contain the name of a user, group, or role

13. An organization is implementing a method of control where the requirements are that employees at different locations are responsible for managing privileges within their administrative areas. Which of the following security management models will they implement?

- ○ **A.** User based
- ○ **B.** Centralized
- ○ **C.** Decentralized
- ○ **D.** Group based

14. An organization is implementing a method of control where the requirements are that employees at one location are responsible for managing privileges for the entire organization. Which of the following security management models can they implement? (Select all correct answers.)

- ○ **A.** User based
- ○ **B.** Centralized
- ○ **C.** Decentralized
- ○ **D.** Group based

15. An administrator is troubleshooting a group policy issue on a computer that is a member of a workgroup rather than a domain member. Which of the following would be the mostly likely reason the policy is not working?

- ○ **A.** Only the local policy is applied.
- ○ **B.** The policy is set to no override.
- ○ **C.** The Block Inheritance setting has been checked.
- ○ **D.** The policy is marked for No Override.

16. GPOs can be associated with or linked to which of the following? (Select all correct answers.)

Quick Answer: **173**
Detailed Answer: **189**

- ○ **A.** Organizational units
- ○ **B.** Domains
- ○ **C.** Sites
- ○ **D.** Forests

17. Which of the following would be the most likely result of a GPO conflict?

Quick Answer: **173**
Detailed Answer: **189**

- ○ **A.** The policy lower in the list takes preference.
- ○ **B.** The GPO that was created first takes preference.
- ○ **C.** The conflict will cause neither policy to be applied.
- ○ **D.** The policy higher up in the list will take preference.

18. Which of the following should be implemented if the organization wants to be sure that all users are off of the network each evening when the backup is run?

Quick Answer: **173**
Detailed Answer: **189**

- ○ **A.** Account expiration
- ○ **B.** Account lockout
- ○ **C.** Time-of-day restrictions
- ○ **D.** Software restriction policies

19. An organization is implementing a domain policy where the employees are temporary and contract workers. Which of the following is the best solution to implement?

Quick Answer: **173**
Detailed Answer: **189**

- ○ **A.** Account expiration
- ○ **B.** Account lockout
- ○ **C.** Time-of-day restrictions
- ○ **D.** Software restriction policies

20. An organization is implementing a domain policy where primary concern is unauthorized attempted access via active user accounts. Which of the following would be the best solution to implement?

Quick Answer: **173**
Detailed Answer: **189**

- ○ **A.** Account expiration
- ○ **B.** Account lockout
- ○ **C.** Time-of-day restrictions
- ○ **D.** Software restriction policies

Objective 3.6: Summarize the various authentication models and identify the components of each.

1. Which of the following best describe the general forms that comprise authentication? (Select all correct answers.)

   ○ **A.** Something you touch

   ○ **B.** Something you have

   ○ **C.** Something you know

   ○ **D.** Something you are

Quick Answer: **173**
Detailed Answer: **190**

2. Which of the following best describes the type of authentication provided by using a logon ID and password?

   ○ **A.** Multifactor authentication

   ○ **B.** Single-factor authentication

   ○ **C.** Mutual authentication

   ○ **D.** On-demand authentication

Quick Answer: **173**
Detailed Answer: **190**

3. Which of the following best describes the type of authentication provided when the client and server verify that the computer with which they are communicating is the proper system?

   ○ **A.** Multifactor authentication

   ○ **B.** Single-factor authentication

   ○ **C.** Mutual authentication

   ○ **D.** On-demand authentication

Quick Answer: **173**
Detailed Answer: **190**

4. Which of the following best describes the type of authentication provided within an ongoing data transmission?

   ○ **A.** Multifactor authentication

   ○ **B.** Single-factor authentication

   ○ **C.** Mutual authentication

   ○ **D.** On-demand authentication

Quick Answer: **173**
Detailed Answer: **190**

5. Which of the following best describes the type of authentication provided by using fingerprint scanning and a password?

   ○ **A.** Multifactor authentication

   ○ **B.** Single-factor authentication

   ○ **C.** Mutual authentication

   ○ **D.** On-demand authentication

Quick Answer: **173**
Detailed Answer: **190**

6. Which of the following best describes the process of determining the identity of the account attempting to access a resource?

- ○ **A.** Authorization
- ○ **B.** Authentication
- ○ **C.** Identification
- ○ **D.** Validation

Quick Answer: **173**
Detailed Answer: **191**

7. Which of the following is one of the most widespread examples of the shortcomings of an authentication system?

- ○ **A.** Lost tokens
- ○ **B.** False positives
- ○ **C.** Weak encryption
- ○ **D.** Easily guessed passwords

Quick Answer: **173**
Detailed Answer: **191**

8. Which of the following authentication methods would most likely be used for access to a library kiosk?

- ○ **A.** A logon identifier and password
- ○ **B.** Anonymous access and password
- ○ **C.** Biometric keys and security token
- ○ **D.** Account logon and security token

Quick Answer: **173**
Detailed Answer: **191**

9. Which of the following authentication methods would most likely be used for access to a governmental financial network?

- ○ **A.** A logon identifier and password
- ○ **B.** Anonymous access and password
- ○ **C.** Biometric keys and security token
- ○ **D.** Account logon and security token

Quick Answer: **173**
Detailed Answer: **191**

10. Which of the following authentication methods would most likely be used for access to an airport kiosk?

- ○ **A.** A security token
- ○ **B.** Anonymous access
- ○ **C.** Biometric keys
- ○ **D.** Account logon

Quick Answer: **173**
Detailed Answer: **191**

11. Which of the following is the correct sequence when a user requests access to a resource?

    ○ **A.** Authentication occurs first and then access is determined.

    ○ **B.** Access rights are determined by authentication method.

    ○ **C.** Authentication and access control occur at the same time.

    ○ **D.** Access must be granted first, and then authentication occurs.

Quick Answer: **173**
Detailed Answer: **192**

12. Which of the following most accurately describes authentication?

    ○ **A.** The presentation of a unique identity

    ○ **B.** A unique identity with a security principal

    ○ **C.** The presentation of credentials

    ○ **D.** A set of resources available

Quick Answer: **173**
Detailed Answer: **192**

13. Which of the following are advantages of implementing a single sign-on solution? (Select all correct answers.)

    ○ **A.** Reduced costs

    ○ **B.** Reduced threats

    ○ **C.** Reduced user support

    ○ **D.** Reduced authentication complexity

Quick Answer: **173**
Detailed Answer: **192**

14. Which of the following authentication methods would most likely be used for access to a corporate network by telecommuters?

    ○ **A.** A logon identifier and password

    ○ **B.** Anonymous access and password

    ○ **C.** Biometric keys and security token

    ○ **D.** Account logon and security token

Quick Answer: **173**
Detailed Answer: **192**

15. Which of the following most accurately describes single sign-on?

    ○ **A.** One account granting access to all services

    ○ **B.** Separate accounts granting access to each service

    ○ **C.** Administrative login granting access to all services

    ○ **D.** Anonymous login granting access to all services

Quick Answer: **173**
Detailed Answer: **192**

Objective 3.7: Deploy various authentication models and identify the components of each.

1. Which of the following are strengths of Kerberos authentication? (Select all correct answers.)

   - ○ **A.** Remote-access connections
   - ○ **B.** Time-synchronized connections
   - ○ **C.** The use of registered clients
   - ○ **D.** The use of registered service keys

Quick Answer: **174**
Detailed Answer: **192**

2. Over which of the following connection types does CHAP function?

   - ○ **A.** LDAP
   - ○ **B.** HTTP
   - ○ **C.** FTP
   - ○ **D.** PPP

Quick Answer: **174**
Detailed Answer: **192**

3. Which of the following best describes TACACS+?

   - ○ **A.** A symmetric-key authentication protocol used to protect the sending of logon information
   - ○ **B.** A remote-access control system providing authentication, authorization, and accounting
   - ○ **C.** A centralized authentication and access control for credentials to resources within an enterprise
   - ○ **D.** An on-demand authentication used at random intervals within an ongoing data transmission

Quick Answer: **174**
Detailed Answer: **193**

4. Which of the following best describes RADIUS?

   - ○ **A.** A symmetric-key authentication protocol used to protect the sending of logon information
   - ○ **B.** A remote-access control system providing authentication, authorization, and accounting
   - ○ **C.** A centralized authentication and access control for credentials to resources within an enterprise
   - ○ **D.** An on-demand authentication used at random intervals within an ongoing data transmission

Quick Answer: **174**
Detailed Answer: **193**

5. Which of the following best describes CHAP?

   ○ **A.** A symmetric-key authentication protocol used to protect the sending of logon information

   ○ **B.** A remote-access control system providing authentication, authorization, and accounting

   ○ **C.** A centralized authentication and access control for
credentials to resources within an enterprise

   ○ **D.** An on-demand authentication used at random intervals
within an ongoing data transmission

Quick Answer: **174**
Detailed Answer: **193**

6. Which of the following best describes Kerberos?

   ○ **A.** A symmetric-key authentication protocol used to protect the sending of logon information

   ○ **B.** A remote-access control system providing authentication, authorization, and accounting

   ○ **C.** A centralized authentication and access control for
credentials to resources within an enterprise

   ○ **D.** An on-demand authentication used at random intervals
within an ongoing data transmission

Quick Answer: **174**
Detailed Answer: **193**

7. Wireless, port-based access control is often paired with which of
the following?

   ○ **A.** Kerberos

   ○ **B.** RADIUS

   ○ **C.** TACACS+

   ○ **D.** CHAP

Quick Answer: **174**
Detailed Answer: **193**

8. Which of the following type of authentication involves comparison
of two values calculated using the message digest (MD5) hashing
algorithm?

   ○ **A.** Kerberos

   ○ **B.** RADIUS

   ○ **C.** TACACS+

   ○ **D.** CHAP

Quick Answer: **174**
Detailed Answer: **194**

9. Which of the following should an organization deploy if the use of
an asymmetric encryption method is required?

   ○ **A.** Kerberos

   ○ **B.** TACACS

   ○ **C.** PKI

   ○ **D.** CHAP

Quick Answer: **174**
Detailed Answer: **194**

10. An organization wants to implement multifactor authentication, which of the following could be used? (Select all correct answers.)

Quick Answer: **174**
Detailed Answer: **194**

- ○ **A.** Smart cards
- ○ **B.** Kerberos authentication
- ○ **C.** Anonymous access
- ○ **D.** Biometric authentication

11. An organization is looking for a biometric method that identifies an individual by using the colored part of the eye surrounding the pupil. Which of the following solutions should they implement?

Quick Answer: **174**
Detailed Answer: **194**

- ○ **A.** Signature
- ○ **B.** Iris profile
- ○ **C.** Facial geometry
- ○ **D.** Retinal scan

12. Which of the following are issues associated with the implementation of biometric authentication methods?

Quick Answer: **174**
Detailed Answer: **194**

- ○ **A.** Error ratios
- ○ **B.** Invasiveness
- ○ **C.** Account lockouts
- ○ **D.** Cross-contamination

13. Which of the following technologies provides a mechanism for the creation of a secured tunnel through a public network?

Quick Answer: **174**
Detailed Answer: **194**

- ○ **A.** VPN
- ○ **B.** RAS
- ○ **C.** LDAP
- ○ **D.** RADIUS

14. Which of the following technologies functions as a gateway through which the remote user may access local resources?

Quick Answer: **174**
Detailed Answer: **194**

- ○ **A.** VPN
- ○ **B.** RAS
- ○ **C.** LDAP
- ○ **D.** RADIUS

15. Which of the following technologies allows authentication of logon identities over TCP/IP connectivity against a hierarchical directory?

   ○ **A.** VPN

   ○ **B.** RAS

   ○ **C.** LDAP

   ○ **D.** RADIUS

Quick Answer: **174**
Detailed Answer: **195**

16. In which of the following technologies is a centralized authentication solution managed through a client/server configuration?

   ○ **A.** VPN

   ○ **B.** RAS

   ○ **C.** LDAP

   ○ **D.** RADIUS

Quick Answer: **174**
Detailed Answer: **195**

17. Which of the following would be implemented if the organization requires a solution for both authentication and authorization? (Select all correct answers.)

   ○ **A.** RADIUS

   ○ **B.** TACACS+

   ○ **C.** LDAP

   ○ **D.** RAS

Quick Answer: **174**
Detailed Answer: **195**

18. Which of the following ports would have to be open if the organization wants to implement a solution that includes LDAP?

   ○ **A.** 161

   ○ **B.** 110

   ○ **C.** 389

   ○ **D.** 162

Quick Answer: **174**
Detailed Answer: **195**

19. Which of the following best describes the part of a packet that is encrypted by RADIUS?

   ○ **A.** The datagram only

   ○ **B.** The entire packet

   ○ **C.** Only the password

   ○ **D.** Only the header

Quick Answer: **174**
Detailed Answer: **195**

20. Which of the following protocols does RADIUS use?

- ○ **A.** TCP
- ○ **B.** UDP
- ○ **C.** FTP
- ○ **D.** SNMP

21. Which of the following protocols does TACACS+ use?

- ○ **A.** TCP
- ○ **B.** UDP
- ○ **C.** FTP
- ○ **D.** SNMP

22. An organization is implementing a technology that only uses CHAP for authentication. Which of the following protocols will be used with CHAP?

- ○ **A.** FTP
- ○ **B.** SPAP
- ○ **C.** PPTP
- ○ **D.** PPP

23. Which of the following best describes the difference between RADIUS and TACACS?

- ○ **A.** TACACS is an actual Internet standard; RADIUS is not.
- ○ **B.** RADIUS is an encryption protocol; TACACS is an authentication protocol.
- ○ **C.** RADIUS is an actual Internet standard; TACACS is not.
- ○ **D.** RADIUS is an authentication protocol; TACACS is an encryption protocol.

24. To which of the following are biometric devices susceptible? (Select all correct answers.)

- ○ **A.** False acceptance
- ○ **B.** False positives
- ○ **C.** False negatives
- ○ **D.** False rejection

25. Which of the following best describes false rejection?

- ○ **A.** The system allows an intrusive action to pass as normal.
- ○ **B.** Allows access to an unauthorized user.
- ○ **C.** Denies access to an authorized user.
- ○ **D.** The system deems a legitimate action a possible intrusion.

Quick Answer: **174**
Detailed Answer: **196**

Objective 3.8: Explain the difference between identification and authentication (identity proofing).

1. Which of the following best describes identity proofing?

- ○ **A.** Controls access to shared computer's processors and memory
- ○ **B.** Model where permissions are uniquely assigned to each account
- ○ **C.** A type of access attempt that causes a security event log record
- ○ **D.** Organizational process that binds users to authentication methods

Quick Answer: **174**
Detailed Answer: **196**

2. Which of the following is true about identity proofing?

- ○ **A.** It is the main component of authentication life cycle management.
- ○ **B.** It must be used in a manner other than online database validation.
- ○ **C.** It is the main component of accounting life cycle management.
- ○ **D.** It is completely separate from any type of integrated biometrics.

Quick Answer: **174**
Detailed Answer: **197**

3. An organization is concerned about secure identification when users forget their hardware token. Which of the following is the primary method to mitigate the vulnerabilities associated with improper authentication?

Quick Answer: **174**
Detailed Answer: **197**

- ○ **A.** Security guards
- ○ **B.** Identity proofing
- ○ **C.** RADIUS authentication
- ○ **D.** Video surveillance

4. Which of the following are authentication forms that can be used with identity proofing? (Select all correct answers.)

Quick Answer: **174**
Detailed Answer: **197**

- ○ **A.** Smart cards
- ○ **B.** Mantraps
- ○ **C.** Biometrics
- ○ **D.** One-time password devices

5. Which of the best describes the purpose of identity proofing?

Quick Answer: **174**
Detailed Answer: **197**

- ○ **A.** Functions as a gateway for remote users to access local resources or Internet connectivity
- ○ **B.** Allows authentication of logon identities over TCP/IP connectivity against a hierarchical directory
- ○ **C.** Gives the organization assurance that the user performing an authentication is the legitimate user
- ○ **D.** Provides for authentication, accounting, and access control for resources for organizational users

Objective 3.9: Explain and apply physical access security methods.

1. Physically unsecured equipment is vulnerable to which of the following type of attacks?

Quick Answer: **174**
Detailed Answer: **197**

- ○ **A.** Brute force
- ○ **B.** Social engineering
- ○ **C.** Malware
- ○ **D.** Rootkits

2. In which of the following types of environments are mandatory physical access controls are commonly found? (Select all correct answers.)

   ○ **A.** Academic institutions

   ○ **B.** Corporate environments

   ○ **C.** Government facilities

   ○ **D.** Military installations

Quick Answer: **174**
Detailed Answer: **197**

3. Which of the following is the primary goal of a physical security plan?

   ○ **A.** To deny access to most users allowing only corporate officers

   ○ **B.** To allow access to all visitors without causing undue duress

   ○ **C.** To allow only trusted use of resources via positive identification

   ○ **D.** To deny access to all except users deemed credible

Quick Answer: **174**
Detailed Answer: **198**

4. Which of the following may be used to prevent an intruder from monitoring users in very high-security areas? (Select all correct answers.)

   ○ **A.** Picket fencing

   ○ **B.** Painted glass

   ○ **C.** Frosted glass

   ○ **D.** Chain-link fencing

Quick Answer: **174**
Detailed Answer: **198**

5. Which of the best describes the physical area known as no-man's land?

   ○ **A.** An area of cleared land surrounding a building

   ○ **B.** An area of bushes surrounding a building

   ○ **C.** A holding area between two entry points

   ○ **D.** A receiver mechanism that reads an access card

Quick Answer: **174**
Detailed Answer: **198**

6. Which of the following best describes a mantrap?

   ○ **A.** An area of cleared land surrounding a building

   ○ **B.** An area of bushes surrounding a building

   ○ **C.** A holding area between two entry points

   ○ **D.** A receiver mechanism that reads an access card

Quick Answer: **174**
Detailed Answer: **198**

7. Which of the following best describes the difference between a cipher lock and a wireless lock?

Quick Answer: **174**
Detailed Answer: **198**

- ○ **A.** A cipher lock is opened by a receiver mechanism, whereas a wireless lock has a punch code entry
- ○ **B.** A cipher lock is opened with a key, whereas a wireless lock has a remote control mechanism
- ○ **C.** A cipher lock is opened with a remote control mechanism, whereas a wireless lock is opened with a key
- ○ **D.** A cipher lock has a punch code entry, whereas a wireless lock is opened by a receiver mechanism

8. Which of the following type of surveillance would the organization implement if it was required that the parking lot be constantly monitored?

Quick Answer: **174**
Detailed Answer: **198**

- ○ **A.** CCTV cameras
- ○ **B.** Security guards
- ○ **C.** Keycard gate
- ○ **D.** Motion detectors

9. Which of the following technologies are used in external motion detectors? (Select all correct answers.)

Quick Answer: **174**
Detailed Answer: **198**

- ○ **A.** Infrared
- ○ **B.** Sound
- ○ **C.** RFID
- ○ **D.** Ultrasonic

10. Which of the following best describes discretionary physical control?

Quick Answer: **174**
Detailed Answer: **198**

- ○ **A.** User access is closely monitored and very restricted with no exceptions.
- ○ **B.** Common needs are predetermined and access is allowed with the same key.
- ○ **C.** Access is delegated to parties responsible for that building or room.
- ○ **D.** Each individual has a unique key that corresponds to his or her access needs.

11. Which of the following best describes mandatory physical control?

Quick Answer: **174**
Detailed Answer: **199**

- ○ **A.** User access is closely monitored and very restricted with no exceptions.
- ○ **B.** Common needs are predetermined and access is allowed with the same key.
- ○ **C.** Access is delegated to parties responsible for that building or room.
- ○ **D.** Each individual has a unique key that corresponds to his or her access needs.

12. Which of the following best describes role-based physical control?

Quick Answer: **174**
Detailed Answer: **199**

- ○ **A.** User access is closely monitored and very restricted with no exceptions.
- ○ **B.** Common needs are predetermined and access is allowed with the same key.
- ○ **C.** Access is delegated to parties responsible for that building or room.
- ○ **D.** Each individual has a unique key that corresponds to his or her access need.

13. Which of the following physical safeguards would provide the best protection for a building that houses top-secret sensitive information and systems?

Quick Answer: **174**
Detailed Answer: **199**

- ○ **A.** Mantrap
- ○ **B.** No-man's land
- ○ **C.** Wooden fence
- ○ **D.** Door access system

14. Which of the following physical safeguards would be most commonly implemented in security for banks?

Quick Answer: **174**
Detailed Answer: **199**

- ○ **A.** Mantraps
- ○ **B.** Security dogs
- ○ **C.** Painted glass
- ○ **D.** Video surveillance

15. Which of the following is the main security concern of implementing motion detectors?

Quick Answer: **174**
Detailed Answer: **199**

- ○ **A.** They can easily be deactivated.
- ○ **B.** They can easily be fooled.
- ○ **C.** They are extremely sensitive.
- ○ **D.** They are extremely expensive.

Quick-Check Answer Key

Objective 3.1: Identify and apply industry best practices for access control methods.

1. B	6. C	11. D
2. B	7. B	12. B
3. A	8. A	13. A
4. C	9. C	14. D
5. D	10. C	15. C

Objective 3.2: Explain common access control models and the differences between each.

1. A	6. C	11. A
2. B	7. A, C	12. A
3. D	8. D	13. B
4. D	9. A, B	14. A
5. A	10. C	15. C

Objective 3.3: Organize users and computers into appropriate security groups and roles while distinguishing between appropriate rights and privileges.

1. A, B, C	6. B	11. A, D
2. C	7. C	12. B
3. B	8. B, D	13. D
4. A, B, C, D	9. D	14. A
5. D	10. B	15. C

Objective 3.4: Apply appropriate security controls to file and print resources.

1. B	**5.** D	**9.** B
2. A, C, D	**6.** C	**10.** B, D
3. B	**7.** A	
4. A	**8.** A, D	

Objective 3.5: Compare and implement logical access control methods.

1. B	**8.** C	**15.** A
2. A	**9.** A	**16.** A, B, C
3. D	**10.** A, B, D	**17.** D
4. C	**11.** C	**18.** C
5. A	**12.** D	**19.** A
6. B	**13.** C	**20.** B
7. D	**14.** B, D	

Objective 3.6: Summarize the various authentication models and identify the components of each.

1. B, C, D	**6.** B	**11.** A
2. B	**7.** D	**12.** B
3. C	**8.** A	**13.** C, D
4. D	**9.** C	**14.** D
5. A	**10.** B	**15.** A

Objective 3.7: Deploy various authentication models and identify the components of each.

1. B, C, D	10. A, B, D	19. C
2. D	11. B	20. B
3. B	12. B	21. A
4. C	13. A	22. D
5. D	14. B	23. C
6. A	15. C	24. A, D
7. B	16. D	25. C
8. D	17. A, B	
9. C	18. C	

Objective 3.8: Explain the difference between identification and authentication (identity proofing).

1. D	4. A, C, D
2. A	5. C
3. B	

Objective 3.9: Explain and apply physical access security methods.

1. B	6. C	11. A
2. C, D	7. D	12. B
3. C	8. A	13. B
4. B, C	9. A, B, D	14. D
5. A	10. C	15. C

Answers and Explanations

Objective 3.1: Identify and apply industry best practices for access control methods.

1. **Answer: B.** The phrase "less is more" is a convenient reminder of the security practice known as the principle of least privilege, where an account is granted no more access rights than the bare minimum needed to perform assigned tasks. Answer A is incorrect because implicit deny is an access control practice wherein resource availability is restricted to only those logons explicitly granted access, remaining unavailable even when not explicitly denied access. Answer C is incorrect because job rotation is an extension of the separation of duties. Rotating administrative users between roles both improves awareness of the mandates of each role and, while also ensuring that fraudulent activity cannot be sustained. Answer D is incorrect; expiration is an access control practice to expire passwords on a regular basis, protecting against brute-force password-guessing attacks, and to expire accounts not used after a certain period of time.

2. **Answer: B.** The User Access Control (UAC) technology used by the Microsoft Vista operating system ensures that software applications cannot perform privileged access without additional authorization from the user. Within the Microsoft environment, lesser accounts may perform privileged processes using the "run as" option to specify the explicit use of a privileged account. Answer A is incorrect because implicit deny is an access control practice wherein resource availability is restricted to only those logons explicitly granted access, remaining unavailable even when not explicitly denied access. Answer C is incorrect because job rotation is an extension of the separation of duties. Rotating administrative users between roles both improves awareness of the mandates of each role and, while also ensuring that fraudulent activity cannot be sustained. Answer D is incorrect; expiration is an access control practice to expire passwords on a regular basis, protecting against brute-force password-guessing attacks, and to expire accounts not used after a certain period of time.

3. **Answer: A.** Implicit deny is an access control practice wherein resource availability is restricted to only those logons explicitly granted access, remaining unavailable even when not explicitly denied access. Answer B is incorrect; the phrase "less is more" is a convenient reminder of the security practice known as the principle of least privilege, where an account is granted no more access rights than the bare minimum needed to perform assigned tasks. Answer C is incorrect because job rotation is an extension of the separation of duties. Rotating administrative users between roles both improves awareness of the mandates of each role and, while also ensuring that fraudulent activity cannot be sustained. Answer D is incorrect; expiration is an access control practice to expire passwords on a regular basis, protecting against brute-force password-guessing attacks, and to expire accounts not used after a certain period of time.

4. **Answer: C.** Separation of duties is an access control practice involving both the separation of logons, such as day-to-day and admin accounts both assigned to the same network admin, as well as the separation of roles, such as security assignment and compliance audit procedures. Answer A is incorrect. Rotating administrative users between roles both improves awareness of the mandates of each role, while also ensuring that fraudulent activity cannot be sustained. This is also the reason that users with administrative access may be required take vacations, allowing other administrators to review standard operating practices in place. Answer B is incorrect; the phrase "less is more" is a convenient reminder of the security practice known as the principle of least privilege, where an account is granted no more access rights than the bare minimum needed to perform assigned tasks. Answer D is incorrect. Rotating administrative users between roles both improves awareness of the mandates of each role, while also ensuring that fraudulent activity cannot be sustained.

5. **Answer: D.** Expiration is an access control practice to expire passwords on a regular basis, protecting against brute-force password-guessing attacks, and to expire accounts not used after a certain period of time. Answer A is incorrect because rotation refers to alternating administrative users between roles to improve awareness of the mandates of each role, and ensure that fraudulent activity cannot be sustained. Answer B is incorrect because purging is an action used to get rid of records. Answer C is incorrect because aging is associated with the length of time a password can be used.

6. **Answer: C.** Job rotation is an extension of the separation of duties. Rotating administrative users between roles both improves awareness of the mandates of each role and, while also ensuring that fraudulent activity cannot be sustained. Answer A is incorrect. Implicit deny is an access control practice wherein resource availability is restricted to only those logons explicitly granted access, remaining unavailable even when not explicitly denied access. Answer B is incorrect; the phrase "less is more" is a convenient reminder of the security practice known as the principle of least privilege, where an account is granted no more access rights than the bare minimum needed to perform assigned tasks. Answer D is incorrect; expiration is an access control practice to expire passwords on a regular basis, protecting against brute-force password-guessing attacks, and to expire accounts not used after a certain period of time.

7. **Answer: B.** The phrase "less is more" is a convenient reminder of the security practice known as the principle of least privilege, where an account is granted no more access rights than the bare minimum needed to perform assigned tasks. Answer A is incorrect because implicit deny is an access control practice wherein resource availability is restricted to only those logons explicitly granted access, remaining unavailable even when not explicitly denied access. Answer C is incorrect because job rotation is an extension of the separation of duties. Rotating administrative users between roles both improves awareness of the mandates of each role, while also ensuring that fraudulent activity cannot be sustained. Answer D is incorrect; expiration is an access control practice to expire passwords on a regular basis, protecting against brute-force password-guessing attacks, and to expire accounts not used after a certain period of time.

8. **Answer: A.** Implicit deny is an access control practice wherein resource availability is restricted to only those logons explicitly granted access, remaining unavailable even when access is not explicitly denied. Answer B is incorrect; the phrase "less is more"

is a convenient reminder of the security practice known as the principle of least privilege, where an account is granted no more access rights than the bare minimum needed to perform assigned tasks. Answer C is incorrect because job rotation is an extension of the separation of duties. Rotating administrative users between roles both improves awareness of the mandates of each role and ensures also that fraudulent activity cannot be sustained. Answer D is incorrect; expiration is an access control practice used for allowing passwords to expire on all accounts on a regular basis. This includes accounts not used after a certain period of time such as contractor accounts. It is also used for protecting against brute-force password-guessing attacks.

9. **Answer: C.** Separation of duties is an access control practice involving both the separation of logons, such as day-to-day and admin accounts both assigned to the same network admin, as well as the separation of roles, such as security assignment and compliance audit procedures. Answer A is incorrect. Rotating administrative users between roles both improves awareness of the mandates of each role, while also ensuring that fraudulent activity cannot be sustained. This is also the reason that users with administrative access may be required take vacations, allowing other administrators to review standard operating practices in place. Answer B is incorrect; the phrase "less is more" is a convenient reminder of the security practice known as the principle of least privilege, where an account is granted no more access rights than the bare minimum needed to perform assigned tasks. Answer D is incorrect. Rotating administrative users between roles both improves awareness of the mandates of each role, while also ensuring that fraudulent activity cannot be sustained.

10. **Answer: C.** Job rotation is an extension of the separation of duties. Rotating administrative users between roles both improves awareness of the mandates of each role, while also ensuring that fraudulent activity cannot be sustained. Answer A is incorrect. Implicit deny is an access control practice wherein resource availability is restricted to only those logons explicitly granted access, remaining unavailable even when not explicitly denied access. Answer B is incorrect; the phrase "less is more" is a convenient reminder of the security practice known as the principle of least privilege, where an account is granted no more access rights than the bare minimum needed to perform assigned tasks. Answer D is incorrect; expiration is an access control practice to expire passwords on a regular basis, protecting against brute-force password-guessing attacks, and to expire accounts not used after a certain period of time.

11. **Answer: D.** Expiration is an access control practice to expire passwords on a regular basis, protecting against brute-force password-guessing attacks, and to expire accounts not used after a certain period of time. Unused accounts often retain weak passwords used in initial assignment, and may be more susceptible to password-guessing routines. Answer A is incorrect. Implicit deny is an access control practice wherein resource availability is restricted to only those logons explicitly granted access, remaining unavailable even when not explicitly denied access. Answer B is incorrect; the phrase "less is more" is a convenient reminder of the security practice known as the principle of least privilege, where an account is granted no more access rights than the bare minimum needed to perform assigned tasks. Answer C is incorrect because job rotation is an extension of the separation of duties. Rotating administrative users between roles both improves awareness of the mandates of each role, while also ensuring that fraudulent activity cannot be sustained.

12. **Answer: B.** Separation of account functionality protects the network by ensuring that an inadvertent malware execution during normal daily operations cannot then attack the network with full administrative privileges. Answer A is incorrect because segregation of duties is an access control practice involving both the separation of logons, such as day-to-day and admin accounts both assigned to the same network admin, and the separation of roles. Answer C is incorrect. Separation of role duties ensures that validation is maintained apart from execution, protecting the network against fraudulent actions or incomplete execution of security mandates. Answer D is incorrect. Segregation of resources would be a separate subnet or a segment separated by a firewall.

13. **Answer: A.** The User Access Control (UAC) technology used by the Microsoft Vista operating system ensures that software applications cannot perform privileged access without additional authorization from the user. Within the Microsoft environment, lesser accounts may perform privileged processes using the "run as" option to specify the explicit use of a privileged account. Answer B is incorrect because the "send to" option is a right-click function used to export files. Answer C is incorrect. Gpresult is used to the see the resultant set of group policies. Answer D is incorrect. The run command is a start menu item option used to run programs.

14. **Answer: D.** Unused accounts often retain weak passwords used in initial assignment, and may be more susceptible to password-guessing routines. Answer A is incorrect because spoofing involves modifying the source address of traffic or source of information. Answer B is incorrect. A null session is a connection without specifying a username or password. Null sessions are a possible security risk because the connection is not really authenticated. Answer C is incorrect because ARP poisoning allows a perpetrator to trick a device into thinking any IP is related to any MAC address.

15. **Answer: C.** Job rotation is an extension of the separation of duties. Rotating administrative users between roles both improves awareness of the mandates of each role and, while also ensuring that fraudulent activity cannot be sustained. Answer A is incorrect. Implicit deny is an access control practice wherein resource availability is restricted to only those logons explicitly granted access, remaining unavailable even when not explicitly denied access. Answer B is incorrect; the phrase "less is more" is a convenient reminder of the security practice known as the principle of least privilege, where an account is granted no more access rights than the bare minimum needed to perform assigned tasks. Answer D is incorrect; expiration is an access control practice to expire passwords on a regular basis, protecting against brute-force password-guessing attacks, and to expire accounts not used after a certain period of time.

Objective 3.2: Explain common access control models and the differences between each.

1. **Answer: A.** Mandatory access control is the most basic form of access control involves the assignment of labels to resources and accounts. If the labels on the account and resource do not match, the resource remains unavailable in a nondiscretionary manner.

Answer B is incorrect. In discretionary access control, a subject has complete control over the objects that it owns. The owner assigns security levels based on objects and subjects. Answer C is incorrect because in a role-based access control scenario, access rights are first assigned to roles, and accounts are then assigned these roles without direct assignment of resource access rights. Answer D is incorrect. In a rule-based access control solution, access rights may vary by account, by time of day, or through other forms of conditional testing.

2. **Answer: B.** In discretionary access control, a subject has complete control over the objects that it owns. The owner assigns security levels based on objects and subjects. Answer A is incorrect. Mandatory access control is the most basic form of access control involves the assignment of labels to resources and accounts. If the labels on the account and resource do not match, the resource remains unavailable in a nondiscretionary manner. Answer C is incorrect because in a role-based access control scenario, access rights are first assigned to roles, and accounts are then assigned these roles without direct assignment of resource access rights. Answer D is incorrect. In a rule-based access control solution, access rights may vary by account, by time of day, or through other forms of conditional testing.

3. **Answer: D.** In a rule-based access control solution, access rights may vary by account, by time of day, or through other forms of conditional testing. The most common form of rule-based access control involves testing against an access control list (ACL) that details systems and accounts with access rights and the limits of its access for the resource. Answer A is incorrect. Mandatory access control is the most basic form of access control involves the assignment of labels to resources and accounts. If the labels on the account and resource do not match, the resource remains unavailable in a nondiscretionary manner. Answer B is incorrect. In discretionary access control, a subject has complete control over the objects that it owns. The owner assigns security levels based on objects and subjects. Answer C is incorrect because in a role-based access control scenario, access rights are first assigned to roles, and accounts are then assigned these roles without direct assignment of resource access rights.

4. **Answer: D.** In a rule-based access control solution, access rights may vary by account, by time of day, or through other forms of conditional testing. The most common form of rule-based access control involves testing against an access control list (ACL) that details systems and accounts with access rights and the limits of its access for the resource. Answer A is incorrect. Mandatory access control is the most basic form of access control involves the assignment of labels to resources and accounts. If the labels on the account and resource do not match, the resource remains unavailable in a nondiscretionary manner. Answer B is incorrect. In discretionary access control, a subject has complete control over the objects that it owns. The owner assigns security levels based on objects and subjects. Answer C is incorrect because in a role-based access control scenario, access rights are first assigned to roles, and accounts are then assigned these roles without direct assignment of resource access rights.

5. **Answer: A.** Mandatory access control is the most basic form of access control involves the assignment of labels to resources and accounts. This type of access control is often used within governmental systems where resources and access may be granted based on categorical assignment such as classified, secret, or top secret. Answer B is incorrect. In discretionary access control, a subject has complete control over the objects that it owns. The owner assigns security levels based on objects and subjects. Answer C is incorrect because in a role-based access control scenario, access rights are first assigned to roles, and accounts are then assigned these roles without direct assignment of resource access rights. Answer D is incorrect. In a rule-based access control solution, access rights may vary by account, by time of day, or through other forms of conditional testing.

6. **Answer: C.** Role-based access control scenario, access rights are first assigned to roles, and accounts are then assigned these roles without direct assignment of resource access rights. This type of access is used with groups for inheritance by group member account. Answer A is incorrect because mandatory access control involves the assignment of labels to resources and accounts. If the labels on the account and resource do not match, the resource remains unavailable in a nondiscretionary manner. Answer B is incorrect. In discretionary access control, a subject has complete control over the objects that it owns. The owner assigns security levels based on objects and subjects. Answer D is incorrect. In a rule-based access control solution, access rights may vary by account, by time of day, or through other forms of conditional testing.

7. **Answer: A, C.** A mandatory access control solution involving labels such as DONOR and DISPLAY would suffice for the user access assignment. A role-based access control solution involving the roles of User and Donor would also be appropriate. Answer B is incorrect because the complexity of assigning by-user access rights over each item's files would involve a large amount of administrative overhead. Answer D is incorrect because the complexity of the requirement is not great enough to involve detailed conditional testing.

8. **Answer: D.** A rule-based access control solution would allow detailed conditional testing of the user's account type and the time of day and day of the week to allow or deny access. Answers A and B are incorrect because both solutions do not allow for conditional testing. Answer C is also incorrect because role-based access control involves testing against role-assigned access rights, rather than by other qualities such as a test for normal working hours.

9. **Answer: A, B.** The TCSEC specification identifies levels of security based on the minimum level of access control used in a network environment by divisions and classes. The four divisions of access control are division D, which is Minimal; division C, which is Discretionary; division B, which is Mandatory; and division A, which is Verified. Category A is the highest level, essentially encompassing all elements of Category B, in addition to formal design and verification techniques. Answers C and D are incorrect; they describe network design methods.

10. **Answer: C.** The TCSEC specification identifies levels of security based on the minimum level of access control used in a network environment. The four divisions of access control are division D, which is Minimal; division C, which is Discretionary;

division B, which is Mandatory; and division A, which is Verified. Category A is the highest level, essentially encompassing all elements of Category B, in addition to formal design and verification techniques. Based in the preceding statement, answers A, B, and D are incorrect.

11. **Answer: A.** In a rule-based access control solution, access rights may vary by account, by time of day, or through other forms of conditional testing. The most common form of rule-based access control involves testing against an access control list (ACL) that details systems and accounts with access rights and the limits of its access for the resource. Answer B is incorrect. In group-based access control, permissions are assigned to groups, and user accounts become members of the groups. Answer C is incorrect because in a role-based access control scenario, access rights are first assigned to roles, and accounts are then assigned these roles without direct assignment of resource access rights. Answer D is incorrect. In a user-based model, permissions are uniquely assigned to each account.

12. **Answer: A.** Mandatory access control is the most basic form of access control involves the assignment of labels to resources and accounts. If the labels on the account and resource do not match, the resource remains unavailable in a nondiscretionary manner. Answer B is incorrect. In discretionary access control, a subject has complete control over the objects that it owns. The owner assigns security levels based on objects and subjects. Answer C is incorrect because in a role-based access control scenario, access rights are first assigned to roles, and accounts are then assigned these roles without direct assignment of resource access rights. Answer D is incorrect. In a rule-based access control solution, access rights may vary by account, by time of day, or through other forms of conditional testing.

13. **Answer: B.** In discretionary access control, a subject has complete control over the objects that it owns. The owner assigns security levels based on objects and subjects. Answer A is incorrect. Mandatory access control is the most basic form of access control involves the assignment of labels to resources and accounts. If the labels on the account and resource do not match, the resource remains unavailable in a nondiscretionary manner. Answer C is incorrect because in a role-based access control scenario, access rights are first assigned to roles, and accounts are then assigned these roles without direct assignment of resource access rights. Answer D is incorrect. In a rule-based access control solution, access rights may vary by account, by time of day, or through other forms of conditional testing.

14. **Answer: A.** Mandatory access control is the most basic form of access control involves the assignment of labels to resources and accounts. This type of access control is often used within governmental systems where resources and access may be granted based on categorical assignment such as classified, secret, or top secret. Answer B is incorrect. In discretionary access control, a subject has complete control over the objects that it owns. The owner assigns security levels based on objects and subjects. Answer C is incorrect because in a role-based access control scenario, access rights are first assigned to roles, and accounts are then assigned these roles without direct assignment of resource access rights. Answer D is incorrect. In a rule-based access control solution, access rights may vary by account, by time of day, or through other forms of conditional testing.

15. **Answer: C.** In role-based access control, rather than providing a mechanism for direct assignment of rights to an account, access rights are assigned to roles, and accounts are then assigned these roles. This solution provides the greatest level of scalability within large enterprise scenarios, where the explicit of rights grant would rapidly incur a significant level of administrative overhead, and the potential for accidental grant of permissions beyond those needed becomes very high. Answer A is incorrect. In a rule-based access control solution, access rights may vary by account, by time of day, or through other forms of conditional testing. The most common form of rule-based access control involves testing against an access control list (ACL) that details systems and accounts with access rights and the limits of its access for the resource. Answer B is incorrect. In group-based access control, permissions are assigned to groups, and user accounts become members of the groups. Answer D is incorrect. In a user-based model, permissions are uniquely assigned to each account.

Objective 3.3: Organize users and computers into appropriate security groups and roles while distinguishing between appropriate rights and privileges.

1. **Answer: A, B, C.** A user account holds information about the specific user. It can contain basic information such as name, password, and the level of permission the user has. Answer D is incorrect because devices are not included in user account information. Device information is more closely associated with SNMP tracking.

2. **Answer: C.** The internal user has the greatest access to data and the opportunity to either deliberately sabotage it or accidentally delete it. Although partnering vendors, contract workers and external users have the opportunity to damage data, they do not have enough permission to accidentally delete data nor do they have access to data as readily as internal users. Based on this information, answers A, B, and D are incorrect.

3. **Answer: B.** Active Directory Services provides flexibility by allowing two types of groups: security groups and distribution groups. Security groups are used to assign rights and permissions to groups for resource access. Distribution groups are assigned to a user list for applications or non-security-related functions. For example, a distribution group can be used by Microsoft Exchange to distribute mail. Answers A and D are incorrect because these groups do not exist. Answer C is incorrect because security groups are used to assign rights and permissions to groups for resource access.

4. **Answer: A, B, C, D.** Users can be placed in universal, global, domain, or local groups.

5. **Answer: D.** Within a user-based model, permissions are uniquely assigned to each account. One example of this is a peer-to-peer network or a workgroup where access is granted based on individual needs. Answer A is incorrect; in a rule-based access control solution, access rights may vary by account, by time of day, or through other forms of conditional testing. Answer B is incorrect; in group-based access control, permissions are assigned to groups, and user accounts become members of the groups. Answer C is incorrect because in role-based access control, rather than

providing a mechanism for direct assignment of rights to an account, access rights are assigned to roles, and accounts are then assigned these roles.

6. **Answer: B.** In group-based access control, permissions are assigned to groups, and user accounts become members of the groups. Access control over large numbers of user accounts can be more easily accomplished by managing the access permissions on each group, which are then inherited by the group's members. Answer A is incorrect; in a rule-based access control solution, access rights may vary by account, by time of day, or through other forms of conditional testing. Answer C is incorrect because in role-based access control, rather than providing a mechanism for direct assignment of rights to an account, access rights are assigned to roles, and accounts are then assigned these roles. Answer D is incorrect; within a user-based model, permissions are uniquely assigned to each account. One example of this is a peer-to-peer network or a workgroup where access is granted based on individual needs.

7. **Answer: C.** Active Directory Services provides flexibility by allowing two types of groups: security groups and distribution groups. Security groups are used to assign rights and permissions to groups for resource access. Answers A and D are incorrect because these groups do not exist. Answer B is incorrect because distribution groups are assigned to a user list for applications or non-security-related functions.

8. **Answer: B, D.** The user rights assignment is twofold: It can grant specific privileges, and it can grant logon rights to users and groups in your computing environment. Logon rights control who and how users log on to the computer, such as the right to log on to a system locally, whereas privileges allow users to perform system tasks such as the right to back up files and directories. Answers A and C are incorrect because the user rights assignment has nothing to do with segregation of users or resources; that is more of an access control function.

9. **Answer: D.** Within a user-based model, permissions are uniquely assigned to each account. One example of this is a peer-to-peer network or a workgroup where access is granted based on individual needs. Answer A is incorrect; in a rule-based access control solution, access rights may vary by account, by time of day, or through other forms of conditional testing. Answer B is incorrect; in group-based access control, permissions are assigned to groups, and user accounts become members of the groups. Answer C is incorrect because in role-based access control, rather than providing a mechanism for direct assignment of rights to an account, access rights are assigned to roles, and accounts are then assigned these roles.

10. **Answer: B.** In group-based access control, permissions are assigned to groups, and user accounts become members of the groups. Access control over large numbers of user accounts can be more easily accomplished by managing the access permissions on each group, which are then inherited by the group's members. Answer A is incorrect; in a rule-based access control solution, access rights may vary by account, by time of day, or through other forms of conditional testing. Answer C is incorrect because in role-based access control, rather than providing a mechanism for direct assignment of rights to an account, access rights are assigned to roles, and accounts are then assigned these roles. Answer D is incorrect; within a user-based model, permissions are uniquely assigned to each account. One example of this is a peer-to-peer network or a workgroup where access is granted based on individual needs.

11. **Answer: A, D.** The user rights assignment is twofold: It can grant specific privileges, and it can grant logon rights to users and groups in your computing environment. Logon rights control who and how users log on to the computer, such as the right to log on to a system locally, whereas permissions allow users to perform system tasks such as the right to back up files and directories. Answers B and C are incorrect because they state the exact opposite of what is true.

12. **Answer: B.** When working with groups, remember a few key items. No matter what OS you are working with, if you are giving a user full access in one group and no access in another group, the result will be no access. However, group permissions are cumulative, so if a user belongs to two groups and one has more liberal access, the user will have the more liberal access, except where the no access right is involved. Therefore, answer A is incorrect. Answers C and D are incorrect because the user would either have full access or no access, read and write are not mentioned in the question.

13. **Answer: D.** Group permissions are cumulative, so if a user belongs to two groups and one has more liberal access, the user will have the more liberal access, except where the no access right is involved. For example, write access has more privileges than just read access. No matter what OS you are working with, if you are giving a user full access in one group and no access in another group, the result will be no access. Therefore, answers A and B are incorrect. Answer C is incorrect because permissions are cumulative.

14. **Answer: A.** Although permissions can apply to individual user accounts, they are best administered by using group accounts. Answer B is incorrect because applying permissions to individual accounts creates administrative overhead and is not good practice. Answers C and D are incorrect because in a domain environment, users are placed in groups, and then permissions are set.

15. **Answer: C.** The administrative account should be used only for the purpose of administering the server. Based on the previous statement, answers A, B, and D are incorrect.

Objective 3.4: Apply appropriate security controls to file and print resources.

1. **Answer: B.** Print and file sharing increases the risk of intruders being able to access any of the files on a computer's hard drive. Locking down these shares is imperative because unprotected network shares are always easy targets and rank high in the list of top security exploits. Answer A is incorrect because logic bombs are based on time or events. Answer C is incorrect because unprotected shares can be detected. Answer D is incorrect because the question asks for the most compelling reason, which is answer B.

2. **Answer: A, C, D.** Recommendations for securing file and print sharing include filter traffic on UDP/TCP ports 137, 138, 139, and 445. Answer B is incorrect; port 135 is used for DCOM-related server/service. Any machines placed behind a NAT router will be inherently safe from attacks on port 135.

3. **Answer: B.** In Windows 2000 and later, Microsoft added the possibility to run SMB directly over TCP/IP. This uses TCP port 445. Recommendations for securing file and print sharing include filter traffic on UDP/TCP ports 137, 138, 139, and 445. Answer A is incorrect because port 110 is used for POP3 mail. Answer C is incorrect; port 135 is used for DCOM-related server/service. Answer D is incorrect; SNMP servers communicate on port 161. They listen for and respond to incoming client requests and commands and are also able to issue alerts, called "traps."

4. **Answer: A.** Print and file sharing increases the risk of intruders being able to access any of the files on a computer's hard drive. Locking down these shares is imperative because unprotected network shares are always easy targets and rank high in the list of top security exploits. Answers B, C, and D are incorrect because they portray just the opposite. Unprotected shares will not mitigate, decrease, or protect against attacks.

5. **Answer: C, D.** Print and file sharing increases the risk of intruders being able to access any of the files on a computer's hard drive. Locking down these shares is imperative because unprotected network shares are always easy targets and rank high in the list of top security exploits. Depending on your operating systems in use, there are two areas to look at: Server Message Block (SMB) file-sharing protocol and Common Internet File System (CIFS). Answer A is incorrect; SMTP is used for email services. Answer B is incorrect; Common Gateway Protocol is used by Citrix. The ICA Client tunnels its ICA traffic inside the Common Gateway Protocol and sends the traffic to port 2598.

6. **Answer: C.** Determine whether file and print sharing is really needed. If it isn't, unbind NetBIOS from TCP/IP. By doing so, you effectively disable Windows SMB file and print sharing. Answer A is incorrect because services may use the default shares to communicate such as the IPC share. Answer B is incorrect because binding NetBIOS to TCP/IP would enable file and print sharing services. Answer D is incorrect because the shares are created by default, and if you remove them, they will be automatically re-created the next time the machine is rebooted.

7. **Answer: A.** As Microsoft operating systems are installed, a number of hidden shares are created by default. An intruder would be aware of this and can map to them if given the chance. Answer B is incorrect because you can restrict user access to read only. Answer C is incorrect because full access has to be granted; it is not automatic. Answer D is incorrect; hidden shares can be detected and users can be restricted from creating shares.

8. **Answer: A, D.** Here are some recommendations for securing file and print sharing: Use an antivirus product that searches for CIFS worms, run intrusion testing tools, filter traffic on UDP/TCP ports 137, 138, 139, 445, and install proper firewalls. Answer B is incorrect because port 135 is used or DCOM services. Answer C is incorrect because binding NetBIOS to TCP/IP would enable file and print sharing services.

9. **Answer: B.** Here are some recommendations for securing file and print sharing: Use an antivirus product that searches for CIFS worms, run intrusion testing tools, filter traffic on UDP/TCP ports 137, 138, 139, 445, and install proper firewalls. Answers A, C, and D are incorrect; securing file and print sharing has nothing to do with SMTP, adware, or logic bombs.

10. **Answer: B, C.** User education and mandatory settings can go a long way toward making sure that file sharing is not enabled unless needed. Answer A is incorrect. Discretionary access control allows the user to control access. Answer D is incorrect. Although written warnings are a method of addressing violations, preventative measures are recommended over reactive measures.

Objective 3.5: Compare and implement logical access control methods.

1. **Answer: B.** In its broadest sense, an access control list (ACL) is the underlying data associated with a network resource that defines the access permissions. The most common privileges include the ability to read, write to, delete, and execute a file. Answer A is incorrect because it describes logical access control. Logical access controls are used in addition to physical security controls to limit access to data. This helps ensure the integrity of information, preserve the confidentiality of data, and maintain the availability of information. Answer C is incorrect because it describes Group Policy. Group Policy enables you to set consistent common security standards for a certain group of computers, enforce common computer and user configurations, simplify computer configuration by distributing applications, and restrict the distribution of applications that may have limited licenses. Answer D is incorrect because it describes a security identifier. A security identifier (SID) is a unique value that identifies a security principal. A SID is issued to every security principal when it is created.

2. **Answer: A.** Logical access controls are used in addition to physical security controls to limit access to data. This helps ensure the integrity of information, preserve the confidentiality of data, and maintain the availability of information. Answer B is incorrect because it describes an access control list. In its broadest sense, an access control list (ACL) is the underlying data associated with a network resource that defines the access permissions. The most common privileges include the ability to read, write to, delete, and execute a file. Answer C is incorrect because it describes Group Policy. Group Policy enables you to set consistent common security standards for a certain group of computers, enforce common computer and user configurations, simplify computer configuration by distributing applications, and restrict the distribution of applications that may have limited licenses. Answer D is incorrect because it describes a security identifier. A security identifier (SID) is a unique value that identifies a security principal. A SID is issued to every security principal when it is created.

3. **Answer: D.** A security identifier (SID) is a unique value that identifies a security principal. A SID is issued to every security principal when it is created. A user's access token includes SIDs of all groups to which the user is a member. When a user logs on and authentication is successful, the logon process returns an SID for the user and a list of SIDs for the user's security groups, and these comprise the access token. Answer A is incorrect because it describes logical access control. Logical access controls are used in addition to physical security controls to limit access to data. This helps ensure the integrity of information, preserve the confidentiality of data, and maintain the availability of information. Answer B is incorrect because it describes an access control list. In its broadest sense, an access control list (ACL) is the underlying data associated with a network resource that defines the access permissions. The

most common privileges include the ability to read, write to, delete, and execute a file. Answer C is incorrect because it describes Group Policy. Group Policy enables you to set consistent common security standards for a certain group of computers, enforce common computer and user configurations, simplify computer configuration by distributing applications, and restrict the distribution of applications that may have limited licenses.

4. **Answer: C.** Group Policy enables you to set consistent common security standards for a certain group of computers, enforce common computer and user configurations, simplify computer configuration by distributing applications, and restrict the distribution of applications that may have limited licenses. Answer A is incorrect because it describes logical access control. Logical access controls are used in addition to physical security controls to limit access to data. This helps ensure the integrity of information, preserve the confidentiality of data, and maintain the availability of information. Answer B is incorrect because it describes an access control list. In its broadest sense, an access control list (ACL) is the underlying data associated with a network resource that defines the access permissions. The most common privileges include the ability to read, write to, delete, and execute a file. Answer D is incorrect because it describes a security identifier. A security identifier (SID) is a unique value that identifies a security principal. A SID is issued to every security principal when it is created

5. **Answer: A.** Implementation of access management is based on one of two models: centralized or decentralized. Both the group-based and role-based methods of access control have a centralized database of accounts and roles or groups to which the accounts are assigned. Decentralized security management is less secure but more scalable. Responsibilities are delegated and employees at different locations are made responsible for managing privileges within their administrative areas. Answers B and C are incorrect; a decentralized solution is less secure than a centralized model. Answer D is incorrect; a decentralized model is more scalable, not less scalable.

6. **Answer: B.** Implementation of access management is based on one of two models: centralized or decentralized. Both the group-based and role-based methods of access control have a centralized database of accounts and roles or groups to which the accounts are assigned. Decentralized security management is less secure but more scalable. Responsibilities are delegated and employees at different locations are made responsible for managing privileges within their administrative areas. Answers A and D are incorrect; a centralized solution is more secure than a decentralized model. Answer C is incorrect; a centralized model is less scalable, not more scalable.

7. **Answer: D.** The order of GPO processing is important because a policy applied later overwrites a policy applied earlier. Group policies get applied from the bottom up, so if there is a conflict, the policy higher up in the list will prevail, unless it meets one of the exceptions such as block inheritance and loopback. Based on the previous statement, answers A, B, and C are incorrect.

8. **Answer: C.** Recommendations for setting a good password policy include making the password length at least eight characters, and require the use of uppercase and lowercase letters, numbers, and special characters. Answers A and B are incorrect because the length is too short and they can easily be compromised. Answer D is incorrect because although it would create a secure password, the length is too long for the average user to remember, causing them to write them down.

9. **Answer: A.** When Group Policy configures these settings, keep in mind that you can have only one domain account policy. The policy is applied at the root of the domain and becomes the policy for any system that is a member of the domain in Windows Server 2003 and earlier server versions. Domain passwords policies affect all users in the domain. The effectiveness of these policies depends on how and where they are applied. Based on this information, answers B, C, and D are incorrect.

10. **Answer: A, B, D.** Good password policies include making the password length at least eight characters; requiring the use of uppercase and lowercase letters, numbers, and special characters; requiring users to change passwords every 60 to 90 days; and setting the server to not allow users to use the same password over and over again. Answer C is incorrect because locking out user accounts after two failed logon attempts will cause undue stress on the help desk staff. Best practices for failed logon attempts is to lock out after three to five bad logon attempts.

11. **Answer: C.** You can assign time-of-day restrictions as a means to ensure that employees are using computers only during specified hours. This setting is useful for organizations where users require supervision, security certification requires it, or employees are mainly temporary or shift workers. Answers A, B, and D are incorrect because all these options affect all employees, not shift workers exclusively.

12. **Answer: D.** In Microsoft operating systems, each ACL has one or more access control entries (ACEs). These are descriptors that contain the name of a user, group, or role. The access privileges are stated in a string of bits called an access mask. Generally, the object owner or the system administrator creates the ACL for an object. Answer A is incorrect because it describes logical access control. Logical access controls are used in addition to physical security controls to limit access to data. This helps ensure the integrity of information, preserve the confidentiality of data, and maintain the availability of information. Answer B is incorrect because it describes Group Policy. Group Policy enables you to set consistent common security standards for a certain group of computers, enforce common computer and user configurations, simplify computer configuration by distributing applications, and restrict the distribution of applications that may have limited licenses. Answer C is incorrect because it describes a security identifier. A security identifier (SID) is a unique value that identifies a security principal. A SID is issued to every security principal when it is created.

13. **Answer: C.** Implementation of access management is based on one of two models: centralized or decentralized. Both the group-based and role-based methods of access control have a centralized database of accounts and roles or groups to which the accounts are assigned. Decentralized security management is less secure but more scalable. Responsibilities are delegated and employees at different locations are made responsible for managing privileges within their administrative areas. Answer A is incorrect because in a user-based model, permissions are uniquely assigned to each account. Answer B is incorrect because in a centralized model, there is one central database of accounts and roles or groups to which the accounts are assigned. Answer D is incorrect because a group-based access method of access control is centralized.

14. **Answer: B, D.** Implementation of access management is based on one of two models: centralized or decentralized. Both the group-based and role-based methods of access control have a centralized database of accounts and roles or groups to which the accounts are assigned. Decentralized security management is less secure but more scalable. Responsibilities are delegated and employees at different locations are made

responsible for managing privileges within their administrative areas. Answer A is incorrect because in a user-based model, permissions are uniquely assigned to each account. Answer C is incorrect because in a decentralized model, responsibilities are delegated and employees at different locations are made responsible for managing privileges within their administrative areas.

15. **Answer: A.** If the computer is a workgroup member rather than a domain member, only the local policy is applied. Based on the previous statement, answers B, C, and D are incorrect. If the computer is a workgroup member, it does not matter what policies are set; only the local policy will apply.

16. **Answer: A, B, C.** GPOs can be associated with or linked to sites, domains, or organizational units. Because Group Policy is so powerful, various levels of administrative roles can be appointed. These include creating, modifying, and linking policies. Answer D is incorrect; forests transverse across domains, and Group Policy is not linked to a forest.

17. **Answer: D.** The order of GPO processing is important because a policy applied later overwrites a policy applied earlier. Group policies get applied from the bottom up; however, if there is a conflict, the policy higher up in the list will prevail. Based on the previous statements, answers A, B, and C are incorrect.

18. **Answer: C.** You can assign time-of-day restrictions as a means to ensure that employees are using computers only during specified hours. This setting is useful for organizations where users require supervision, security certification requires it, or employees are mainly temporary or shift workers. Answer A is incorrect because the account expiration attribute specifies when an account expires. This setting may be used under the same conditions as the time-of-day restrictions. Answer B is incorrect because the account lockout policy can be used to secure the system against attacks by disabling the account after a certain number of attempts, for a certain period of time. Answer D is incorrect because the software restriction policy has to do with application installations.

19. **Answer: A.** The account expiration attribute specifies when an account expires. This setting may be used under the same conditions as the time-of-day restrictions. Answer B is incorrect because the account lockout policy can be used to secure the system against attacks by disabling the account after a certain number of attempts, for a certain period of time. Answer C is incorrect. You can assign time-of-day restrictions as a means to ensure that employees are using computers only during specified hours. This setting is useful for organizations where users require supervision, security certification requires it, or employees are mainly temporary or shift workers. Answer D is incorrect because the software restriction policy has to do with application installations.

20. **Answer: B.** The account lockout policy can be used to secure the system against attacks by disabling the account after a certain number of attempts, for a certain period of time. Answer A is incorrect. The account expiration attribute specifies when an account expires. This setting may be used under the same conditions as the time-of-day restrictions. Answer C is incorrect. You can assign time-of-day restrictions as a means to ensure that employees are using computers only during specified hours. This setting is useful for organizations where users require supervision, security certification requires it, or employees are mainly temporary or shift workers. Answer D is incorrect because the software restriction policy has to do with application installations.

Objective 3.6: Summarize the various authentication models and identify the components of each.

1. **Answer: B, C, D.** Authentication can be generally broken into three basic forms, depending on what is required to authorize access: something you know, something you have, or something you are. Answer A is incorrect because something you touch may be a method used for validation, not a basic form.

2. **Answer: B.** Using a login and password is single-factor because it consists of only what you know. Therefore, it is not considered multifactor authentication. Multifactor authentication involves the use of two or more different forms of authentication. Different forms include what you know (logon, password, PIN), what you have (keycard, SecureID number generator), or what you are (biometrics). Therefore, answer A is incorrect. Answer C is incorrect; Kerberos v5 includes support for a process known as mutual authentication, where both the identity of the client that is requesting authentication and the server that is providing authentication are verified. Answer D is incorrect; Challenge-Handshake Authentication Protocol (CHAP) provides on-demand authentication.

3. **Answer: C.** Kerberos v5 includes support for a process known as mutual authentication, where both the identity of the client that is requesting authentication and the server that is providing authentication are verified. Multifactor authentication involves the use of two or more different forms of authentication. Different forms include what you know (logon, password, PIN), what you have (keycard, SecureID number generator), or what you are (biometrics). Therefore, answer A is incorrect. Answer B is incorrect. Using a login and password is not considered multifactor authentication. It is single-factor because it consists of only what you know. Answer D is incorrect; Challenge-Handshake Authentication Protocol (CHAP) provides on-demand authentication.

4. **Answer: D.** Challenge-Handshake Authentication Protocol (CHAP) provides on-demand authentication. Multifactor authentication involves the use of two or more different forms of authentication. Different forms include what you know (logon, password, PIN), what you have (keycard, SecureID number generator), or what you are (biometrics). Therefore, answer A is incorrect. Answer B is incorrect. Using a login and password is not considered multifactor authentication. It is single-factor because it consists of only what you know. Answer C is incorrect; Kerberos v5 includes support for a process known as mutual authentication, where both the identity of the client that is requesting authentication and the server that is providing authentication are verified.

5. **Answer: A.** Multifactor authentication involves the use of two or more different forms of authentication. Different forms include what you know (logon, password, PIN), what you have (keycard, SecureID number generator), or what you are (biometrics). Answer B is incorrect. Using a login and password is not considered multifactor authentication. It is single-factor because it consists of only what you know. Answer C is incorrect; Kerberos v5 includes support for a process known as mutual authentication,

where both the identity of the client that is requesting authentication and the server that is providing authentication are verified. Answer D is incorrect; Challenge-Handshake Authentication Protocol (CHAP) provides on-demand authentication.

6. **Answer: B.** Before authorization may occur for anything other than anonymous access to wholly public resources, the identity of the account attempting to access a resource must first be determined. This process is known as authentication. The most well-known form of authentication is the use of a logon account identifier and password combination to access controlled resources. Access is not possible without both parts required for account authentication, so a level of protection is provided. Therefore, answers A, C, and D are incorrect.

7. **Answer: D.** The shortcoming of any authentication system is that the keys used may be easily falsified and access rights may be granted to an unauthorized access attempt. Null or easily guessed passwords are one of the most widespread examples of the potential for this weakness. Answer A is incorrect because lost tokens are associated with biometric methods or multifactor authentication. Answer B is incorrect; false positives are associated with intrusion detection systems. Answer C is incorrect because weak encryption is most closely associated with wireless networks.

8. **Answer: A.** Most libraries require the creation of an account or a library card to use the computers and kiosks. Anonymous or open access represents the weakest possible form of authentication, whereas the requirement for both a logon identifier and password combination may be considered the most basic of actual account verification. The highest levels of authentication may involve not only account logon, but also when the logon is occurring from specific network addresses or whether a security token such as an access smart card is present. Answer B is incorrect because although anonymous access is a possibility, as a publicly funded institution, the library should have some due diligence to prevent the use of the computer for illegal purposes. Answers C and D are incorrect; these types of authentication are extremely expensive and restrictive for access to library resources.

9. **Answer: C.** The highest levels of authentication may involve not only account logon, but also when the logon is occurring from specific network addresses or whether a security token such as an access smart card is present. Most governmental financial systems would require some type of biometric verification a security token. Answers A, B, and D are incorrect; they are not restrictive enough. Anonymous or open access represents the weakest possible form of authentication, whereas the requirement for both a logon identifier and password combination may be considered the most basic of actual account verification.

10. **Answer: B.** Millions of travelers access kiosks at airports daily. Although anonymous access is the weakest possible form of authentication, it is the only solution due to the volume of traffic. Whereas the requirement for both a logon identifier and password combination may be considered the most basic of actual account verification, requiring each traveler to use a login and password, would create an unbearable backlog of travelers. Answer A is incorrect. Issuing security tokens is not cost-effective or administratively manageable in a kiosk environment. Answers C and D are incorrect; these types of authentication are extremely expensive and restrictive for access to airport kiosks.

11. **Answer: A.** Before access rights can be determined a user must first be authenticated. Answer B is incorrect because the processes of authentication and access rights determination are not explicitly dependent on one another. Answers C and D are incorrect; authentication must precede access rights determination to avoid granting an unauthorized account access rights.

12. **Answer: B.** Authentication is the mechanism by which the unique identity is associated with a security principal (a specific user or service). Answer A is incorrect because it describes identification, which is the presentation of a unique identity. Answer C is incorrect; it is a description of identification. Identification presents credentials. Answer D is incorrect because it describes access control. Access control provides a set of resources available to the authenticated identity.

13. **Answer: C, D.** To reduce user support and authentication complexity, a single sign-on (SSO) capable of granting access to all services is desirable. SSO solutions may employ a central directory service like Microsoft's Active Directory or Novell's eDirectory service, or may sequester services behind a series of proxy applications as in the Service-Oriented Architecture approach. Answer A is incorrect because implementing single sign-on solutions is can be costly. Answer B is incorrect. When single sign-on is used, if an account is compromised, there are more resources at risk.

14. **Answer: D.** Most access for telecommuters will involve not only account logon, but also when the logon is occurring from specific network addresses or whether a security token such as an access smart card is present. Answer A is incorrect; the requirement for both a logon identifier and password combination may be considered the most basic of actual account verification and not strong enough for home users with always on network connections. Answer B is incorrect. Anonymous access is a very weak solution for home users with always on network connectors and should not be used. Answers C is incorrect; this type of authentication is extremely expensive and does make sense for the users.

15. **Answer: A.** To reduce user support and authentication complexity, a single sign-on (SSO) capable of granting access to all services is desirable. Based on the previous information, answer B is incorrect. Answer B is incorrect. Anonymous access is a very weak solutions for home users with always on network connectors and should not be used. Answers C and D are incorrect because neither administrative nor anonymous access should be used.

Objective 3.7: Deploy various authentication models and identify the components of each.

1. **Answer: B, C, D.** The strengths of Kerberos authentication come from its time-synchronized connections and the use of registered client and service keys within the Key Distribution Center (KDC). The Key Distribution Center (KDC) is a trusted third party that consists of two logically separate parts: an Authentication Server (AS) and a Ticket-Granting Server (TGS). Answer A is incorrect because Kerberos is not used with remote-access connections.

2. **Answer: D.** Challenge-Handshake Authentication Protocol (CHAP) functions over Point-to-Point Protocol (PPP) connections. CHAP can be used to provide on-demand authentication within an ongoing data transmission. Based on the previous information, answers A, B, and C are incorrect.

3. **Answer: B.** TACACS+ is a remote-access control system providing authentication, authorization, and accounting (AAA). Answer A is incorrect; it describes Kerberos. Kerberos is a symmetric-key authentication protocol used to protect sending actual logon information across an unsecured network. Answer C is incorrect; it describes RADIUS. RADIUS provides centralized authentication and access control for credentials to resources within an extended enterprise. Answer D is incorrect; it describes CHAP. The Challenge-Handshake Authentication Protocol (CHAP) can be used to provide on-demand authentication within an ongoing data transmission.

4. **Answer: C.** RADIUS provides centralized authentication and access control for credentials to resources within an extended enterprise Answer A is incorrect; it describes Kerberos. Kerberos is a symmetric-key authentication protocol used to protect sending actual logon information across an unsecured network. Answer B is incorrect; it describes TACACS+. TACACS+ is a remote-access control system providing authentication, authorization, and accounting (AAA). Answer D is incorrect; it describes CHAP. The Challenge-Handshake Authentication Protocol (CHAP) can be used to provide on-demand authentication within an ongoing data transmission.

5. **Answer: D.** The Challenge-Handshake Authentication Protocol (CHAP) can be used to provide on-demand authentication within an ongoing data transmission. Answer A is incorrect; it describes Kerberos. Kerberos is a symmetric-key authentication protocol used to protect sending actual logon information across an unsecured network. Answer B is incorrect; it describes TACACS+. TACACS+ is a remote-access control system providing authentication, authorization, and accounting (AAA). Answer C is incorrect; it describes RADIUS. RADIUS provides centralized authentication and access control for credentials to resources within an extended enterprise.

6. **Answer: A.** Kerberos is a symmetric-key authentication protocol used to protect sending actual logon information across an unsecured network. Answer B is incorrect; it describes TACACS+. TACACS+ is a remote-access control system providing authentication, authorization, and accounting (AAA). Answer C is incorrect; it describes RADIUS. RADIUS provides centralized authentication and access control for credentials to resources within an extended enterprise. Answer D is incorrect; it describes CHAP. The Challenge-Handshake Authentication Protocol (CHAP) can be used to provide on-demand authentication within an ongoing data transmission.

7. **Answer: B.** The IEEE 802.1x standard for wireless port-based access control can be used to provide authentication as well as access control, but is often paired with a RADIUS server to facilitate enterprise-wide access management. Answer A is incorrect; Kerberos is a symmetric-key authentication protocol used to protect sending actual logon information across an unsecured network. Answer C is incorrect; RADIUS provides centralized authentication and access control for credentials to resources within an extended enterprise. Answer D is incorrect; it describes CHAP. The

Challenge-Handshake Authentication Protocol (CHAP) can be used to provide on-demand authentication within an ongoing data transmission.

8. **Answer: D.** The Challenge-Handshake Authentication Protocol uses two compared values created using the MD5 hashing algorithm. Answer A is incorrect; Kerberos is a symmetric-key authentication protocol used to protect sending actual logon information across an unsecured network. Answer B is incorrect; TACACS+ is a remote-access control system providing authentication, authorization, and accounting (AAA). Answer C is incorrect; RADIUS provides centralized authentication and access control for credentials to resources within an extended enterprise.

9. **Answer: C.** A Public Key Infrastructure (PKI) solution involves an asymmetric encryption scheme in which a public key is used to encrypt data and a separate private key is used to decrypt the data. Answer A is incorrect; Kerberos is a symmetric-key authentication protocol used to protect sending actual logon information across an unsecured network. Answer B is incorrect; TACACS is a remote-access control system providing authentication, authorization, and accounting (AAA). Answer D is incorrect; RADIUS provides centralized authentication and access control for credentials to resources within an extended enterprise.

10. **Answer: A, B, D.** Any combination of authentication methods may be used in a multifactor solution. Multifactor authentication just refers to solutions including more than a single type of authentication. Answer C is incorrect. Anonymous access is the weakest form of authentication and is not combined with other authentication methods.

11. **Answer: B.** Iris profile biometric devices identify an individual by using the colored part of the eye that surrounds the pupil. Answer A is incorrect because signature matches an individual's electronic signature to a database by comparing electronic signals created by the speed and manner in which a document is signed. Answer C is incorrect because facial geometry Identifies a user based on the profile and characteristics of his face. Answer D is incorrect because a retina scan identifies an individual by using the blood-vessel pattern at the back of the eyeball.

12. **Answer: A, B.** When using biometrics, remember that each method has its own degree of error ratios, and some methods may seem invasive to the users and may not be accepted gracefully. Answer C is incorrect because account lockouts have to do with passwords. Answer D is incorrect because cross-contamination is a physical concern not associated with biometric solutions.

13. **Answer: A.** Virtual private network (VPN) connections provide a mechanism for the creation of a secured "tunnel" through a public network such as the Internet, which then encapsulates data packets to prevent sniffing over the public network. Answer B is incorrect because a remote-access service (RAS) server functions as a gateway through which the remote user may access local resources or gain connectivity to the Internet. Answer C is incorrect because the Lightweight Directory Access Protocol (LDAP) allows authentication of logon identities over TCP/IP connectivity against a hierarchical directory. Answer D is incorrect; RADIUS provides centralized authentication and access control for credentials to resources within an extended enterprise.

14. **Answer: B.** Client systems equipped with a modem can connect using normal dial-up

acoustic connections to a properly equipped remote-access service (RAS) server, which functions as a gateway through which the remote user may access local resources or gain connectivity to the Internet. Answer A is incorrect; virtual private network (VPN) connections provide a mechanism for the creation of a secured "tunnel" through a public network such as the Internet, which then encapsulates data packets to prevent sniffing over the public network. Answer C is incorrect because the Lightweight Directory Access Protocol (LDAP) allows authentication of logon identities over TCP/IP connectivity against a hierarchical directory. Answer D is incorrect; RADIUS provides centralized authentication and access control for credentials to resources within an extended enterprise.

15. **Answer: C.** The Lightweight Directory Access Protocol (LDAP) allows authentication of logon identities over TCP/IP connectivity against a hierarchical directory. Answer A is incorrect; virtual private network (VPN) connections provide a mechanism for the creation of a secured "tunnel" through a public network such as the Internet, which then encapsulates data packets to prevent sniffing over the public network. Answer B is incorrect because a remote-access service (RAS) server functions as a gateway through which the remote user may access local resources or gain connectivity to the Internet. Answer D is incorrect; RADIUS provides centralized authentication and access control for credentials to resources within an extended enterprise.

16. **Answer: D.** RADIUS provides centralized authentication and access control for credentials to resources within an extended enterprise. Answer A is incorrect; virtual private network (VPN) connections provide a mechanism for the creation of a secured "tunnel" through a public network such as the Internet, which then encapsulates data packets to prevent sniffing over the public network. Answer B is incorrect because a remote-access service (RAS) server functions as a gateway through which the remote user may access local resources or gain connectivity to the Internet. Answer C is incorrect because the Lightweight Directory Access Protocol (LDAP) allows authentication of logon identities over TCP/IP connectivity against a hierarchical directory.

17. **Answer: A, B.** Modern solutions provide for both user authentication and authorization, including the Remote Authentication Dial-In User Service (RADIUS) or Terminal Access Controller Access-Control System Plus (TACACS+) protocols. Answer C is incorrect because the Lightweight Directory Access Protocol (LDAP) allows authentication of logon identities over TCP/IP connectivity against a hierarchical directory. Answer D is incorrect because remote-access service (RAS) functions as a gateway through which the remote user may access local resources or gain connectivity to the Internet.

18. **Answer: C.** Remember that LDAP is a TCP/IP-based protocol connecting by default to TCP port 389. Answers A and D are incorrect; ports 161 and 162 are used by SNMP. Answer B is incorrect because port 110 is used by POP3 for email.

19. **Answer: C.** RADIUS encrypts only the password in the access-request packet, from the client to the server. The remainder of the packet is unencrypted. Based on this information, answers A, B, and D are incorrect.

20. **Answer: B.** RADIUS, which was developed originally for modem-based connectivity access control uses User Datagram Protocol (UDP) transport. Answer A is incorrect;

RADIUS uses UDP, which is connectionless oriented, whereas TCP is a connection-oriented protocol. Answer C is incorrect. File Transfer Protocol is not connected with the use of RADIUS. Answer D is incorrect. SMTP is used for email communication.

21. **Answer: A.** TACACS+ is similar to Remote Authentication Dial-In User Service (RADIUS), but relies on Transmission Control Protocol (TCP) rather than RADIUS's User Datagram Protocol (UDP) transport developed originally for modem-based connectivity access control. Therefore, answer B is incorrect. Answer C is incorrect. File Transfer Protocol is not connected with the use of TACACS+. Answer D is incorrect. SMTP is used for email communication.

22. **Answer: D.** CHAP functions over Point-to-Point Protocol (PPP) connections. PPP is a protocol for communicating between two points using a serial interface, provides service at the second layer of the OSI model: the data link layer. PPP can handle both synchronous and asynchronous connections. Answer A is incorrect. File Transfer Protocol is not connected with the use of CHAP. Answer B is incorrect; PPTP is not used as a connection protocol for CHAP. Answer C is incorrect; Shiva Password Authentication Protocol (SPAP) was designed by Shiva and is an older, two-way reversible encryption protocol that encrypts the password data sent between client and server.

23. **Answer: C.** TACACS is a client/server protocol that provides the same functionality as RADIUS, except that RADIUS is an actual Internet standard; therefore, answer A is incorrect. Answers B and D are incorrect because both RADIUS and TACACS are authentication protocols.

24. **Answer: A, D.** Biometric devices are susceptible to false acceptance and false rejection rates. The false acceptance rate (FAR) is a measure of the likelihood that the access system will wrongly accept an access attempt. In other words, it will allow access to an unauthorized user. The false rejection rate (FRR) is the percentage of identification instances in which false rejection occurs. In false rejection, the system fails to recognize an authorized person and rejects that person as unauthorized. Answers B and C are incorrect because false positives and negatives are associated with intrusion detection systems.

25. **Answer: C.** Biometric devices are susceptible to false acceptance and false rejection rates. The false rejection rate (FRR) is the percentage of identification instances in which false rejection occurs. In false rejection, the system fails to recognize an authorized person and rejects that person as an authorized. Answer A is incorrect because it describes false negative. The false acceptance rate (FAR) is a measure of the likelihood that the access system will wrongly accept an access attempt. In other words, it will allow access to an unauthorized user. Therefore, answer B is incorrect. Answer D is incorrect because it describes a false positive.

Objective 3.8: Explain the difference between identification and authentication (identity proofing).

1. **Answer: D.** Identity proofing gives the organization assurance that the user performing an authentication is the legitimate user. Answer A is incorrect because a hypervisor controls how access to a computer's processors and memory is shared. Answer B is incorrect because in a user-based model, permissions are uniquely assigned to each account. Answer C is incorrect because access control entries specify the types of access attempts that cause the system to generate a record in the security event log.

2. **Answer: A.** Identity proofing is the main component of authentication life cycle management. The first link in the chain of trust is established when a person is issued a credential establishing identity or privileges. It must provide a firm assurance that persons are who they say they are. This technique can include integrated biometrics or online database validation. Identity proofing comes in a variety of forms. Answers B and D are incorrect; when establishing identity or privileges, the method must provide a firm assurance that the person is who they say they are. This can include integrated biometrics or online database validation. Answer C is incorrect because identity proofing is based on authentication, not accounting. Accounting is associated with TACACS+.

3. **Answer: B.** Identity proofing is an organizational process that binds users to authentication methods. Identity proofing gives the organization assurance that the user performing an authentication is the legitimate user. Identity proofing is especially important in emergency access (for example, when users accidentally leave their hardware tokens at home). Answers A, C, and D are incorrect because these methods will not provide adequate identification if a hardware token is forgotten.

4. **Answer: A, C, D.** Authenticators for identity proofing include smart cards, biometrics, and one-time password (OTP) devices. Answer B is incorrect because a mantrap is a physical security device.

5. **Answer: C.** Identity proofing is an organizational process that binds users to authentication methods. Identity proofing gives the organization assurance that the user performing an authentication is the legitimate user. Identity proofing is the main component of authentication lifecycle management. Answer A is incorrect because it describes RAS. Answer B is incorrect because it describes LDAP. Answer D is incorrect because it describes TACACS+.

Objective 3.9: Explain and apply physical access security methods.

1. **Answer: B.** Unsecured equipment is vulnerable to social-engineering attacks. It is much easier for an attacker to walk into a reception area, say she is here to do some work on the server, and get access server than to get into a physically secured area with a guest sign-in and sign-out sheet. Brute-force attacks, malware, and rootkits can be installed or launched without physical access. Therefore, answers A, C, and D are incorrect.

2. **Answer: C, D.** Mandatory physical access controls are commonly found in govern-

ment facilities and military installations where users are closely monitored and very restricted. Answers A and B are incorrect because academic institutions and most corporate environments use a discretionary or role-based access control method.

3. **Answer: C.** The goal of a physical security policy is to allow only trusted use of resources via positive identification that the entity accessing the systems is someone or something that has permission to do so based on the security model the organization has chosen. Answers A, B, and D are incorrect because only allowing officers, only what is deemed to be credible users is discretionary, while allowing all visitors will create an unsecure environment.

4. **Answer: B, C.** In very high-security areas, frosted or painted glass can be used to eliminate direct visual observation of user actions, and very high-security scenarios may mandate the use of electromagnetic shielding to prevent remote monitoring of emissions generated by video monitors, network switching, and system operation. Answers A and D are incorrect; picket and chain-link fencing should not be used in high-security areas.

5. **Answer: A.** Buildings that house sensitive information and systems usually have an area of cleared land surrounding them. This area is referred to as no-man's land. The purpose of this area is to eliminate the possibility of an intruder hiding in the bushes or behind another building. Answer B is incorrect because it increases the chances of an intruder hiding. Answer C is incorrect; it describes a mantrap. Answer D is incorrect because it describes a wireless lock entry.

6. **Answer: C.** A mantrap is a holding area between two entry points that gives security personnel time to view a person before allowing him into the internal building. Answer A is incorrect because it describes no-man's land. The purpose of this area is to eliminate the possibility of an intruder hiding in the bushes or behind another building. Answer B is incorrect because it increases the chances of an intruder hiding. Answer D is incorrect because it describes a wireless lock entry.

7. **Answer: D.** A cipher lock has a punch code entry system. A wireless lock is opened by a receiver mechanism that reads the card when it is held close to the receiver. Based on this information, answers A, B, and C are incorrect.

8. **Answer: A.** Video or CCTV cameras should be posted in key locations so that the entire area is covered. Place cameras near entrances and exits to capture each visitor who comes in and out of the parking lot. Place cameras strategically so that every area of the parking lot can be seen by a camera's field of vision. Answer B is incorrect. If the parking lot covers a large area, security guard coverage may not be enough. Answer C is incorrect because a keycard entry point can easily be compromised. Answer D incorrect because motion detection is not feasible for a parking lot.

9. **Answer: A, B, D.** External motion detectors can be based on light, sound, infrared, or ultrasonic technology. Answer C is incorrect because radio-frequency identification (RFID) is an automatic identification method.

10. **Answer: C.** Discretionary physical control to a building or room is delegated to parties responsible for that building or room. Answer A is incorrect. Mandatory physical

access controls are commonly found in government facilities and military installations, where users are closely monitored and very restricted. Because they are being monitored by security personnel and devices, users cannot modify entry methods or let others in. Answer B is incorrect. In role-based access methods for physical control, groups of people who have common access needs are predetermined, and access to different locations is allowed with the same key or swipe card. Answer D is incorrect. Allowing access based on individual needs is both costly and causes extensive administrative overhead.

11. **Answer: A.** Mandatory physical access controls are commonly found in government facilities and military installations, where users are closely monitored and very restricted. Because they are being monitored by security personnel and devices, users cannot modify entry methods or let others in. Answer B is incorrect. In role-based access methods for physical control, groups of people who have common access needs are predetermined, and access to different locations is allowed with the same key or swipe card. Answer C is incorrect. Discretionary physical control to a building or room is delegated to parties responsible for that building or room. Answer D is incorrect. Allowing access based on individual needs is both costly and causes extensive administrative overhead.

12. **Answer: B.** In role-based access methods for physical control, groups of people who have common access needs are predetermined, and access to different locations is allowed with the same key or swipe card. Answer A is incorrect. Mandatory physical access controls are commonly found in government facilities and military installations, where users are closely monitored and very restricted. Because they are being monitored by security personnel and devices, users cannot modify entry methods or let others in. Answer C is incorrect. Discretionary physical control to a building or room is delegated to parties responsible for that building or room. Answer D is incorrect. Allowing access based on individual needs is both costly and causes extensive administrative overhead.

13. **Answer: B.** Buildings that house sensitive information and systems usually have an area of cleared land surrounding them. This area is referred to as no-man's land. Answer A is incorrect because a mantrap is a holding area between two entry points that gives security personnel time to view a person before allowing him into the internal building. Answer C is incorrect because a fence keeps out unwanted vehicles and people. Answer D is incorrect because door access systems include biometric access, proximity access, and coded access systems, and modular door entry systems.

14. **Answer: D.** Video surveillance such as closed-circuit television (CCTV) is the most common method of surveillance. The picture is viewed or recorded, but not broadcast. It was originally developed as a means of security for banks. Answer A is incorrect because a mantrap is a holding area between two entry points that gives security personnel time to view a person before allowing him into the internal building. Answer B is incorrect security dogs are not a good solution for a bank. Answer C is incorrect because painted glass is used a method of obscuring views. This it is not a sufficient method of security for a bank.

15. **Answer: C.** Motion detectors can alert security personnel of intruders or suspicious activity on the company's premises. They can be based on light, sound, infrared, or ultrasonic technology. These devices must be properly configured because they are

CHAPTER FOUR

Domain 4.0: Assessments & Audits

To secure a network, it is important to identify the normal operating parameters so that you can recognize atypical variations from this baseline operational level. The first step toward minimizing the potential damage that may result from unauthorized access attempts is the detection and identification of an unauthorized intrusion. Intrusion detection requires a detailed understanding of all operational aspects of the network, along with a means to identify variations and bring these changes to the attention of the proper responsible parties. Auditing is done to protect the validity and reliability of organizational information and systems. As a security professional, you can audit a vast amount of data. Auditing can create a large repository of information that has to be filtered through. Monitoring can be as simple or complex as you want to make it. Many organizations monitor an extensive amount of information, whereas others may monitor little or nothing. As a prospective security professional, you should also take every opportunity you may find to expand your skill base beyond these basic foundational elements. The following list includes the key areas from Domain 4 that you need to master for the exam:

▶ Conduct risk assessments and implement risk mitigation.

▶ Carry out vulnerability assessments using common tools.

▶ Within the realm of vulnerability assessments, explain the proper use of penetration testing versus vulnerability scanning.

- ► Use monitoring tools on systems and networks and detect security-related anomalies.

- ► Compare and contrast various types of monitoring methodologies.

- ► Execute proper logging procedures and evaluate the results.

- ► Conduct periodic audits of system security settings.

Practice Questions

Objective 4.1: Conduct risk assessments and implement risk mitigation.

1. Metrics for security baselines and hardening efforts rely on which of the following?

    - ○ **A.** Mitigation of threats and attacks
    - ○ **B.** Identification of security measures and policies
    - ○ **C.** Identification of vulnerability and risk
    - ○ **D.** Mitigation of vulnerability and risk

Quick Answer: **229**
Detailed Answer: **232**

2. When the risk of equipment loss is covered by a full-replacement insurance policy, which of the following best describes the risk?

    - ○ **A.** Accepted
    - ○ **B.** Transferred
    - ○ **C.** Eliminated
    - ○ **D.** Mitigated

Quick Answer: **229**
Detailed Answer: **232**

3. An organization removes legacy dial-up telephony modem devices to prevent war-dialing attacks. Which of the following best describes the risk?

    - ○ **A.** Accepted
    - ○ **B.** Transferred
    - ○ **C.** Eliminated
    - ○ **D.** Mitigated

Quick Answer: **229**
Detailed Answer: **232**

4. When an organization installs a firewall to prevent attacks, which of the following best describes the risk?

- ○ **A.** Accepted
- ○ **B.** Transferred
- ○ **C.** Eliminated
- ○ **D.** Mitigated

Quick Answer: **229**
Detailed Answer: **232**

5. When an organization decides the cost of an IDS is too expensive to implement, which of the following best describes the risk?

- ○ **A.** Accepted
- ○ **B.** Transferred
- ○ **C.** Eliminated
- ○ **D.** Mitigated

Quick Answer: **229**
Detailed Answer: **232**

6. Which of the following best describes the primary purpose of a risk assessment?

- ○ **A.** To collect user logins and passwords for administrative purposes
- ○ **B.** To scan the network to find and address vulnerabilities
- ○ **C.** To properly store and protect personally identifiable information
- ○ **D.** To identify existing threats and potential mitigation mechanisms

Quick Answer: **229**
Detailed Answer: **233**

7. Which of the following is the correct formula for calculating annual loss expectancy?

- ○ **A.** $SLE \times ARO$
- ○ **B.** $ALE \times SLE$
- ○ **C.** $ALE \times ARO$
- ○ **D.** $CLE \times SLE$

Quick Answer: **229**
Detailed Answer: **233**

8. Which of the following best describes how single loss expectancy is calculated?

- ○ **A.** Loss prevented minus the total cost of the solution
- ○ **B.** Asset value multiplied by the threat exposure factor
- ○ **C.** Threat factor multiplied by potential vulnerability
- ○ **D.** Annualized rate of occurrence multiplied by threat factor

Quick Answer: **229**
Detailed Answer: **233**

9. An organization has identified and reduced risk to a level that is comfortable and then implemented controls to maintain that level. Which of the following best describes this action?

  ○ **A.** Risk management
  ○ **B.** Risk acceptance
  ○ **C.** Risk analysis
  ○ **D.** Risk transference

Quick Answer: 229
Detailed Answer: 233

10. An organization identified risks, estimated the impact of potential threats, and identified ways to reduce the risk without the cost of the prevention outweighing the risk. Which of the following best describes this action?

  ○ **A.** Risk management
  ○ **B.** Risk acceptance
  ○ **C.** Risk analysis
  ○ **D.** Risk transference

Quick Answer: 229
Detailed Answer: 233

11. Which of the following best describes risk?

  ○ **A.** Probability of threat exposure
  ○ **B.** Cumulative loss expectancy
  ○ **C.** Possibility of loss or danger
  ○ **D.** Mitigation of loss or danger

Quick Answer: 229
Detailed Answer: 233

12. During the process of risk assessment, which of the following would be reviewed? (Select all correct answers.)

  ○ **A.** Audit policies
  ○ **B.** Access methods
  ○ **C.** Financial records
  ○ **D.** Hiring procedures

Quick Answer: 229
Detailed Answer: 234

13. Which of the following best describes return on investment?

  ○ **A.** Estimating the impact of potential threats and identifying ways to reduce the risk
  ○ **B.** Implemented controls to maintain a level of risk that is comfortable for the organization
  ○ **C.** A measure of how effectively a company uses the money invested in its operations
  ○ **D.** The ratio of money realized on an investment relative to the amount of money invested

Quick Answer: 229
Detailed Answer: 234

14. When the return on investment is calculated, if the result is a negative number, which of the following is true?

    ○ **A.** Less money was spent than the loss prevented.

    ○ **B.** More money was spent than the loss prevented.

    ○ **C.** The money spent was not a worthwhile investment.

    ○ **D.** The money spent was an excellent investment.

Quick Answer: **229**
Detailed Answer: **234**

15. Which of the following best describes exposure factor or probability?

    ○ **A.** The weakness that allows an attacker to violate the integrity of a system

    ○ **B.** The actual amount of loss prevented by implementing a total cost solution

    ○ **C.** The percentage of loss that a realized threat could have on a certain asset

    ○ **D.** The estimated possibility of a specific threat taking place in a one-year period

Quick Answer: **229**
Detailed Answer: **234**

Objective 4.2: Carry out vulnerability assessments using common tools.

1. Which of the following is a software utility that will scan a single machine or a range of IP addresses checking for a response on service connections?

    ○ **A.** Port scanner

    ○ **B.** Network mapper

    ○ **C.** Protocol analyzer

    ○ **D.** Vulnerability scanner

Quick Answer: **229**
Detailed Answer: **234**

2. Which of the following is a software utility that will scan a range of IP addresses testing for the present of known weaknesses in software configuration and accessible services?

    ○ **A.** Port scanner

    ○ **B.** Network mapper

    ○ **C.** Protocol analyzer

    ○ **D.** Vulnerability scanner

Quick Answer: **229**
Detailed Answer: **234**

3. Which of the following is a software utility that is used on a hub, a switch supervisory port, or in line with network connectivity to allow the analysis of network communications?

- ○ **A.** Port scanner
- ○ **B.** Network mapper
- ○ **C.** Protocol analyzer
- ○ **D.** Vulnerability scanner

Quick Answer: **229**
Detailed Answer: **235**

4. Which of the following is a software utility that is used to conduct network assessments over a range of IP addresses and compiles a listing of all systems, devices, and hardware present within a network segment?

- ○ **A.** Port scanner
- ○ **B.** Network mapper
- ○ **C.** Protocol analyzer
- ○ **D.** Vulnerability scanner

Quick Answer: **229**
Detailed Answer: **235**

5. Which of the following best describes the purpose of OVAL?

- ○ **A.** An abstract description for layered communications and computer network protocol design
- ○ **B.** A family of standards dealing with local area networks and metropolitan area networks
- ○ **C.** An international standard setting body composed of representatives from various national standards organizations
- ○ **D.** An international language for representing vulnerability information allowing the development of vulnerability test tools

Quick Answer: **229**
Detailed Answer: **235**

6. An administrator working in the Department of Homeland Security needs to document standards for the assessment process of systems. Which of the following would be most useful to the administrator?

- ○ **A.** OVAL
- ○ **B.** IEEE
- ○ **C.** ISO
- ○ **D.** ISSA

Quick Answer: **229**
Detailed Answer: **235**

7. An organization wants to select an assessment tool for creating an inventory of services hosted on networked systems. Which of the following should the organization choose?

- ○ **A.** Port scanner
- ○ **B.** Network mapper
- ○ **C.** Protocol analyzer
- ○ **D.** Vulnerability scanner

Quick Answer: **229**
Detailed Answer: **235**

8. An organization wants to select an assessment tool that will examine individual protocols and specific endpoints. Which of the following should the organization choose?

- ○ **A.** Port scanner
- ○ **B.** Network mapper
- ○ **C.** Protocol analyzer
- ○ **D.** Vulnerability scanner

Quick Answer: **229**
Detailed Answer: **236**

9. An organization wants to select an assessment tool for checking particular versions and patch levels of a service. Which of the following should the organization choose?

- ○ **A.** Port scanner
- ○ **B.** Network mapper
- ○ **C.** Protocol analyzer
- ○ **D.** Vulnerability scanner

Quick Answer: **229**
Detailed Answer: **236**

10. An organization wants to select an assessment tool that will create graphical details suitable for reporting on network configurations. Which of the following should the organization choose?

- ○ **A.** Port scanner
- ○ **B.** Network mapper
- ○ **C.** Protocol analyzer
- ○ **D.** Vulnerability scanner

Quick Answer: **229**
Detailed Answer: **236**

11. An organization wants to select an assessment tool that will directly test user logon password strength. Which of the following should the organization choose?

- ○ **A.** Password Locker
- ○ **B.** Password generator
- ○ **C.** Password cracker
- ○ **D.** Password keychain

Quick Answer: **229**
Detailed Answer: **236**

12. Which of the following best describes the difference between a port scanner and a vulnerability scanner?

Quick Answer: 229
Detailed Answer: 236

○ **A.** Port scanners only test for the availability of services; vulnerability scanners check for a particular version or patch level of a service.

○ **B.** Port scanners compile a listing of all hardware present within a network segment; vulnerability scanners check for the availability of services.

○ **C.** Vulnerability scanners only test for the availability of services; port scanners check for a particular version or patch level of a service.

○ **D.** Vulnerability scanners compile a listing of all hardware present within a network segment; port scanners test for the availability of services.

13. When using a password cracker to test mandatory complexity guidelines, which of the following should the password cracker provide?

Quick Answer: 229
Detailed Answer: 237

○ **A.** The password only

○ **B.** The password and hash value

○ **C.** The username and password

○ **D.** The strength of the password

14. An organization wants to select an assessment tool that will report information used to identify single points of failure. Which of the following should the organization choose?

Quick Answer: 229
Detailed Answer: 237

○ **A.** Port scanner

○ **B.** Network mapper

○ **C.** Protocol analyzer

○ **D.** Vulnerability scanner

15. Which of the following tools is often referred to as a packet sniffer?

Quick Answer: 229
Detailed Answer: 237

○ **A.** Port scanner

○ **B.** Network mapper

○ **C.** Protocol analyzer

○ **D.** Vulnerability scanner

Objective 4.3: Within the realm of vulnerability assessments, explain the proper use of penetration testing versus vulnerability scanning.

1. Which of the following is best described as a friendly attack against a network to test the security measures put into place?

   ○ **A.** Vulnerability assessment

   ○ **B.** Penetration test

   ○ **C.** Security assessment

   ○ **D.** Compliance test

Quick Answer: **229**
Detailed Answer: **237**

2. Which of the following are the most serious downsides to conducting a penetration test? (Select all correct answers.)

   ○ **A.** They can cause some disruption to network operations.

   ○ **B.** The help desk can be flooded by affected users.

   ○ **C.** They can generate false data in IDS systems.

   ○ **D.** External users can have difficulty accessing resources.

Quick Answer: **229**
Detailed Answer: **237**

3. Which of the following is true about inexperienced internal systems administrators performing penetration tests against the organizational network? (Select all correct answers.)

   ○ **A.** It is a safe practice.

   ○ **B.** It is a bad practice.

   ○ **C.** It may be a violation of privacy laws.

   ○ **D.** It does not violate any privacy laws.

Quick Answer: **229**
Detailed Answer: **238**

4. Which of the following is true about the relationship between vulnerability assessment and penetration testing?

   ○ **A.** They are inversely related.

   ○ **B.** They are contradictory.

   ○ **C.** They are separate functions.

   ○ **D.** They are complementary.

Quick Answer: **229**
Detailed Answer: **238**

5. Which of the following is the main security risk of penetration testing?

 ❍ **A.** It can conceal aggression that is unrelated to the test.

 ❍ **B.** It can affect user connectivity and resource access.

 ❍ **C.** It can disrupt the normal business environment.

 ❍ **D.** It can weaken the network's security level.

Quick Answer: **229**
Detailed Answer: **238**

Objective 4.4: Use monitoring tools on systems and networks and detect security-related anomalies.

1. Which of the following would most likely be used as a troubleshooting tool to tell whether a route is available to a host?

 ❍ **A.** tracert

 ❍ **B.** netstat

 ❍ **C.** nslookup

 ❍ **D.** ping

Quick Answer: **230**
Detailed Answer: **238**

2. Which of the following would most likely be used as a troubleshooting tool in a Windows environment to test the connectivity path a packet takes to arrive at the destination?

 ❍ **A.** tracert

 ❍ **B.** netstat

 ❍ **C.** nslookup

 ❍ **D.** ping

Quick Answer: **230**
Detailed Answer: **238**

3. Which of the following would most likely be used to troubleshoot a Domain Name System (DNS) server database?

 ❍ **A.** tracert

 ❍ **B.** netstat

 ❍ **C.** nslookup

 ❍ **D.** ping

Quick Answer: **230**
Detailed Answer: **238**

4. Which of the following would most likely be used to display all the ports on which the computer is currently listening?

 ❍ **A.** tracert

 ❍ **B.** netstat

 ❍ **C.** nslookup

 ❍ **D.** ping

Quick Answer: **230**
Detailed Answer: **239**

5. Which of the following is used in a Windows environment to verify the Transmission Control Protocol/Internet Protocol (TCP/IP) configuration?

- ○ **A.** traceroute
- ○ **B.** ipconfig
- ○ **C.** netstat
- ○ **D.** ifconfig

6. Which of the following is the most likely reason the ping command returns a time out when trying to contact an external host?

- ○ **A.** The host is unavailable.
- ○ **B.** DNS traffic is blocked.
- ○ **C.** The host network is unavailable.
- ○ **D.** ICMP traffic is blocked.

7. Which of the following best describes benchmarking?

- ○ **A.** A measuring of normal activity
- ○ **B.** The improving of system performance
- ○ **C.** Determining how much load a server can handle
- ○ **D.** Spreading work between two or more computers

8. Which of the following best describes a baseline?

- ○ **A.** A measure of normal activity
- ○ **B.** The improvement of system performance
- ○ **C.** A comparison of how much load a server can handle
- ○ **D.** The distribution of work between two or more computers

9. Which of the following protocols is used by the ping utility?

- ○ **A.** ICMP
- ○ **B.** SNMP
- ○ **C.** SMTP
- ○ **D.** NNTP

10. Which of the following is used for tracking and viewing the utilization of operating system resources?

- ○ **A.** Event Viewer
- ○ **B.** Performance console
- ○ **C.** Network Monitor
- ○ **D.** Task Manager

11. Which of the following is used for system monitoring by allowing an administrator to view actions that occur on the system?

Quick Answer: **230**
Detailed Answer: **240**

- ○ **A.** Event Viewer
- ○ **B.** Performance console
- ○ **C.** Network Monitor
- ○ **D.** Task Manager

12. Which of the following is Microsoft's version of a protocol analyzer that comes with Windows Server operating systems?

Quick Answer: **230**
Detailed Answer: **240**

- ○ **A.** Event Viewer
- ○ **B.** Performance console
- ○ **C.** Network Monitor
- ○ **D.** Task Manager

13. Which of the following gives you an instant history view of CPU and memory usage?

Quick Answer: **230**
Detailed Answer: **240**

- ○ **A.** Event Viewer
- ○ **B.** Performance console
- ○ **C.** Network Monitor
- ○ **D.** Task Manager

14. The network administrator for the organization attempts to access the security log in Event Viewer on the file server, but the log file does not contain any entries. Which of the following is the most likely reason the security log is missing?

Quick Answer: **230**
Detailed Answer: **240**

- ○ **A.** Logging is not enabled.
- ○ **B.** The security log is not shared.
- ○ **C.** Auditing is not enabled.
- ○ **D.** The security log is not stored on the server.

15. Which of the following is an application layer protocol used to collect statistics from TCP/IP devices?

Quick Answer: **230**
Detailed Answer: **240**

- ○ **A.** ICMP
- ○ **B.** SNMP
- ○ **C.** SMTP
- ○ **D.** NNTP

16. At which of the following levels should the operating system be monitored to detect rootkits?

- ○ **A.** Kernel
- ○ **B.** Network
- ○ **C.** Application
- ○ **D.** Shell

17. An organization is concerned about unauthorized users attempting to access network resources. Which of the following tools will the organization use to monitor user access activity?

- ○ **A.** Event Viewer
- ○ **B.** Performance console
- ○ **C.** Network Monitor
- ○ **D.** Task Manager

18. An organization is concerned about high I/O and CPU usage on the servers. Which of the following tools will the organization use to monitor resource activity?

- ○ **A.** Event Viewer
- ○ **B.** Performance console
- ○ **C.** Network Monitor
- ○ **D.** Task Manager

19. An organization is concerned about high memory and CPU usage on the local user machines. Which of the following tools will the organization use to spot check resource activity?

- ○ **A.** Event Viewer
- ○ **B.** Performance console
- ○ **C.** Network Monitor
- ○ **D.** Task Manager

20. An organization is having internal network connectivity issues and would like to implement a packet sniffer. Which of the following tools will the organization use to conduct this activity?

- ○ **A.** Event Viewer
- ○ **B.** Performance console
- ○ **C.** Network Monitor
- ○ **D.** Task Manager

21. Several users appear to be having internal network connectivity issues. The systems administrator is not exactly sure where the problem lies. Upon going to a workstation and opening a command prompt, which of the following commands would most likely be typed first?

○ **A.** tracert

○ **B.** netstat

○ **C.** nslookup

○ **D.** ipconfig

Quick Answer: **230**
Detailed Answer: **241**

22. The users appear to be having connectivity issues to a vendor's web hosted application. The systems administrator is not exactly sure where the problem lies. Upon going to a workstation and opening a command prompt, which of the following commands would most likely be typed first?

○ **A.** tracert

○ **B.** netstat

○ **C.** nslookup

○ **D.** ipconfig

Quick Answer: **230**
Detailed Answer: **241**

23. No one seems to be able to contact the intranet using DNS names but the intranet can be contacted by using the IP address. After opening a command prompt, which of the following commands would most likely be typed first?

○ **A.** tracert

○ **B.** netstat

○ **C.** nslookup

○ **D.** ipconfig

Quick Answer: **230**
Detailed Answer: **241**

24. A user reports slowness and intermittent odd activity on their workstation. After opening a command prompt, which of the following commands would most likely be typed first?

○ **A.** tracert

○ **B.** netstat

○ **C.** nslookup

○ **D.** ipconfig

Quick Answer: **230**
Detailed Answer: **241**

25. Which of the following is true about baselines? (Select all correct answers.)

- ○ **A.** An initial baseline should be done for the network but not applications.
- ○ **B.** Baselines must be updated on a regular basis.
- ○ **C.** Baselines do not need to be updated when new technology is added.
- ○ **D.** Baselines must be updated when the network has changed.

Quick Answer: **230**
Detailed Answer: **242**

Objective 4.5: Compare and contrast various types of monitoring methodologies.

1. Which of the following best describes behavior-based monitoring?

- ○ **A.** Looks at patterns of access that have been established
- ○ **B.** Looks at the way certain executable files make a computer act
- ○ **C.** Looks for specific byte sequences that appear in attack traffic
- ○ **D.** Looks for traffic behavior that is new or unusual

Quick Answer: **230**
Detailed Answer: **242**

2. Which of the following best describes anomaly-based monitoring?

- ○ **A.** Looks at patterns of access that have been established
- ○ **B.** Looks at the way certain executable files make a computer act
- ○ **C.** Looks for specific byte sequences that appear in attack traffic
- ○ **D.** Looks for traffic behavior that is new or unusual

Quick Answer: **230**
Detailed Answer: **242**

3. Which of the following best describes signature-based monitoring?

- ○ **A.** Looks at patterns of access that have been established
- ○ **B.** Looks at the way certain executable files make a computer act
- ○ **C.** Looks for specific byte sequences that appear in attack traffic
- ○ **D.** Looks for traffic behavior that is new or unusual principal

Quick Answer: **230**
Detailed Answer: **242**

4. An organization is concerned about buffer overflow attacks. Which of the following monitoring methods will best suit the organization?

Quick Answer: **230**
Detailed Answer: **242**

- ○ **A.** Signature-based monitoring
- ○ **B.** Anomaly-based monitoring
- ○ **C.** Performance-based monitoring
- ○ **D.** Behavior-based monitoring

5. An organization is concerned about internal misuse. Which of the following monitoring methods will best suit the organization?

Quick Answer: **230**
Detailed Answer: **243**

- ○ **A.** Signature-based monitoring
- ○ **B.** Anomaly-based monitoring
- ○ **C.** Performance-based monitoring
- ○ **D.** Behavior-based monitoring

6. An organization is concerned about system compromises from older known attacks on unpatched systems. Which of the following monitoring methods will best suit the organization?

Quick Answer: **230**
Detailed Answer: **243**

- ○ **A.** Signature-based monitoring
- ○ **B.** Anomaly-based monitoring
- ○ **C.** Performance-based monitoring
- ○ **D.** Behavior-based monitoring

7. An organization wants to implement a monitoring solution that returns few false positives and does not use a lot of system resources. Which of the following monitoring methods will best suit the organization?

Quick Answer: **230**
Detailed Answer: **243**

- ○ **A.** Signature-based monitoring
- ○ **B.** Anomaly-based monitoring
- ○ **C.** Performance-based monitoring
- ○ **D.** Behavior-based monitoring up

8. An organization wants to implement a monitoring solution that can be used in a mixed operating system environment and not dependent on OS-specific mechanisms. Which of the following monitoring methods will best suit the organization?

Quick Answer: **230**
Detailed Answer: **243**

- ○ **A.** Signature-based monitoring
- ○ **B.** Anomaly-based monitoring
- ○ **C.** Performance-based monitoring
- ○ **D.** Behavior-based monitoring

9. An organization wants to implement a monitoring solution that includes video surveillance. Which of the following monitoring methods will best suit the organization?

- ○ **A.** Signature-based monitoring
- ○ **B.** Anomaly-based monitoring
- ○ **C.** Performance-based monitoring
- ○ **D.** Behavior-based monitoring

Quick Answer: **230**
Detailed Answer: **243**

10. An organization wants to implement a monitoring solution that does not require a lot of software updating and can be self-learning. Which of the following monitoring methods will best suit the organization?

- ○ **A.** Signature-based monitoring
- ○ **B.** Anomaly-based monitoring
- ○ **C.** Performance-based monitoring
- ○ **D.** Behavior-based monitoring

Quick Answer: **230**
Detailed Answer: **244**

11. An organization wants to implement a monitoring solution that returns a low number of false positives. Which of the following monitoring methods will best suit the organization?

- ○ **A.** Signature-based monitoring
- ○ **B.** Anomaly-based monitoring
- ○ **C.** Performance-based monitoring
- ○ **D.** Behavior-based monitoring

Quick Answer: **230**
Detailed Answer: **244**

12. An organization that issues credit cards requires spending profiles for their customers. Which of the following monitoring methods will best suit the organization?

- ○ **A.** Signature-based monitoring
- ○ **B.** Anomaly-based monitoring
- ○ **C.** Performance-based monitoring
- ○ **D.** Behavior-based monitoring

Quick Answer: **230**
Detailed Answer: **244**

13. An organization requires a monitoring solution that determines if program is malicious by inspecting the stream of system calls that the program issues to the operating system. Which of the following monitoring method will best suit the organization?

- ○ **A.** Signature-based monitoring
- ○ **B.** Anomaly-based monitoring
- ○ **C.** Performance-based monitoring
- ○ **D.** Behavior-based monitoring

Quick Answer: **230**
Detailed Answer: **244**

14. Which of the following are disadvantages of using a behavior-based monitoring solution? (Select all correct answers.)

Quick Answer: **230**
Detailed Answer: **244**

- ○ **A.** The rule sets need constant updating.
- ○ **B.** It can generate false positives.
- ○ **C.** File checking is quite slow.
- ○ **D.** It is based on passive monitoring.

15. Which of the following are disadvantages of using a signature-based monitoring solution? (Select all correct answers.)

Quick Answer: **230**
Detailed Answer: **244**

- ○ **A.** The rule sets need constant updating.
- ○ **B.** It can generate false positives.
- ○ **C.** File checking is quite slow.
- ○ **D.** It is based on passive monitoring.

16. Which of the following are advantages of using a behavior-based monitoring solution? (Select all correct answers.)

Quick Answer: **230**
Detailed Answer: **245**

- ○ **A.** Can monitor for malware activities
- ○ **B.** Triggers a low number of false positives
- ○ **C.** Can identify polymorphic viruses
- ○ **D.** Uses very few system resources

17. Which of the following are advantages of using a signature-based monitoring solution? (Select all correct answers.)

Quick Answer: **230**
Detailed Answer: **245**

- ○ **A.** Can monitor for malware activities
- ○ **B.** Triggers a low number of false positives
- ○ **C.** Can identify polymorphic viruses
- ○ **D.** Uses very few system resources

18. An organization requires a monitoring solution for a highly secure environment in which the individual use patterns for each user profile can be identified. Which of the following monitoring method will best suit the organization?

Quick Answer: **230**
Detailed Answer: **245**

- ○ **A.** Signature-based monitoring
- ○ **B.** Anomaly-based monitoring
- ○ **C.** Performance-based monitoring
- ○ **D.** Behavior-based monitoring

19. Which of the following types of attacks are anomaly-based monitoring solutions best at detecting? (Select all correct answers.)

  ○ **A.** DoS attacks based on payloads

  ○ **B.** Protocol and port exploitation

  ○ **C.** Documented malicious software

  ○ **D.** Known intrusive activity

Quick Answer: **230**
Detailed Answer: **245**

20. Which of the following types of attacks are signature-based monitoring solutions best at detecting? (Select all correct answers.)

  ○ **A.** DoS attacks based on payloads or volume

  ○ **B.** Protocol and port exploitation

  ○ **C.** Documented malicious software

  ○ **D.** Known intrusive activity

Quick Answer: **230**
Detailed Answer: **245**

Objective 4.6: Execute proper logging procedures and evaluate the results.

1. Which of the following best describes system logging?

  ○ **A.** The process of measuring the performance of a network

  ○ **B.** The process of collecting data to be used for monitoring

  ○ **C.** The process of tracking users and actions on the network

  ○ **D.** The process of observing of the state of a system

Quick Answer: **230**
Detailed Answer: **245**

2. To get an accurate view of a network, which of the following must precede logging?

  ○ **A.** Baselining

  ○ **B.** Auditing

  ○ **C.** Monitoring

  ○ **D.** Archiving

Quick Answer: **230**
Detailed Answer: **245**

3. Which of the following best describes the way logging should be implemented?

Quick Answer: **230**
Detailed Answer: **245**

- ○ **A.** Only the user events should be logged.
- ○ **B.** Only pertinent events should be logged.
- ○ **C.** All events should be logged so nothing is missed.
- ○ **D.** Nothing should be logged until there is a need for it.

4. Which of the following would be considered a best practice for improved server performance when deciding where to store log files?

Quick Answer: **230**
Detailed Answer: **246**

- ○ **A.** Store in the system directory of a machine in the DMZ
- ○ **B.** Store in the system directory on the local machine
- ○ **C.** Store on a nonsystem striped or mirrored disk volume
- ○ **D.** Store on a nonsystem disk volume on the local machine

5. Which of the following would be considered a best security practice when deciding where to store log files?

Quick Answer: **230**
Detailed Answer: **246**

- ○ **A.** Stored in the system directory on the local machine
- ○ **B.** Stored in a data directory on a server in the Intranet
- ○ **C.** Stored in the system directory of a machine in the DMZ
- ○ **D.** Stored in a centralized repository of an offline volume

6. An organization requires the implementation of an enterprise application logging strategy. Which of the following would be a critical analysis consideration when choosing a solution?

Quick Answer: **230**
Detailed Answer: **246**

- ○ **A.** A proprietary custom-built solution
- ○ **B.** Already built-in application logging solutions
- ○ **C.** A solution that uses standard protocols and formats
- ○ **D.** A variety of solutions that each use different formats

7. An organization chooses to implement a manual application logging strategy and desires to use a format that can readily be parsed. Which of the following formats will meet the organizational requirements?

Quick Answer: **230**
Detailed Answer: **246**

- ○ **A.** CSV
- ○ **B.** HTML
- ○ **C.** TXT
- ○ **D.** SQL

8. Application logging standards should be implemented for the types of events the organization logs based on which of the following? (Select all correct answers.)

    ○ **A.** User requirements

    ○ **B.** Vendor requirements

    ○ **C.** Business requirements

    ○ **D.** Regulatory requirements

Quick Answer: **230**
Detailed Answer: **246**

9. Which of the following is pertinent in addition to reading the log files?

    ○ **A.** Knowing how to correlate events

    ○ **B.** Knowing how to parse log files

    ○ **C.** Knowing how to delete events

    ○ **D.** Knowing how to export log files

Quick Answer: **230**
Detailed Answer: **246**

10. Internet Information Services (IIS) logs can be used for which of the following purposes? (Select all correct answers.)

    ○ **A.** Assess content

    ○ **B.** Identify bottlenecks

    ○ **C.** End processes

    ○ **D.** Investigate attacks

Quick Answer: **230**
Detailed Answer: **246**

11. Which of the following most accurately describes best practice for using Microsoft DNS logging?

    ○ **A.** Only the user events should be logged.

    ○ **B.** Only pertinent events should be logged.

    ○ **C.** All events should be logged so nothing is missed.

    ○ **D.** Nothing should be logged until there is a need for it.

Quick Answer: **230**
Detailed Answer: **246**

12. Which of the following would be the first place an administrator would look when troubleshooting Microsoft DNS-related issues?

    ○ **A.** The DNS debug log file

    ○ **B.** The Event Viewer DNS server log file

    ○ **C.** Syslog channel log.msgs

    ○ **D.** The Event Viewer Application log file

Quick Answer: **230**
Detailed Answer: **246**

13. Which of the following would be the first place an administrator would look when troubleshooting UNIX- or Linux-based systems?

- ○ **A.** Mtools.conf
- ○ **B.** Msconfig
- ○ **C.** Event Viewer
- ○ **D.** Syslogd

14. Which of the following would be considered best practices for system logging? (Select all correct answers.)

- ○ **A.** For easy compilation, keep log files in plain text.
- ○ **B.** When permissible, encrypt the log files.
- ○ **C.** Store log files on a stand-alone system.
- ○ **D.** Store log files on individual system data partitions.

15. Which of the following would an administrator use to end applications that get hung up without having to reboot the machine?

- ○ **A.** Network Monitor
- ○ **B.** Task Manager
- ○ **C.** Event Viewer
- ○ **D.** Performance Console

16. Which of the following would provide information for troubleshooting remote-access policy issues?

- ○ **A.** Internet Information Services logging
- ○ **B.** Critical and error level logging
- ○ **C.** Authentication and accounting logging
- ○ **D.** Event Viewer Application logging

17. Which of the following are events in the firewall log that require additional examination? (Select all correct answers.)

- ○ **A.** Traffic on port 25
- ○ **B.** HTTP traffic
- ○ **C.** Blocked attempts
- ○ **D.** Suspicious signatures

18. The organizational firewall log shows repeated traffic to port 53. This could be an indication of which of the following types of attacks? (Select all correct answers.)

    ○ **A.** Cross-site scripting

    ○ **B.** Denial of service

    ○ **C.** Distributed denial of service

    ○ **D.** SQL injection

19. Which of the following types of logging events are most commonly found in antivirus software? (Select all correct answers.)

    ○ **A.** Updates

    ○ **B.** Dropped packets

    ○ **C.** Quarantined viruses

    ○ **D.** Update history

20. An organization primarily contracts workers and is concerned about remote-access usage and remote authentication attempts. Which of the following would the organization implement to track this type of activity?

    ○ **A.** Firewall logging

    ○ **B.** RRAS logging

    ○ **C.** IIS logging

    ○ **D.** System logging

Objective 4.7: Conduct periodic audits of system security settings.

1. Which of the following best describes auditing?

    ○ **A.** The process of measuring the performance of a network

    ○ **B.** The process of collecting data to be used for monitoring

    ○ **C.** The process of tracking users and actions on the network

    ○ **D.** The process of observing the state of a system

224   Chapter 4

2. Which of the following are unintended consequences when auditing is not clear-cut or built around the organizational goals and policies? (Select all correct answers.)

   ○ **A.** Irrelevant information is gathered.

   ○ **B.** Important security events are deleted.

   ○ **C.** User hard drives quickly run out of space.

   ○ **D.** System administrators have reduced workloads.

Quick Answer: **231**
Detailed Answer: **248**

3. A systems administrator is tasked with auditing user privileges. Which of the following steps must be taken? (Select two correct answers.)

   ○ **A.** Enable logging within the operating system.

   ○ **B.** Enable auditing within the operating system.

   ○ **C.** Specify the resources to be audited.

   ○ **D.** Specify the audit file storage directory.

Quick Answer: **231**
Detailed Answer: **248**

4. An organization has primarily contract workers and is concerned about unauthorized and unintentional access on these accounts. Which of the following would the organization audit to track this type of activity?

   ○ **A.** Group policies

   ○ **B.** Retention polices

   ○ **C.** DHCP events and changes

   ○ **D.** Access use and rights changes

Quick Answer: **231**
Detailed Answer: **248**

5. Which of the following are user rights used by processes? (Select all correct answers.)

   ○ **A.** Process tracking

   ○ **B.** Create a token object

   ○ **C.** Bypass traverse checking

   ○ **D.** Account management

Quick Answer: **231**
Detailed Answer: **248**

6. Which of the following is true about the auditing of failed logon events and successful login events?

   ○ **A.** Only failed events should be audited.

   ○ **B.** Only successful events should be audited.

   ○ **C.** Both successful and failed events should be audited.

   ○ **D.** Neither one should be audited unless absolutely necessary.

Quick Answer: **231**
Detailed Answer: **248**

7. Which of the following best describes the activity that involves collecting information used for monitoring and reviewing purposes?

- ○ **A.** Auditing
- ○ **B.** Logging
- ○ **C.** Baselining
- ○ **D.** Inspecting

8. Which of the following best describes the unintended consequence of turning on all auditing counters for all objects?

- ○ **A.** Reduced user productivity
- ○ **B.** Reduced I/O activity on user machines
- ○ **C.** Reduced administrative overhead
- ○ **D.** Reduced server performance

9. Which of the following would an organization include in its retention and disposal policies? (Select all correct answers.)

- ○ **A.** Security evaluations
- ○ **B.** Commercial software manuals
- ○ **C.** Operational documentation
- ○ **D.** Vendor user manuals

10. Which of the following most accurately describes the maintenance of data-retention and storage polices?

- ○ **A.** Once in place, they are good for many years.
- ○ **B.** They need to be updated on a monthly basis.
- ○ **C.** They need to be updated on a quarterly basis.
- ○ **D.** They need to be updated when business goals change.

11. An organization does not have a data-retention policy in place when it becomes involved in a lawsuit. Many of the employees have kept emails for a period of up to ten years. As a general rule, which of the following is true about the discovery of these emails?

- ○ **A.** All are discoverable regardless of time frame or format.
- ○ **B.** None are discoverable because they are electronic format.
- ○ **C.** They are discoverable only going back three years.
- ○ **D.** Only the emails the organization deems necessary are discoverable.

Quick Check

12. Which of the following are pertinent for an organization to review before formulating data-retention policy? (Select all correct answers.)

    ○ **A.** ISP requirements

    ○ **B.** Regulatory requirements

    ○ **C.** User requirements

    ○ **D.** Business requirements

Quick Answer: **231**
Detailed Answer: **249**

13. Which of the following best describes how settings will actually be applied to an object in a group policy?

    ○ **A.** Individually applied to the object and only from the last policy

    ○ **B.** A combination of all the settings that can affect the object

    ○ **C.** Only from settings within the domain where the object is located

    ○ **D.** A combination of only local group polices that affect the object

Quick Answer: **231**
Detailed Answer: **249**

14. An administrator is attempting to resolve some issue with multiple group policies on several computers. Which of the following tools would be used to script GPO troubleshooting of multiple computers?

    ○ **A.** Gpupdate

    ○ **B.** Gpresult

    ○ **C.** Resultant Set of Policy

    ○ **D.** Group Policy object

Quick Answer: **231**
Detailed Answer: **249**

15. Which of the following tools is used to review the effects of Group Policy settings on a particular computer?

    ○ **A.** Resultant Set of Policy

    ○ **B.** Group Policy object

    ○ **C.** Gpupdate

    ○ **D.** Local Security settings

Quick Answer: **231**
Detailed Answer: **249**

16. An organization is concerned with knowing about any unusual activity that would indicate modification to the local security authority (LSA). Which of the following event categories should be audited?

   ○ **A.** Audit success events in the account management

   ○ **B.** Success events in the policy change on domain controllers

   ○ **C.** Success and failure events in the system events

   ○ **D.** Audit success events in the logon event category

Quick Answer: **231**
Detailed Answer: **250**

17. An organization is concerned with unusual activity indicating that an intruder is attempting to gain access to the network. Which of the following event categories should be audited?

   ○ **A.** Audit success events in the account management

   ○ **B.** Success events in the policy change on domain controllers

   ○ **C.** Success and failure events in the system events

   ○ **D.** Audit success events in the logon event category

Quick Answer: **231**
Detailed Answer: **250**

18. An organization wants to verify changes that are made to user account and group properties. Which of the following event categories should be audited?

   ○ **A.** Audit success events in the account management

   ○ **B.** Success events in the policy change on domain controllers

   ○ **C.** Success and failure events in the system events

   ○ **D.** Audit success events in the logon event category

Quick Answer: **231**
Detailed Answer: **250**

19. An organization wants a record of when each user logs on to or logs off from any computer. Which of the following event categories should be audited?

   ○ **A.** Audit success events in the account management event

   ○ **B.** Success events in the policy change on domain controllers

   ○ **C.** Success and failure events in the system events

   ○ **D.** Audit success events in the logon event category

Quick Answer: **231**
Detailed Answer: **250**

20. An organization wants to verify when users log on to or log off
    from the domain. Which of the following event categories should
    be audited?

Quick Answer: 231
Detailed Answer: 250

- ○ **A.** Audit success events in the account management
       event
- ○ **B.** Success events in the policy change on domain con-
       trollers
- ○ **C.** Success events in the account logon on domain con-
       trollers
- ○ **D.** Audit success events in the logon event category

Quick-Check Answer Key

Objective 4.1: Conduct risk assessments and implement risk mitigation.

1. C	**6.** D	**11.** C
2. B	**7.** A	**12.** A, B, D
3. C	**8.** B	**13.** D
4. D	**9.** A	**14.** B
5. A	**10.** C	**15.** C

Objective 4.2: Carry out vulnerability assessments using common tools.

1. A	**6.** A	**11.** C
2. D	**7.** A	**12.** A
3. C	**8.** C	**13.** D
4. B	**9.** D	**14.** B
5. D	**10.** B	**15.** C

Objective 4.3: Within the realm of vulnerability assessments, explain the proper use of penetration testing versus vulnerability scanning.

1. B	**4.** D
2. A, C	**5.** A
3. B, C	

Objective 4.4: Use monitoring tools on systems and networks and detect security-related anomalies.

1. D	10. B	19. D
2. A	11. A	20. C
3. C	12. C	21. D
4. B	13. D	22. A
5. B	14. C	23. C
6. D	15. B	24. B
7. C	16. A	25. B, D
8. A	17. A	
9. A	18. B	

Objective 4.5: Compare and contrast various types of monitoring methodologies.

1. B	8. D	15. A, D
2. D	9. B	16. A, C
3. C	10. B	17. B, D
4. B	11. A	18. B
5. D	12. B	19. A, B
6. A	13. D	20. C, D
7. A	14. B, C	

Objective 4.6: Execute proper logging procedures and evaluate the results.

1. B	8. C, D	15. B
2. A	9. A	16. C
3. B	10. A, B, D	17. C, D
4. C	11. D	18. B, C
5. D	12. B	19. A, C, D
6. C	13. D	20. B
7. A	14. B, C	

Objective 4.7: Conduct periodic audits of system security settings.

1. C	**8.** D	**15.** A
2. A, B	**9.** A, C	**16.** B
3. C	**10.** D	**17.** C
4. D	**11.** A	**18.** A
5. B, C	**12.** B, D	**19.** D
6. C	**13.** B	**20.** C
7. B	**14.** B	

Answers and Explanations

Objective 4.1 Conduct risk assessments and implement risk mitigation.

1. **Answer: C.** Metrics for security baselines and hardening efforts rely on identification of vulnerability and risk. It is necessary to have some mechanism for measuring vulnerability to determine whether a baseline has been met, or if a new security measure has been effective. Answer A is incorrect because mitigation of threats and attacks are not related to metrics. Answer B is incorrect because security policies are not related to metrics. Answer D is incorrect; mitigation of vulnerability and risk is not related to metrics.

2. **Answer: B.** A risk, once identified, can be dealt with in several ways. A risk may be transferred, such as when the risk of equipment loss is covered by a full-replacement insurance policy. Answer A is incorrect because some risks cannot be addressed within a reasonable time or cost constrained and may be accepted, with proper documentation as to the reasons why the risk is acceptable. Answer C is incorrect because some risks can be eliminated through a change in the technology, policy, or mechanism of employment. For example, the risk of "war-dialing" attacks can be eliminated by removing legacy dial-up telephony modem devices. Answer D is incorrect; most risks fall into the mitigated response area, where the application of additional effort may reduce the risk to a level documented as acceptable.

3. **Answer: C.** A risk, once identified, can be dealt with in several ways. Some risks can be eliminated through a change in the technology, policy, or mechanism of employment. For example, the risk of "war-dialing" attacks can be eliminated by removing legacy dial-up telephony modem devices. Answer A is incorrect because some risks cannot be addressed within a reasonable time or cost constrained and may be accepted, with proper documentation as to the reasons why the risk is acceptable. Answer B is incorrect; a risk may be transferred, such as when the risk of equipment loss is covered by a full-replacement insurance policy. Answer D is incorrect; most risks fall into the mitigated response area, where the application of additional effort may reduce the risk to a level documented as acceptable.

4. **Answer: D.** A risk, once identified, can be dealt with in several ways. Most risks fall into the mitigated response area, where the application of additional effort may reduce the risk to a level documented as acceptable. Answer A is incorrect because some risks cannot be addressed within a reasonable time or cost constrained and may be accepted, with proper documentation as to the reasons why the risk is acceptable. Answer B is incorrect; a risk may be transferred, such as when the risk of equipment loss is covered by a full-replacement insurance policy. Answer C is incorrect because some risks can be eliminated through a change in the technology, policy, or mechanism of employment. For example, the risk of "war-dialing" attacks can be eliminated by removing legacy dial-up telephony modem devices.

5. **Answer: A.** A risk, once identified, can be dealt with in several ways. Some risks cannot be addressed within a reasonable time or cost constrained and may be accepted,

with proper documentation as to the reasons why the risk is acceptable. Answer B is incorrect; a risk may be transferred, such as when the risk of equipment loss is covered by a full-replacement insurance policy. Answer C is incorrect because some risks can be eliminated through a change in the technology, policy, or mechanism of employment. For example, the risk of "war-dialing" attacks can be eliminated by removing legacy dial-up telephony modem devices. Answer D is incorrect; most risks fall into the mitigated response area, where the application of additional effort may reduce the risk to a level documented as acceptable.

6. **Answer: D.** Before any baseline can be established, beyond those developed by regulatory bodies outside of the business entity, a risk assessment must be conducted to identify existing risks and potential mitigation mechanisms. Answer A is incorrect. This is not a good policy and is not included is a risk assessment. Answer B is incorrect; it describes a vulnerability assessment. Answer C is incorrect; personally identifiable information may be part of the risk assessment, but is it not the main purpose.

7. **Answer: A.** Annual loss expectancy (ALE) equals the single loss expectancy (SLE) times the annualized rate of occurrence (ARO): SLE × ARO = ALE. Based on the previous formula, answers B, C, and D are incorrect.

8. **Answer: B.** SLE equals asset value multiplied by the threat exposure factor or probability. Answer A is incorrect because it describes return on investment (ROI). Answer C is incorrect because it describes risk. Answer D is incorrect because it describes annualized rate of occurrence. The ARO is the estimated possibility of specific threat taking place in a one-year time frame.

9. **Answer: A.** Risk management is the process of identifying and reducing risk to a level that is comfortable, and then implementing controls to maintain that level. Answer B is incorrect because some risks cannot be addressed within a reasonable time or cost constrained and may be accepted, with proper documentation as to the reasons why the risk is acceptable. Answer C is incorrect because risk analysis helps align security objectives with business objectives. Answer D is incorrect; a risk may be transferred, such as when the risk of equipment loss is covered by a full-replacement insurance policy because risk is the possibility of loss or danger.

10. **Answer: C.** Risk analysis helps align security objectives with business objectives. Risk analysis identifies risks, estimates the impact of potential threats, and identifies ways to reduce the risk without the cost of the prevention outweighing the risk. Answer A is incorrect. Risk management is the process of identifying and reducing risk to a level that is comfortable, and then implementing controls to maintain that level. Answer B is incorrect because some risks cannot be addressed within a reasonable time or cost constrained and may be accepted, with proper documentation as to the reasons why the risk is acceptable. Answer D is incorrect; a risk may be transferred, such as when the risk of equipment loss is covered by a full-replacement insurance policy because risk is the possibility of loss or danger.

11. **Answer: C.** Risk is the possibility of loss or danger. Answer A is incorrect because the exposure factor or probability is the percentage of loss that a realized threat could have on a certain asset. Answer B is incorrect; the cumulative loss expectancy (CLE) is a risk model that calculates risk based on single systems. Answer D is incorrect because mitigation comes after risk is identified and assessed.

12. **Answer: A, B, D.** During the process of risk assessment, it is necessary to review many areas, such as the following: methods of access, authentication schemes, audit policies, hiring and release procedures, isolated services that may provide a single point of failure or avenue of compromise and data or services requiring special backup or automatic failover support. Answer C is incorrect. Financial records review is not a necessary part of risk assessment, but how well that data is protected may be.

13. **Answer: D.** Return on investment is the ratio of money realized or unrealized on an investment relative to the amount of money invested. Answer A is incorrect because it describes risk analysis. Answer B is incorrect because it describes risk management. Answer C is incorrect because it describes return on capital.

14. **Answer: B.** Return in investment is equal to the loss prevented minus the cost of solution. If the result of this formula is a negative number, you spent more than the loss prevented. Therefore, answer A is incorrect. Answers C and D are incorrect because depending on what the investment is, it may or may not be a good investment and might be necessary due to regulations.

15. **Answer: C.** The exposure factor or probability is the percentage of loss that a realized threat could have on a certain asset. Answer A is incorrect because it describes vulnerability. Answer B is incorrect because it describes reduced risk on investment. Answer D is incorrect because it describes annual rate of occurrence.

Objective 4.2: Carry out vulnerability assessments using common tools.

1. **Answer: A.** A port-scanning software utility will scan a single machine or a range of IP addresses, checking for a response on service ports. Answer B is incorrect. A network mapper is a software utility used to conduct network assessments over a range of IP addresses. The network mapper compiles a listing of all systems, devices, and network hardware present within a network segment. Answer C is incorrect because a protocol analyzer is a software utility is used on a hub, a switch supervisory port, or in line with network connectivity to allow the analysis of network communications. Answer D is incorrect. A vulnerability scanner is a software utility that will scan a range of IP addresses, testing for the presence of known vulnerabilities in software configuration and accessible services.

2. **Answer: D.** A vulnerability scanner is a software utility that will scan a range of IP addresses, testing for the presence of known vulnerabilities in software configuration and accessible services. Answer A is incorrect. A port-scanning software utility will scan a single machine or a range of IP addresses, checking for a response on service ports. Answer B is incorrect. A network mapper is a software utility used to conduct network assessments over a range of IP addresses. The network mapper compiles a listing of all systems, devices, and network hardware present within a network segment. Answer C is incorrect because a protocol analyzer is a software utility is used on a hub, a switch supervisory port, or in line with network connectivity to allow the analysis of network communications.

3. **Answer: C.** A protocol analyzer is a software utility is used on a hub, a switch supervisory port, or in line with network connectivity to allow the analysis of network communications. Answer A is incorrect. A port-scanning software utility will scan a single machine or a range of IP addresses, checking for a response on service ports. Answer B is incorrect. A network mapper is a software utility used to conduct network assessments over a range of IP addresses. The network mapper compiles a listing of all systems, devices, and network hardware present within a network segment. Answer D is incorrect. A vulnerability scanner is a software utility that will scan a range of IP addresses, testing for the present of known vulnerabilities in software configuration and accessible services.

4. **Answer: B.** A network mapper is a software utility used to conduct network assessments over a range of IP addresses. The network mapper compiles a listing of all systems, devices, and network hardware present within a network segment. Answer A is incorrect. A port-scanning software utility will scan a single machine or a range of IP addresses, checking for a response on service ports. Answer C is incorrect because a protocol analyzer is a software utility is used on a hub, a switch supervisory port, or in line with network connectivity to allow the analysis of network communications. Answer D is incorrect. A vulnerability scanner is a software utility that will scan a range of IP addresses testing for the present of known vulnerabilities in software configuration and accessible services.

5. **Answer: D.** Open Vulnerability Assessment Language (OVAL) is intended as an international language for representing vulnerability information using an XML schema for expression, allowing tools to be developed to test for identified vulnerabilities in the OVAL repository. Answer A is incorrect because it describes the Open Systems Interconnection reference model (OSI model). Answer B is incorrect because it describes IEEE 802 standards. Answer C is incorrect because it describes the International Organization for Standardization (ISO).

6. **Answer: A.** Within U.S. Governmental agencies, vulnerability may be discussed using the Open Vulnerability Assessment Language (OVAL) sponsored by the Department of Homeland Security's National Cyber Security Division (NCSD). Answer B is incorrect because IEEE refers to a family of IEEE standards dealing with local area networks and metropolitan area networks. Answer C is incorrect because the International Organization for Standardization, widely known as ISO, is an international-standard-setting body composed of representatives from various national standards organizations. Answer D is incorrect because the Information Systems Security Association is a security-focused group.

7. **Answer: A.** A port-scanning software utility will scan a single machine or a range of IP addresses, checking for a response on service ports. Port scanners are useful in creating an inventory of services hosted on networked systems. Answer B is incorrect. A network mapper is a software utility used to conduct network assessments over a range of IP addresses. The network mapper compiles a listing of all systems, devices, and network hardware present within a network segment. Answer C is incorrect because a protocol analyzer is a software utility is used on a hub, a switch supervisory port, or in line with network connectivity to allow the analysis of network communications. Answer D is incorrect. A vulnerability scanner is a software utility that will scan a range of IP addresses, testing for the present of known vulnerabilities in software configuration and accessible services.

8. **Answer: C.** A protocol analyzer is a software utility is used on a hub, a switch supervisory port, or in line with network connectivity to allow the analysis of network communications. Individual protocols, specific endpoints, or sequential access attempts may be identified using this utility, which is often referred to as a packet sniffer. Answer A is incorrect. A port-scanning software utility will scan a single machine or a range of IP addresses, checking for a response on service ports. Answer B is incorrect. A network mapper is a software utility used to conduct network assessments over a range of IP addresses. The network mapper compiles a listing of all systems, devices, and network hardware present within a network segment. Answer D is incorrect. A vulnerability scanner is a software utility that will scan a range of IP addresses, testing for the present of known vulnerabilities in software configuration and accessible services.

9. **Answer: D.** A vulnerability scanner is a software utility that will scan a range of IP addresses, testing for the present of known vulnerabilities in software configuration and accessible services. Unlike port scanners, which only test for the availability of services, vulnerability scanners may check for the particular version or patch level of a service to determine its level of vulnerability. Answer A is incorrect. A port-scanning software utility will scan a single machine or a range of IP addresses, checking for a response on service ports. Answer B is incorrect. A network mapper is a software utility used to conduct network assessments over a range of IP addresses. The network mapper compiles a listing of all systems, devices, and network hardware present within a network segment. Answer C is incorrect because a protocol analyzer is a software utility is used on a hub, a switch supervisory port, or in line with network connectivity to allow the analysis of network communications.

10. **Answer: B.** A network mapper is a software utility used to conduct network assessments over a range of IP addresses. The network mapper compiles a listing of all systems, devices, and network hardware present within a network segment. Answer A is incorrect. A port-scanning software utility will scan a single machine or a range of IP addresses, checking for a response on service ports. Answer C is incorrect because a protocol analyzer is a software utility is used on a hub, a switch supervisory port, or in line with network connectivity to allow the analysis of network communications. Answer D is incorrect. A vulnerability scanner is a software utility that will scan a range of IP addresses, testing for the present of known vulnerabilities in software configuration and accessible services.

11. **Answer: C.** A password cracker is a software utility that allows direct testing of user logon password strength by conducting a brute-force password test using dictionary terms, specialized lexicons, or mandatory complexity guidelines. Answer A is incorrect. Password Locker is a commercial program that lets you save passwords, recover passwords, and manage and form-fill all your usernames and passwords. Answer B is incorrect because a password generator creates random passwords. Answer D is incorrect. A password keychain, most commonly found on Apple computers, keeps track of your passwords for any type of account.

12. **Answer: A.** Unlike port scanners, which only test for the availability of services, vulnerability scanners may check for the particular version or patch level of a service to determine its level of vulnerability. Answers B, C, and D are incorrect because they do not accurately describe port scanners or vulnerability scanners.

13. **Answer: D.** Password crackers should provide only the relative strength of a password, rather than the password itself, to avoid weakening logon responsibility under evidentiary discovery actions. Answers A, B, and C are incorrect because password crackers should not provide the password itself to avoid disclosure under e-discovery proceedings.

14. **Answer: B.** The network mapper compiles a listing of all systems, devices, and network hardware present within a network segment. This information can be used to identify single points of failure, conduct a network inventory, and create graphical details suitable for reporting on network configurations. Answer A is incorrect. A port-scanning software utility will scan a single machine or a range of IP addresses, checking for a response on service ports. Answer C is incorrect because a protocol analyzer is a software utility is used on a hub, a switch supervisory port, or in line with network connectivity to allow the analysis of network communications. Answer D is incorrect. A vulnerability scanner is a software utility that will scan a range of IP addresses, testing for the present of known vulnerabilities in software configuration and accessible services.

15. **Answer: C.** A protocol analyzer is a software utility is used on a hub, a switch supervisory port, or in line with network connectivity to allow the analysis of network communications. Individual protocols, specific endpoints, or sequential access attempts may be identified using this utility, which is often referred to as a packet sniffer. Answer A is incorrect. A port-scanning software utility will scan a single machine or a range of IP addresses, checking for a response on service ports. Answer B is incorrect. A network mapper is a software utility used to conduct network assessments over a range of IP addresses. The network mapper compiles a listing of all systems, devices, and network hardware present within a network segment. Answer D is incorrect. A vulnerability scanner is a software utility that will scan a range of IP addresses, testing for the present of known vulnerabilities in software configuration and accessible services.

Objective 4.3: Within the realm of vulnerability assessments, explain the proper use of penetration testing versus vulnerability scanning.

1. **Answer: B.** Friendly attacks against a network to test the security measures put into place. Such attacks are referred to as penetration tests or simply "pen tests." Answer A and C are incorrect because a vulnerability assessment or a security assessment are not directed efforts to exploit vulnerabilities in an attempt to gain access to networked resources. Answer D is incorrect because a compliance test has nothing to do with penetration testing.

2. **Answer: A, C.** Penetration tests may cause some disruption to network operations as a result of the actual penetration efforts conducted. Penetration tests can also make legitimate attacks by generating false data in intrusion detection systems/intrusion prevention systems (IDS/IPS). Answers B and D are incorrect; although internal and external users may be affected, these are not the most serious downsides of penetration testing.

3. **Answer: B, C.** Some systems administrators may perform amateur pen tests against networks in an attempt to prove a particular vulnerability exists or to evaluate the overall security exposure of a network. This is a bad practice because it generates false intrusion data, may weaken the network's security level, and may be a violation of privacy laws, regulatory mandates, or business entity guidelines. Answers A and D are incorrect because the statements are contrary to the correct answers.

4. **Answer: D.** Vulnerability assessments may be complemented by directed efforts to exploit vulnerabilities in an attempt to gain access to networked resources. Penetration testing includes all of the process in vulnerability assessment plus an important extra step, which is to exploit the vulnerabilities found in the discovery phase. Based in the previous information, answers A, B, and C are incorrect.

5. **Answer: A.** Penetration tests can also make legitimate attacks by generating false data in IDS systems, concealing aggression that is otherwise unrelated to the officially sanctioned penetration test. Answers B and C are incorrect; although they are both concerns, they are not the main security risk. Answer D is incorrect; penetration testing itself does not weaken the network's security level; however amateur pen testing can.

Objective 4.4: Use monitoring tools on systems and networks and detect security-related anomalies.

1. **Answer: D.** Packet Internet Grouper (ping) is a utility that tests network connectivity by sending an Internet Control Message Protocol (ICMP) echo request to a host. It is a good troubleshooting tool to tell whether a route is available to a host. Answer A is incorrect because the `traceroute` utility traces the route a packet takes and records the hops along the way. Answer B is incorrect because `netstat` displays all the ports on which the computer is currently listening. Answer C is incorrect because `nslookup` is a command-line utility used to troubleshoot a Domain Name System (DNS) server database.

2. **Answer: A.** The `traceroute` utility traces the route a packet takes and records the hops along the way. This is a good tool to use to find out where a packet is getting hung up. Answer B is incorrect because `netstat` displays all the ports on which the computer is currently listening. Answer C is incorrect because `nslookup` is a command-line utility used to troubleshoot a Domain Name System (DNS) server database. Answer D is incorrect. Packet Internet Grouper (`ping`) is a utility that tests network connectivity by sending an Internet Control Message Protocol (ICMP) echo request to a host.

3. **Answer: C.** `nslookup` is a command-line utility used to troubleshoot a Domain Name System (DNS) server database. Answer A is incorrect because the `traceroute` utility traces the route a packet takes and records the hops along the way. Answer B is incorrect because `netstat` displays all the ports on which the computer is currently listening. Answer D is incorrect. Packet Internet Grouper (`ping`) is a utility that tests network connectivity by sending an Internet Control Message Protocol (ICMP) echo request to a host.

4. **Answer: B.** `netstat` displays all the ports on which the computer is currently listening. Answer A is incorrect because the `traceroute` utility traces the route a packet takes and records the hops along the way. Answer C is incorrect because `nslookup` is a command-line utility used to troubleshoot a Domain Name System (DNS) server database. Answer D is incorrect. Packet Internet Grouper (`ping`) is a utility that tests network connectivity by sending an Internet Control Message Protocol (ICMP) echo request to a host.

5. **Answer: B.** `ipconfig` is used to display the TCP/IP settings on a Windows machine. Answer A is incorrect; the `traceroute` utility traces the route a packet takes and records the hops along the way. Answer C is incorrect because `netstat` displays all the ports on which the computer is currently listening. Answer D is incorrect; `ifconfig` is used to display the TCP/IP settings on a UNIX machine.

6. **Answer: D.** It is common practice to block ICMP traffic on routers and firewalls. The devices can be configured to block ICMP PING request packets. Answers A and C are incorrect because the host and the host network may be available. Answer B is incorrect because DNS traffic has nothing to do with ping.

7. **Answer: C.** Benchmarking determines how much of a load the server can handle by comparing two or more systems or components of a system. Answer A is incorrect because it describes a baseline. Answer B is incorrect because it describes performance tuning. Answer D is incorrect; load balancing is a technique to spread work between two or more computers, network links, CPUs, hard drives, or other resources.

8. **Answer: A.** The measure of normal activity is known as a baseline. Answer B is incorrect because it describes performance tuning. Answer C is incorrect because it describes a benchmark. Answer D is incorrect; load balancing is a technique to spread work between two or more computers, network links, CPUs, hard drives, or other resources.

9. **Answer: A.** Ping uses the Internet Control Message Protocol (ICMP) and is a network layer test of whether a remote host is alive. A small packet containing an ICMP echo request message is sent through the network to a particular IP address. Answer B is incorrect because Simple Network Management Protocol (SNMP) is an application layer protocol whose purpose is to collect statistics from TCP/IP devices. Answer C is incorrect because Simple Mail Transfer Protocol is used for email. Answer D is incorrect; Network News Transport Protocol is used for newsgroups.

10. **Answer: B.** Microsoft's Performance console is used for tracking and viewing the utilization of operating system resources. Answer A is incorrect. Event Viewer enables you to view certain events that occur on the system. Answer C is incorrect. Windows Server operating systems come with a protocol analyzer called Network Monitor. Answer D is incorrect. Although Task Manager does not actually log performance, it gives you an instant history view of CPU and memory usage and can be extremely useful in determining where further investigation is needed.

11. **Answer: A.** Event Viewer enables you to view certain events that occur on the system. Answer B is incorrect. Microsoft's Performance console is used for tracking and viewing the utilization of operating system resources. Answer C is incorrect. Windows Server operating systems come with a protocol analyzer called Network Monitor. Answer D is incorrect. Although Task Manager does not actually log performance, it gives you an instant history view of CPU and memory usage and can be extremely useful in determining where further investigation is needed.

12. **Answer: C.** Windows Server operating systems come with a protocol analyzer called Network Monitor. Answer A is incorrect. Event Viewer enables you to view certain events that occur on the system. Answer B is incorrect. Microsoft's Performance console is used for tracking and viewing the utilization of operating system resources. Answer D is incorrect. Although Task Manager does not actually log performance, it gives you an instant history view of CPU and memory usage and can be extremely useful in determining where further investigation is needed.

13. **Answer: D.** Although Task Manager does not actually log performance, it gives you an instant history view of CPU and memory usage and can be extremely useful in determining where further investigation. Answer A is incorrect. Event Viewer enables you to view certain events that occur on the system. Answer B is incorrect. Microsoft's Performance console is used for tracking and viewing the utilization of operating system resources. Answer C is incorrect. Windows Server operating systems come with a protocol analyzer called Network Monitor.

14. **Answer: C.** The security log records security events and is available for viewing only by administrators. For security events to be monitored, you must enable auditing. Based on this information, answers A, B, and D are incorrect.

15. **Answer: B.** Simple Network Management Protocol (SNMP) is an application layer protocol whose purpose is to collect statistics from TCP/IP devices. Answer A is incorrect Internet Control Message Protocol (ICMP) and is a network layer protocol used to test remote connectivity. Answer C is incorrect because Simple Mail Transfer Protocol is used for email. Answer D is incorrect; Network News Transport Protocol is used for newsgroups.

16. **Answer: A.** The kernel level is the execution profile. It is here that malicious software such as rootkits operate. Answer B is incorrect; the network-level profile consists of the assembly and transport of data packets. Answer C is incorrect because all applications generate a normal profile of behavior. Changes in the normal application behavior warrants further investigation for a compromise. Answer D is incorrect; at the shell level, each user generates a standard profile representing the normal activities that are routine for that person.

17. **Answer: A.** Event Viewer enables you to view certain events that occur on the system. Event Viewer maintains three log files: one for system processes, one for security information, and one for applications. Answer B is incorrect. Microsoft's Performance console is used for tracking and viewing the utilization of system resources. Answer C is incorrect because Network Monitor is used to capture network traffic and generate statistics for creating reports. Answer D is incorrect because Task Manager gives you an instant history view of CPU and memory usage and can be extremely useful in determining where further investigation is needed.

18. **Answer: B.** Microsoft's Performance console is used for tracking and viewing the utilization of system resources. Answer A is incorrect. Event Viewer enables you to view certain events that occur on the system. Answer C is incorrect because Network Monitor is used to capture network traffic and generate statistics for creating reports. Answer D is incorrect because Task Manager gives you an instant history view of CPU and memory usage and can be extremely useful in determining where further investigation is needed.

19. **Answer: D.** Although Task Manager does not actually log performance, it gives you an instant history view of CPU and memory usage and can be extremely useful in determining where further investigation. Answer A is incorrect. Event Viewer enables you to view certain events that occur on the system. Answer B is incorrect. Microsoft's Performance console is used for tracking and viewing the utilization of operating system resources. Answer C is incorrect. Windows Server operating systems come with a protocol analyzer called Network Monitor.

20. **Answer: C.** Windows Server operating systems come with a protocol analyzer called Network Monitor. A protocol analyzer, otherwise known as a packet sniffer, is used to capture network traffic and generate statistics for creating reports. Answer A is incorrect. Event Viewer enables you to view certain events that occur on the system. Answer B is incorrect. Microsoft's Performance console is used for tracking and viewing the utilization of operating system resources. Answer D is incorrect. Although Task Manager does not actually log performance, it gives you an instant history view of CPU and memory usage and can be extremely useful in determining where further investigation.

21. **Answer: D.** `ipconfig` is used to display the TCP/IP settings on a Windows machine. Answer A is incorrect because the `traceroute` utility traces the route a packet takes and records the hops along the way. Answer B is incorrect because `netstat` displays all the ports on which the computer is currently listening. Answer C is incorrect because `nslookup` is a command-line utility used to troubleshoot a Domain Name System (DNS) server database.

22. **Answer: A.** The `traceroute` utility traces the route a packet takes and records the hops along the way. Answer B is incorrect because `netstat` displays all the ports on which the computer is currently listening. Answer C is incorrect because `nslookup` is a command-line utility used to troubleshoot a Domain Name System (DNS) server database. Answer D is incorrect. `ipconfig` is used to display the TCP/IP settings on a Windows machine.

23. **Answer: C.** `nslookup` is a command-line utility used to troubleshoot a Domain Name System (DNS) server database. Answer A is incorrect because the `traceroute` utility traces the route a packet takes and records the hops along the way. Answer B is incorrect because `netstat` displays all the ports on which the computer is currently listening. Answer D is incorrect. `ipconfig` is used to display the TCP/IP settings on a Windows machine.

24. **Answer: B.** `netstat` displays all the ports on which the computer is currently listening. Answer A is incorrect. The `traceroute` utility traces the route a packet takes and records the hops along the way. Answer C is incorrect because `nslookup` is a command-line utility used to troubleshoot a Domain Name System (DNS) server database. Answer D is incorrect. `ipconfig` is used to display the TCP/IP settings on a Windows machine.

25. **Answer: B, D.** Baselines must be updated on a regular basis, and certainly when the network has changed or new technology has been deployed. An initial baseline should be done for both network and application processes so that you can tell whether you have a hardware or software issue. Based on the previous statement, answers A and C are incorrect.

Objective 4.5: Compare and contrast various types of monitoring methodologies.

1. **Answer: B.** Behavior-based scanning works by looking at the way certain executable files make your computer behave. Answer A is incorrect because it describes knowledge-based IDSs. These devices may monitor for patterns of access that have been established as never being appropriate within the monitored network. Answer C is incorrect because it describes signature-based monitoring. This type of monitoring method looks for specific byte sequences or signatures that are known to appear in attack traffic. Answer D is incorrect because it describes anomaly-based monitoring. Anomaly-based monitoring detects any traffic behavior that is new or unusual.

2. **Answer: D.** Anomaly-based monitoring detects any traffic behavior that is new or unusual. Answer A is incorrect because it describes knowledge-based IDSs. These devices may monitor for patterns of access that have been established as never being appropriate within the monitored network. Answer B is incorrect. Behavior-based scanning works by looking at the way certain executable files make your computer behave. Answer C is incorrect because it describes signature-based monitoring. This type of monitoring method looks for specific byte sequences or signatures that are known to appear in attack traffic.

3. **Answer: C.** Signature-based monitoring looks for specific byte sequences or signatures that are known to appear in attack traffic. Answer A is incorrect because it describes knowledge-based IDSs. These devices may monitor for patterns of access that have been established as never being appropriate within the monitored network. Answer B is incorrect. Behavior-based scanning works by looking at the way certain executable files make your computer behave. Answer D is incorrect because it describes anomaly-based monitoring. Anomaly-based monitoring detects any traffic behavior that is new or unusual.

4. **Answer: B.** Anomaly-based monitoring detects any traffic behavior that is new or unusual. Anomaly-based monitoring is useful for detecting these types of attacks: protocol and port exploitation, new exploits or buffer overflow attacks, and DoS attacks based on payloads or volume. Answer A is incorrect because it describes signature-based monitoring. This type of monitoring method looks for specific byte sequences or signatures that are known to appear in attack traffic. Answer C is incorrect because performance-based monitoring is an automated data system that reports annually on the performance of a system. Answer D is incorrect. Behavior-based scanning works by looking at the way certain executable files make your computer behave.

5. **Answer: D.** Behavior-based scanning works by looking at the way certain executable files make your computer behave. This monitoring method can be used to identify internal misuse by recognizing actions outside of normal access patterns or authorized events occurring outside of normal profile usage, such as the access of protected files during off-hours. Answer A is incorrect because it describes signature-based monitoring. This type of monitoring method looks for specific byte sequences or signatures that are known to appear in attack traffic. Answer B is incorrect because it describes anomaly-based monitoring. Anomaly-based monitoring detects any traffic behavior that is new or unusual. Answer C is incorrect because performance-based monitoring is an automated data system that reports annually on the performance of a system.

6. **Answer: A.** Signature-based monitoring looks for specific byte sequences or signatures that are known to appear in attack traffic. Signature-based systems have an advantage because of their simplicity and their ability to operate online in real time. The problem is that they can detect only known attacks with identified signatures. Answer B is incorrect because it describes anomaly-based monitoring. Anomaly-based monitoring detects any traffic behavior that is new or unusual. Answer C is incorrect because performance-based monitoring is an automated data system that reports annually on the performance of a system. Answer D is incorrect. Behavior-based scanning works by looking at the way certain executable files make your computer behave.

7. **Answer: A.** Signature-based systems have an advantage because of their simplicity and their ability to operate online in real time. The advantages for this type of monitoring include the following: low number of false positives, detailed text logs, and use of few system resources. Answer B is incorrect because it describes anomaly-based monitoring. Anomaly-based monitoring detects any traffic behavior that is new or unusual. Answer C is incorrect because performance-based monitoring is an automated data system that reports annually on the performance of a system. Answer D is incorrect. Behavior-based scanning works by looking at the way certain executable files make your computer behave.

8. **Answer: D.** Behavior-based scanning works by looking at the way certain executable files make your computer behave. It is not dependent on OS-specific mechanisms. Answer A is incorrect because it describes signature-based monitoring. This type of monitoring method looks for specific byte sequences or signatures that are known to appear in attack traffic. Answer B is incorrect because it describes anomaly-based monitoring. Anomaly-based monitoring detects any traffic behavior that is new or unusual. Answer C is incorrect because performance-based monitoring is an automated data system that reports annually on the performance of a system.

9. **Answer: B.** Anomaly-based monitoring detects any traffic behavior that is new or unusual. Detection of anomalies is used in many security domains, ranging from video surveillance and security systems to intrusion detection and fraudulent transactions. Answer A is incorrect because it describes signature-based monitoring. This type of monitoring method looks for specific byte sequences or signatures that are known to appear in attack traffic. Answer C is incorrect because performance-based monitoring is an automated data system that reports annually on the performance of a system. Answer D is incorrect. Behavior-based scanning works by looking at the way certain executable files make your computer behave.

10. **Answer: B.** The classifications of anomaly detection techniques include statistical methods, rule-based methods, distance-based methods, profiling methods, and model-based approaches. For example, under the profiling method, normal behavior can be programmed based on offline research, or the system can learn behavior while processing network traffic. Answer A is incorrect because it describes signature-based monitoring. This type of monitoring method looks for specific byte sequences or signatures that are known to appear in attack traffic. Answer C is incorrect because performance-based monitoring is an automated data system that reports annually on the performance of a system. Answer D is incorrect. Behavior-based scanning works by looking at the way certain executable files make your computer behave.

11. **Answer: A.** Signature-based systems have an advantage because of their simplicity and their ability to operate online in real time. The advantages for this type of monitoring include the following: low number of false positives, detailed text logs, and use of few system resources. Answer B is incorrect because it describes anomaly-based monitoring. Anomaly-based monitoring detects any traffic behavior that is new or unusual. Answer C is incorrect because performance-based monitoring is an automated data system that reports annually on the performance of a system. Answer D is incorrect. Behavior-based scanning works by looking at the way certain executable files make your computer behave.

12. **Answer: B.** Anomaly-based monitoring detects any traffic behavior that is new or unusual. Anomaly detection is analogous to credit card fraud detection. Credit card companies maintain "spending profiles" for their customers. Answer A is incorrect because it describes signature-based monitoring. This type of monitoring method looks for specific byte sequences or signatures that are known to appear in attack traffic. Answer C is incorrect because performance-based monitoring is an automated data system that reports annually on the performance of a system. Answer D is incorrect. Behavior-based scanning works by looking at the way certain executable files make your computer behave.

13. **Answer: D.** Behavior-based scanning works by looking at the way certain executable files make your computer behave. A behavior-based detector determines whether a program is malicious by inspecting the stream of system calls that the program issues to the operating system. Answer A is incorrect because it describes signature-based monitoring. This type of monitoring method looks for specific byte sequences or signatures that are known to appear in attack traffic. Answer B is incorrect because it describes anomaly-based monitoring. Anomaly-based monitoring detects any traffic behavior that is new or unusual. Answer C is incorrect because performance-based monitoring is an automated data system that reports annually on the performance of a system.

14. **Answers: B, C.** Behavior based detection has several limitations, including high incidence of false alarms and slow file checking. Answers A and D are incorrect because they are associated with signature-based monitoring solutions.

15. **Answer: A, D.** Signature-based detection has several limitations, including being based excessively on passive monitoring and the rule sets need constant updating. Answers B and C are incorrect because they are associated with behavior-based monitoring solutions.

16. **Answer: A, C.** Behavior-based monitoring advantages include the following: It can identify malware before it is added to signature files, monitor for malware activities, and learn about malware based on previous detection. Answers B and D are incorrect because they are advantages associated with signature-based monitoring.

17. **Answer: B, D.** Signature-based monitoring advantages include the following: It can identify malware before it is added to signature files, monitor for malware activities, and learn about malware based on previous detection. Answers A and C are incorrect because they are advantages associated with behavior-based monitoring.

18. **Answer: B.** Anomaly-based monitoring detects any traffic behavior that is new or unusual. Because this method detects anomalies, it is also called statistical anomaly detection. Highly secure environments might use complex patterns of behavior analysis, in some cases learning individual patterns of use common to each user profile, so that variations can be identified. Answer A is incorrect because it describes signature-based monitoring. This type of monitoring method looks for specific byte sequences or signatures that are known to appear in attack traffic. Answer C is incorrect because performance-based monitoring is an automated data system that reports annually on the performance of a system. Answer D is incorrect. Behavior-based scanning works by looking at the way certain executable files make your computer behave.

19. **Answer: A, B.** Anomaly-based monitoring is useful for detecting these types of attacks: protocol and port exploitation, new exploits or buffer overflow attacks, DoS attacks based on payloads or volume, normal network failures, and variants of existing attacks in new environments. Answers C and D are incorrect; they are associated with signature-based monitoring.

20. **Answer: C, D.** In signature-based monitoring, the user can examine the signature database, and quickly determine which intrusive activity the misuse detection system is programmed to alert on. Another benefit is that it can accurate detect know malicious software. Answers A and B are incorrect; they are associated with anomaly-based monitoring.

Objective 4.6: Execute proper logging procedures and evaluate the results.

1. **Answer: B.** Logging is the process of collecting data to be used for monitoring and auditing purposes. Answer A is incorrect because it describes baselining. Answer C is incorrect because it describes auditing. Answer D is incorrect because it describes monitoring.

2. **Answer: A.** Logging procedures and evaluation are an important part of keeping your network safe. However, before you can configure logging, it is essential to identify what is typical behavior for your network. Answers B, C, and D are incorrect; all these functions are performed after logging is enabled.

3. **Answer: B.** When choosing what to log, be sure you choose carefully. Logs take up disk space and use system resources. They also have to be read; and if you log too much, will bog down the system, and it will take a long time to weed through the log files to determine what is important. Therefore, answers A, C, and D are incorrect.

4. **Answer: C.** To improve server performance, logs should be stored on a nonsystem striped or striped/mirrored disk volume. Answer A is incorrect. Storing the log files in the DMZ is poor practice as the servers located here are generally more vulnerable. Answers B and D are incorrect; storing the log files on the local machine will not improve performance.

5. **Answer: D.** Log files should be stored in a centralized repository of an offline volume or on a standalone computer. Answer A is incorrect; storing the log files on the local machine will not improve security. Answer B is incorrect. Storing the log files on the Intranet is poor practice as the information is visible and more vulnerable. Answer C is incorrect. Storing the log files in the DMZ is poor practice as the servers located here are generally more vulnerable.

6. **Answer: C.** When implementing an application logging strategy, look for a solution that uses standard protocols and formats so that analysis is simpler. Therefore, answers A, B, and D are incorrect.

7. **Answer: A.** Should you choose to use manual analysis, consider creating the logs in a format that is can readily be parsed, such as comma-separated value (CSV). Doing so will allow for more flexibility when importing the information into applications for analysis. Answers B, C, and D are incorrect because none of these formats are readily parsed.

8. **Answer: C, D.** Standards should be implemented for the types of events you want to log based on business, technical, and regulatory requirements, and the threats the organization faces. Answer A is incorrect because although user needs should be considered, logging standards should not be based on them. Answer B is incorrect; vendor requirements have nothing to do with organizational logging standards.

9. **Answer: A.** Not only do you need to read the logs, you may also have to know how to correlate events examining output. Answers B, C, and D are incorrect; they are not pertinent to being able to decipher log files.

10. **Answer: A, B, D.** IIS logs may include information about site visitors and their viewing habits. They can be used to assess content, identify bottlenecks, or investigate attacks. Answer C is incorrect. Task Manager is a tool that you can use to end processes.

11. **Answer: D.** DNS logging may cause performance degradation on the server. It should be used only for troubleshooting purposes. By enabling DNS debug logging, you can log all DNS-related information. Based on this information, answers A, B, and C are incorrect.

12. **Answer: B.** The DNS server log contains events logged by the DNS Server service. For example, when the DNS server starts or stops, a corresponding event message is written to this log. This should be the first place you look when troubleshooting DNS-related issues. Answer A is incorrect. By enabling DNS debug logging, you can log all DNS-related information. Answer C is incorrect. Syslog channels are used for BIND logging. Answer D is incorrect. The Event Viewer Application log will not provide enough detailed information.

13. **Answer: D.** In UNIX- or Linux-based systems, programs send log entries to the system logging daemon, syslogd. Answer A is incorrect because mtools.conf is a configuration file for all the operations. Answers B and C are incorrect; both Msconfig and Event Viewer are tools used on Windows-based systems.

14. **Answer: B, C.** You should employ strict access controls on all logging servers. If allowable, encrypt the log files and store log files on a stand-alone system. Answer A is incorrect; it is not good practice to store log files in plain text. Answer D is incorrect; log files should not be stored on data partitions of individual systems.

15. **Answer: B.** Task Manager is a tool that you can use to end processes or applications that get hung up or cause the operating system to become unstable, without having to reboot the machine. It also gives you an instant view of CPU and memory usage. Answer A is incorrect because Network Monitor is used to capture network traffic and generate statistics for creating reports. Answer C is incorrect because Event Viewer enables you to view certain events that occur on the system. Event Viewer maintains three log files: one for system processes, one for security information, and one for applications. Answer D is incorrect because Microsoft's Performance console is used for tracking and viewing the utilization of system resources.

16. **Answer: C.** Authentication and accounting logging is particularly useful for troubleshooting remote-access policy issues. Answer A is incorrect because Internet Information Services (IIS) logging is designed to be more detailed than the event-logging or performance-monitoring features of Windows Server operating systems. The IIS logs can include information such as who has visited your site, what they viewed, and when the information was viewed last. Answer B is incorrect because critical and error level logging is one of the eight different logging levels available for Cisco logging devices. Answer D is incorrect because authentication and accounting logging information is used to track remote-access usage and authentication attempts. This logging is separate from the events recorded in the system event log.

17. **Answer: C, D.** The following are some events you should to take a closer look at: repeated traffic to particular ports, blocked attempts, and suspicious signatures. Answer A is incorrect because port 25 is used for SMTP traffic. Answer B is incorrect because HTTP traffic is used for web access.

18. **Answer: B, C.** If a firewall log shows repeated traffic to particular ports, this can indicate a DoS or distributed DoS (DDoS) attack. When there is repeated traffic on port 53, the attacker is probably trying to overwhelm the DNS service. Answers A and D are incorrect because these attacks are associated with web browsers and servers.

19. **Answer: A, C, D.** Antivirus software, just like other software applications, usually contain a folder within the application for logging events such as updates, quarantined viruses, and update history. Answer B is incorrect. Dropped packets are normally found in router logs.

20. **Answer: B.** Routing and remote access logging information is used to track remote-access usage and authentication attempts. This logging is separate from the events recorded in the system event log. Therefore, Answer D is incorrect. Answer A is incorrect; firewall logging will not log remote access and authentication. Answer C is incorrect; IIS logging will not log remote access and authentication.

Objective 4.7: Conduct periodic audits of system security settings.

1. **Answer: C.** Auditing is the process of tracking users and their actions on the network. Answer A is incorrect because it describes baselining. Answer B is incorrect because it describes logging. Answer D is incorrect because it describes monitoring.

2. **Answer: A, B.** Without proper planning and policies, you probably will quickly fill your log files and hard drives with useless or unused information. The more quickly you fill up your log files, the more frequently you need to check the logs; otherwise, important security events may get deleted unnoticed. Answer C is incorrect because log files should not be stored on user hard drives. Answer D is incorrect. When auditing is not clear-cut, the workload of the system administrator increases.

3. **Answer: B, C.** Auditing user privileges is generally a two-step process that involves enabling auditing within the operating system and then specifying the resources to be audited. Answer A is incorrect; auditing not logging needs to be enabled. Answer D is incorrect; the log file storage directory is specified not the audit file directory.

4. **Answer: D.** Auditing of access use and rights changes should be implemented to prevent unauthorized or unintentional access for a guest or restricted user account access to sensitive or protected resources. Answer A is incorrect; group policy controls access to resources. Answer B is incorrect; retention polices concern data not user access. Answer C is incorrect; DHCP deals with the issuing of IP addresses not access to accounts.

5. **Answer: B, C.** The following user rights are never audited, mainly because they are used by processes: bypass traverse checking, generate security audits, create a token object, debug programs and replace a process-level token. However, the assignment of these rights can be audited. Answers A and D are incorrect; these are audit polices set at a domain level. They are not user right assignments.

6. **Answer: C.** It is equally important to audit both failed and successful events because both may reveal unauthorized access or an unexpected escalation of access rights. Answers A and B are incorrect because it is important to audit both types of events. Answer D is incorrect because auditing is an important part of securing the network.

7. **Answer: B.** Logging is the process of collecting data to be used for monitoring and reviewing purposes. Auditing is the process of verification that normally involves going through log files; therefore, answer A is incorrect. Answer C is incorrect. Baselining is measuring and rating the performance of a network. Typically, the log files are frequently inspected, and inspection is not the process of collecting the data; therefore, answer D is incorrect.

8. **Answer: D.** Turning on all audit counters for all objects could significantly impact server performance. Answer A is incorrect; auditing is done in the background and does not affect user productivity. Answer B is incorrect; if the I/O activity were affected at all, it would be increased. Answer C is incorrect; as with I/O activity, if there were change, it would be an increase, not a decrease.

9. **Answer: A, C.** Log files, physical records, security evaluations, and other operational documentation should be managed within an organization's retention and disposal policies. These should include specifications for access authorization, term of retention, and requirements for disposal. Answers B and D are incorrect; software and user manuals are readily available from the vendors website and are not required in a retention and disposal policy.

10. **Answer: D.** The organization should change and adjust a data-retention policy when and as needed (with emphasis on when and as needed). There may be a reason to make new classifications as business goals change, but make sure this gets into the documentation. Answer A is incorrect. Data-retention policies must be reviewed on a regular basis. Answers B and C are incorrect; these review cycles are too short a period of time.

11. **Answer: A.** If an organization is sued by a former employee for wrongful termination, the department may be compelled during the discovery phase of the suit to produce all documents related to that individual's work performance. This used to mean the records and copies of any written correspondence (memos, letters, and so on) concerning the performance of that employee. All data is subject to discovery regardless of storage format or location. Therefore, answers B and C are incorrect. Answer D is incorrect because the organizations can never arbitrarily decide what is and what is not discoverable.

12. **Answer: B and D.** The organization should have a legal hold policy in place, have an understanding of statutory and regulatory document retention requirements, understand the varying statues of limitations, have a policy, and have a records-retention and destruction schedule. Answer A is incorrect because ISPs do not impose data-retention requirements on customers. Answer C is incorrect because user requirements may be a consideration, but it not pertinent.

13. **Answer: B.** In Group Policy, the settings that will actually be applied to an object will be a combination of all the settings that can affect the object. Answer A is incorrect because all group policies are applied to the object. Answer C is incorrect; in a universal group, the policies may be applied from different domains. Answer D is incorrect; this would only apply if there was not a domain environment.

14. **Answer: B.** You can use gpresult to see what policy is in effect and to troubleshoot problems. Answer A is incorrect; you can use gpupdate to refresh policy immediately and to specify certain options at the command line. Answer C is incorrect the Resultant Set of Policy (RSoP) tool is used to determine the effective settings on the computer that you are working from or any other computer in a Windows Server 2003 Active Directory domain. Answer D is incorrect; the Group Policy object is used to create group polices.

15. **Answer: A.** You can use the Resultant Set of Policy (RSoP) tool to determine the effective settings on the computer that you are working from or any other computer in a Windows Server 2003 Active Directory domain. Answer B is incorrect; the Group Policy object is used to create group polices. Answer C is incorrect; you can use gpupdate to refresh policy immediately and to specify certain options at the command line. Answer D is incorrect; the local security settings are used on the local machine only.

16. **Answer: B.** The organization should audit success events in the policy change event category on domain controllers. A logged event indicates someone has changed the local security authority (LSA). Answer A is incorrect. Auditing success events in the policy change event category will record success and failure events in the system events. Answer C is incorrect; auditing success events in the account management event category is used to verify changes that were made to account properties and group properties. Answer D is incorrect; auditing success events in the logon event category records when each user logs on to or logs off from the computer.

17. **Answer: C.** Auditing success events in the account management event category can be used to verify changes that were made to account properties and group properties. Answer A is incorrect. Auditing success events in the policy change event category will record success and failure events in the system events. Answer B is incorrect. Auditing success events in the policy change event category on domain controllers indicates someone has changed the local security authority (LSA). Answer D is incorrect; auditing success events in the logon event category records when each user logs on to or logs off from the computer.

18. **Answer: A.** Auditing success events in the policy change event category will record success and failure events in the system events. Answer B is incorrect. Auditing success events in the policy change event category on domain controllers indicates someone has changed the local security authority (LSA). Answer C is incorrect; auditing success events in the account management event category is used to verify changes that were made to account properties and group properties. Answer D is incorrect; auditing success events in the logon event category records when each user logs on to or logs off from the computer.

19. **Answer: D.** Auditing success events in the logon event category records when each user logs on to or logs off from the computer. Answer A is incorrect. Auditing success events in the policy change event category will record success and failure events in the system events. Answer B is incorrect. Auditing success events in the policy change event category on domain controllers indicates someone has changed the local security authority (LSA). Answer C is incorrect; auditing success events in the account management event category is used to verify changes that were made to account properties and group properties.

20. **Answer: C.** Auditing success events in the account logon event category on domain controllers is used to verify when users log on to or log off from the domain. Answer A is incorrect. Auditing success events in the policy change event category will record success and failure events in the system events. Answer B is incorrect. Auditing success events in the policy change event category on domain controllers indicates someone has changed the local security authority (LSA). Answer D is incorrect; auditing success events in the logon event category records when each user logs on to or logs off from the computer.

CHAPTER FIVE

Domain 5.0: Cryptography

Recently, modern cryptography has become increasingly important and ubiquitous. There has been increasing concern about the security of data, which continues to rapidly grow across information systems and traverse and reside in many different locations. This combined with more sophisticated attacks and a growing economy around computer-related fraud and data theft makes the need to protect the data itself even more important than in the past. A public key infrastructure (PKI) makes use of both public and private keys. It also provides the foundation for binding keys to an identity via a certificate authority (CA), thus providing the system for the secure exchange of data over a network through the use of an asymmetric key system. This system for the most part consists of digital certificates and the CAs that issue the certificates. These certificates identify individuals, systems, and organizations that have been verified as authentic and trustworthy. As a prospective security professional, you should also take every opportunity you may find to expand your skill base beyond these basic foundational elements. The following list includes the key areas from Domain 5 that you need to master for the exam:

▶ Explain general cryptography concepts.

▶ Explain basic hashing concepts and map various algorithms to appropriate applications.

▶ Explain basic encryption concepts and map various algorithms to appropriate applications.

▶ Explain and implement protocols.

▶ Explain core concepts of public key cryptography.

▶ Implement PKI and certificate management.

Practice Questions

Objective 5.1: Explain general cryptography concepts.

1. Which of the following best describes a cryptography key?

   ○ **A.** Plaintext data converted into an unreadable format

   ○ **B.** Messages hidden from unintended recipients

   ○ **C.** A string of bits used to encrypt and decrypt data

   ○ **D.** Mathematical sequence used to perform encryption and decryption

   Quick Answer: **278**
   Detailed Answer: **281**

2. Which of the following best describes steganography?

   ○ **A.** Plaintext data converted into an unreadable format

   ○ **B.** Messages hidden from unintended recipients

   ○ **C.** A string of bits used to encrypt and decrypt data

   ○ **D.** Mathematical sequence used to perform encryption and decryption

   Quick Answer: **278**
   Detailed Answer: **281**

3. Which of the following best describes an algorithm?

   ○ **A.** Plaintext data converted into an unreadable format

   ○ **B.** Messages hidden from unintended recipients

   ○ **C.** A string of bits used to encrypt and decrypt data

   ○ **D.** Mathematical sequence used to perform encryption and decryption

   Quick Answer: **278**
   Detailed Answer: **281**

4. Which of the following best describes encryption?

   ○ **A.** Plaintext data converted into an unreadable format

   ○ **B.** Messages hidden from unintended recipients

   ○ **C.** A string of bits used to encrypt and decrypt data

   ○ **D.** Mathematical sequence used to perform encryption and decryption

   Quick Answer: **278**
   Detailed Answer: **281**

5. Which of the following best describes why cryptography has become increasingly important? (Select all correct answers.)

   ○ **A.** Concerns over the security of data

   ○ **B.** Steganography has become more prevalent

   ○ **C.** Attacks have become more sophisticated

   ○ **D.** Concerns over increasing virus infections

   Quick Answer: **278**
   Detailed Answer: **281**

6. Which of the following are fundamental types of encryption algorithms? (Select all correct answers.)

- ○ **A.** Hash function
- ○ **B.** Asymmetric key
- ○ **C.** Trusted platform
- ○ **D.** Symmetric key

Quick Answer: **278**
Detailed Answer: **282**

7. Which of the following best describes symmetric key cryptography?

- ○ **A.** A hashing algorithm that uses a common shared key between the sender and receiver
- ○ **B.** An encryption system that uses a common shared key between the sender and receiver
- ○ **C.** An encryption system where each user has a pair of keys, one public and one private
- ○ **D.** A hashing algorithm that uses a common shared key between the sender and receiver

Quick Answer: **278**
Detailed Answer: **282**

8. Which of the following best describes asymmetric key cryptography?

- ○ **A.** A hashing algorithm that uses a common shared key between the sender and receiver
- ○ **B.** An encryption system that uses a common shared key between the sender and receiver
- ○ **C.** An encryption system where each user has a pair of keys, one public and one private
- ○ **D.** A hashing algorithm that uses a common shared key between the sender and receiver

Quick Answer: **278**
Detailed Answer: **282**

9. Which of the following best describes where the user's public key is maintained in an asymmetric encryption?

- ○ **A.** On a centralized server so that anyone can access it
- ○ **B.** Maintained on the host system or application
- ○ **C.** In the cryptographic vault of the organization
- ○ **D.** In the users shared network folder for easy access

Quick Answer: **278**
Detailed Answer: **282**

10. Which of the following best describes where the user's private key is maintained in an asymmetric encryption?

- ○ **A.** On a centralized server so that anyone can access it
- ○ **B.** Maintained on the host system or application
- ○ **C.** In the cryptographic vault of the organization
- ○ **D.** In the user's shared network folder for easy access

Quick Answer: **278**
Detailed Answer: **282**

11. Which of the following is another name for asymmetric algorithms?

    ○   **A.** Private key algorithms

    ○   **B.** Shared key algorithms

    ○   **C.** Public key algorithms

    ○   **D.** Secret key algorithms

Quick Answer: **278**
Detailed Answer: **282**

12. Which of the following is another name for symmetric algorithms? (Select all correct answers.)

    ○   **A.** Private key algorithms

    ○   **B.** Shared key algorithms

    ○   **C.** Public key algorithms

    ○   **D.** Secret key algorithms

Quick Answer: **278**
Detailed Answer: **282**

13. Which of the following best describes how a message encrypted with the private key is decrypted?

    ○   **A.** The public key can never decrypt the message.

    ○   **B.** The public key can always decrypt the message.

    ○   **C.** The public key can sometimes decrypt the message.

    ○   **D.** The public key can decrypt the message only when used by an administrator.

Quick Answer: **278**
Detailed Answer: **282**

14. Which of the following best describes the function of the public key in asymmetric algorithms?

    ○   **A.** The public key can never decrypt a message that it was used to encrypt with.

    ○   **B.** The public key can always decrypt a message that it was used to encrypt with.

    ○   **C.** The public key can sometimes decrypt a message that it was used to encrypt with.

    ○   **D.** The public key can decrypt a message that it was used to encrypt with only when used by an administrator.

Quick Answer: **278**
Detailed Answer: **282**

15. Which of the following best describes the difference between steganography and cryptography?

Quick Answer: **278**
Detailed Answer: **283**

   O **A.** Steganography seeks to expose the presence of a hidden message; cryptography transforms a message from a readable form to unreadable form.

   O **B.** Cryptography seeks to hide the presence of a message; steganography transforms a message from a readable form to unreadable form.

   O **C.** Cryptography seeks to expose the presence of a hidden message; steganography transforms a message from an unreadable form to a readable form.

   O **D.** Steganography seeks to hide the presence of a message; cryptography transforms a message from a readable form to unreadable form.

16. Which of the following best describes the coding used by many printers consisting of tiny dots that reveal serial numbers and time stamps?

Quick Answer: **278**
Detailed Answer: **283**

   O **A.** Phishing

   O **B.** Steganography

   O **C.** Cryptography

   O **D.** Hashing

17. Which of the following best describes the main concern of confidentiality?

Quick Answer: **278**
Detailed Answer: **283**

   O **A.** Unauthorized disclosure of sensitive information

   O **B.** Unauthorized modification of information or systems

   O **C.** Specifying if an identity should be granted access to a resource

   O **D.** Maintaining continuous operations without service disruptions

18. Which of the following best describes the main concern of integrity?

Quick Answer: **278**
Detailed Answer: **283**

   O **A.** Unauthorized disclosure of sensitive information

   O **B.** Unauthorized modification of information or systems

   O **C.** Specifying if an identity should be granted access to a resource

   O **D.** Maintaining continuous operations without service disruptions

Quick Check

19. Which of the following best describes the main concern of availability?

Quick Answer: **278**
Detailed Answer: **283**

- ○ **A.** Unauthorized disclosure of sensitive information
- ○ **B.** Unauthorized modification of information or systems
- ○ **C.** Specifying if an identity should be granted access to a resource
- ○ **D.** Maintaining continuous operations without service disruptions

20. An organization implements PGP. This is an example of which of the following? (Select all correct answers.)

Quick Answer: **278**
Detailed Answer: **283**

- ○ **A.** Integrity
- ○ **B.** Availability
- ○ **C.** Confidentiality
- ○ **D.** Authorization

21. Which of the following best describes the assurance that data and information can only be modified by those authorized to do?

Quick Answer: **278**
Detailed Answer: **283**

- ○ **A.** Integrity
- ○ **B.** Availability
- ○ **C.** Confidentiality
- ○ **D.** Authorization

22. Which of the following best describes limiting the disclosure of private information?

Quick Answer: **278**
Detailed Answer: **284**

- ○ **A.** Integrity
- ○ **B.** Availability
- ○ **C.** Confidentiality
- ○ **D.** Authorization

23. Which of the following best describes requiring the accessibility of information and information systems?

Quick Answer: **278**
Detailed Answer: **284**

- ○ **A.** Integrity
- ○ **B.** Availability
- ○ **C.** Confidentiality
- ○ **D.** Authorization

24. Which of the following best describes the main intent of nonrepudiation?

Quick Answer: **278**
Detailed Answer: **284**

- ❍ **A.** To prevent unauthorized modification of information or systems
- ❍ **B.** To prevent unauthorized disclosure of sensitive information
- ❍ **C.** To specify if an identity should be granted access to a specific resource
- ❍ **D.** To provide an irrefutable method of accountability for the source of data

25. Which of the following are key elements that nonrepudiation services provide? (Select all correct answers.)

Quick Answer: **278**
Detailed Answer: **284**

- ❍ **A.** Proof of service
- ❍ **B.** Proof of origin
- ❍ **C.** Proof of delivery
- ❍ **D.** Proof of receipt

26. An organization is implementing a security solution that attempts to guarantee the identity of the person sending the data from one point to another. Which of the following best describes this implementation?

Quick Answer: **278**
Detailed Answer: **284**

- ❍ **A.** Hashing function
- ❍ **B.** Steganography
- ❍ **C.** Cryptography
- ❍ **D.** Digital signature

27. Which of the following would be the best implementation solution for an organization to mitigate the risks associated with lost or stolen laptops and the accompanying disclosure laws?

Quick Answer: **278**
Detailed Answer: **284**

- ❍ **A.** Whole disk encryption
- ❍ **B.** Trusted Platform Module
- ❍ **C.** Digital signatures
- ❍ **D.** Hashing functions

28. Which of the following would an organization implement to secure the storage of keys, passwords, and digital certificates at the hardware level?

   ○ **A.** Whole disk encryption

   ○ **B.** Trusted Platform Module

   ○ **C.** Digital signatures

   ○ **D.** Hashing functions

29. When conducting an online banking transaction, one can be assured they are at the legitimate site by verifying the server-side certificate. Which of the following best describes this type of certificate?

   ○ **A.** Digital signature

   ○ **B.** Hashing function

   ○ **C.** Single sided

   ○ **D.** Dual sided

30. An organization is concerned about back doors and flaws undermining encryption algorithms. Which of the following technologies should the organization choose?

   ○ **A.** An algorithm based on DES

   ○ **B.** An already proven algorithm

   ○ **C.** A proprietary vendor algorithm

   ○ **D.** An in-house-developed algorithm

Objective 5.2: Explain basic hashing concepts and map various algorithms to appropriate applications.

1. Which of the following best describes a hash?

   ○ **A.** Plaintext data converted into an unreadable format

   ○ **B.** A generated summary from a mathematical rule

   ○ **C.** A string of bits used to encrypt and decrypt data

   ○ **D.** Mathematical sequence used to perform encryption and decryption

2. Which of the following best describes how hashing functions work?

Quick Answer: **278**
Detailed Answer: **285**

- ○ **A.** By taking a string of any length and producing a string the exact same length for output
- ○ **B.** By taking a string of any length and encrypting it bit by bit one at a time
- ○ **C.** By taking a string of any length and producing a fixed-length string for output
- ○ **D.** By taking a string of any length and encrypting it in fixed-length chunks

3. Which of the following is correct about a hash created from a document?

Quick Answer: **278**
Detailed Answer: **285**

- ○ **A.** The document can be unencrypted using the same hash.
- ○ **B.** The document can be re-created from the hash.
- ○ **C.** The document can be re-created by using the same encryption.
- ○ **D.** The document cannot be re-created from the hash.

4. Which of the following is the correct strength hash that SHA can generate?

Quick Answer: **278**
Detailed Answer: **285**

- ○ **A.** 160 bits in length
- ○ **B.** 64 bits in length
- ○ **C.** 128 bits in length
- ○ **D.** 256 bits in length

5. Which of the following is the correct strength hash that the MD series can generate?

Quick Answer: **278**
Detailed Answer: **286**

- ○ **A.** 160 bits in length
- ○ **B.** 64 bits in length
- ○ **C.** 128 bits in length
- ○ **D.** 256 bits in length

6. Which of the following best describes message authentication code?

Quick Answer: **278**
Detailed Answer: **286**

- ○ **A.** An encryption system that uses a common shared key between the sender and receiver

- ○ **B.** A piece of data derived by applying a message combined with a secret key to a cryptographic algorithm

- ○ **C.** An encryption system where each user has a pair of keys, one public and one private

- ○ **D.** A hash algorithm pioneered by the National Security Agency and widely used in the U.S. government

7. Which of the following are primary weaknesses of the LM hash? (Select all correct answers.)

Quick Answer: **278**
Detailed Answer: **286**

- ○ **A.** Before being hashed, all lowercase characters in the password are converted to uppercase characters.

- ○ **B.** The authenticity of the public key can easily be forged by an attacker.

- ○ **C.** Passwords longer than seven characters are broken down into two chunks.

- ○ **D.** Management of the keys is often overlooked and they can easily be compromised.

8. An organization wants to select a hashing method that will be able to resist forgery and is not open to man in the middle attacks. Which of the following would be the most appropriate choice for the organization?

Quick Answer: **278**
Detailed Answer: **286**

- ○ **A.** SHA
- ○ **B.** NTLM
- ○ **C.** MD
- ○ **D.** MAC

9. Which of the following hashing algorithms is the most resource intensive?

Quick Answer: **278**
Detailed Answer: **286**

- ○ **A.** MD5
- ○ **B.** SHA
- ○ **C.** LM
- ○ **D.** NTLM

10. An organization wants to select the most appropriate hashing method that can be used to secure Windows authentication. Which of the following should the organization choose?

○ **A.** MD5

○ **B.** SHA

○ **C.** LM

○ **D.** NTLM

Objective 5.3: Explain basic encryption concepts and map various algorithms to appropriate applications.

1. Which of the following are classifications of symmetric algorithms? (Select all correct answers.)

○ **A.** Classical cipher

○ **B.** Block cipher

○ **C.** Stream cipher

○ **D.** Simple cipher

2. DES is which of the following types of cipher?

○ **A.** Classical cipher

○ **B.** Block cipher

○ **C.** Stream cipher

○ **D.** Simple cipher

3. Which of the following is the total effective key length of 3DES?

○ **A.** 168 bit in length

○ **B.** 64 bit in length

○ **C.** 128 bit in length

○ **D.** 256 bit in length

4. Which of the following is a stream cipher?

○ **A.** RC5

○ **B.** Blowfish

○ **C.** IDEA

○ **D.** RC4

5. Which of the following block ciphers can perform encryption with any length key up to 448-bits?

- ⃝ **A.** RC5
- ⃝ **B.** Blowfish
- ⃝ **C.** IDEA
- ⃝ **D.** RC4

Quick Answer: **279**
Detailed Answer: **287**

6. An organization wants to be able to export encrypted files to a country that only allows 56-bit encryption. Which of the following would the organization choose?

- ⃝ **A.** 3DES
- ⃝ **B.** RC5
- ⃝ **C.** DES
- ⃝ **D.** AES

Quick Answer: **279**
Detailed Answer: **287**

7. An organization wants to use an encryption method that uses a 168-bit key length. Which of the following would the organization choose?

- ⃝ **A.** 3DES
- ⃝ **B.** RC5
- ⃝ **C.** DES
- ⃝ **D.** AES

Quick Answer: **279**
Detailed Answer: **287**

8. An organization wants to use an encryption method that uses a 256-bit key length. Which of the following could the organization choose? (Select all correct answers.)

- ⃝ **A.** 3DES
- ⃝ **B.** RC5
- ⃝ **C.** DES
- ⃝ **D.** AES

Quick Answer: **279**
Detailed Answer: **287**

9. Which of the following ciphers has earned the mark of being completely unbreakable?

- ⃝ **A.** RC5
- ⃝ **B.** OTP
- ⃝ **C.** IDEA
- ⃝ **D.** DES

Quick Answer: **279**
Detailed Answer: **287**

10. In an implementation of Advanced Encryption Standard (AES), which of the following is the correct number of layers that the data passes through?

- ○ **A.** Five
- ○ **B.** Four
- ○ **C.** Three
- ○ **D.** Two

11. An organization wants to use an encryption algorithm that uses little overhead. Which of the following could the organization? (Select all correct answers.)

- ○ **A.** ECC
- ○ **B.** RSA
- ○ **C.** RC5
- ○ **D.** DES

12. An organization wants to use system that incorporates a mixed approach, using both asymmetric and symmetric encryption. Which of the following meets this requirement?

- ○ **A.** OTP
- ○ **B.** PGP
- ○ **C.** DES
- ○ **D.** ECC

13. Which of the following asymmetric algorithm is considered by many to be the standard for encryption and core technology that secures most business conducted on the Internet?

- ○ **A.** RSA
- ○ **B.** ECC
- ○ **C.** OTP
- ○ **D.** DES

14. An organization wants to use an encryption algorithm that combines a compact design with extreme difficulty to break. Which of the following meets this requirement?

- ○ **A.** RSA
- ○ **B.** ECC
- ○ **C.** OTP
- ○ **D.** DES

15. Which of the following ciphers has the highest storage and transmission costs?

Quick Answer: **279**
Detailed Answer: **288**

    ◯ **A.** RC5

    ◯ **B.** OTP

    ◯ **C.** IDEA

    ◯ **D.** DES

16. For most environments today, which of the following encryption key strengths is considered adequate?

Quick Answer: **279**
Detailed Answer: **288**

    ◯ **A.** 1024 bit in length

    ◯ **B.** 56 bit in length

    ◯ **C.** 128 bit in length

    ◯ **D.** 256 bit in length

17. An organization wants to use a system for the encryption and decryption of email along with digitally signing emails. Which of the following meets this requirement?

Quick Answer: **279**
Detailed Answer: **289**

    ◯ **A.** OTP

    ◯ **B.** PGP

    ◯ **C.** DES

    ◯ **D.** ECC

18. Which of the following AES encryption key strengths is most commonly found today on secure USB sticks?

Quick Answer: **279**
Detailed Answer: **289**

    ◯ **A.** 128 bit in length

    ◯ **B.** 192 bit in length

    ◯ **C.** 256 bit in length

    ◯ **D.** 1024 bit in length

19. Which of the following ciphers does TKIP use?

Quick Answer: **279**
Detailed Answer: **289**

    ◯ **A.** RC5

    ◯ **B.** Blowfish

    ◯ **C.** IDEA

    ◯ **D.** RC4

20. Which of the following ciphers does WEP use?

Quick Answer: **279**
Detailed Answer: **289**

    ◯ **A.** RC5

    ◯ **B.** Blowfish

    ◯ **C.** IDEA

    ◯ **D.** RC4

Objective 5.4: Explain and implement protocols.

1. Which of the following are the most commonly used cryptographic protocols for managing secure communication between a client and server over the Web? (Select all correct answers.)

   ○ **A.** SSL

   ○ **B.** TLS

   ○ **C.** PPTP

   ○ **D.** WEP

Quick Answer: **279**
Detailed Answer: **289**

2. An organization wants to use an encapsulated tunneling protocol the does not send authentication information in cleartext to support the creation of VPNs. Which of the following meets this requirement?

   ○ **A.** HTTP

   ○ **B.** PPTP

   ○ **C.** MIME

   ○ **D.** L2TP

Quick Answer: **279**
Detailed Answer: **289**

3. An organization wants to use a network protocol that enables the secure transfer of data from a remote client to a private enterprise server. Which of the following meets this requirement?

   ○ **A.** HTTP

   ○ **B.** PPTP

   ○ **C.** MIME

   ○ **D.** L2TP

Quick Answer: **279**
Detailed Answer: **289**

4. Which of the following supports on-demand, multiprotocol, and virtual private networking over public networks?

   ○ **A.** HTTP

   ○ **B.** PPTP

   ○ **C.** MIME

   ○ **D.** L2TP

Quick Answer: **279**
Detailed Answer: **290**

5. Which of the following cryptographic methods is used by SSH?

   ○ **A.** RSA

   ○ **B.** ECC

   ○ **C.** OTP

   ○ **D.** PGP

Quick Answer: **279**
Detailed Answer: **290**

6. Which of the following algorithms can SSH use for data encryption? (Select all correct answers.)

   ○ **A.** IDEA

   ○ **B.** Blowfish

   ○ **C.** DES

   ○ **D.** Diffie-Hellman

Quick Answer: **279**
Detailed Answer: **290**

7. Which of the following secure utilities are encapsulated in the SSH suite? (Select all correct answers.)

   ○ **A.** slogin

   ○ **B.** rlogin

   ○ **C.** rsh

   ○ **D.** scp

Quick Answer: **279**
Detailed Answer: **290**

8. Which of the following protocols does IPsec use to provide authentication services, as well as encapsulation of data?

   ○ **A.** HTTP

   ○ **B.** PPTP

   ○ **C.** IKE

   ○ **D.** PKI

Quick Answer: **279**
Detailed Answer: **290**

9. An organization wants to use a protocol that has connectionless integrity and data origin authentication for IP packets. Which of the following meets this requirement?

   ○ **A.** IKE

   ○ **B.** SSH

   ○ **C.** IP

   ○ **D.** AH

Quick Answer: **279**
Detailed Answer: **290**

10. If IPsec is configured to use AH only, which of the following protocol traffic must be permitted to pass through the firewall?

    ○ **A.** Protocol 255

    ○ **B.** Protocol 51

    ○ **C.** Protocol 50

    ○ **D.** Protocol 2

Quick Answer: **279**
Detailed Answer: **291**

11. If IPsec is configured to use ESP only, which of the following protocol traffic must be permitted to pass through the firewall?

Quick Answer: **279**
Detailed Answer: **291**

- ○ **A.** Protocol 255
- ○ **B.** Protocol 51
- ○ **C.** Protocol 50
- ○ **D.** Protocol 2

12. If IPsec is configured for nested AH and ESP, IP can be configured
to let only which of the following protocol's traffic to pass through
the firewall?

Quick Answer: **279**
Detailed Answer: **291**

- ○ **A.** Protocol 255
- ○ **B.** Protocol 51
- ○ **C.** Protocol 50
- ○ **D.** Protocol 2

13. Which of the following encryption schemes does S/MIME use?

Quick Answer: **279**
Detailed Answer: **291**

- ○ **A.** RSA
- ○ **B.** ECC
- ○ **C.** OTP
- ○ **D.** PGP

14. Which of the following protocols was developed to support connectivity for banking transactions and other secure web communications, but is not commonly used?

Quick Answer: **279**
Detailed Answer: **291**

- ○ **A.** HTTP
- ○ **B.** PPTP
- ○ **C.** S-HTTP
- ○ **D.** S/MIME

15. Which of the following is a specification that provides email privacy using encryption and authentication via digital signatures?

Quick Answer: **279**
Detailed Answer: **291**

- ○ **A.** HTTP
- ○ **B.** PPTP
- ○ **C.** S-HTTP
- ○ **D.** S/MIME

16. Which of the following encrypts and decrypts email messages using asymmetric encryptions schemes such as RSA?

Quick Answer: **279**
Detailed Answer: **292**

- ○ **A.** S/MIME
- ○ **B.** PGP/MIME
- ○ **C.** HTTP
- ○ **D.** PPTP

17. Which of the following TLS protocols allows the client and server to authenticate to one another?

Quick Answer: **279**
Detailed Answer: **292**

- ○ **A.** Record protocol
- ○ **B.** Alert protocol
- ○ **C.** Application protocol
- ○ **D.** Handshake protocol

18. Which of the following TLS protocols provides connection security?

Quick Answer: **279**
Detailed Answer: **292**

- ○ **A.** Record protocol
- ○ **B.** Alert protocol
- ○ **C.** Application protocol
- ○ **D.** Handshake protocol

19. An organization is concerned about web-based connections and wants to implement encryption and authentication. Which of the following ports will the organization typically use for secured communication?

Quick Answer: **279**
Detailed Answer: **292**

- ○ **A.** 8080
- ○ **B.** 80
- ○ **C.** 443
- ○ **D.** 445

20. An organization is concerned about the cleartext communications of a Telnet session. Which of the following will the organization implement to authenticate and encrypt the data stream?

Quick Answer: **279**
Detailed Answer: **292**

- ○ **A.** SSL
- ○ **B.** TLS
- ○ **C.** WEP
- ○ **D.** SSH

Objective 5.5: Explain core concepts of public key cryptography.

1. Which of the following best describes a public key infrastructure?

   ○ **A.** A de facto standard that defines a framework for authentication services by a directory

   ○ **B.** A collection of varying technologies and policies for the creation and use of digital certificates

   ○ **C.** The de facto cryptographic message standards developed and published by RSA Laboratories

   ○ **D.** The development of Internet standards for X.509-based key infrastructures

Quick Answer: **279**
Detailed Answer: **292**

2. Which of the following best describes the scenario where all certificates are issued by a third-party certificate authority (CA) and if one party trusts the CA, then it automatically trusts the certificates that CA issues?

   ○ **A.** Certificate trust model

   ○ **B.** Certificate authority

   ○ **C.** Registration authority

   ○ **D.** Certificate practice statement

Quick Answer: **279**
Detailed Answer: **293**

3. Which of the following best describes the Public Key Cryptography Standards?

   ○ **A.** A de facto standard that defines a framework for authentication services by a directory

   ○ **B.** A collection of varying technologies and policies for the creation and use of digital certificates

   ○ **C.** The de facto cryptographic message standards developed and published by RSA Laboratories

   ○ **D.** The development of Internet standards for X.509-based key infrastructure

Quick Answer: **279**
Detailed Answer: **293**

4. Which of the following provides authentication to the CA as to the validity of a client's certificate request?

   ○ **A.** Certificate trust model

   ○ **B.** Certificate authority

   ○ **C.** Registration authority

   ○ **D.** Certificate practice statement

Quick Answer: **279**
Detailed Answer: **293**

5. Which of the following is true about the validity period of X.509 standard digital certificates?

Quick Answer: **279**
Detailed Answer: **293**

- ○ **A.** It can be of any duration period.
- ○ **B.** It is renewed on a six-month period.
- ○ **C.** It can only be one year.
- ○ **D.** It cannot be more than three years.

6. Which of the following information is contained in a X.509 standard digital certificate? (Select all correct answers.)

Quick Answer: **279**
Detailed Answer: **293**

- ○ **A.** User's private key
- ○ **B.** Signature algorithm identifier
- ○ **C.** User's public key
- ○ **D.** Serial number

7. Which of the following issue certificates, verifies the holder of a digital certificate, and ensures that the holder of the certificate is who they claim to be?

Quick Answer: **279**
Detailed Answer: **293**

- ○ **A.** Certificate trust model
- ○ **B.** Certificate authority
- ○ **C.** Registration authority
- ○ **D.** Certificate practice statement

8. Which of the following best describes the X.509 standard?

Quick Answer: **279**
Detailed Answer: **294**

- ○ **A.** A de facto standard that defines a framework for authentication services by a directory
- ○ **B.** A collection of varying technologies and policies for the creation and use of digital certificates
- ○ **C.** The de facto cryptographic message standards developed and published by RSA Laboratories
- ○ **D.** The development of Internet standards for X.509-based key infrastructures

9. Which of the following is a legal document created and published by a CA for the purpose of conveying information?

Quick Answer: **279**
Detailed Answer: **294**

- ○ **A.** Certificate trust model
- ○ **B.** Certificate authority
- ○ **C.** Registration authority
- ○ **D.** Certificate practice statement

10. Which of the following best describes PKIX?

- ○ **A.** A de facto standard that defines a framework for authentication services by a directory
- ○ **B.** A collection of varying technologies and policies for the creation and use of digital certificates
- ○ **C.** The de facto cryptographic message standards developed and published by RSA Laboratories
- ○ **D.** The development of Internet standards for X.509-based certificate infrastructures

Quick Answer: **279**
Detailed Answer: **294**

11. Which of the following are functions of a registration authority? (Select all correct answers.)

- ○ **A.** Serves as an aggregator of information
- ○ **B.** Conveys information in the form of a legal document
- ○ **C.** Ensures that the holder of the certificate is who they claim to be
- ○ **D.** Provides authentication about the validity of a certificate request

Quick Answer: **279**
Detailed Answer: **294**

12. An organization determines that some clients have fraudulently obtained certificates. Which of the following would be the most likely action the organization will take?

- ○ **A.** Use a recovery agent
- ○ **B.** Revoke the certificates
- ○ **C.** Change the trust model
- ○ **D.** Implement key escrow

Quick Answer: **279**
Detailed Answer: **294**

13. Which of the following provides the rules indicating the purpose and use of an assigned digital certificate?

- ○ **A.** Registration authority
- ○ **B.** Key escrow
- ○ **C.** Trust model
- ○ **D.** Certificate policy

Quick Answer: **279**
Detailed Answer: **294**

14. Which of the following is used to describe the situation where a CA or other entity maintains a copy of the private key associated with the public key signed by the CA?

- ○ **A.** Registration authority
- ○ **B.** Key escrow
- ○ **C.** Trust model
- ○ **D.** Certificate policy

Quick Answer: **279**
Detailed Answer: **295**

15. Which of the following best describes the difference between a certificate policy and a certificate practice statement?

Quick Answer: 279
Detailed Answer: 295

- ○ **A.** The focus of a certificate policy is on the CA; the focus of a CPS is on the certificate.
- ○ **B.** The focus of a certificate policy is on the private key; the focus of a CPS is on the public key.
- ○ **C.** The focus of a certificate policy is on the certificate; the focus of a CPS is on the CA.
- ○ **D.** The focus of a certificate policy is on the public key; the focus of a CPS is on the private key.

16. An organization determines that some clients have fraudulently obtained certificates. Which of the following is used to distribute certificate revocation information?

Quick Answer: 279
Detailed Answer: 295

- ○ **A.** CPS
- ○ **B.** CRL
- ○ **C.** ACL
- ○ **D.** PKI

17. Which of the following CA models is most closely related to a web of trust?

Quick Answer: 279
Detailed Answer: 295

- ○ **A.** Cross-certification model
- ○ **B.** Hierarchical model
- ○ **C.** Bridge model
- ○ **D.** Virtual bridge model

18. An organization requires a process that can be used for restoring a key pair from a backup and re-creating a digital certificate using the recovered keys. Which of the following will meet the organizational requirement?

Quick Answer: 279
Detailed Answer: 295

- ○ **A.** Key storage
- ○ **B.** Key revocation
- ○ **C.** Key escrow
- ○ **D.** Key recovery

19. An organization decides to implement a single CA architecture. Which of the following is the greatest potential issue the organization will face in using this model?

    ○ **A.** Sole point of compromise

    ○ **B.** Multiple points of compromise

    ○ **C.** Difficult key management

    ○ **D.** Complex certificate management

Quick Answer: **279**
Detailed Answer: **295**

20. An organization is implementing a certificate architecture. Which of the following CAs would the organization take offline?

    ○ **A.** Subordinate CA

    ○ **B.** Secondary CA

    ○ **C.** Bridge CA

    ○ **D.** Root CA

Quick Answer: **279**
Detailed Answer: **296**

Objective 5.6: Implement PKI and certificate management.

1. An organization is formulating policies for the certificate lifecycle. Which of the following documents will the organization include? (Select all correct answers.)

    ○ **A.** Certificate revocation statement

    ○ **B.** Certificate policy

    ○ **C.** Key escrow

    ○ **D.** Certification practice statement

Quick Answer: **279**
Detailed Answer: **296**

2. An organization decides to implement a centralized key management system. Which of the following are the greatest potential issues the organization will face in implementing this system? (Select all correct answers.)

    ○ **A.** Need for a secure channel to transmit the private key

    ○ **B.** Additional required infrastructure

    ○ **C.** Additional administrative overhead

    ○ **D.** Need for secure channel to transmit the public key

Quick Answer: **280**
Detailed Answer: **296**

3. An organization wishes to allow a CA to have access to all the information that is encrypted using the public key from a user's certificate, as well as create digital signatures on behalf of the user. Which of the following best meets this requirement?

- ○ **A.** Key storage
- ○ **B.** Key revocation
- ○ **C.** Key escrow
- ○ **D.** Key recovery

4. An administrator is tasked with checking the state of several digital certificates. Which of the following will the administrator use to perform this function? (Select all correct answers.)

- ○ **A.** Certificate policy
- ○ **B.** Certificate revocation lists
- ○ **C.** Online Certificate Status Protocol
- ○ **D.** Certification practice statement

5. An organization discovers that some clients may have fraudulently obtained certificates. The organization wants to allow the certificates to stay in place until the validity can be verified. Which of the following is the most appropriate action for the organization?

- ○ **A.** Certificate revocation
- ○ **B.** Certificate suspension
- ○ **C.** Key recovery
- ○ **D.** Key escrow

6. An organization discovers that some clients may have corrupt key pairs but the keys are still considered valid and trusted. Which of the following is the most appropriate action for the organization?

- ○ **A.** Certificate revocation
- ○ **B.** Certificate suspension
- ○ **C.** Key recovery
- ○ **D.** Key escrow

7. An organization chooses to implement a decentralized key management system. For which of the following functions will a user be responsible?

- ○ **A.** Revocation of the digital certificate
- ○ **B.** Creation of the digital certificate
- ○ **C.** Key recovery and archiving
- ○ **D.** Creation of the private and public keys

8. An organization wants to reduce the complexity of using a large cross-certification model. Which of the following will meet this requirement?

- ○ **A.** A subordinate CA model
- ○ **B.** A hierarchical model
- ○ **C.** A bridge CA model
- ○ **D.** A root CA model

9. A reorder associate needs a key pair for signing and sending encrypted messages and a key pair for restricted equipment ordering limited to a specific dollar amount. Which of the following is true about the number of key pairs required in this situation?

- ○ **A.** Only one key pair is needed.
- ○ **B.** Two key pairs are required.
- ○ **C.** Three key pairs are required.
- ○ **D.** Four key pairs are required.

10. The key usage extension of the certificate specifies which of the following?

- ○ **A.** The cryptographic algorithm used
- ○ **B.** How the private key can be used
- ○ **C.** The time frame the key can be used
- ○ **D.** How the public key can be used

11. Which of the following are best practices regarding key destruction if the key pair is used for digital signatures? (Select all correct answers.)

- ○ **A.** The certificate should be added to the CRL.
- ○ **B.** The public key portion should be destroyed first.
- ○ **C.** The private key portion should be destroyed first.
- ○ **D.** The certificate should be added to the CPS.

12. Which of the following are correct functions of the certificate key usage extension? (Select all correct answers.)

- ○ **A.** Peer negotiation
- ○ **B.** Creation of digital signatures
- ○ **C.** Exchange of sensitive information
- ○ **D.** Securing of connections

13. Which of the following is true regarding the encryption and decryption of email using an asymmetric encryption algorithm?

- ○ **A.** The public key is used to either encrypt or decrypt.
- ○ **B.** The private key is used to decrypt data encrypted with the public key.
- ○ **C.** The private key is used to encrypt and the public key is used to decrypt.
- ○ **D.** A secret key is used to perform both encrypt and decrypt operations.

14. Which of the following best describes what happens when a certificate expires?

- ○ **A.** It gets automatically renewed.
- ○ **B.** It can be extended for another equal period.
- ○ **C.** A new certificate must be issued.
- ○ **D.** A new identity is issued for the current one.

15. Which of the following events comprise the certificate lifecycle? (Select all correct answers.)

- ○ **A.** Creation
- ○ **B.** Preservation
- ○ **C.** Usage
- ○ **D.** Destruction

16. An organization had an incident where a private key was compromised. Which of the following methods can the organization use to notify the community that the certificate is no longer valid? (Select all correct answers.)

- ○ **A.** Certificate policy statement
- ○ **B.** Certificate revocation list
- ○ **C.** Certification practice statement
- ○ **D.** Online Certificate Status Protocol

17. Which of the following best describes the difference between certificate suspension and certificate revocation?

Quick Answer: **280**
Detailed Answer: **298**

 ○ **A.** In suspension, new credentials are not needed; in revocation, new credentials are issued.

 ○ **B.** In suspension, new credentials are issued; in revocation, new credentials are not needed.

 ○ **C.** In suspension, the key pair is restored from backup; in revocation, the key pair is restored from escrow.

 ○ **D.** In suspension, the key pair is restored from escrow; in revocation, the key pair is restored from backup.

18. The organizational wants to implement the backing up the public and private key across multiple systems. Which of the following satisfies this requirement?

Quick Answer: **280**
Detailed Answer: **298**

 ○ **A.** Key escrow

 ○ **B.** M of N control

 ○ **C.** Key recovery

 ○ **D.** Version control

19. Which of the following are basic status levels existing in most PKI solutions? (Select all correct answers.)

Quick Answer: **280**
Detailed Answer: **299**

 ○ **A.** Active

 ○ **B.** Valid

 ○ **C.** Revoked

 ○ **D.** Suspended

20. Which of the following problems does key escrow enable an organization to overcome?

Quick Answer: **280**
Detailed Answer: **299**

 ○ **A.** Forgotten passwords

 ○ **B.** Forged signatures

 ○ **C.** Phishing emails

 ○ **D.** Virus infection

Quick-Check Answer Key

Objective 5.1: Explain general cryptography concepts.

1. C	11. C	21. A
2. B	12. A, C, D	22. C
3. D	13. B	23. B
4. A	14. A	24. D
5. A, C	15. D	25. B, C, D
6. B, D	16. B	26. D
7. B	17. A	27. A
8. C	18. B	28. B
9. A	19. D	29. C
10. B	20. A, C	30. B

Objective 5.2: Explain basic hashing concepts and map various algorithms to appropriate applications.

1. B	5. C	9. B
2. C	6. B	10. D
3. D	7. A, C	
4. A	8. D	

Objective 5.3: Explain basic encryption concepts and map various algorithms to appropriate applications.

1. B, C	8. B, D	15. B
2. B	9. B	16. C
3. A	10. C	17. B
4. D	11. C, D	18. C
5. B	12. B	19. D
6. C	13. A	20. D
7. A	14. B	

Objective 5.4: Explain and implement protocols.

1. A, B	8. C	15. D
2. D	9. D	16. B
3. B	10. B	17. D
4. B	11. C	18. A
5. A	12. B	19. C
6. A, B, C	13. A	20. D
7. A, D	14. C	

Objective 5.5: Explain core concepts of public key cryptography.

1. B	8. A	15. C
2. A	9. D	16. B
3. C	10. D	17. A
4. C	11. A, D	18. D
5. A	12. B	19. A
6. B, C, D	13. D	20. D
7. B	14. B	

Objective 5.6: Implement PKI and certificate management.

1. B, D

2. A, B

3. C

4. B, C

5. B

6. C

7. D

8. C

9. B

10. B

11. A, C

12. B, C

13. B

14. C

15. A, C, D

16. B, D

17. A

18. B

19. B, C, D

20. A

Answers and Explanations

Objective 5.1: Explain general cryptography concepts.

1. **Answer: C.** A cryptography key describes a string of bits, which are used for encrypting and decrypting data. These keys can also be thought of as a password or table. Answer A is incorrect because it describes encryption. Encryption takes plaintext data and converts it into an unreadable format (ciphertext) by using an algorithm (cipher). Answer B is incorrect because it describes steganography. Steganography is a method for hiding messages so that unintended recipients aren't even aware of any message. Answer D is incorrect; an algorithm is the mathematical procedure or sequence of steps taken to perform encryption and decryption.

2. **Answer: B.** Steganography is a method for hiding messages so that unintended recipients aren't even aware of any message. Answer A is incorrect because it describes encryption. Encryption takes plaintext data and converts it into an unreadable format (ciphertext) by using an algorithm (cipher). Answer C is incorrect because it describes a cryptography key. A cryptography key is a string of bits, which are used for encrypting and decrypting data. Answer D is incorrect; an algorithm is the mathematical procedure or sequence of steps taken to perform encryption and decryption.

3. **Answer: D.** An algorithm is the mathematical procedure or sequence of steps taken to perform encryption and decryption. Answer A is incorrect because it describes encryption. Encryption takes plaintext data and converts it into an unreadable format (ciphertext) by using an algorithm (cipher). Answer B is incorrect because it describes steganography. Steganography is a method for hiding messages so that unintended recipients aren't even aware of any message. Answer C is incorrect because it describes a cryptography key. A cryptography key is a string of bits, which are used for encrypting and decrypting data.

4. **Answer: A.** Encryption takes plaintext data and converts it into an unreadable format (ciphertext) by using an algorithm (cipher). Answer B is incorrect because it describes steganography. Steganography is a method for hiding messages so that unintended recipients aren't even aware of any message. Answer C is incorrect because it describes a cryptography key. A cryptography key is a string of bits, which are used for encrypting and decrypting data. Answer D is incorrect; an algorithm is the mathematical procedure or sequence of steps taken to perform encryption and decryption.

5. **Answer: A, C.** There has been growing concerns over the security of data, which continues to rapidly grow across information systems and reside in many different locations. Combining this with more sophisticated attacks and a growing economy around computer related fraud and data theft, make the need to protect the data itself even more important than in the past. Answers B and D are incorrect; the increase in virus infections and use of steganography has nothing to do with cryptography.

6. **Answer: B, D.** There are two fundamental types of encryption algorithms: symmetric key and asymmetric key. Answer A is incorrect. Hashing algorithms are not encryption methods, but offer additional system security via a "signature" for data confirming the original content. Answer C is incorrect; Trusted Platform is the name of a published specification detailing a secure cryptoprocessor that can store cryptographic keys that protect information.

7. **Answer: B.** Symmetric key cryptography is an encryption system that uses a common shared key between the sender and receiver. Answers A and D are incorrect because hashing is different from encryption. Answer C is incorrect because it describes asymmetric key cryptography.

8. **Answer: C.** The asymmetric encryption algorithm has two keys: a public one and a private one. Answers A and D are incorrect because hashing is different from encryption. Answer B is incorrect because it describes symmetric key cryptography.

9. **Answer: A.** The asymmetric encryption algorithm has two keys: a public one and a private one. The public key is made available to whoever is going to encrypt the data sent to the holder of the private key. Often the public encryption key is made available in a number of fashions, such as email or centralized servers that host a pseudo address book of published public encryption keys. Answer B is incorrect because this is where the private key is stored. Answer C is incorrect because a cryptographic vault is used for theft resistance. It is a small crypto file system containing all the secrets in unencrypted form. Answer D is incorrect; the user shared network folder is not used to store the public key.

10. **Answer: B.** The asymmetric encryption algorithm has two keys: a public one and a private one. The private key is maintained on the host system or application. Answer A is incorrect because this is where the public key is stored. The public encryption key is made available in a number of fashions, such as email or centralized servers that host a pseudo address book of published public encryption keys. Answer C is incorrect because a cryptographic vault is used for theft resistance. It is a small crypto file system containing all the secrets in unencrypted form. Answer D is incorrect; the user shared network folder is not used to store the public key.

11. **Answer: C.** Asymmetric algorithms are often referred to as public key algorithms because of their use of the public key as the focal point for the algorithm. Answers A, B, and D are incorrect; symmetric key algorithms are often referred to as secret key algorithms, private key algorithms, and shared secret algorithms.

12. **Answer: A, C, D.** Symmetric key algorithms are often referred to as secret key algorithms, private key algorithms, and shared secret algorithms. Answer B is incorrect. Asymmetric algorithms are often referred to as public key algorithms because of their use of the public key as the focal point for the algorithm.

13. **Answer: B.** Some general rules for asymmetric algorithms include the following: the public key can never decrypt a message that it was used to encrypt with, private keys should never be able to be determined through the public key (if it is designed properly), and each key should be able to decrypt a message made with the other. For instance, if a message is encrypted with the private key, the public key should be able to decrypt it; therefore, answers A and C are incorrect. Answer D is incorrect because the public key can never be used to decrypt a message even by an administrator.

14. **Answer: A.** Some general rules for asymmetric algorithms include the following: the public key can never decrypt a message that it was used to encrypt with, private keys should never be able to be determined through the public key (if it is designed properly), and each key should be able to decrypt a message made with the other. For instance, if a message is encrypted with the private key, the public key should be able to decrypt it; therefore, answers B and C are incorrect. Answer D is incorrect because the public key can never be used to decrypt a message even by an administrator.

15. **Answer: D.** Steganography seeks to hide the presence of a message, whereas the purpose of cryptography is to transform a message from readable plaintext into an unreadable form known as ciphertext. Answer A is incorrect because steganography seeks to hide the presence of a message not expose it. Answers B and C are incorrect because the descriptions of each are reversed and cryptography has nothing to do with hiding or exposing hidden messages.

16. **Answer: B.** Steganography has been used by many printers, using tiny dots that reveal serial numbers and time stamps. Answer A is incorrect; phishing is the fraudulent process of attempting to acquire sensitive information. Answer C is incorrect; cryptography transforms a message from readable plaintext into an unreadable form known as ciphertext. Answer D is incorrect; a hash is a generated summary from a mathematical rule or algorithm.

17. **Answer: A.** Confidentiality is concerned with the unauthorized disclosure of sensitive information. Answer B is incorrect; integrity pertains to preventing unauthorized modifications of information or systems. Answer C is incorrect; authorization is the function of specifying access rights to resources. Answer D is incorrect; availability is about maintaining continuous operations and preventing service disruptions.

18. **Answer: B.** Integrity pertains to preventing unauthorized modifications of information or systems. Answer A is incorrect; confidentiality is concerned with the unauthorized disclosure of sensitive information. Answer C is incorrect; authorization is the function of specifying access rights to resources. Answer D is incorrect; availability is about maintaining continuous operations and preventing service disruptions.

19. **Answer: D.** Availability is about maintaining continuous operations and preventing service disruptions. Answer A is incorrect; confidentiality is concerned with the unauthorized disclosure of sensitive information. Answer B is incorrect; integrity pertains to preventing unauthorized modifications of information or systems. Answer C is incorrect; authorization is the function of specifying access rights to resources.

20. **Answer: A, C.** Pretty Good Privacy (PGP) is a computer program used for signing, encrypting, and decrypting email messages. PGP is used to send and receive emails in a confidential, secure fashion. Answer B is incorrect. Availability is about maintaining continuous operations and preventing service disruptions. Answer D is incorrect; authorization is the function of specifying access rights to resources.

21. **Answer: A.** Integrity is the assurance that data and information can only be modified by those authorized to do so. Answer B is incorrect; availability refers to the accessibility of information and information systems, when they are needed. Answer C is incorrect; confidentiality describes the act of limiting disclosure of private information. Answer D is incorrect because authorization is the function of specifying access rights to resources.

22. **Answer: C.** Confidentiality describes the act of limiting disclosure of private information. Answer A is incorrect; integrity is the assurance that data and information can only be modified by those authorized to do so. Answer B is incorrect; availability refers to the accessibility of information and information systems, when they are needed. Answer D is incorrect because authorization is the function of specifying access rights to resources.

23. **Answer: B.** Availability refers to the accessibility of information and information systems, when they are needed. Answer A is incorrect; integrity is the assurance that data and information can only be modified by those authorized to do so. Answer C is incorrect; confidentiality describes the act of limiting disclosure of private information. Answer D is incorrect because authorization is the function of specifying access rights to resources.

24. **Answer: D.** Nonrepudiation is intended to provide, through encryption, a method of accountability in which there is no refute from where data has been sourced (or arrived from). Answer A is incorrect because it describes integrity. Answer B is incorrect because it describes confidentiality. Answer C is incorrect because it describes authorization.

25. **Answer: B, C, D.** The four key elements that nonrepudiation services provide are proof of origin, proof of submission, proof of delivery, and proof of receipt. Answer A is incorrect because proof of service is a court paper filed by a process server as evidence that the witness or party to the lawsuit was served with the court papers as instructed.

26. **Answer: D.** Digital signatures attempt to guarantee the identity of the person sending the data from one point to another. Answer A is incorrect; a hash is a generated summary from a mathematical rule or algorithm. Answer B is incorrect; steganography seeks to hide the presence of a message. Answer C is incorrect; cryptography transforms a message from readable plaintext into an unreadable form known as ciphertext.

27. **Answer: A.** Whole disk encryption helps mitigate the risks associated with lost or stolen laptops and accompanying disclosure laws when the organization is required to report data breaches. Answer B is incorrect; Trusted Platform Module is the name of a published specification detailing a secure cryptoprocessor that can store cryptographic keys that protect information. Answer C is incorrect; digital signatures attempt to guarantee the identity of the person sending the data from one point to another. Answer D is incorrect; a hash is a generated summary from a mathematical rule or algorithm.

28. **Answer: B.** At the most basic level, TPM provides for the secure storage of keys, passwords, and digital certificates, and is hardware based, typically attached to the circuit board of the system. Answer A is incorrect because whole disk encryption helps mitigate the risks associated with lost or stolen laptops and accompanying disclosure laws. Answer C is incorrect; digital signatures attempt to guarantee the identity of the person sending the data from one point to another. Answer D is incorrect; a hash is a generated summary from a mathematical rule or algorithm.

29. **Answer: C.** In most cases, the use of SSL and TLS is single sided. Only the server is being authenticated as valid with a verifiable certificate. For example, when conducting an online banking transaction, one can be assured they are at the legitimate site by verifying the server side certificate, whereas the client is verified by a means other than a certificate, such as a username and password. Answer A is incorrect; digital signatures attempt to guarantee the identity of the person sending the data from one point to another. Answer B is incorrect; a hash is a generated summary from a mathematical rule or algorithm. Answer D is incorrect; in a dual-sided scenario, not only is the server authenticated using a certificate, but the client side is as well. This certainly can provide for a more secure environment, but additional overhead is created. Furthermore, a unique client side certificate now needs to be created and managed for every client rather than just a single server.

30. **Answer: B.** Because of the sensitive nature behind the uses of cryptography, the use of well-known, proven technologies is crucial. Back doors and flaws, for example, can undermine any encryption algorithm, which is why proven algorithms should always be considered. Although various vendors might have their own encryption solutions, most of these depend upon well-known, time-tested algorithms, and generally speaking one should be skeptical of any vendor using a proprietary nonproven algorithm; therefore, answers C and D are incorrect. Answer A is incorrect; DES is only a 56-bit encryption key algorithm and is considered weak.

Objective 5.2: Explain basic hashing concepts and map various algorithms to appropriate applications.

1. **Answer: B.** A hash is a generated summary from a mathematical rule or algorithm, and is used commonly as a "digital fingerprint" to verify the integrity of files and messages as well as to ensure message integrity and provide authentication verification. Answer A is incorrect; encryption takes plaintext data and converts it into an unreadable format (ciphertext) by using an algorithm (cipher). Answer C is incorrect because a cryptography key describes a string of bits, which are used for encrypting and decrypting data. Answer D is incorrect. An algorithm is the mathematical procedure or sequence of steps taken to perform a variety of functions. Hashing and encryption are examples of how algorithms can be used.

2. **Answer: C.** Hash functions work by taking a string (for example, a password or email) of any length, and producing a fixed-length string for output. Based on this information, answers A, B, and D are incorrect.

3. **Answer: D.** Although you can create a hash from a document, you cannot re-create the document from the hash. Keep in mind that hashing is a one-way function. Based on this information, answers A, B, and C are incorrect.

4. **Answer: A.** Secure Hash Algorithm (SHA, SHA-1) are hash algorithms pioneered by the National Security Agency and widely used in the U.S. government. SHA-1 can generate a 160-bit hash from any variable length string of data, making it very secure but also resource intensive. Based on this information, answers B, C, and D are incorrect.

5. **Answer: C.** Message Digest Series Algorithms MD2, MD4, and MD5 are a series of encryption algorithms created by Ronald Rivest (founder of RSA Data Security, Inc.), that are designed to be fast, simple, and secure. The MD series generates a hash of up to a 128-bit strength out of any length of data. Based on this information, answers A, B, and D are incorrect.

6. **Answer: B.** A Message Authentication Code (MAC) is similar to a hash function. The MAC is a small piece of data known as an authentication tag, which is derived by applying a message or file combined with a secret key to a cryptographic algorithm. The resulting MAC value can ensure the integrity of the data as well as its authenticity as one in possession of the secret key can subsequently detect if there are any changes from the original. Answer A is incorrect because it describes symmetric encryption. Answer C is incorrect because it describes asymmetric encryption. Answer D is incorrect because it describes the Secure Hash Algorithm.

7. **Answer: A, C.** The two primary weaknesses of LM hash are that first all passwords longer than seven characters are broken down into two chunks, from which each piece is hashed separately. Second, before the password is hashed, all lowercase characters are converted to uppercase characters. Answers B and D are incorrect; LM hashes have nothing to do with encryption keys.

8. **Answer: D.** A Message Authentication Code (MAC) is similar to a hash function, but is able to resist forgery and is not open to man in the middle attacks. A MAC can be thought of as an encrypted hash, combining an encryption key and a hashing algorithm. Based on this information, answers A, B, and C are incorrect.

9. **Answer: B.** Both SHA and the MD series are similar in design; however, keep in mind that because of the higher bit strength of the SHA-1 algorithm, it will be in the range of 20% to 30% slower to process than the MD family of algorithms; therefore, answer A is incorrect. Answer C is incorrect; LM hash is based on DES encryption. Answer D is incorrect; NTLM hashing makes use of the MD4 hashing algorithm.

10. **Answer: D.** NTLM hashing makes use of the MD4 hashing algorithm, and is used on more recent versions of the Windows operating system. Answers A and B are incorrect; MD5 and SHA are typically not used in place of NTLM. Answer C is incorrect; the NTLM hash is an improvement over the LM hash. LM hash is based on DES encryption, yet it is not considered to be effective (and is technically not truly a hashing algorithm) due to a weaknesses in the design implementation.

Objective 5.3: Explain basic encryption concepts and map various algorithms to appropriate applications.

1. **Answer: B, C.** Symmetric algorithms can be classified into either being a block cipher or a stream cipher. A stream cipher, as the name implies, encrypts the message bit by bit, one at a time; whereas, a block cipher encrypts the message in chunks. Answer A is incorrect; historical pen and paper ciphers used in the past are sometimes known as classical ciphers. Answer D is incorrect because simple substitution ciphers and transposition ciphers are considered classical ciphers.

2. **Answer: B.** DES is a block cipher that uses a 56-bit key and 8 bits of parity on each 64-bit chuck of data. Based on this information, answers A, C, and D are incorrect.

3. **Answer: A.** Triple Data Encryption Standard (3DES), also known as Triple-DES, dramatically improves upon the DES by using the DES algorithm three times with three distinct keys. This provides a total effective key length of 168 bits. Based on this information, answers B, C, and D are incorrect.

4. **Answer: D.** RC4 is a stream cipher that uses a 1 to 2048 bits key length. Answers A, B, and C are incorrect because they are all block ciphers.

5. **Answer: B.** Blowfish Encryption Algorithm is a block cipher that can encrypt using any size chunk of data. Blowfish can also perform encryption with any length encryption key up to 448-bits, making it a very flexible and secure symmetric encryption algorithm. Answers A and C are incorrect; although they are block ciphers, the maximum key length of RC5 is 256 and the maximum key length of International Data Encryption Algorithm (IDEA) is 128. Answer D is incorrect; RC4 is a stream cipher.

6. **Answer: C.** Data Encryption Standard (DES) is a block cipher that uses a 56-bit key and 8 bits of parity on each 64-bit chuck of data. Answer A is incorrect; with Triple Data Encryption Standard (3DES), the DES algorithm is used three times with three distinct keys. This provides a total effective key length of 168 bits. Answer B is incorrect; the key length of RC5 is 128 to 256 bits. Answer D is incorrect; the key length of Advanced Encryption Standard (AES) is 128 to 256 bits.

7. **Answer: A.** Triple Data Encryption Standard (3DES), also known as Triple-DES, dramatically improves upon the Data Encryption Standard (DES) by using the DES algorithm three times with three distinct keys. This provides a total effective key length of 168 bits. Answer B is incorrect; the key length of RC5 is 128 to 256 bits. Answer C is incorrect; DES is a block cipher that uses a 56-bit key and 8 bits of parity on each 64-bit chuck of data. Answer D is incorrect; the key length of Advanced Encryption Standard (AES) is 128 to 256 bits.

8. **Answer: B, D.** The key length of both RC5 and AES is 128 to 256 bits. Answer A is incorrect; Triple Data Encryption Standard (3DES), also known as Triple-DES, dramatically improves upon the Data Encryption Standard (DES) by using the DES algorithm three times with three distinct keys. This provides a total effective key length of 168 bits. Answer C is incorrect; DES is a block cipher that uses a 56-bit key and 8 bits of parity on each 64-bit chuck of data.

9. **Answer: B.** There is one type of cipher that perhaps has earned the mark as being completely unbreakable: one-time pad (OTP). Unfortunately, the OTP currently has the tradeoff of requiring a key as long as the message, thus having significant storage and transmission costs. Answer A is incorrect; the key length of RC5 is 128 to 256 bits. Answer C is incorrect; the maximum key length of IDEA is 128. Answer D is incorrect; Data Encryption Standard (DES) is a block cipher that uses a 56-bit key and 8 bits of parity on each 64-bit chuck of data.

10. **Answer: C.** Advanced Encryption Standard (AES) is similar to Data Encryption Standard (DES) in that it can create keys from 128-bit to 256-bit in length and can perform the encryption and decryption of data up to 128-bit chunks of data. Similar to Triple Data Encryption Standard (3DES), the data is passed through three layers, each with a specific task, such as generating random keys based on the data and the bit strength being used. Based on this information, answers A, B, and D are incorrect.

11. **Answer: C, D.** Because of the additional overhead generated by using one key for encryption and another for decryption, using asymmetric algorithms requires far more resources than symmetric algorithms. Answers A and B are incorrect; both ECC and RSA are asymmetric algorithms.

12. **Answer: B.** PGP was originally designed to provide for the encryption/decryption of email, as well as for digitally signing emails. PGP follows the OpenPGP format using a combination of public key and private key encryption. Answer A is incorrect; one-time pad (OTP) is a type of cipher that perhaps has earned the mark as being completely unbreakable. Answer C is incorrect; Data Encryption Standard (DES) is a symmetric algorithm. Answer D is incorrect; Elliptic Curve Cryptography (ECC) is an asymmetric algorithm.

13. **Answer: A.** Rivest, Shamir, Adleman (RSA) is a well-known cryptography system used for encryption and digital signatures. In fact, the RSA algorithm is considered by many to be the standard for encryption and core technology that secures most business conducted on the Internet. Answer B is incorrect; Elliptic Curve Cryptography (ECC) is an asymmetric algorithm. Answer C is incorrect. One-time pad (OTP) is one type of cipher that perhaps has earned the mark as being completely unbreakable. Answer D is incorrect; Data Encryption Standard (DES) is a symmetric algorithm.

14. **Answer: B.** Elliptic Curve Cryptography (ECC) techniques utilize a method in which elliptic curves could be used to calculate simple, but very difficult to break, encryption keys to use in general purpose encryption. One of the key benefits of ECC encryption algorithms is that they have a very compact design because of the advanced mathematics involved in ECC. Answer A is incorrect. The Rivest, Shamir, Adleman (RSA) algorithm, named after its inventors at MIT, is considered by many to be the standard for encryption and core technology that secures most business conducted on the Internet. Answer C is incorrect; one-time pad (OTP) is one type of cipher that perhaps has earned the mark as being completely unbreakable. Answer D is incorrect; Data Encryption Standard (DES) is a symmetric algorithm.

15. **Answer: B.** There is one type of cipher that perhaps has earned the mark as being completely unbreakable: one-time pad (OTP). Unfortunately, the OTP currently has the tradeoff of requiring a key as long as the message, thus having significant storage and transmission costs. Answer A is incorrect; the key length of RC5 is 128 to 256 bits. Answer C is incorrect; the maximum key length of IDEA is 128. Answer D is incorrect; Data Encryption Standard (DES) is a block cipher that uses a 56-bit key and 8 bits of parity on each 64-bit chuck of data.

16. **Answer: C.** For most environments today, 128-bit encryption key strength is considered adequate; therefore, symmetric encryption may often suffice. However, if you want to simplify how you distribute keys, asymmetric encryption may be the better choice. Answer A is incorrect because Rivest, Shamir, Adleman (RSA) key generation on smart cards shows that the generation of up to 1024 bit prime numbers is costly

both in terms of time and energy. Answer B is incorrect because 56-bit encryption is considered weak. Answer D is incorrect; although many USB drives now come with 256-bit encryption, 128 bit is sufficient for an enterprise organization.

17. **Answer: B.** Pretty Good Privacy (PGP) was originally designed to provide for the encryption/decryption of email, as well as for digitally signing emails. PGP follows the OpenPGP format using a combination of public key and private key encryption. Answer A is incorrect. One-time pad (OTP) is one type of cipher that perhaps has earned the mark as being completely unbreakable. Answer C is incorrect; Data Encryption Standard (DES) is a symmetric algorithm. Answer D is incorrect; Elliptic Curve Cryptography (ECC) is an asymmetric algorithm.

18. **Answer: C.** Advanced Encryption Standard (AES) supports key lengths of 128, 192, and 256 bits, and many commercial offerings, to encrypt laptops or USB sticks for example, supply AES at the maximum 256-bit key length. Based on this information, answers A, B, and D are incorrect.

19. **Answer: D.** TKIP uses the RC4 algorithm, and does not require an upgrade to existing hardware. Based on this information, answers A, B, and C are incorrect.

20. **Answer: D.** Wired Equivalent Privacy (WEP) uses the RC4 cipher for confidentiality; however, the WEP algorithm, although still widely used, is no longer considered secure and has been replaced. Based on this information, answers A, B, and C are incorrect.

Objective 5.4: Explain and implement protocols.

1. **Answer: A, B.** Secure Sockets Layer (SSL) and Transport Layer Security (TLS) are the most widely used cryptographic protocols for managing secure communication between a client and server over the Web. Both essentially serve the same purpose with TLS being the successor to SSL. Answer C is incorrect; Point-to-Point Tunneling Protocol (PPTP) is not cryptographic. Answer D is incorrect because Wired Equivalent Privacy (WEP) is inherently unsecure and is not used specifically for client server connections.

2. **Answer: D.** Layer 2 Tunneling Protocol (L2TP) is an encapsulated tunneling protocol often used to support the creation of virtual private networks (VPNs). Answer A is incorrect because Hypertext Transfer Protocol (HTTP) is used for web-based communications. Answer B is incorrect because Point-to-Point Tunneling Protocol (PPTP) is a network protocol that enables the secure transfer of data from a remote client to a private enterprise server. PPTP sends authentication information in cleartext. Answer C is incorrect because Multipurpose Internet Mail Extensions (MIME) is used in email communications.

3. **Answer: B.** Point-to-Point Tunneling Protocol (PPTP) is a network protocol that enables the secure transfer of data from a remote client to a private enterprise server by creating a virtual private network (VPN) across TCP/IP-based data networks. Answer A is incorrect because Hypertext Transfer Protocol (HTTP) is used for web-based communications. Answer C is incorrect because Multipurpose Internet Mail Extensions (MIME) is used in email communications. Answer D is incorrect; Layer 2 Tunneling Protocol (L2TP) is an encapsulated tunneling protocol not a network protocol.

4. **Answer: B.** Point Tunneling Protocol (PPTP) is a network protocol that enables the secure transfer of data from a remote client to a private enterprise server by creating a virtual private network (VPN) across TCP/IP-based data networks. PPTP supports on-demand, multiprotocol, and virtual private networking over public networks, such as the Internet. Answer A is incorrect because Hypertext Transfer Protocol (HTTP) is used for web-based communications. Answer C is incorrect because Multipurpose Internet Mail Extensions (MIME) is used in email communications. Answer D is incorrect. Layer 2 Tunneling Protocol (L2TP) is an encapsulated tunneling protocol not a network protocol.

5. **Answer: A.** Secure Shell (SSH) utilizes the asymmetric (public key) Rivest, Shamir, Adleman (RSA) cryptography method to provide both connection and authentication. Answer B is incorrect; Elliptic Curve Cryptography (ECC) techniques utilize a method in which elliptic curves could be used to calculate simple, but very difficult to break, encryption keys to use in general purpose encryption. Answer C is incorrect. One-time pad (OTP) is one type of cipher that perhaps has earned the mark as being completely unbreakable. Answer D is incorrect; Pretty Good Privacy (PGP) was originally designed to provide for the encryption/decryption of email, as well as for digitally signing emails.

6. **Answer: A, B, C.** Data encryption with SSH is accomplished using one of the following algorithms: International Data Encryption Algorithm (IDEA), Blowfish, or Data Encryption Standard (DES). Answer D is incorrect because Diffie-Hellman is a mathematical algorithm that allows two computers to generate an identical shared secret on both systems, even though those systems may never have communicated with each other before.

7. **Answer: A, D.** Secure Shell (SSH) provides an authenticated and encrypted data stream, as opposed to the cleartext communications of a telnet session. The SSH suite encapsulates three secure utilities: slogin, ssh, and scp. Answers B and C are incorrect because rlogin and rsh are earlier nonsecure UNIX utilities.

8. **Answer: C.** IPsec provides authentication services, as well as encapsulation of data through support of the Internet Key Exchange (IKE) protocol. Answer A is incorrect because Hypertext Transfer Protocol (HTTP) is used for web-based communications. Answer B is incorrect. Point-to-Point Tunneling Protocol (PPTP) is a network protocol that enables the secure transfer of data from a remote client to a private enterprise server by creating a virtual private network (VPN) across TCP/IP-based data networks. Answer D is incorrect; a public key infrastructure (PKI) is a vast collection of varying technologies and policies for the creation and use of digital certificates.

9. **Answer: D.** Authentication Header (AH) provides connectionless integrity and data origin authentication for IP packets. Answer A is incorrect because the Internet Key Exchange (IKE) protocol provides for additional features and ease of configuration. IKE specifically provides authentication for IPsec peers and negotiates IPsec keys and security associations. Answer B is incorrect because Secure Shell (SSH) provides an authenticated and encrypted data stream, as opposed to the cleartext communications of a telnet session. Answer C is incorrect; Internet Protocol (IP) is part of the TCP/IP suite.

10. Answer: B. If IPsec is configured to do authentication only (AH), you must permit protocol 51 traffic to pass through the stateful firewall or packet filter. Answer A is incorrect; Protocol 255 is an Internet Assigned Numbers Authority (IANA) reserved value. Answer C is incorrect; in an IP header, ESP can be identified as IP protocol number 50. Answer D is incorrect; Protocol 2 is Internet Group Management (IGMP).

11. Answer: C. Encapsulating Security Payload (ESP) provides encryption and limited traffic flow confidentiality, or connectionless integrity, data origin authentication, and an antireplay service. In an IP header, ESP can be identified as IP protocol number 50. Answer A is incorrect; Protocol 255 is a IANA reserved value. Answer B is incorrect; Authentication Header (AH) provides connectionless integrity and data origin authentication for IP packets. In an IP header, AH can be identified as IP protocol number 51. Answer D is incorrect; Protocol 2 is Internet Group Management (IGMP).

12. Answer: B. If IPsec uses nested Authentication Header (AH) and Encapsulating Security Payload (ESP), IP can be configured to let only protocol 51 (AH) traffic pass through the stateful firewall or packet filter. Answer A is incorrect; Protocol 255 is an Internet Assigned Numbers Authority (IANA) reserved value. Answer C is incorrect; IP can be configured to let only protocol 51 (AH) traffic pass. Answer D is incorrect; Protocol 2 is Internet Group Management (IGMP).

13. Answer: A. S/MIME utilizes the Rivest, Shamir, Adleman (RSA) asymmetric encryption scheme to encrypt electronic mail transmissions over public networks. Answer B is incorrect; Elliptic Curve Cryptography (ECC) techniques utilize a method in which elliptic curves could be used to calculate simple, but very difficult to break, encryption keys to use in general purpose encryption. Answer C is incorrect. One-time pad (OTP) is one type of cipher that perhaps has earned the mark as being completely unbreakable. Answer D is incorrect; Pretty Good Privacy (PGP) was originally designed to provide for the encryption/decryption of email, as well as for digitally signing emails.

14. Answer: C. An alternative to HTTPS is the Secure Hypertext Transport Protocol (S-HTTP), which was developed to support connectivity for banking transactions and other secure web communications. Answer A is incorrect because HTTP is used for unsecured web-based communications. Answer B is incorrect because Point-to-Point Tunneling Protocol (PPTP) is a network protocol that enables the secure transfer of data from a remote client to a private enterprise server by creating a virtual private network (VPN) across TCP/IP-based data networks. Answer D is incorrect. S/MIME is used to encrypt electronic mail transmissions over public networks.

15. Answer: D. S/MIME utilizes the Rivest, Shamir, Adleman (RSA) asymmetric encryption scheme is a specification that provides email privacy using encryption and authentication via digital signatures. Answer A is incorrect because Hypertext Transfer Protocol (HTTP) is used for unsecured web-based communications. Answer B is incorrect because Point-to-Point Tunneling Protocol (PPTP) is a network protocol that enables the secure transfer of data from a remote client to a private enterprise server by creating a virtual private network (VPN) across TCP/IP-based data networks. Answer C is incorrect. An alternative to HTTPS is the Secure Hypertext Transport Protocol (S-HTTP), which was developed to support connectivity for banking transactions and other secure web communications.

16. **Answer: B.** PGP/MIME derives from the Pretty Good Privacy application and is an alternative to S/MIME. Basically, it encrypts and decrypts email messages using asymmetric encryptions schemes such as RSA. Answer A is incorrect; Multipurpose Internet Mail Extensions (MIME) does not encrypt email. MIME extends the original Simple Mail Transfer Protocol (SMTP) to allow the inclusion of nontextual data within an email message. Answer C is incorrect because Hypertext Transfer Protocol (HTTP) is used for unsecured web-based communications. Answer D is incorrect because Point-to-Point Tunneling Protocol (PPTP) is a network protocol that enables the secure transfer of data from a remote client to a private enterprise server by creating a virtual private network (VPN) across TCP/IP-based data networks.

17. **Answer: D.** Transport Layer Security (TLS) consist of two additional protocols: the TLS record protocol and the TLS handshake protocol. The handshake protocol allows the client and server to authenticate to one another and the record protocol provides connection security. Therefore, Answer A is incorrect. Answer B is incorrect; the alert protocol is used to signal errors. Answer C is incorrect; application protocol is a generic term that can be used to describe TLS.

18. **Answer: A.** Transport Layer Security (TLS) consist of two additional protocols: the TLS record protocol and the TLS handshake protocol. The handshake protocol allows the client and server to authenticate to one another and the record protocol provides connection security; therefore, Answer D is incorrect. Answer B is incorrect; the alert protocol is used to signal errors. Answer C is incorrect; application protocol is a generic term that can be used to describe TLS.

19. **Answer: C.** Hypertext Transfer Protocol Secure (HTTPS) traffic typically occurs over port 443. Answer A is incorrect; port 8080 is a popular alternative to port 80 for offering web services. Answer B is incorrect; the default port for unencrypted HTTP traffic is port 80. Answer D is incorrect; TCP port 445 is used for Server Message Block (SMB) over TCP.

20. **Answer: D.** Secure Shell (SSH) provides an authenticated and encrypted data stream, as opposed to the cleartext communications of a Telnet session. Answers A and B are incorrect; Secure Socket Layer (SSL) and Transport Layer Security (TLS) are best known for protecting Hypertext Transfer Protocol (HTTP) web traffic and transactions, commonly known as Hypertext Transfer Protocol over SSL (HTTPS), which is a secure HTTP connection. Answer C is incorrect; Wired Equivalent Privacy (WEP) uses the RC4 cipher for confidentiality of wireless communications.

Objective 5.5: Explain core concepts of public key cryptography.

1. **Answer: B.** A public key infrastructure is a vast collection of varying technologies and policies for the creation and use of digital certificates. Answer A is incorrect because it describes the X.509 standard. Answer C is incorrect because it describes Public Key Cryptography Standards (PKCS). Answer D is incorrect because it describes public key infrastructure (X.509) (PKIX).

2. **Answer: A.** In a certificate trust model, everybody's certificate is issued by a third party called certificate authority (CA). If one trusts the CA, he automatically trusts the certificates that CA issues. Answer B is incorrect; certificate authorities (CAs) are trusted entities and are an important concept within PKI. The CA's job is to issue certificates, as well as to verify the holder of a digital certificate, and ensure that the holder of the certificate is who they claim to be. Answer C is incorrect because a registration authority (RA) provides authentication to the CA as to the validity of a client's certificate request; in addition, the RA serves as an aggregator of information. Answer D is incorrect; a certificate practice statement (CPS) is a legal document created and published by a CA for the purpose of conveying information to those depending on the CA's issued certificates.

3. **Answer: C.** The Public Key Cryptography Standards (PKCS) are the de facto cryptographic message standards developed and published by RSA Laboratories. Answer B is incorrect because it describes a public key infrastructure (PKI). Answer A is incorrect because it describes the X.509 standard. Answer D is incorrect because it describes public key infrastructure (X.509) (PKIX).

4. **Answer: C.** A registration authority (RA) provides authentication to the CA as to the validity of a client's certificate request; in addition, the RA serves as an aggregator of information. Answer A is incorrect because in a certificate trust model, everybody's certificate is issued by a third party called the certificate authority (CA). If one trusts the CA, then he automatically trusts the certificates that CA issues. Answer B is incorrect; certificate authorities (CAs) are trusted entities and are an important concept within PKI. The CA's job is to issue certificates, as well as to verify the holder of a digital certificate, and ensure that the holder of the certificate is who they claim to be. Answer D is incorrect; a certificate practice statement (CPS) is a legal document created and published by a CA for the purpose of conveying information to those depending on the CA's issued certificates.

5. **Answer: A.** The validity period identifies the time frame for which the private key is valid, if the private key has not been compromised. This period is indicated with both a start and an end time, and may be of any duration, but it is often set to one year. Based on this information, answers B, C, and D are incorrect.

6. **Answer: B, C, D.** Information about the signature algorithm identifier, user's public key, and serial number of the issuing certificate authority (CA) is all included within a digital certificate. A user's private key should never be contained within the digital certificate and should remain under tight control; therefore, answer A is incorrect.

7. **Answer: B.** Certificate authorities (CAs) are trusted entities and are an important concept within public key infrastructure (PKI). The CA's job is to issue certificates, as well as to verify the holder of a digital certificate, and ensure that the holder of the certificate is who they claim to be. Answer A is incorrect because in a certificate trust model, everybody's certificate is issued by a third party called certificate authority (CA). If one trusts the CA, then he automatically trusts the certificates that CA issues. Answer C is incorrect because a registration authority (RA) provides authentication to the CA as to the validity of a client's certificate request; in addition, the RA serves as an aggregator of information. Answer D is incorrect; a certificate practice statement (CPS) is a legal document created and published by a CA for the purpose of conveying information to those depending on the CA's issued certificates.

8. **Answer: A.** The X.509 standard defines a framework for authentication services by a directory and the format of required data for digital certificates. Answer B is incorrect because it describes a public key infrastructure (PKI). Answer C is incorrect because it describes Public Key Cryptography Standards (PKCS). Answer D is incorrect because it describes public key infrastructure (X.509) (PKIX).

9. **Answer: D.** A certificate practice statement (CPS) is a legal document created and published by a CA for the purpose of conveying information to those depending on the CA's issued certificates. Answer A is incorrect because in a certificate trust model, everybody's certificate is issued by a third party called a certificate authority (CA). If one trusts the CA, he automatically trusts the certificates that CA issues. Answer B is incorrect; certificate authorities (CAs) are trusted entities and are an important concept within PKI. The CA's job is to issue certificates, as well as to verify the holder of a digital certificate, and ensure that the holder of the certificate is who they claim to be. Answer C is incorrect because a registration authority (RA) provides authentication to the CA as to the validity of a client's certificate request; in addition, the RA serves as an aggregator of information.

10. **Answer: D.** Public key infrastructure (X.509) (PKIX) describes the development of Internet standards for X.509-based public key infrastructure (PKI). Answer B is incorrect because it describes a PKI. Answer A is incorrect because it describes the X.509 standard. Answer C is incorrect because it describes Public Key Cryptography Standards (PKCS).

11. **Answer: A, D.** A registration authority (RA) provides authentication to the CA as to the validity of a client's certificate request; in addition, the RA serves as an aggregator of information. Answer B is incorrect because a certificate practice statement (CPS) is a legal document created and published by a CA for the purpose of conveying information to those depending on the CA's issued certificates. Answer C is incorrect because the CA's job is to issue certificates, as well as to verify the holder of a digital certificate, and ensure that the holder of the certificate is who they claim to be.

12. **Answer: B.** Revoking a certificate invalidates a certificate before its expiration date. Revocation typically occurs because the certificate is no longer considered trustworthy. For example, if a certificate holder's private key is compromised, the certificate is most likely to be revoked. Answer A is incorrect because recovery is necessary if a certifying key is compromised but the certificate holder is still considered valid and trusted. In this case, it is not true. Answer C is incorrect because changing the trust model would necessitate unneeded changes. Answer D is incorrect. Key escrow occurs when a certificate authority (CA) or other entity maintains a copy of the private key associated with the public key signed by the CA.

13. **Answer: D.** A certificate policy indicates specific uses applied to a digital certificate, as well as other technical details. Thus, the certificate policy provides the rules that indicate the purpose and use of an assigned digital certificate. Answer A is incorrect because a registration authority (RA) provides authentication to the certificate authority (CA) as to the validity of a client's certificate request; in addition, the RA serves as an aggregator of information. Answer B is incorrect; key escrow occurs when a CA or other entity maintains a copy of the private key associated with the public key signed by the CA. Answer C is incorrect because a trust model is an architecture within a public key infrastructure (PKI) for certificate authorities.

14. **Answer: B.** Key escrow occurs when a CA or other entity maintains a copy of the private key associated with the public key signed by the CA. Answer A is incorrect because a registration authority (RA) provides authentication to the CA as to the validity of a client's certificate request; in addition, the RA serves as an aggregator of information. Answer C is incorrect because a trust model is an architecture within a PKI for certificate authorities. Answer D is incorrect; a certificate policy indicates specific uses applied to a digital certificate, as well as other technical details. Thus, the certificate policy provides the rules that indicate the purpose and use of an assigned digital certificate.

15. **Answer: C.** The focus of a certificate policy is on the certificate, whereas the focus of a certificate practice statement is on the certificate authority (CA) and the way that the CA issues certificates. Answer A is incorrect because the focus in the given statement is reversed. Answers B and D are incorrect; neither a certificate policy nor a CPS focuses solely on the keys.

16. **Answer: B.** A component of public key infrastructure (PKI) includes a mechanism for distributing certificate revocation information, called certificate revocation lists (CRLs). A CRL is used when verification of digital certificate takes place to ensure the validity of a digital certificate. Answer A is incorrect because a certificate practice statement (CPS) is a legal document created and published by a CA for the purpose of conveying information to those depending on the CA's issued certificates. Answer C is incorrect because an access control list is used to control object permissions. Answer D is incorrect because a public key infrastructure is a vast collection of varying technologies and policies for the creation and use of digital certificates.

17. **Answer: A.** An alternative to the hierarchical model is the cross-certification model, often referred to as a Web of Trust. In this model, certificate authorities (CAs) are considered peers to one another. Answer B is incorrect in a hierarchical CA model, an initial root CA exists at the top of the hierarchy with subordinate CAs below. Answer C is incorrect; a solution to the complexity of a large cross-certification model is to implement what is known as a bridge CA model. By implementing bridging, you can have a single CA, known as the bridge CA, be the central point of trust. Answer D is incorrect; a virtual bridge certificate authority model is used to overcome the bridge certificate authority compromise problem and removes the cross certificates among trust domains.

18. **Answer: D.** Key recovery is the process of restoring a key pair from a backup and re-creating a digital certificate using the recovered keys. Answer A is incorrect; after the key pairs are generated and a digital certificate has been issued by the CA, both keys must be stored appropriately to ensure their integrity is maintained. However, the key use must still be easy and efficient. Answer B is incorrect once a certificate is no longer valid, certificate revocation occurs. Answer C is incorrect. Key escrow occurs when a certificate authority (CA) or other entity maintains a copy of the private key associated with the public key signed by the CA.

19. **Answer: A.** In the single certificate authority (CA) architecture, only one CA exists to issue and maintain certificates. Although this model may be beneficial to smaller organizations because of its administrative simplicity, it has the potential to present problems. If the private key of the CA becomes compromised, all the issued certificates from that CA would then be invalid; therefore, answer B is incorrect. Answers C and D are incorrect; a single CA architecture is based on simplicity.

20. **Answer: D**. A root certificate authority (CA) differs from subordinate CAs in that the root CA is taken offline to reduce the risk of key compromise, and the root CA should be made available only to create and revoke certificates for subordinate CAs. Remember, if the root CA is compromised, then the entire architecture is compromised. If a subordinate CA is compromised, however, the root CA can revoke the subordinate CA. Based on this information, answer A is incorrect. Answer B is incorrect; a secondary CA is treated the same as a subordinate CA. Answer C is incorrect because a bridge CA is a solution to the complexity of a large cross-certification model.

Objective 5.6: Implement PKI and certificate management.

1. **Answer: B, D**. The certificate lifecycle is typically based on two documents: the certificate policy and the certification practice statement (CPS). Answer A is incorrect because certificate revocation statement is an incorrect term. The correct term is a certificate revocation list (CRL). A CRL is used when verification of digital certificate takes place to ensure the validity of a digital certificate. Answer C is incorrect because key escrow allows the certificate authority (CA) or escrow agent to have access to all the information that is encrypted using the public key from a user's certificate, as well as create digital signatures on behalf of the user.

2. **Answer: A, B**. Although the benefit of central control may be seen as an advantage, a centralized system also has other disadvantages, which include additional required infrastructure, a need to positively authenticate the end entity prior to transmitting the private key, as well as the need for a secure channel to transmit the private key. Answer C is incorrect; additional overhead is reduced with a centralized system. Answer D is incorrect; the public key does not need a secure channel.

3. **Answer: C**. Key escrow allows the certificate authority (CA) or escrow agent to have access to all the information that is encrypted using the public key from a user's certificate, as well as create digital signatures on behalf of the user. Answer A is incorrect; after the key pairs are generated and a digital certificate has been issued by the CA, both keys must be stored appropriately to ensure their integrity is maintained. However, the key use must still be easy and efficient. Answer B is incorrect because once a certificate is no longer valid, certificate revocation occurs. Answer D is incorrect; key recovery is the process of restoring a key pair from a backup and re-creating a digital certificate using the recovered keys.

4. **Answer: B, C**. Both Online Certificate Status Protocol (OSCP) and certificate revocation lists (CRLs) are used to verify the status of a certificate Answer A is incorrect. The certificate policy provides the rules that indicate the purpose and use of an assigned digital certificate. Answer D is incorrect because a certificate practice statement (CPS) is a legal document created and published by a certificate authority (CA) for the purpose of conveying information to those depending on the CA's issued certificates.

5. **Answer: B**. Certificate suspension occurs when a certificate is under investigation to determine if it should be revoked. This mechanism allows a certificate to stay in place, but it is not valid for any type of use during the suspension. Answer A is incorrect;

revoking a certificate invalidates a certificate before its expiration date. Revocation typically occurs because the certificate is no longer considered trustworthy. Answer C is incorrect; key escrow occurs when a certificate authority (CA) or other entity maintains a copy of the private key associated with the public key signed by the CA. Answer D is incorrect; key recovery is the process of restoring a key pair from a backup and re-creating a digital certificate using the recovered keys.

6. **Answer: C.** Key recovery is the process of restoring a key pair from a backup and re-creating a digital certificate using the recovered keys. Answer A is incorrect; revoking a certificate invalidates a certificate before its expiration date. Revocation typically occurs because the certificate is no longer considered trustworthy. Answer B is incorrect; certificate suspension occurs when a certificate is under investigation to determine if it should be revoked. This mechanism allows a certificate to stay in place, but it is not valid for any type of use during the suspension. Answer D is incorrect; key escrow occurs when a certificate authority (CA) or other entity maintains a copy of the private key associated with the public key signed by the CA.

7. **Answer: D.** In a decentralized key system, the end user generates his or her own key pair. The other functions, such as creation of the certificate, the revocation of the certificate, and key recovery and archiving are still handled by the certificate authority; therefore, Answers A, B, and C are incorrect.

8. **Answer: C.** A solution to the complexity of a large cross-certification model is to implement what is known as a bridge certificate authority (CA) model. Remember that in the cross-certification model, each CA must trust the others; however, by implementing bridging, it is possible to have a single CA, known as the bridge CA, be the central point of trust. Answers A and D are incorrect because these are CA server types not models. Answer B is incorrect; in the hierarchical CA model, an initial root CA exists at the top of the hierarchy, and subordinate CAs reside beneath the root.

9. **Answer: B.** In some circumstances, dual or multiple key pairs might be used to support distinct and separate services. For example, a reorder associate may have one key pair to be used for signing and sending encrypted messages, and might have another restricted to ordering equipment worth no more than a specific dollar amount. Multiple key pairs require multiple certificates, because the X.509 certificate format does not support multiple keys; therefore, answers A, C, and D are incorrect.

10. **Answer: B.** The key usage extension of the certificate specifies how the private key can be used. It is used to either to enable the exchange of sensitive information or to create digital signatures. Answer A is incorrect because it describes the signature algorithm identifier. Answer C is incorrect because it describes the validity period. Answer D is incorrect because the public key is not of consequence to the extension usage.

11. **Answer: A, C.** If the key pair to be destroyed is used for digital signatures, the private key portion should be destroyed first, to prevent future signing activities with the key. In addition, a digital certificate associated with key that are no longer valid should be added to the CRL regardless of whether the key is actually destroyed or archived. Answer B is incorrect because is concern is the private key. Answer D is incorrect because a certificate practice statement (CPS) is a legal document created and published by a CA for the purpose of conveying information to those depending on the CA's issued certificates.

12. **Answer: B, C.** The key usage extension of the certificate specifies how the private key can be used. It is used to either to enable the exchange of sensitive information or to create digital signatures. Answer A is incorrect because peer negotiation is associated with SSL/TLS. Answer D is incorrect because securing connections is associated with PPTP.

13. **Answer: B.** In asymmetric encryption, the private key decrypts data encrypted with the public key. Answer A is incorrect because the public key cannot decrypt the same data it encrypted. Answer C is incorrect because the public key would be used to encrypt and the private key to decrypt. Answer D is incorrect because this describes symmetric encryption.

14. **Answer: C.** Every certificate is issued with an expiration date. When the certificate expires, a new certificate needs to be reissued. So long as the certificate holder's needs or identity information has not changed, the process is relatively simple. After the issuing certificate authority (CA) validates the entity's identity, a new certificate can be generated based on the current public key; therefore, answers A, B, and D are incorrect.

15. **Answer: A, C, D.** The certificate lifecycle refers to those events required to create, use, and destroy public keys and the digital certificates with which they are associated. The certificate lifecycle is typically based on two documents: the certificate policy and the certification practice statement (CPS). Answer B is incorrect; preservation is not included in the certificate lifecycle.

16. **Answer: B, D.** Revoking a certificate is just not enough. The community that trusts these certificates must be notified that the certificates are no longer valid. This is accomplished via a certificate revocation list (CRL) or the Online Certificate Status Protocol (OCSP). Answer A is incorrect; it should read certificate policy. The certificate policy provides the rules that indicate the purpose and use of an assigned digital certificate. Answer C is incorrect because a certificate practice statement (CPS) is a legal document created and published by a CA for the purpose of conveying information to those depending on the CA's issued certificates.

17. **Answer: A.** Certificate suspension occurs when a certificate is under investigation to determine whether it should be revoked. Like the status checking that occurs with revoked certificates, users and systems are notified of suspended certificates in the same way. The primary difference is that new credentials will not need to be retrieved; it is only necessary to be notified that current credentials have had a change in status and are temporarily not valid for use. Answer B is incorrect because the proper usage is reversed. Answers C and D are incorrect because both revocation and suspension have to do with credentials not key pair restoration.

18. **Answer: B.** M of N control as it relates to public key infrastructure (PKI) refers to the concept of backing up the public and private key across multiple systems. This multiple backup provides a protective measure to ensure that no one individual can re-create his or her key pair from the backup. Answer A is incorrect; key escrow occurs when a certificate authority (CA) or other entity maintains a copy of the private key associated with the public key signed by the CA. Answer C is incorrect; key recovery is

the process of restoring a key pair from a backup and re-creating a digital certificate using the recovered keys. Answer D is incorrect; version control is associated software development.

19. **Answer: B, C, D.** Three basic status levels exist in most public key infrastructure (PKI) solutions: valid, suspended, and revoked. Answer A is incorrect; active status is a generic term that is not specifically associated with status levels in a PKI.

20. **Answer: A.** Key escrow enables an organization to overcome the large problem of forgotten passwords. Rather than revoke and reissue new keys, an organization can generate a new certificate using the private key stored in escrow. Answers B, C, and D are incorrect; forged signatures, phishing, and virus infections have nothing to do with key escrow.

CHAPTER SIX

Domain 6.0: Organizational Security

Network security and system hardening provide the strongest possible levels of security against directed attacks, but organizational security must also be considered when planning an organization's data security. Concerns such as redundancy planning, disaster recovery, backup, and restoration policies need to be addressed. After planning for disaster and recovery procedures, it is necessary to plan for incident response, forensics investigations, and protecting the organizations from malice from both external and internal damages. This includes environmental controls and user security awareness training. Although only 12% of the exam is based on the organizational security domain, this is a growing area of security planning. As a prospective security professional, you should also take every opportunity you may find to expand your skill base beyond these basic foundational elements. The following list includes the key areas from Domain 6 that you need to master for the exam:

▶ Explain redundancy planning and its components.

▶ Implement disaster recovery procedures.

▶ Differentiate between and execute appropriate incident response procedures.

▶ Identify and explain applicable legislation and organizational policies.

▶ Explain the importance of environmental controls.

▶ Explain the concept of and how to reduce the risks of social engineering.

Practice Questions

Objective 6.1: Explain redundancy planning and its components.

1. An organization is planning site redundancy. In the event of a catastrophe, the employees simply need to drive to the site, log on, and begin working. Which of the following best meets these requirements?

   ○ **A.** Hot site

   ○ **B.** Warm site

   ○ **C.** Cold site

   ○ **D.** Mirror site

Quick Answer: **328**
Detailed Answer: **330**

2. An organization is planning site redundancy. In the event of a catastrophe, electricity, bathrooms, and space will be provided. Which of the following best meets these requirements?

   ○ **A.** Hot site

   ○ **B.** Warm site

   ○ **C.** Cold site

   ○ **D.** Mirror site

Quick Answer: **328**
Detailed Answer: **330**

3. An organization is planning site redundancy. Currently, the organization does not have much money in the budget and requires the most inexpensive solution possible. Which of the following best meets these requirements?

   ○ **A.** Hot site

   ○ **B.** Warm site

   ○ **C.** Cold site

   ○ **D.** Mirror site

Quick Answer: **328**
Detailed Answer: **330**

4. An organization is planning site redundancy. In the event of a catastrophe, the site should already be configured with power, phone, and network jacks. Which of the following best meets these requirements?

   ○ **A.** Hot site

   ○ **B.** Warm site

   ○ **C.** Cold site

   ○ **D.** Mirror site

Quick Answer: **328**
Detailed Answer: **330**

5. An organization is planning site redundancy. It has been determined that the organization will contract with a third party for configuring devices, installing applications, and activating resources. All facility supplies should already be intact at the site. Which of the following best meets these requirements?

   ○ **A.** Hot site

   ○ **B.** Warm site

   ○ **C.** Cold site

   ○ **D.** Mirror site

Quick Answer: **328**
Detailed Answer: **331**

6. An organization is planning site redundancy. It is mandatory that all business operations are available 7 days a week for 24 hours per day. Which of the following best meets these requirements?

   ○ **A.** Hot site

   ○ **B.** Warm site

   ○ **C.** Cold site

   ○ **D.** Mirror site

Quick Answer: **328**
Detailed Answer: **331**

7. An organization is planning site redundancy. It is mandatory that live operations and recovery testing occurs before an actual catastrophic event happens. Which of the following best meets these requirements?

   ○ **A.** Hot site

   ○ **B.** Warm site

   ○ **C.** Cold site

   ○ **D.** Mirror site

Quick Answer: **328**
Detailed Answer: **331**

8. An organization operates in an area subject to rolling blackouts. Which of the following is the best method to provide continuous operations?

   ○ **A.** An uninterruptible power supply

   ○ **B.** A generator

   ○ **C.** A redundant electric connection

   ○ **D.** A RAID configuration

Quick Answer: **328**
Detailed Answer: **331**

9. An organization operates in an area that has frequent brownouts. Which of the following is the best method to provide continuous operations?

   ○ **A.** An uninterruptible power supply

   ○ **B.** A generator

   ○ **C.** A redundant electric connection

   ○ **D.** A RAID configuration

Quick Answer: **328**
Detailed Answer: **331**

10. An organization is located in an industrial area where there is a large amount of electromagnetic interference (EMI). Which of the following is the best method to provide continuous operations?

Quick Answer: **328**
Detailed Answer: **332**

- ○ **A.** An uninterruptible power supply
- ○ **B.** A generator
- ○ **C.** A redundant electric connection
- ○ **D.** A RAID configuration

11. A small organization is located in a remote area. When the power is interrupted, it often takes some time for the electric company to restore it. Which of the following is the best method to provide continuous operations?

Quick Answer: **328**
Detailed Answer: **332**

- ○ **A.** An uninterruptible power supply
- ○ **B.** A generator
- ○ **C.** A redundant electric connection
- ○ **D.** A RAID configuration

12. An organization requires a UPS solution that provides the best isolation from power line problems. Which of the following is the best method to provide continuous operations?

Quick Answer: **328**
Detailed Answer: **332**

- ○ **A.** Surge protector
- ○ **B.** Standby power supply
- ○ **C.** Ferroresonant UPS system
- ○ **D.** Continuous UPS

13. An organization is located in an area that requires protection against line noise and electromagnetic interference (EMI). Which of the following would best provide the protection required for the organization?

Quick Answer: **328**
Detailed Answer: **332**

- ○ **A.** Surge protector
- ○ **B.** Standby power supply
- ○ **C.** Ferroresonant UPS system
- ○ **D.** Continuous UPS

14. An organization requires a UPS solution that only activates when the power actually fails. Which of the following is the best method to meet this requirement?

Quick Answer: **328**
Detailed Answer: **332**

- ○ **A.** Surge protector
- ○ **B.** Standby power supply
- ○ **C.** Ferroresonant UPS system
- ○ **D.** Continuous UPS

15. An organization that operates a nonprofit donation hotline is planning for redundancy. Which of the following would be the most
critical component in providing continuous operations?

Quick Answer: **328**
Detailed Answer: **333**

- ○ **A.** Server redundancy
- ○ **B.** ISP redundancy
- ○ **C.** Phone system redundancy
- ○ **D.** Data disk redundancy

16. An organization that operates a web-based book business is planning for redundancy. Which of the following is the most critical
component in providing continuous customer access?

Quick Answer: **328**
Detailed Answer: **333**

- ○ **A.** Server redundancy
- ○ **B.** ISP redundancy
- ○ **C.** Phone system redundancy
- ○ **D.** Data disk redundancy

17. An organization that operates a small photo backup business is
planning for redundancy. Which of the following would be the
most critical component in providing continuous operations?

Quick Answer: **328**
Detailed Answer: **333**

- ○ **A.** Server redundancy
- ○ **B.** ISP redundancy
- ○ **C.** Phone system redundancy
- ○ **D.** Data disk redundancy

18. An organization that operates a large data warehousing business
is planning for redundancy using load balancing. Which of the following would best meet the organizational goals?

Quick Answer: **328**
Detailed Answer: **333**

- ○ **A.** Server redundancy
- ○ **B.** ISP redundancy
- ○ **C.** Phone system redundancy
- ○ **D.** Data disk redundancy

19. An organization that operates a small web-based photo backup business is evaluating single points of failure. The organization has three servers, four switches, and one hundred client systems. Which of the following would be the most likely component(s) to be the single point of failure?

   ○ **A.** Servers

   ○ **B.** ISP connection

   ○ **C.** Client systems

   ○ **D.** Switches

Quick Answer: **328**
Detailed Answer: **333**

20. An organization is implementing a data availability solution based on a striped disk array without redundancy. Which of the following best describes this implementation?

   ○ **A.** RAID 0

   ○ **B.** RAID 1

   ○ **C.** RAID 5

   ○ **D.** RAID 10

Quick Answer: **328**
Detailed Answer: **333**

21. An organization requires a solution based on high reliability combined with high performance. Which of the following would best meet the organizational requirements?

   ○ **A.** RAID 0

   ○ **B.** RAID 1

   ○ **C.** RAID 5

   ○ **D.** RAID 10

Quick Answer: **328**
Detailed Answer: **334**

22. An organization requires a solution that has the best small read, large write performance of any redundancy disk array. Which of the following would best meet the organizational requirements?

   ○ **A.** RAID 0

   ○ **B.** RAID 1

   ○ **C.** RAID 5

   ○ **D.** RAID 10

Quick Answer: **328**
Detailed Answer: **334**

23. An organization is implementing a simple data redundancy solution that offers 100% redundancy with a tradeoff of 50% disk utilization. Which of the following best describes this implementation?

   ○ **A.** RAID 0

   ○ **B.** RAID 1

   ○ **C.** RAID 5

   ○ **D.** RAID 10

Quick Answer: **328**
Detailed Answer: **334**

24. An organization is implementing a redundancy plan and is concerned about the need to restore equipment and parts. Which of the following is the best cost-effective method to ensure the availability of replacement parts?

- ○ **A.** Creating an area for broken equipment that can be used for parts
- ○ **B.** Purchasing exact duplicates of the equipment
- ○ **C.** Signing a service level agreement
- ○ **D.** Contracting for a hot site

25. An organization that operates a tax service requires that all branch offices have access to each office's client files for easier tax preparation. Which of the following would be the most critical component in providing continuous operations?

- ○ **A.** Multiple network cards in each machine
- ○ **B.** Redundant connections between sites
- ○ **C.** Redundant data disks
- ○ **D.** Multiple Internet Service Providers

Objective 6.2: Implement disaster recovery procedures.

1. Which of the following best describes the difference between a disaster recovery plan and a business continuity plan?

- ○ **A.** A disaster recovery plan covers natural disasters while a business continuity plan covers man-made disasters.
- ○ **B.** A disaster recovery plan is a more comprehensive approach than a business continuity plan.
- ○ **C.** A disaster recovery plan covers man-made disasters while a business continuity plan covers natural disasters.
- ○ **D.** A business continuity plan is a more comprehensive approach than a disaster recovery plan.

2. Full data backups are performed weekly on Saturday at 3:00 a.m., and incremental backups are performed each weekday at 3:00 a.m. If a drive failure causes a total loss of data at 9:00 a.m. on Tuesday morning, what is the minimum number of backup tapes that must be used to restore the lost data?

- ○ **A.** One
- ○ **B.** Two
- ○ **C.** Three
- ○ **D.** Four

Quick Answer: **328**
Detailed Answer: **335**

3. Full data backups are performed weekly on Saturday at 3:00 a.m., and differential backups are performed each weekday at 3:00 a.m. If a drive failure causes a total loss of data at 9:00 a.m. on Thursday morning, what is the minimum number of backup tapes that must be used to restore the lost data?

- ○ **A.** One
- ○ **B.** Two
- ○ **C.** Three
- ○ **D.** Four

Quick Answer: **328**
Detailed Answer: **335**

4. An organization is formulating a backup strategy. In the event of a total loss of data, which of the following backup methods will provide the fastest data restoration?

- ○ **A.** Incremental
- ○ **B.** Differential
- ○ **C.** Copy
- ○ **D.** Full

Quick Answer: **328**
Detailed Answer: **335**

5. An organization is implementing a backup strategy using three sets of backup tapes with backup sets rotated on a daily, weekly, and monthly basis. Which of the following best describes this implementation?

- ○ **A.** Grandfather, father, son
- ○ **B.** Grandmother, mother, daughter
- ○ **C.** Tower of Druaga
- ○ **D.** Tower of Hanoi

Quick Answer: **328**
Detailed Answer: **335**

6. An organization is planning a backup strategy that requires cost-effective solution that will provide backup data for more than a two week time period. Which of the following would best meet the organizational requirements?

   ◯ **A.** Grandfather, father, son

   ◯ **B.** Ten-tape rotation

   ◯ **C.** Tower of Druaga

   ◯ **D.** Tower of Hanoi

Quick Answer: **328**
Detailed Answer: **335**

7. A small organization is planning a backup strategy that requires a simple and cost-effective solution. Which of the following would best meet the organizational requirements?

   ◯ **A.** Grandfather, father, son

   ◯ **B.** Ten-tape rotation

   ◯ **C.** Tower of Druaga

   ◯ **D.** Tower of Hanoi

Quick Answer: **328**
Detailed Answer: **335**

8. Which of the following best describes a written document that defines how an organization will recover from a catastrophe and how it will restore business with minimum delay?

   ◯ **A.** Impact analysis

   ◯ **B.** Business continuity plan

   ◯ **C.** Disaster recovery plan

   ◯ **D.** Risk analysis

Quick Answer: **328**
Detailed Answer: **336**

9. Which of the following is true about the data-restoration process? (Select all correct answers.)

   ◯ **A.** It should be stored in a secure manner.

   ◯ **B.** It should be stored alongside the servers.

   ◯ **C.** It should be included in the employee manual.

   ◯ **D.** It should be properly documented.

Quick Answer: **328**
Detailed Answer: **336**

10. Which of the following is the most secure storage place for back-up media?

   ◯ **A.** Next to the backup server

   ◯ **B.** Locked in a proper safe

   ◯ **C.** In the desk of the HR manager

   ◯ **D.** In the home of the IT manager

Quick Answer: **328**
Detailed Answer: **336**

Objective 6.3: Differentiate between and execute appropriate incident response procedures.

1. Which of the following best describes the application of investigative and analytical techniques to acquire and protect potential legal evidence?

   ○ **A.** Due diligence

   ○ **B.** Chain of custody

   ○ **C.** Due process

   ○ **D.** Computer forensics

   Quick Answer: **328**
   Detailed Answer: **336**

2. Which of the following best describes the documentation of how evidence traveled from the crime scene to the courtroom?

   ○ **A.** Due diligence

   ○ **B.** Chain of custody

   ○ **C.** Due process

   ○ **D.** Computer forensics

   Quick Answer: **328**
   Detailed Answer: **336**

3. Which of the following are concepts behind computer forensics? (Select all correct answers.)

   ○ **A.** Identifying the evidence

   ○ **B.** Identifying the suspect

   ○ **C.** Determining how to preserve the evidence

   ○ **D.** Determining how to prosecute the suspect

   Quick Answer: **328**
   Detailed Answer: **336**

4. Which of the following best describes the documentation of how evidence was collected and preserved?

   ○ **A.** Incident response

   ○ **B.** Chain of custody

   ○ **C.** Due process

   ○ **D.** Due diligence

   Quick Answer: **328**
   Detailed Answer: **337**

5. As a first responder, which of the following is true about the han-
dling of a suspect's workspace?

- ○ **A.** The IT department should be allowed to remove the
computer.

- ○ **B.** The suspect's manager should be allowed to examine
the area.

- ○ **C.** The suspect should be allowed to remove personal
items.

- ○ **D.** No one should be allowed to remove any items from
the scene.

Quick Answer: **328**
Detailed Answer: **337**

6. As a first responder, which of the following is true about the han-
dling of a suspect's computer?

- ○ **A.** The computer should only be inspected by a trained
professional.

- ○ **B.** The suspect's manager should be allowed to inspect
the computer.

- ○ **C.** You should immediately begin to identify suspicious
computer files.

- ○ **D.** The IT department should be allowed to inspect the
computer.

Quick Answer: **328**
Detailed Answer: **337**

7. An organization has determined that an incident occurred. Which
of the following is the next step the organization would take in the
incident analysis process?

- ○ **A.** Contact the press
- ○ **B.** Contact affected vendors
- ○ **C.** Determine the scope
- ○ **D.** Mitigate the risk

Quick Answer: **328**
Detailed Answer: **337**

8. When an incident occurs, which of the following actions would the
organization take first to mitigate the impact?

- ○ **A.** Analysis
- ○ **B.** Containment
- ○ **C.** Remediation
- ○ **D.** Reporting

Quick Answer: **328**
Detailed Answer: **337**

9. An organization needs help formulating best practices for reporting and disclosing computer security incidents. Which of the following would be of the most help to the organization?

- ○ **A.** Operating system user manuals
- ○ **B.** FBI investigative guidelines
- ○ **C.** Request For Comments (RFC) 2350
- ○ **D.** Request For Comments (RFC) 50

Quick Answer: **328**
Detailed Answer: **337**

10. Which of the following best describes why it is important to accurately determine the cause of each incident?

- ○ **A.** To update the disaster recovery plan
- ○ **B.** To prevent similar incidents from occurring
- ○ **C.** To catch and prosecute the perpetrator
- ○ **D.** To notify the press and any affected vendors

Quick Answer: **328**
Detailed Answer: **337**

Objective 6.4: Identify and explain applicable legislation and organizational policies.

1. Which of the following will have the greatest effect on the formulation of organizational policies?

- ○ **A.** The board of directors
- ○ **B.** The needs of the users
- ○ **C.** Current and pending vendor contracts
- ○ **D.** Current and pending legislation

Quick Answer: **329**
Detailed Answer: **338**

2. An organization is formulating a policy that will define requirements for the classification and security of data and hardware resources based on the harm inflicted if it is disclosed to nonemployees. Which of the following best describes this policy?

- ○ **A.** Information sensitivity policy
- ○ **B.** Acceptable use policy
- ○ **C.** Change management policy
- ○ **D.** Computer security policy

Quick Answer: **329**
Detailed Answer: **338**

3. An organization is formulating a policy that will provide details that specify what users may do with their network access, including Internet access. Which of the following best describes this policy?

   - ○ **A.** Information sensitivity policy
   - ○ **B.** Acceptable use policy
   - ○ **C.** Change management policy
   - ○ **D.** Computer security policy

Quick Answer: **329**
Detailed Answer: **338**

4. An organization is formulating a policy that will define specific details on any configuration alterations to machines or operating systems. Which of the following best describes this policy?

   - ○ **A.** Information sensitivity policy
   - ○ **B.** Acceptable use policy
   - ○ **C.** Change management policy
   - ○ **D.** Computer security policy

Quick Answer: **329**
Detailed Answer: **338**

5. Upon logon to the network, an organization displays a statement stating that network access is granted under certain conditions and that all activities may be monitored. Which of the following best describes this policy?

   - ○ **A.** Information sensitivity policy
   - ○ **B.** Acceptable use policy
   - ○ **C.** Change management policy
   - ○ **D.** Computer security policy

Quick Answer: **329**
Detailed Answer: **338**

6. At the customer service desk of an electronics vendor, return items are entered by the desk clerk. Before refunds are issued, a manager must review the refund request and enter a password into the system to complete the transaction. Which of the following best describes this action?

   - ○ **A.** Due care
   - ○ **B.** Due diligence
   - ○ **C.** Principle of least privilege
   - ○ **D.** Separation of duties

Quick Answer: **329**
Detailed Answer: **339**

Quick Check

7. An organization has set forth in policies a statement regarding reasonable care a person should take before entering into an agreement or a transaction with another party. Which of the following best describes this statement?

- ○ **A.** Due care
- ○ **B.** Due diligence
- ○ **C.** Due process
- ○ **D.** Due course

Quick Answer: **329**
Detailed Answer: **339**

8. An organization has set forth in policies a statement regarding knowledge and actions that a reasonable and prudent person would possess or act upon. Which of the following best describes this statement?

- ○ **A.** Due care
- ○ **B.** Due diligence
- ○ **C.** Due process
- ○ **D.** Due course

Quick Answer: **329**
Detailed Answer: **339**

9. An organization has set forth in policies a statement stating that any employee legal proceedings must be fair. Which of the following best describes this statement?

- ○ **A.** Due care
- ○ **B.** Due diligence
- ○ **C.** Due process
- ○ **D.** Due course

Quick Answer: **329**
Detailed Answer: **339**

10. An employee entered into a large contract with a vendor without reviewing any of the terms of the contract. The organization suffered a huge financial loss as a result of the terms of the contract. Which of the following principles was violated by this action?

- ○ **A.** Due care
- ○ **B.** Due diligence
- ○ **C.** Due process
- ○ **D.** Due course

Quick Answer: **329**
Detailed Answer: **339**

11. A network administrator disabled the network firewall to allow his department to post materials to his personal FTP site. During this period of time, a denial of service attack was launched against the network. The organization suffered several hours of downtime. Which of the following principles was violated by this action?

- ○ **A.** Due care
- ○ **B.** Due diligence
- ○ **C.** Due process
- ○ **D.** Due course

12. An employee accused of sexual harassment was promptly dismissed by the immediate supervisor without any notification to human resources or discussion with the accused employee. As a result, the organization became involved in a lengthy lawsuit. Which of the following principles was violated by the immediate supervisor's actions?

- ○ **A.** Due care
- ○ **B.** Due diligence
- ○ **C.** Due process
- ○ **D.** Due course

13. An organization is establishing policies for dealing with the proper disposal of obsolete hardware. Which of the following specifications does the organization need to consider?

- ○ **A.** Sarbanes-Oxley
- ○ **B.** ISO 9000
- ○ **C.** IEEE specifications
- ○ **D.** ISO 17799

14. An organization is establishing policies for dealing with the proper disposal of obsolete hardware. Which of the following would be appropriate considerations?

- ○ **A.** Accessibility to remnants of legacy data
- ○ **B.** Breaches of health and safety requirements
- ○ **C.** Cost of disposal versus recycling
- ○ **D.** Old equipment necessary to read archived data

15. An organization is establishing policies for dealing with proper media disposal. Which of the following processes would the organization use if it wanted to remove the contents from the media as fully as possible, making it extremely difficult to restore before disposal?

- ○ **A.** Declassification
- ○ **B.** Sanitization
- ○ **C.** Degaussing
- ○ **D.** Destruction

16. Which of the following policies would an organization implement to help protect the network passwords from hackers?

- ○ **A.** Password complexity
- ○ **B.** Random generated passwords
- ○ **C.** Password storage in reversible encryption
- ○ **D.** Default passwords

17. An organization is formulating a change management policy. After a system change has been requested, documented, and approved, which of the following should occur?

- ○ **A.** Implementation
- ○ **B.** Management notification
- ○ **C.** User notification
- ○ **D.** Workarounds

18. An organization is implementing information classification levels. Confidential information that could influence the organization's operational effectiveness and cause financial loss if it became public, is considered which of the following classifications?

- ○ **A.** Class 1
- ○ **B.** Class 2
- ○ **C.** Class 3
- ○ **D.** Class 4

19. An organization is implementing information classification levels. High-security internal information that defines the way in which the organization operates is considered which of the following classifications?

- ○ **A.** Top secret
- ○ **B.** Proprietary
- ○ **C.** Internal use only
- ○ **D.** Public documents

20. An organization is implementing information classification levels. Highly sensitive internal documents and data to which very few employees should have access is considered which of the following classifications?

- ○　**A.** Top secret
- ○　**B.** Proprietary
- ○　**C.** Internal use only
- ○　**D.** Public documents

21. An organization is implementing information classification levels. Restricted information that is unlikely to result in financial loss or serious damage to the organization is considered which of the following classifications?

- ○　**A.** Top secret
- ○　**B.** Proprietary
- ○　**C.** Internal use only
- ○　**D.** Public documents

22. A financial institution is establishing policies that address balance of power. Which of the following principles is the financial institution most likely to implement?

- ○　**A.** Due care
- ○　**B.** Due diligence
- ○　**C.** Principle of least privilege
- ○　**D.** Separation of duties

23. A financial institution is establishing policies that outline the manner in which a user is associated with necessary information and system resources. It has been discovered that due to the nature of the position, the systems administrators never have scheduled time off and are on call during any scheduled days off. Which of the following principles will the institution implement to remedy this situation?

- ○　**A.** Mandatory vacations
- ○　**B.** Security compliance
- ○　**C.** Principle of least privilege
- ○　**D.** Due diligence

24. A financial institution is establishing policies that address balance of power. Which of the following actions can the financial institution implement to keep one person from having complete control of a transaction from beginning to end? (Select all correct answers.)

- ○ **A.** Job rotation
- ○ **B.** Change management
- ○ **C.** Mandatory vacations
- ○ **D.** Cross-training

25. An organization is establishing a policy for dealing with privacy-sensitive information. Which of the following information would have to be included in the policy? (Select all correct answers.)

- ○ **A.** Email address
- ○ **B.** Name
- ○ **C.** Address
- ○ **D.** Group membership

26. Which of the following aspects of security policy planning details how fast a vendor must have a new server delivered onsite?

- ○ **A.** Business impact analysis
- ○ **B.** Service level agreement
- ○ **C.** Disaster recovery plan
- ○ **D.** Disaster recovery policies

27. Which of the following aspects of security policy planning spells out the processes, service expectations, and service metrics expected by parties involved in a cooperative partnership?

- ○ **A.** Business impact analysis
- ○ **B.** Service level agreement
- ○ **C.** Disaster recovery plan
- ○ **D.** Disaster recovery policies

28. When termination involves a power user with high-level access rights or knowledge of service administrator passwords, which of the following should the organization do?

- ○ **A.** Immediately wipe the user's computer
- ○ **B.** Conduct a thorough exit interview
- ○ **C.** Institute password and security updates
- ○ **D.** Thoroughly search the user's work area

29. An organization is implementing a user-awareness training program. Valuable information can be gathered by hackers and other agents seeking unauthorized access through information posted on the organizational website about which of the following groups?

   ○ **A.** Executives

   ○ **B.** IT administrators

   ○ **C.** Organizational users

   ○ **D.** Security guards

Quick Answer: **329**
Detailed Answer: **342**

30. An organization is implementing a user-awareness training program. Which of the following groups can provide the most valuable support for security initiatives to ensure that published security training and other requirements are applied to all users equally?

   ○ **A.** Executives

   ○ **B.** IT administrators

   ○ **C.** Organizational users

   ○ **D.** Security guards

Quick Answer: **329**
Detailed Answer: **342**

Objective 6.5: Explain the importance of environmental controls.

1. An organization is planning to purchase a fire-suppression system. Certain areas of the building require a system that has water under pressure in it at all times. Which of the following best describes this type of system?

   ○ **A.** Dry pipe

   ○ **B.** Wet pipe

   ○ **C.** Deluge

   ○ **D.** Preaction

Quick Answer: **329**
Detailed Answer: **343**

2. Which of the following best describes the difference between a wet-pipe and a dry-pipe fire-suppression system?

Quick Answer: **329**
Detailed Answer: **343**

- ○ **A.** A wet-pipe system uses wet chemicals that deploy after the pipe loses air pressure, whereas a dry-pipe system uses dry chemicals that deploy before the pipe loses air pressure.
- ○ **B.** A dry-pipe system uses dry chemicals, whereas a wet-pipe system uses wet chemicals.
- ○ **C.** A dry-pipe system uses air to suppress fire, whereas a wet-pipe system uses water.
- ○ **D.** A wet-pipe system has water in the pipe at all times, whereas in a dry-pipe system water is used but is held back by a valve until a certain temperature is reached.

3. Class A fires involve which of the following?

Quick Answer: **329**
Detailed Answer: **343**

- ○ **A.** Energized electrical equipment, electrical fire, and burning wires
- ○ **B.** Flammable liquids, gases, and greases
- ○ **C.** Trash, wood, and paper
- ○ **D.** Combustible metals such as magnesium, titanium, and sodium

4. An organization is evaluating its environmental controls. Which of the following cable types carries an inherent danger due to the fact that it is easy to add devices to the network via open ports on unsecured hubs and switches? (Select all correct answers.)

Quick Answer: **329**
Detailed Answer: **343**

- ○ **A.** Shielded twisted pair
- ○ **B.** Coaxial
- ○ **C.** Unshielded twisted pair
- ○ **D.** Fiber optic

5. Class C fires involve which of the following?

Quick Answer: **329**
Detailed Answer: **343**

- ○ **A.** Energized electrical equipment, electrical fire, and burning wires
- ○ **B.** Flammable liquids, gases, and greases
- ○ **C.** Trash, wood, and paper
- ○ **D.** Combustible metals such as magnesium, titanium, and sodium

6. Class D fires involve which of the following?

　　○ **A.** Energized electrical equipment, electrical fire, and burning wires

　　○ **B.** Flammable liquids, gases, and greases

　　○ **C.** Trash, wood, and paper

　　○ **D.** Combustible metals such as magnesium, titanium, and sodium

Quick Answer: **329**
Detailed Answer: **343**

7. Class A fires can be extinguished using which of the following?

　　○ **A.** Foam

　　○ **B.** Water

　　○ **C.** Sodium chloride

　　○ **D.** Carbon dioxide

Quick Answer: **329**
Detailed Answer: **343**

8. Class B fires can be extinguished using which of the following?

　　○ **A.** Foam

　　○ **B.** Water

　　○ **C.** Sodium chloride

　　○ **D.** Carbon dioxide

Quick Answer: **329**
Detailed Answer: **344**

9. Class C fires can be extinguished using which of the following?

　　○ **A.** Foam

　　○ **B.** Water

　　○ **C.** Sodium chloride

　　○ **D.** Carbon dioxide

Quick Answer: **329**
Detailed Answer: **344**

10. Class D fires can be extinguished using which of the following?

　　○ **A.** Foam

　　○ **B.** Water

　　○ **C.** Sodium chloride

　　○ **D.** Carbon dioxide

Quick Answer: **329**
Detailed Answer: **344**

11. In fire-suppression systems, which of the following has replaced halon?

　　○ **A.** Foam

　　○ **B.** Water

　　○ **C.** Sodium chloride

　　○ **D.** Carbon dioxide

Quick Answer: **329**
Detailed Answer: **344**

12. When selecting a location for a building, an organization should investigate which of the following? (Select all correct answers.)

    ○ **A.** Crime rate

    ○ **B.** Proximity to an electronics store

    ○ **C.** Type of neighborhood

    ○ **D.** Emergency response times

Quick Answer: **329**
Detailed Answer: **344**

13. An organization that has several small branches in North Dakota, Minnesota, and Ontario, Canada, is planning for a fire-suppression system installation. Which of the following will best fit the needs of the organization?

    ○ **A.** Dry pipe

    ○ **B.** Wet pipe

    ○ **C.** Deluge

    ○ **D.** Preaction

Quick Answer: **329**
Detailed Answer: **344**

14. Which of the following is an inherent risk to equipment associated with overcooling?

    ○ **A.** RFI

    ○ **B.** Condensation

    ○ **C.** EMF

    ○ **D.** Static

Quick Answer: **329**
Detailed Answer: **344**

15. Which of the following is an inherent risk to equipment associated with using dehumidifiers?

    ○ **A.** RFI

    ○ **B.** Condensation

    ○ **C.** EMF

    ○ **D.** Static

Quick Answer: **329**
Detailed Answer: **345**

16. Which of the following is an inherent risk to equipment components associated with high levels of humidity?

    ○ **A.** Rust

    ○ **B.** ESD

    ○ **C.** EMF

    ○ **D.** Solidification

Quick Answer: **329**
Detailed Answer: **345**

17. An organization requires a cable types that is secure and can only be tapped by interrupting the service or using specially constructed equipment. Which of the following will best fit the needs of the organization?

   ○ **A.** Shielded twisted pair

   ○ **B.** Coaxial

   ○ **C.** Unshielded twisted pair

   ○ **D.** Fiber optic

Quick Answer: **329**
Detailed Answer: **345**

18. An organization is planning to protect the environment through the use of shielding. Which of the following can be an efficient and cost-effective way to protect a large quantity of equipment from electronic eavesdropping?

   ○ **A.** Electron configuration table

   ○ **B.** Electromagnetic field

   ○ **C.** Faraday cage

   ○ **D.** TEMPEST

Quick Answer: **329**
Detailed Answer: **345**

19. An organization is planning to protect the environment through the use of shielding. The equipment is in a corporate environment that process government and military highly classified information. Which of the following best meets the requirements of the organization?

   ○ **A.** Electron configuration table

   ○ **B.** Electromagnetic field

   ○ **C.** Faraday cage

   ○ **D.** TEMPEST

Quick Answer: **329**
Detailed Answer: **345**

20. An organization requires a cabling solution that is not susceptible to eavesdropping. Which of the following cable types should automatically be eliminated from the list of viable solutions?

   ○ **A.** Shielded twisted pair

   ○ **B.** Coaxial

   ○ **C.** Unshielded twisted pair

   ○ **D.** Fiber optic

Quick Answer: **329**
Detailed Answer: **345**

Objective 6.6: Explain the concept of and how to reduce the risks of social engineering.

1. A help desk employee receives a call from someone who is posing as a technical aide attempting to update some type of information, and asks for identifying user details that may then be used to gain access. Which of the following type of attack has occurred?

   ○ **A.** Pharming

   ○ **B.** Social engineering

   ○ **C.** Phishing

   ○ **D.** Shoulder surfing

Quick Answer: **329**
Detailed Answer: **346**

2. A help desk employee receives a call from the administrative assistant. She has received an email stating if she doesn't respond within 48 hours with certain personal information, the corporate bank account will be closed. Which of the following type of attack has occurred?

   ○ **A.** Pharming

   ○ **B.** Social engineering

   ○ **C.** Phishing

   ○ **D.** Shoulder surfing

Quick Answer: **329**
Detailed Answer: **346**

3. An organization recently has experienced large volumes of phishing scans. Which of the following is the best defense against this type of attack?

   ○ **A.** S/MIME

   ○ **B.** Antivirus software

   ○ **C.** Email filtering

   ○ **D.** User education

Quick Answer: **329**
Detailed Answer: **346**

4. The help desk is flooded with calls from users that received an email warning them of a new virus. The mail instructed the users to search for and delete several files from their systems. Many of the users who attempted to reboot their systems after deleting the specified files are having difficulties and the machines are not rebooting properly. Which of the following type of attack has occurred?

   ○ **A.** Pharming

   ○ **B.** Hoax

   ○ **C.** Phishing

   ○ **D.** Spam

Quick Answer: **329**
Detailed Answer: **346**

5. An organization discovers that many employees have been responding to chain letter emails. Which of the following is the greatest concern to the organization?

Quick Answer: **329**
Detailed Answer: **346**

- ○ **A.** Undue burden on resources.
- ○ **B.** They may contain viruses.
- ○ **C.** Theft of proprietary information.
- ○ **D.** Nothing, chain letters are harmless.

6. An organization discovers that city laws do not require special disposal of computer equipment. As a result, when equipment fails, employees throw it in the trash. Which of the following is the greatest concern to the organization?

Quick Answer: **329**
Detailed Answer: **347**

- ○ **A.** Health hazards
- ○ **B.** Social engineering
- ○ **C.** Dumpster diving
- ○ **D.** Shoulder surfing

7. An organization does not have a document disposal policy in place, nor does it have recycling or shredding bins. As a result, when employees no longer need printed information it is throw it in the trash. Which of the following is the greatest concern to the organization?

Quick Answer: **329**
Detailed Answer: **347**

- ○ **A.** Fire hazards
- ○ **B.** Social engineering
- ○ **C.** Dumpster diving
- ○ **D.** Shoulder surfing

8. An organization allows employees to access confidential data remotely. Many of the sales staff spend extended time in public places and use this downtime to catch up on work. Which of the following is the greatest concern to the organization?

Quick Answer: **329**
Detailed Answer: **347**

- ○ **A.** Virus infection
- ○ **B.** Social engineering
- ○ **C.** Dumpster diving
- ○ **D.** Shoulder surfing

9. An organization using keypad entry for all external doors is located in a busy and congested complex. The organization is concerned about shoulder surfing. Which of the following would provide the best defense against this type of attack?

Quick Answer: **329**
Detailed Answer: **347**

- ○ **A.** Hand cupping
- ○ **B.** Biometrics
- ○ **C.** Security guards
- ○ **D.** Deadbolts

10. An attacker disconnects several cables from an unattended reception area then offers the receptionist his business card as a computer repair technician when she returns. While waiting to see whether the IT manager is available to see him, the receptionist's computer appears to fail. Which of the following type of attack has occurred?

Quick Answer: **329**
Detailed Answer: **347**

- ○ **A.** Reverse social engineering
- ○ **B.** Denial of service
- ○ **C.** Shoulder surfing
- ○ **D.** Phishing

11. An organization using keypad entry for all external doors is located in a busy and congested complex. The organization is concerned about shoulder surfing. Which of the following would provide an immediate defense against this type of attack?

Quick Answer: **329**
Detailed Answer: **348**

- ○ **A.** Hand cupping
- ○ **B.** Biometrics
- ○ **C.** Security guards
- ○ **D.** Deadbolts

12. Which of the following are examples of social engineering? (Select all correct answers.)

Quick Answer: **329**
Detailed Answer: **348**

- ○ **A.** An attacker pretends to be an executive who forgot his password to gain access to credentials.
- ○ **B.** An attacker presents a fake UPS ID to gain entrance to a specific floor of the building.
- ○ **C.** An attacker uses a wireless packet sniffer to monitor user credentials.
- ○ **D.** An attacker piggybacks into the building behind an unsuspecting employee.

13. Which of the following is true regarding the scope of security awareness training for management?

◯ **A.** The focus should be the same as for users.

◯ **B.** The focus should be on program costs.

◯ **C.** The focus should be on business impact.

◯ **D.** The focus should be the same as for IT staff.

14. Which of the following are essential components in an organizational security awareness program that attempts to minimize vulnerabilities created by social engineering? (Select all correct answers.)

◯ **A.** Security posters

◯ **B.** Regular reminders

◯ **C.** Scheduled training

◯ **D.** Clear policies

15. Which of the following would be items addressed in a user security awareness training program? (Select all correct answers.)

◯ **A.** How to react to someone who has piggybacked into the building

◯ **B.** How to properly exit the building when the fire alarm is activated

◯ **C.** What to do when their computer is suspected of having a malware infection

◯ **D.** What to do when an administrator calls and asks for a user's password

Quick-Check Answer Key

Objective 6.1: Explain redundancy planning and its components.

1. A	10. A	19. B
2. C	11. B	20. A
3. C	12. D	21. D
4. B	13. C	22. C
5. B	14. B	23. B
6. A	15. C	24. C
7. A	16. B	25. B
8. B	17. D	
9. A	18. A	

Objective 6.2: Implement disaster recovery procedures.

1. D	5. A	9. A, D
2. C	6. D	10. B
3. B	7. B	
4. D	8. C	

Objective 6.3: Differentiate between and execute appropriate incident response procedures.

1. D	5. D	9. C
2. B	6. A	10. B
3. A, C	7. C	
4. B	8. B	

Objective 6.4: Identify and explain applicable legislation and organizational policies.

1. D	11. A	21. C
2. A	12. C	22. D
3. B	13. D	23. A
4. C	14. A, B, D	24. A, C, D
5. B	15. B	25. A, B, C
6. D	16. A	26. B
7. B	17. C	27. B
8. A	18. C	28. C
9. C	19. B	29. A
10. B	20. A	30. A

Objective 6.5: Explain the importance of environmental controls.

1. B	8. A	15. D
2. D	9. D	16. A
3. C	10. C	17. D
4. A, C	11. D	18. C
5. A	12. A, C, D	19. D
6. D	13. A	20. B
7. B	14. B	

Objective 6.6: Explain the concept of and how to reduce the risks of social engineering.

1. B	6. C	11. A
2. C	7. C	12. A, B
3. D	8. D	13. C
4. B	9. B	14. B, C, D
5. A	10. A	15. A, D

Answers and Explanations

Objective 6.1: Explain redundancy planning and its components.

1. **Answer: A.** A hot site is similar to the original site in that it has all the equipment needed for the organization to continue operations. This type of site is similar to the original site in that it is equipped with all necessary hardware, software, network, and Internet connectivity fully installed, configured, and operational. Answer B is incorrect because a warm site is a scaled-down version of a hot site. The site is generally configured with power, phone, and network jacks. The site may have computers and other resources, but they are not configured and ready to go. Answer C is incorrect because a cold site does not provide any equipment. These sites are merely a prearranged request to use facilities if needed. Electricity, bathrooms, and space are about the only facilities provided in a cold site contract. Answer D is incorrect because a mirror site is an exact copy of another Internet site.

2. **Answer: C.** A cold site does not provide any equipment. These sites are merely a prearranged request to use facilities if needed. Electricity, bathrooms, and space are about the only facilities provided in a cold site contract. Answer A is incorrect. A hot site is similar to the original site in that it has all the equipment needed for the organization to continue operations. This type of site is similar to the original site in that it is equipped with all necessary hardware, software, network, and Internet connectivity fully installed, configured, and operational. Answer B is incorrect because a warm site is a scaled-down version of a hot site. The site is generally configured with power, phone, and network jacks. The site may have computers and other resources, but they are not configured and ready to go. Answer D is incorrect because a mirror site is an exact copy of another Internet site.

3. **Answer: C.** A cold site is the weakest of the recovery plan options but also the cheapest. These sites are merely a prearranged request to use facilities if needed. Electricity, bathrooms, and space are about the only facilities provided in a cold site contract. Answer A is incorrect. A hot site is similar to the original site in that it has all the equipment needed for the organization to continue operations, such as hardware and furnishings. Answer B is incorrect because a warm site is a scaled-down version of a hot site. The site is generally configured with power, phone, and network jacks. The site may have computers and other resources, but they are not configured and ready to go. Answer D is incorrect because a mirror site is an exact copy of another Internet site.

4. **Answer: B.** A warm site is a scaled-down version of a hot site. The site is generally configured with power, phone, and network jacks. The site may have computers and other resources, but they are not configured and ready to go. Answer A is incorrect. A hot site is similar to the original site in that it has all the equipment needed for the organization to continue operations, such as hardware and furnishings. Answer C is incorrect because a cold site does not provide any equipment. These sites are merely a prearranged request to use facilities if needed. Answer D is incorrect because a mirror site is an exact copy of another Internet site.

5. **Answer: B.** A warm site is a scaled-down version of a hot site. The site may have computers and other resources, but they are not configured and ready to go. It is assumed that the organization itself will configure the devices, install applications, and activate resources or that it will contract with a third party for these services. Answer A is incorrect because a hot site is similar to the original site in that it has all the equipment needed for the organization to continue operations, such as hardware and furnishings. Answer C is incorrect because a cold site does not provide any equipment. These sites are merely a prearranged request to use facilities if needed. Answer D is incorrect because a mirror site is an exact copy of another Internet site.

6. **Answer: A.** A hot site is a site location that is already running and is available 7 days a week for 24 hours per day. Answer B is incorrect because a warm site is a scaled-down version of a hot site. The site is generally configured with power, phone, and network jacks. The site may have computers and other resources, but they are not configured and ready to go. Answer C is incorrect because a cold site does not provide any equipment. These sites are merely a prearranged request to use facilities if needed. Answer D is incorrect because a mirror site is an exact copy of another Internet site.

7. **Answer: A.** A hot site is similar to the original site in that it has all the equipment needed for the organization to continue operations. This type of site is similar to the original site in that it is equipped with all necessary hardware, software, network, and Internet connectivity fully installed, configured, and operational. Hot sites are traditionally more expensive, but they can be used for operations and recovery testing before an actual catastrophic event occurs. Answer B is incorrect because a warm site is a scaled-down version of a hot site. The site is generally configured with power, phone, and network jacks. Answer C is incorrect because a cold site does not provide any equipment. These sites are merely a prearranged request to use facilities if needed. Answer D is incorrect because a mirror site is an exact copy of another Internet site.

8. **Answer: B.** Backup power is a power supply that will run the power for your organization in the case of a power outage. This can be done through the use of a gas-powered generator. A generator can be used for rolling blackouts, emergency blackouts, or electrical problems. Answer A is incorrect because an interruptible power supply protects the environment from damaging fluctuations in power and cannot sustain power outages for a long period of time. Answer C is incorrect because most electric companies only service one area. If it is possible to contract with another service provider, the cost will most likely be prohibitive. Answer D is incorrect because RAID does not protect against electrical failures.

9. **Answer: A.** Brownouts are short-term decreases in voltage levels that most often occur when motors are started or are triggered by faults on the utility provider's system. To protect your environment from such damaging fluctuations in power, always connect your sensitive electronic equipment to power conditioners, surge protectors, and a UPS, which provides the best protection of all. Answer B is incorrect because a generator is used for rolling blackouts, emergency blackouts, or electrical problems. Answer C is incorrect because most electric companies only service one area. If it is possible to contract with another service provider, the cost will most likely be prohibitive. Answer D is incorrect because RAID does not protect against electrical failures.

10. **Answer: A.** Power variations called noise are also referred to as electromagnetic interference (EMI). To protect your environment from such damaging fluctuations in power, always connect your sensitive electronic equipment to power conditioners, surge protectors, and a UPS, which provides the best protection of all. Answer B is incorrect because a generator is used for rolling blackouts, emergency blackouts, or electrical problems. Answer C is incorrect because most electric companies only service one area. If it is possible to contract with another service provider, the cost will most likely be prohibitive. Answer D is incorrect because RAID does not protect against electrical failures.

11. **Answer: B.** Backup power is a power supply that will run the power for your organization in the case of a power outage. This can be done through the use of a gas-powered generator. A generator can be used for rolling blackouts, emergency blackouts, or electrical problems. Answer A is incorrect because an interruptible power supply protects the environment from damaging fluctuations in power and cannot sustain power levels for a long period of time. Answer C is incorrect because most electric companies only service one area. If it is possible to contract with another service provider, the cost will most likely be prohibitive. Answer D is incorrect because RAID does not protect against electrical failures.

12. **Answer: D.** In a continuous UPS, also called an "online" UPS, the computer is always running off of battery power, and the battery is continuously being recharged. There is no switchover time, and these supplies generally provide the best isolation from power line problems. Answer A is incorrect. A surge protector is designed to protect electrical devices from voltage spikes by limiting the surge to acceptable levels that electronic equipment can handle. This device does not regulate or supply any power in the event of sags. Answer B is incorrect. A standby power supply (SPS) is also referred to as an "offline" UPS. In this type of supply, power usually derives directly from the power line, until power fails. Answer C is incorrect because a ferroresonant UPS system maintains a constant output voltage even with a varying input voltage and provides good protection against line noise.

13. **Answer: C.** A ferroresonant UPS system maintains a constant output voltage even with a varying input voltage and provides good protection against line noise. Answer A is incorrect; a surge protector is designed to protect electrical devices from voltage spikes, not supply power. Answer B is incorrect; a standby power supply (SPS) is also referred to as an "offline" UPS. In this type of supply, power usually derives directly from the power line, until power fails. Answer D is incorrect; in a continuous UPS, also called an "online" UPS, the computer is always running off of battery power, and the battery is continuously being recharged. There is no switchover time, and these supplies generally provide the best isolation from power line problems.

14. **Answer: B.** A standby power supply (SPS) is also referred to as an "offline" UPS. In this type of supply, power usually derives directly from the power line, until power fails. Answer A is incorrect because a surge protector is designed to protect electrical devices from voltage spikes, not supply power. Answer C is incorrect; a ferroresonant UPS system maintains a constant output voltage even with a varying input voltage and provides good protection against line noise. Answer D is incorrect; in a continuous UPS, also called an "online" UPS, the computer is always running off of battery power, and the battery is continuously being recharged. There is no switchover time, and these supplies generally provide the best isolation from power line problems.

15. **Answer: C.** If the majority of your business is telephone based, you might look for redundancy in the phone system as opposed to the ISP. Therefore, Answer B is incorrect. Answer A is incorrect because if the servers failed, phone donations could still be taken via pen and paper. Answer D is incorrect because while data disk redundancy for the storage of data is important, without a phone system, the business could not function.

16. **Answer: B.** If all your business is web based, to provide continued customer access it is a good idea to have some redundancy in the event the Internet connection goes down. Answer A is incorrect because if one of the servers failed, business could still be conducted. Answer C is incorrect. If the majority of your business is telephone based, you might look for redundancy in the phone system as opposed to the ISP and this is not the case. Answer D is incorrect because while data disk redundancy for the storage of data is important, without an Internet connection, the business could not function.

17. **Answer: D.** The primary function of the business is to provide a backup service. Without data disk redundancy, the business could not operate. Answer A is incorrect because if one of the servers failed, business could be conducted. Answer B is incorrect because the main business purpose is to provide backup service. The temporary loss of the Internet connection going down is not as damaging as losing a data disk. Answer C is incorrect; if the majority of your business is telephone based, you might look for redundancy in the phone system, and this is not the case.

18. **Answer: A.** It might be necessary to set up redundant servers so that the business can still function in the event of hardware or software failure. If a single server hosts vital applications, a simple equipment failure might result in days of downtime as the problem is repaired. Answer B is incorrect; the main business purpose is to provide data warehousing. The temporary loss of the Internet connection going down is not as damaging as losing a vital server. Answer C is incorrect because if the majority of your business is telephone based, you might look for redundancy in the phone system and this is not the case. Answer D is incorrect because while data disk redundancy for the storage of data is important, the business could still function if a disk was lost.

19. **Answer: B.** Neglecting single points of failure can prove disastrous. A single point of failure is any piece of equipment that can bring your operation down if it stops working. Based on this, the Internet connection would be the single point of failure. Answers A, C, and D are incorrect; there is more than one of each of these pieces of equipment, so they are not single points of failure.

20. **Answer: A.** RAID Level 0 is a striped disk array without fault tolerance. Answer B is incorrect. RAID Level 1 is mirroring and duplexing. This solution requires a minimum of two disks and offers 100% redundancy because all data is written to both disks. Answer C is incorrect; RAID Level 5 consists of independent data disks with distributed parity blocks. In RAID 5, each entire block of the data and the parity is striped. Answer D is incorrect; RAID Level 10 is high reliability combined with high performance. This solution is a striped array that has RAID 1 arrays.

21. **Answer: D.** RAID Level 10 is high reliability combined with high performance. This solution is a striped array that has RAID 1 arrays. Answer A is incorrect because RAID Level 0 is a striped disk array without fault tolerance. Answer B is incorrect because RAID Level 1 is mirroring and duplexing. This solution requires a minimum of two disks and offers 100% redundancy because all data is written to both disks. Answer C is incorrect because RAID Level 5 consists of independent data disks with distributed parity blocks. In RAID 5, each entire block of the data and the parity is striped.

22. **Answer: C.** In RAID 5, each entire block of the data and the parity is striped. Because it writes both the data and the parity over all the disks, it has the best small read, large write performance of any redundancy disk array. Answer A is incorrect because RAID Level 0 is a striped disk array without fault tolerance. Answer B is incorrect because RAID Level 1 is mirroring and duplexing. This solution requires a minimum of two disks and offers 100% redundancy because all data is written to both disks. Answer D is incorrect; RAID Level 10 is high reliability combined with high performance. This solution is a striped array that has RAID 1 arrays.

23. **Answer: B.** RAID Level 1 is mirroring and duplexing. This solution requires a minimum of two disks and offers 100% redundancy because all data is written to both disks. RAID 1 disk usage is 50% as the other 50% is for redundancy. Answer A is incorrect because RAID Level 0 is a striped disk array without fault tolerance. Answer C is incorrect because RAID Level 5 consists of independent data disks with distributed parity blocks. In RAID 5, each entire block of the data and the parity is striped. Answer D is incorrect because RAID Level 10 is high reliability combined with high performance. This solution is a striped array that has RAID 1 arrays.

24. **Answer: C.** In the event of a disaster, an organization might also need to restore equipment (in addition to data). One of the best ways to ensure the availability of replacement parts is through service level agreements (SLAs). Answer A is incorrect because this solution consumes space and does not ensure that correct replacement parts will be available. Answers B and D are incorrect; they are too costly.

25. **Answer: B.** In disaster recovery planning, you might need to consider redundant connections between branches or sites. Because the records must be available between offices, this is the single point of failure that requires redundancy. Based on this information, answers A, C, and D are incorrect.

Objective 6.2: Implement disaster recovery procedures.

1. **Answer: D.** Business continuity planning is a more comprehensive approach to provide guidance so the organization can continue making sales and collecting revenue. As with disaster recovery planning, it covers natural and man-made disasters. Based on this information, answers A, B, and C are incorrect.

2. **Answer: C.** Saturday's full backup must be installed, followed by Monday's incremental backup, and finally Tuesday morning's incremental backup. This will recover all data as of 3:00 a.m. Tuesday morning. Answer A is incorrect because a full backup Tuesday morning would be required to allow a single tape recovery of all data. Answer B is incorrect because A differential backup on Tuesday morning would be required in addition to the full backup so that only two backup tapes would be needed. Answer D is incorrect because four tapes would not be required.

3. **Answer: B.** A differential backup on Thursday morning would be required in addition to the full backup so that only two backup tapes would be needed. Answer A is incorrect because a full backup Thursday morning would be required to allow a single tape recovery of all data. Answer C is incorrect; Saturday's full backup must be installed, followed by Monday's, Tuesday's, Wednesday's, and Thursday's incremental backup tapes. Answer D is incorrect because four tapes would not be required.

4. **Answer: D.** In the event of a total loss of data, restoration from a full backup will be faster than other methods. Answers A and B are incorrect; each of these methods will require more than one tape and take longer than restoring from a full backup. Answer C is incorrect because a copy backup copies all the selected files, but does not mark the files as having been backed up. This backup type is useful for backing up single files between normal and incremental backups because it does not affect these operations.

5. **Answer: A.** Grandfather-father-son backup refers to the most common rotation scheme for rotating backup media. Originally designed for tape backup, it works well for any hierarchical backup strategy. The basic method is to define three sets of backups, such as daily, weekly, and monthly. Answers B and C are incorrect; neither of these are valid backup methods. Answer D is incorrect because the Tower of Hanoi is based on the mathematics of the Tower of Hanoi puzzle, with what is essentially a recursive method.

6. **Answer: D.** The Tower of Hanoi is based on the mathematics of the Tower of Hanoi puzzle, with what is essentially a recursive method. It is a "smart" way of archiving an effective number of backups and provides the ability to go back over time. The Tower of Hanoi is more difficult to implement and manage but costs less than the grandfather-father-son scheme. Answer A is incorrect; grandfather-father-son backup refers to the most common rotation scheme for rotating backup media. Originally designed for tape backup, it works well for any hierarchical backup strategy. Answer B is incorrect because ten-tape rotation is a simpler and more cost-effective method for small businesses. It provides a data history of up to two weeks. Answer C is incorrect; this is not a valid backup method.

7. **Answer: B.** Ten-tape rotation is a simpler and more cost-effective method for small businesses. It provides a data history of up to two weeks. Friday backups are full backups. Monday through Thursday backups are incremental. Answer A is incorrect; grandfather-father-son backup refers to the most common rotation scheme for rotating backup media. Originally designed for tape backup, it works well for any hierarchical backup strategy. Answer C is incorrect; this is not a valid backup method. Answer D is incorrect; the Tower of Hanoi is based on the mathematics of the Tower of Hanoi puzzle, with what is essentially a recursive method. The Tower of Hanoi is more difficult to implement and manage but costs less than the grandfather-father-son scheme.

8. **Answer: C.** A disaster recovery plan is a written document that defines how the organization will recover from a disaster and how to restore business with minimum delay. Answer A is incorrect because an impact analysis is an analytic process that aims to reveal business and operational impacts stemming from any number of incidents or events. Answer B is incorrect because business continuity planning is a comprehensive approach to provide guidance so that the organization can continue making sales and collecting revenue. Answer D is incorrect because a risk analysis helps determine which security controls are appropriate and cost-effective.

9. **Answers: A, D.** Restoration planning documentation, backup scheduling, and backup media must include protections against unauthorized access or potential damage and critical procedures should be properly documented so that another equally trained individual can manage the restoration process. Answer B is incorrect; although this is convenient, it is not secure. Answer C is incorrect because this information does not belong in the employee manual.

10. **Answer: B.** A common practice is to have removable storage media locked in a proper safe or container at the end of the day. Answer A is incorrect; although this is convenient, it is not secure. Answer C is incorrect because this information does not belong in the desk of the HR manager. Answer D is incorrect because storing backup tapes in the home of the IT manager is a liability for the organization.

Objective 6.3: Differentiate between and execute appropriate incident response procedures.

1. **Answer: D.** Computer forensics review involves the application of investigative and analytical techniques to acquire and protect potential legal evidence. Answer A is incorrect; due diligence refers to the care a reasonable person should take before entering into an agreement or a transaction with another party. Answer B is incorrect because a chain of custody is the documentation of all transfers of evidence from one person to another. Answer C is incorrect because due process is the concept that laws and legal proceedings must be fair.

2. **Answer: B.** A chain of custody tells how the evidence made it from the crime scene to the courtroom, including documentation of how the evidence was collected, preserved, and analyzed. Answer A is incorrect; due diligence refers to the care a reasonable person should take before entering into an agreement or a transaction with another party. Answer C is incorrect because due process is the concept that laws and legal proceedings must be fair. Answer D is incorrect because computer forensics review involves the application of investigative and analytical techniques to acquire and protect potential legal evidence.

3. **Answers: A, C.** The major concepts behind computer forensics are to identify the evidence, determine how to preserve the evidence, extract, process, and interpret the evidence and ensure that the evidence is acceptable in a court of law This provides a total effective key length of 168 bits. Answers B and D are incorrect; identification and prosecution of the suspect are left to law enforcement.

4. **Answer: B.** A chain of custody tells how the evidence made it from the crime scene to the courtroom, including documentation of how the evidence was collected, preserved, and analyzed. Answer A is incorrect; a disaster recovery plan is a written document that defines how the organization will recover from a disaster and how to restore business with minimum delay. Answer C is incorrect because due process is the concept that laws and legal proceedings must be fair. Answer D is incorrect; due diligence refers to the care a reasonable person should take before entering into an agreement or a transaction with another party.

5. **Answer: D.** The entire work area is a potential crime scene, not just the computer itself. There might be evidence such as removable media, voicemail messages, or handwritten notes. The work area should be secured and protected to maintain the integrity of the area. Under no circumstances should you touch the computer or should anyone be allowed to remove any items from the scene. Based on this information, answers A, B, and C are incorrect.

6. **Answer: A.** If you are an untrained first responder, touch nothing and contact someone trained in these matters for help. Although it seems that simply viewing the files or directories on a system would not change the original media, merely browsing a file can change it. Based on this information, answers B, C, and D are incorrect.

7. **Answer: C.** When the response team has determined that an incident occurred, the next step in incident analysis involves taking a comprehensive look at the incident activity to determine the scope, priority, and threat of the incident. Answer A is incorrect; the press should not be contacted unless it is absolutely necessary, and then only after the scope has been determined. Answer B is incorrect because affected vendors should only be contacted after the scope has been determined. Answer D is incorrect because the risk cannot be mitigated until the scope is determined.

8. **Answer: B.** In keeping with the severity of the incident, the organization can act to mitigate the impact of the incident by containing it and eventually restoring operations back to normal. Answers A, C, and D are incorrect; analysis, remediation, and reporting happen after containment.

9. **Answer: C.** Request For Comments (RFC) 2350, "Expectations for Computer Security Incident Response," spells out the expectations for computer security incident response. This RFC can be helpful in formulating organizational best practices for reporting and disclosure. Answer A is incorrect; organizational best practices for reporting and disclosure are not found in operating system manuals. Answer B is incorrect; FBI Investigative Guidelines are the guidelines on general crimes, national security investigative guidelines, and the confidential supplemental foreign intelligence guidelines. Answer D is incorrect because RFC 50 is comments on the Meyer Proposal.

10. **Answer: B.** It is important to accurately determine the cause of each incident so that it can be fully contained and the exploited vulnerabilities can be mitigated to prevent similar incidents from occurring in the future. Answer A is incorrect; the incident response plan would be updated, not the disaster recovery plan. Answer C is incorrect; apprehension and prosecution is the job of law enforcement. Answer D is incorrect; depending on the incident, press and vendor notification may not be necessary.

Objective 6.4: Identify and explain applicable legislation and organizational policies.

1. **Answer: D.** To ensure that proper incident response planning is managed and maintained, it is important to establish clear and detailed security policies that are ratified by an organization's management and brought to the attention of its users. Current and pending legislation will affect the formulation of those policies. Answers A, B, and C are incorrect; although each of these factors may have influence on organizational policies, legislation will have the greatest effect.

2. **Answer: A.** An organization's information sensitivity policy will define requirements for the classification and security of data and hardware resources based on their relative level of sensitivity. Answer B is incorrect because an acceptable use policy provides details that specify what users may do with their network access. Answer C is incorrect because a change management policy specifies details about system changes such as the files being replaced, the configuration being changed, and the machines or operating systems affected. Answer D is incorrect; a computer security policy defines the goals for securing and protecting an organization's computer systems.

3. **Answer: B.** An acceptable use policy provides details that specify what users may do with their network access, including email and instant messaging usage for personal purposes, limitations on access times, and the storage space available to each user. Answer A is incorrect because an organization's information sensitivity policy will define requirements for the classification and security of data and hardware resources based on their relative level of sensitivity. Answer C is incorrect because a change management policy specifies details about system changes such as the files being replaced, the configuration being changed, and the machines or operating systems affected. Answer D is incorrect because a computer security policy defines the goals and elements of an organization's computer systems.

4. **Answer: C.** A change management policy specifies details about system changes such as the files being replaced, the configuration being changed, and the machines or operating systems affected. Answer A is incorrect because an organization's information sensitivity policy will define requirements for the classification and security of data and hardware resources based on their relative level of sensitivity. Answer B is incorrect because an acceptable use policy provides details that specify what users may do with their network access. Answer D is incorrect because a computer security policy defines the goals and elements of an organization's computer systems.

5. **Answer: B.** An acceptable use policy example is that upon logon, a statement that network access is granted under certain conditions and that all activities may be monitored is displayed. Answer A is incorrect because an organization's information sensitivity policy will define requirements for the classification and security of data and hardware resources based on their relative level of sensitivity. Answer C is incorrect because a change management policy specifies details about system changes such as the files being replaced, the configuration being changed, and the machines or operating systems affected. Answer D is incorrect because a computer security policy defines the goals and elements of an organization's computer systems.

6. **Answer: D.** The idea of separation of duties hinges on the concept that multiple people conspiring to corrupt a system is less likely than a single person corrupting it. Answer A is incorrect; due care is the knowledge and actions that a reasonable and prudent person would possess or act upon. Answer B is incorrect because due diligence refers to the care a reasonable person should take before entering into an agreement or a transaction with another party. Answer C is incorrect; principle of least privilege refers to the concept that all users at all times should run with as few privileges as possible.

7. **Answer: B.** Due diligence refers to the care a reasonable person should take before entering into an agreement or a transaction with another party. Answer A is incorrect; due care is the knowledge and actions that a reasonable and prudent person would possess or act upon. Answer C is incorrect; due process is the concept that laws and legal proceedings must be fair. Answer D is incorrect; due course is an onward movement in a particular direction.

8. **Answer: A.** Due care is the knowledge and actions that a reasonable and prudent person would possess or act upon. Answer B is incorrect because due diligence refers to the care a reasonable person should take before entering into an agreement or a transaction with another party. Answer C is incorrect; due process is the concept that laws and legal proceedings must be fair. Answer D is incorrect; due course is an onward movement in a particular direction.

9. **Answer: C.** Due process is the concept that laws and legal proceedings must be fair. Answer A is incorrect; due care is the knowledge and actions that a reasonable and prudent person would possess or act upon. Answer B is incorrect because due diligence refers to the care a reasonable person should take before entering into an agreement or a transaction with another party. Answer D is incorrect; due course is an onward movement in a particular direction.

10. **Answer: B.** Due diligence refers to the care a reasonable person should take before entering into an agreement or a transaction with another party. Answer A is incorrect; due care is the knowledge and actions that a reasonable and prudent person would possess or act upon. Answer C is incorrect; due process is the concept that laws and legal proceedings must be fair. Answer D is incorrect; due course is an onward movement in a particular direction.

11. **Answer: A.** Due care is the knowledge and actions that a reasonable and prudent person would possess or act upon. Answer B is incorrect because due diligence refers to the care a reasonable person should take before entering into an agreement or a transaction with another party. Answer C is incorrect because due process is the concept that laws and legal proceedings must be fair. Answer D is incorrect because due course is an onward movement in a particular direction.

12. **Answer: C.** Due process is the concept that laws and legal proceedings must be fair. Answer A is incorrect; due care is the knowledge and actions that a reasonable and prudent person would possess or act upon. Answer B is incorrect because due diligence refers to the care a reasonable person should take before entering into an agreement or a transaction with another party. Answer D is incorrect; due course is an onward movement in a particular direction.

13. **Answer: D.** ISO 17799, particularly sections 7 and 8, has established standards for dealing with the proper disposal of obsolete hardware. Answer A is incorrect; Sarbanes-Oxley (SOX) governs financial and accounting disclosure information. Answer B is incorrect; ISO 9000 is a family of standards for quality management systems. Answer C is incorrect; the IEEE specifications are the central source for standardization in a broad range of emerging technologies.

14. **Answers: A, B, D.** Breaches of health and safety requirements, inadequate disposal planning results in severe business loss, remnants of legacy data from old systems that may still be accessible, and disposal of old equipment that is necessary to read archived data should be considered when formulating a policy on the secure disposal of outdated equipment. Answer C is incorrect because it is addressing a cost, not a disposal consideration.

15. **Answer: B.** Sanitization is the process of removing the contents from the media as fully as possible, making it extremely difficult to restore. Answer A is incorrect because declassification is a formal process of assessing the risk involved in discarding particular information. Answer C is incorrect because degaussing is a method that uses an electrical device to reduce the magnetic flux density of the storage media to zero. Answer D is incorrect because destruction is the process of physically destroying the media and the information stored on it.

16. **Answer: A.** Strong password policies help protect the network from hackers and define the responsibilities of users who have been given access to company resources. Answer B is incorrect; if the passwords are too difficult to remember, users will write them down and post them on monitors, keyboards, and any number of easy-to-find places. Answer C is incorrect because enabling Store Passwords Using Reversible Encryption is essentially the same as storing passwords in plaintext, which is unsecure and not recommended. The purpose of this policy setting is to provide support for applications that use protocols that require knowledge of the user's password for authentication purposes. Answer D is incorrect because default passwords can easily be guessed by an intruder.

17. **Answer: C.** After the change has been requested, documented, and approved, you should then send out notification to the users so that they will know what to expect when the change has been implemented. Therefore, Answer A is incorrect; notification happens before implementation. Answer B is incorrect; often management doesn't need notification. Answer D is incorrect; once changes are approved, there should not be workarounds.

18. **Answer: C.** Class 3 is confidential information that if the data become public, it could influence the organization's operational effectiveness and cause financial loss. Answer A is incorrect because Class 1 is data available in the public domain. Answer B is incorrect because Class 2 is internal information that should the data become public, the consequences are not critical. Answer D is incorrect because Class 4 is secret information. This data is critical to the company, should be accessed by very few, and should never become public.

19. **Answer: B.** Proprietary classification is internal information that defines the way in which the organization operates. Security should be high. Answer A is incorrect because top-secret classification is highly sensitive internal documents and data. This

is the highest security level possible. Answer C is incorrect because internal use only classification is information that is unlikely to result in financial loss or serious damage to the organization. This is a restricted but normal security level. Answer D is incorrect because public documents classification is information in the public domain. This is a minimal security level.

20. **Answer: A.** Top-secret classification is highly sensitive internal documents and data. This is the highest security level possible. Answer B is incorrect because proprietary classification is internal information that defines the way in which the organization operates. Security should be high. Answer C is incorrect because internal use only classification is information that is unlikely to result in financial loss or serious damage to the organization. This is a restricted but normal security level. Answer D is incorrect because public documents classification is information in the public domain. This is a minimal security level.

21. **Answer: C.** Internal use only classification is information that is unlikely to result in financial loss or serious damage to the organization. This is a restricted but normal security level. Answer A is incorrect because top-secret classification is highly sensitive internal documents and data. This is the highest security level possible. Answer B is incorrect because proprietary classification is internal information that defines the way in which the organization operates. Security should be high. Answer D is incorrect because public documents classification is information in the public domain. This is a minimal security level.

22. **Answer: D.** The idea of separation of duties hinges on the concept that multiple people conspiring to corrupt a system is less likely than a single person corrupting it. Often you will find this in financial institutions, where in order to violate the security controls, all the participants in the process would have to agree to compromise the system. Answer A is incorrect; due care is the knowledge and actions that a reasonable and prudent person would possess or act upon. Answer B is incorrect because due diligence refers to the care a reasonable person should take before entering into an agreement or a transaction with another party. Answer C is incorrect; principle of least privilege refers to the concept that all users at all times should run with as few privileges as possible.

23. **Answer: A.** For security purposes, organizations should avoid having one individual who has complete control of a transaction or process from beginning to end, and implement policies such as job rotation, mandatory vacations, and cross-training. Answer B is incorrect; security compliance deals with adhering to regulations and standards. Answer C is incorrect; principle of least privilege refers to the concept that all users at all times should run with as few privileges as possible. Answer D is incorrect because due diligence refers to the care a reasonable person should take before entering into an agreement or a transaction with another party.

24. **Answers: A, C, D.** For security purposes, organizations should avoid having one individual who has complete control of a transaction or process from beginning to end, and implement policies such as job rotation, mandatory vacations, and cross-training. Answer B is incorrect because a change management policy specifies details about system changes such as the files being replaced, the configuration being changed, and the machines or operating systems affected.

25. **Answers: A, B, C.** Privacy-sensitive information is referred to as personally identifiable information (PII). This is any information that identifies or can be used to identify, contact, or locate the person to whom such information pertains. Examples of PII are name, address, phone number, fax number, email address, financial profiles, Social Security number, and credit card information. Answer D is incorrect because group membership does not expose privacy-sensitive information.

26. **Answer: B.** Service level agreements establish the contracted requirements for service through utilities, facility management, and ISPs. Answer A is incorrect a business impact analysis is an analytic process that aims to reveal business and operational impacts stemming from any number of incidents or events. Answer C is incorrect because a disaster recovery plan is a written document that defines how the organization will recover from a disaster and how to restore business with minimum delay. Answer D is incorrect because a disaster recovery policy outlines what to do during a disaster.

27. **Answer: B.** Service level agreements establish the contracted requirements for service through utilities, facility management, and ISPs. The purpose of an SLA is to establish a cooperative partnership, bring both sides together, and map out each party's responsibilities. Answer A is incorrect a business impact analysis is an analytic process that aims to reveal business and operational impacts stemming from any number of incidents or events. Answer C is incorrect because a disaster recovery plan is a written document that defines how the organization will recover from a disaster and how to restore business with minimum delay. Answer D is incorrect because a disaster recovery policy outlines what to do during a disaster.

28. **Answer: C.** When termination involves power users with high-level access rights or knowledge of service administrator passwords, it is critical to institute password and security updates to exclude known avenues of access while also increasing security monitoring for possible reprisals against the organization. Answer A is incorrect; immediately wiping the computer could delete necessary information. Answer B is incorrect; although an exit interview is part of normal HR processes, the concern is access after termination. Answer D is incorrect; searching the user's work area should be done by proper authority and procedures.

29. **Answer: A.** Hackers and other agents seeking unauthorized access often search for highly placed users within an organization who have exempted themselves from standard security policies. Information about the profiles and positions of high-level users is often available on organizational websites which can provide hackers with more directed information. Answers B and D are incorrect; these two groups should have a heightened sense of security awareness and not divulge confidential information. Answer C is incorrect because users can provide valuable information, but high-level employees have access to more valuable information.

30. **Answer: A.** It is important to locate a suitable upper-level sponsor for security initiatives to ensure that published security training and other requirements are applied to all users equally. Without management buy-in, the program will have a difficult time being successful. Based on this information, answers B, C, and D are incorrect.

Objective 6.5: Explain the importance of environmental controls.

1. **Answer: B.** The pipe in the wet-pipe system has water under pressure in it at all times. Answer A is incorrect because dry-pipe systems work in exactly the same fashion as wet-pipe systems, except that the pipes are filled with pressurized air rather than water. Conventional deluge and preaction fire protection systems include a control valve, commonly called a deluge valve, which normally prevents water from flowing into a sprinkler line. Therefore, answers C and D are incorrect.

2. **Answer: D.** A wet-pipe system constantly has water in it. In dry-pipe systems, water is used but is held back by a valve until a certain temperature is reached. Therefore, answers A, B, and C are incorrect.

3. **Answer: C.** Class A fires are trash, wood, and paper. Answer A is incorrect because Class C fires are energized electrical equipment, electrical fire. Answer B is incorrect because Class B fires are flammable liquids, gases, and greases. Answer D is incorrect because Class D fires are fires that involve combustible metals such as magnesium, titanium, and sodium.

4. **Answers: A, C.** With UTP and STP, an inherent danger lies in the fact that it is easy to add devices to the network via open ports on unsecured hubs and switches. Answer B is incorrect because coax cables have no physical transmission security and are very simple to tap without interrupting regular transmissions or being noticed. Answer D is incorrect because it is impossible to tap fiber without interrupting the service and using specially constructed equipment. This makes it more difficult to eavesdrop or steal service.

5. **Answer: A.** Class C fires are energized electrical equipment, electrical fire. Answer B is incorrect because Class B fires are flammable liquids, gases, and greases. Answer C is incorrect. Class A fires are trash, wood, and paper. Answer D is incorrect. Class D fires are fires that involve combustible metals such as magnesium, titanium, and sodium.

6. **Answer: D.** Class D fires are fires that involve combustible metals such as magnesium, titanium, and sodium. Answer A is incorrect because Class C fires are energized electrical equipment, electrical fire. Answer B is incorrect because Class B fires are flammable liquids, gases, and greases. Answer C is incorrect because Class A fires are trash, wood, and paper.

7. **Answer: B.** Class B fires, which are flammable liquids, gases, and greases, are usually put out using foam. Answer A is incorrect; for Class A fires, which are trash, wood, and paper, water will decrease the fire's temperature and extinguish its flames. Answer C is incorrect because the two types of extinguishing agents for Class D fires are sodium chloride and a copper-based dry powder. Answer D is incorrect; Class C fires, which are energized electrical equipment, electrical fire, and burning wires, are put out using extinguishes based on carbon dioxide or halon.

8. **Answer: A.** For Class A fires, which are trash, wood, and paper, water will decrease the fire's temperature and extinguish its flames. Answer B is incorrect. Class B fires, which are flammable liquids, gases, and greases, are usually put out using foam. Answer C is incorrect because the two types of extinguishing agents for Class D fires are sodium chloride and a copper-based dry powder. Answer D is incorrect; Class C fires, which are energized electrical equipment, electrical fire, and burning wires, are put out using extinguishes based on carbon dioxide or halon.

9. **Answer: D.** Class C fires, which are energized electrical equipment, electrical fire, and burning wires, are put out using extinguishes based on carbon dioxide or halon. Answer A is incorrect. For Class A fires, which are trash, wood, and paper, water will decrease the fire's temperature and extinguish its flames. Answer B is incorrect; Class B fires, which are flammable liquids, gases, and greases, are usually put out using foam. Answer C is incorrect because the two types of extinguishing agents for Class D fires are sodium chloride and a copper-based dry powder.

10. **Answer: C.** The two types of extinguishing agents for Class D fires are sodium chloride and a copper-based dry powder. Answer A is incorrect. For Class A fires, which are trash, wood, and paper, water will decrease the fire's temperature and extinguish its flames. Answer B is incorrect; Class B fires, which are flammable liquids, gases, and greases, are usually put out using foam. Answer D is incorrect; Class C fires, which are energized electrical equipment, electrical fire, and burning wires, are put out using extinguishers based on carbon dioxide or halon.

11. **Answer: D.** In 1987, an international agreement known as the Montreal Protocol mandated, because of emissions, the phase out of halons in developed countries by the year 2000 and in less-developed countries by 2010. Therefore, carbon dioxide extinguishers have replaced halon ones. They don't leave a harmful residue, making them a good choice for an electrical fire on a computer or other electronic devices. Based on this information, answers A, B, and C are incorrect.

12. **Answers: A, C, D.** When choosing a location for a building, an organization should investigate the type of neighborhood, population, crime rate, and emergency response times. Answer B is incorrect because the proximity to an electronic store may be a consideration, but it should not one of the deciding factors.

13. **Answer: A.** One of the reasons for using a dry-pipe system is that when the outside temperature drops below freezing, any water in the pipes will freeze, causing them to burst. Therefore, answer B is incorrect. Answer C is incorrect because deluge systems are used in places that are considered high hazard areas such as power plants, aircraft hangars and chemical storage or processing facilities. Deluge systems are needed where high velocity suppression is necessary to prevent fire spread. Answer D is incorrect; conventional preaction systems are relatively complex and expensive, tending to preclude the benefits of their use in low-cost water-sensitive applications such as small areas and residential applications where the need to avoid inadvertent water damage is as important as providing protection against fire damage.

14. **Answers: B.** Overcooling causes condensation on equipment, and too dry leads to excessive static. Therefore, answer D is incorrect. Answers A and C are incorrect because electromagnetic interference (EMI), also called radio frequency interference (RFI), is a disturbance that affects an electrical circuit due to either electromagnetic conduction or electromagnetic radiation emitted from an external source.

15. **Answer: D.** Overcooling causes condensation on equipment, and too dry leads to excessive static. Therefore, Answer B is incorrect. Answers A and C are incorrect because electromagnetic interference (EMI), also called radio frequency interference (RFI), is a disturbance that affects an electrical circuit due to either electromagnetic conduction or electromagnetic radiation emitted from an external source.

16. **Answer: A.** A high level of humidity can cause components to rust and degrade electrical resistance or thermal conductivity. Answer B is incorrect because a low level of humidity can subject components to electrostatic discharge (ESD), causing damage. Answer C is incorrect because EMF is associated with the electricity that comes out of every power sockets and higher-frequency radio waves that create electromagnetic fields. Answer D is incorrect because solidification is the crystallization of a large amount of material from a single point of nucleation results in a single crystal.

17. **Answer: D.** It is impossible to tap fiber without interrupting the service and using specially constructed equipment. This makes it more difficult to eavesdrop or steal service. Answers A and C are incorrect. With UTP and STP, an inherent danger lies in the fact that it is easy to add devices to the network via open ports on unsecured hubs and switches. Answer B is incorrect because coax cables have no physical transmission security and are very simple to tap without interrupting regular transmissions or being noticed.

18. **Answer: C.** An efficient way to protect a large quantity of equipment from electronic eavesdropping is to place the equipment into a well-grounded metal box called a Faraday cage. Answer A is incorrect; an electron configuration table is a type of code that describes how many electrons are in each energy level of an atom and how the electrons are arranged within each energy level. Answer B is incorrect because EMF is associated with the electricity that comes out of every power sockets and higher-frequency radio waves that create electromagnetic fields. Answer D is incorrect because TEMPEST can be costly to implement and protecting an area within a building makes more sense than protecting individual pieces of equipment.

19. **Answer: D.** You are most likely to find TEMPEST equipment in government, military, and corporate environments that process government/military classified information. Answer A is incorrect; an electron configuration table is a type of code that describes how many electrons are in each energy level of an atom and how the electrons are arranged within each energy level. Answer B is incorrect because EMF is associated with the electricity that comes out of every power sockets and higher-frequency radio waves that create electromagnetic fields. Answer C is incorrect because although a Faraday cage is an option, it protects an area within a building not individual pieces of equipment.

20. **Answer: B.** Coax cables have no physical transmission security and are very simple to tap without interrupting regular transmissions or being noticed. Answers A and C are incorrect; both UTP and STP are possible to tap, although it is physically a little trickier than tapping coax cable because of the physical structure of STP and UTP cable. Answer D is incorrect because it is impossible to tap fiber without interrupting the service and using specially constructed equipment. This makes it more difficult to eavesdrop or steal service.

Objective 6.6: Explain the concept of and how to reduce the risks of social engineering.

1. **Answer: B.** Social engineering is a process by which an attacker may extract useful information from users who are often just tricked into helping the attacker. Answer A is incorrect because pharming is a hacker's attack aiming to redirect a website's traffic to another, bogus website. Answer C is incorrect because phishing is an attempt to acquire sensitive information by masquerading as a trustworthy entity via an electronic communication, usually email. Answer D is incorrect because shoulder surfing uses direct observation techniques. It gets its name from looking over someone's shoulder to get information.

2. **Answer: C.** Phishing is an attempt to acquire sensitive information by masquerading as a trustworthy entity via an electronic communication, usually email. Answer A is incorrect because pharming is a hacker's attack aiming to redirect a website's traffic to another, bogus website. Answer B is incorrect. Social engineering is a process by which an attacker may extract useful information from users who are often just tricked into helping the attacker. Answer D is incorrect because shoulder surfing uses direct observation techniques. It gets its name from looking over someone's shoulder to get information.

3. **Answer: D.** For best protection, proper security technologies and techniques must be deployed at the client side, the server side, and the enterprise level. Ideally, users should not be able to directly access email attachments from within the email application. However, the best defense is user education. Answer A is incorrect; S/MIME is a standard for public key encryption and signing of email. Answer B is incorrect because antivirus software cannot identify phishing scams. Answer C is incorrect because email filtering cannot catch all unwanted email.

4. **Answer: B.** Hoax messages may warn of emerging threats that do not exist. They might instruct users to delete certain files to ensure their security against a new virus, while actually only rendering the system more susceptible to later viral agents. Answer A is incorrect because pharming is a hacker's attack aiming to redirect a website's traffic to another, bogus website. Answer C is incorrect because phishing is an attempt to acquire sensitive information by masquerading as a trustworthy entity via an electronic communication, usually email. Answer D is incorrect because spam is unwanted email communication.

5. **Answer: A.** Although hoaxes present issues such as loss of functionality or security vulnerabilities, they also use system resources and consume users' time. This results in lost productivity and an undue burden on the organization's resources, especially if many employees respond. Answer B is incorrect; although virus may be a concern, the idea behind a chain letter is to occupy time and resources. Answer C is incorrect because hoaxes try to occupy time and resources, not garner proprietary information. Answer D is incorrect because this statement is simply not true.

6. **Answer: C.** Equipment sometimes is put in the garbage because city laws do not require special disposal. Because intruders know this, they can scavenge through discarded equipment and documents, called dumpster diving, and extract sensitive information from it without ever contacting anyone in the company. Answer A is incorrect; health hazards are a concern; however, the real danger is the organizational information that is readily accessible. Answer B is incorrect; social engineering is a process by which an attacker may extract useful information from users who are often just tricked into helping the attacker. Answer D is incorrect because shoulder surfing uses direct observation techniques. It gets its name from looking over someone's shoulder to get information.

7. **Answer: C.** Equipment sometimes is put in the garbage because city laws do not require special disposal. Because intruders know this, they can scavenge through discarded equipment and documents, called dumpster diving, and extract sensitive information from it without ever contacting anyone in the company. Answer A is incorrect; fire hazards are a concern. However, the real danger is the organizational information that is readily accessible. Answer B is incorrect because social engineering is a process by which an attacker may extract useful information from users who are often just tricked into helping the attacker. Answer D is incorrect because shoulder surfing uses direct observation techniques. It gets its name from looking over someone's shoulder to get information.

8. **Answer: D.** Shoulder surfing uses direct observation techniques. It gets its name from looking over someone's shoulder to get information. Shoulder surfing is an effective way to get information in crowded places such as airports, conventions, or coffee shops because it's relatively easy to stand next to someone and watch as the person enters a PIN or a password. Answer A is incorrect; virus infection is a concern. However, the real danger is the organizational information that is readily accessible. Answer B is incorrect because social engineering is a process by which an attacker may extract useful information from users who are often just tricked into helping the attacker. Answer C is incorrect because dumpster diving is scavenging through discarded equipment and documents and extract sensitive information from it without ever contacting anyone in the company.

9. **Answer: B.** The immediate solution to prevent shoulder surfing is to shield paperwork or your keypad from view by using your body or cupping your hand. Biometrics and gaze-based password entry makes gleaning password information difficult for the unaided observer while retaining the simplicity and ease of use for the user. Answer A is incorrect because it is an immediate solution, not the best defense. Answer C is incorrect because security guards won't necessarily prevent shoulder surfing. Answer D is incorrect because switching to deadbolts is not a viable solution.

10. **Answer: A.** Reverse social engineering involves an attacker convincing the user that he is a legitimate IT authority, causing the user to solicit his assistance. Answer B is incorrect because denial of service is a type of network attack. Answer C is incorrect because shoulder surfing uses direct observation techniques. It gets its name from looking over someone's shoulder to get information. Answer D is incorrect because phishing is an attempt to acquire sensitive information by masquerading as a trustworthy entity via an electronic communication, usually email.

11. **Answer: A.** The immediate solution to prevent shoulder surfing is to shield paperwork or your keypad from view by using your body or cupping your hand. Biometrics and gaze-based password entry makes gleaning password information difficult for the unaided observer while retaining the simplicity and ease of use for the user. Answer B is incorrect because it is the best defense, not an immediate solution. Answer C is incorrect because security guards won't necessarily prevent shoulder surfing. Answer D is incorrect because switching to deadbolts is not a viable solution.

12. **Answers: A, B.** Social engineering attacks involve tricking a user into providing the attacker with access rights or operational details. Answer C is incorrect because packet sniffing is a form of a network security threat. Answer D is incorrect because this is a physical access control risk rather than social engineering.

13. **Answer: C.** Management training should focus on the ramifications of social engineering, such as the liability of the company when a breach happens, the financial damage that can happen, and how this can affect the reputation or credibility of the company. Answer A is incorrect because the user-based training will be more prevention oriented. Answer B is incorrect because to focus the training on costs rather than benefits is not promoting education. Answer D is incorrect because this training will be technical.

14. **Answers: B, C, D.** Planning, training, regular reminders, and firm and clear security policies are important when you're attempting to minimize vulnerabilities created by social engineering. Answer A is incorrect; security posters might be a part of training, but are not an essential element.

15. **Answers: A, D.** Some guidelines for information to be included in user training may consist of the following points: how to address someone who has her hands full and asks for help getting into a secure area, how to react to someone who has piggybacked into the building, what to say to a vice president who has forgotten his password and needs it right away, and what to do when an administrator calls and asks for a user's password. Answer B is incorrect; this is a part of fire safety education. Answer C is incorrect; virus education should be addressed separately from security awareness training.

FREE Online Edition

Your purchase of **CompTIA Security+ SY0-201 Practice Questions Exam Cram** includes access to a free online edition for 45 days through the Safari Books Online subscription service. Nearly every Exam Cram book is available online through Safari Books Online, along with more than 5,000 other technical books and videos from publishers such as Addison-Wesley Professional, Cisco Press, IBM Press, O'Reilly, Que, Prentice Hall, and Sams.

SAFARI BOOKS ONLINE allows you to search for a specific answer, cut and paste code, download chapters, and stay current with emerging technologies.

Activate your FREE Online Edition at www.informit.com/safarifree

> **STEP 1:** Enter the coupon code: ZFVTPVH.

> **STEP 2:** New Safari users, complete the brief registration form. Safari subscribers, just log in.

If you have difficulty registering on Safari or accessing the online edition, please e-mail customer-service@safaribooksonline.com